The Origins
of Capitalism
in Russia

Joseph T. Fuhrmann

The Origins
of Capitalism
in Russia

*Industry and Progress
in the
Sixteenth and Seventeenth
Centuries*

Chicago: **Quadrangle Books,** 1972

Acknowledgments

THIS BOOK BEGAN AS a dissertation at Indiana University on Russian iron manufacturing during the seventeenth century. I am indebted to many people and organizations for aid at that stage of its development, above all to my adviser and dissertation director, John M. Thompson, for his careful readings of early manuscripts and all but countless suggestions for their improvement. Professor G. A. Novitskii of Moscow University gave much help with early Russian technical terminology. The Foreign Area Fellowship Program provided financial support during 1963-1965 and the summer of 1967. The Inter-University Committee on Travel Grants made it possible for me to spend nine months at Moscow University during the academic year 1965-1966, and the librarians of Moscow University's Gorkii Library enabled me to gather most of the information contained in these pages. I must also thank the inter-library loan staffs of Indiana University and of the University of Texas at Arlington, and my gracious dissertation typist, Mrs. Theta Stovall of Winchester, Tennessee.

Producing a book beyond the dissertation necessitated a complete revision of earlier material, preparation of a new Introduction and Conclusion, and the addition of four entirely new chapters (I, IX, XI, and XII). In achieving this I am much indebted to a fine secretary, Mrs. Glyndean La Plante, and to Ivan R. Dee, managing editor of Quadrangle Books, for his many useful editorial recommendations. But I must express special gratitude to my lovely wife Mary for her general encouragement, and also for compiling the Index. Any errors or interpretative inadequacies are solely my responsibility.

J.T.F.
Greeneville, Tennessee
· *October 1970*

List of Bibliographical Abbreviations

D.k A.I.	*Dopolnenie k Aktam Istorichestim*
E.H.R.	*English Historical Review*
E.S.	*Entsiklopedicheskii Slovar'* (Brokgauz-Efron)
I.z.	*Istoricheskie zapiski*
I.zh.	*Istoricheskii zhurnal*
J.G.O.	*Jahrbucher fur Geschichte Osteuropas*
K.m.	*Krepostnaia manufaktura*
O.S.P.	*Oxford Slavonic Papers*
P.S.Z.R.I.	*Polnoe Sobranie Zakonov Rossiiskoi Imperii*
R.I.B.	*Russkaia Istoricheskaia Biblioteka*
R.S.	*Russkaia Starina*
S.E.E.R.	*Slavonic and East European Review*
S.G.G.i D.	*Sobranie Gosudarstvennykh Gramot i Dogovorov*
S.R.	*Slavic Review*
V.i.	*Voprosy istorii*
Zh.m.n.p.	*Zhurnal ministerstva narodnago prosveshcheniia*

Contents

Maps

Early Modern Russia

Some Seventeenth-Century Manufactories
of the Moscow Area

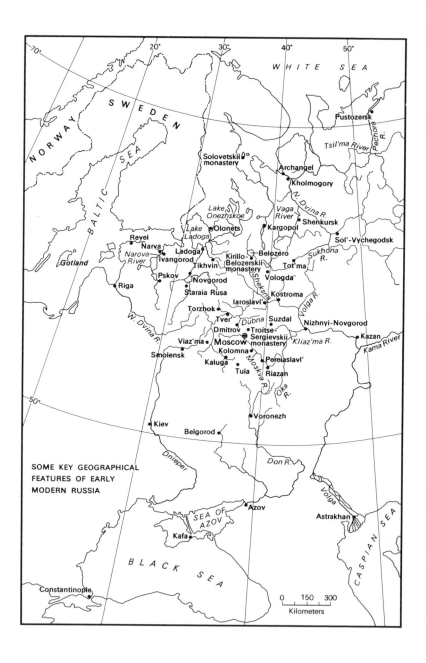

SOME KEY GEOGRAPHICAL
FEATURES OF EARLY
MODERN RUSSIA

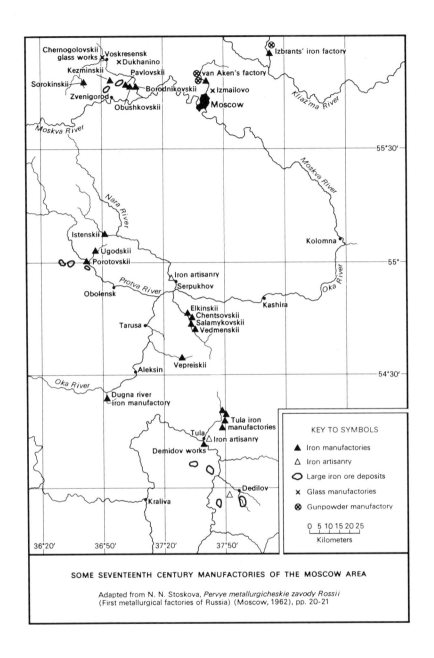

SOME SEVENTEENTH CENTURY MANUFACTORIES OF THE MOSCOW AREA

Adapted from N. N. Stoskova, *Pervye metallurgicheskie zavody Rossii*
(First metallurgical factories of Russia) (Moscow, 1962), pp. 20-21

The Origins
of Capitalism
in Russia

Introduction

BECAUSE THE aim of this book is to study the beginnings of capitalism in Russia, it is crucial at the outset to define what we mean by *capitalism*. This is not a simple task, nor one which economic historians have attempted without provoking among themselves intense disagreements. Some students, for example, have employed narrow definitions which have had the effect of restricting the study of capitalism to a few geographical areas and time periods; other scholars have favored a broader concept of the term, expanding considerably the scope of their work on the history of capitalism. Among the latter, many historians have viewed capitalism simply as "production for the market" or the "purchase and sale of commodities for profit," and on the basis of this approach have concluded that "capitalism" was a basic or emerging feature of some of the earliest civilizations. In this way Michael Rostovtzeff finds much to say about capitalism in Greco-Roman times, and Henri Pirenne does not hesitate to apply the term to certain pre-Renaissance societies.[1]

3

For a variety of reasons I am dissatisified with any use of the word "capitalism" which equates ancient Mesopotamia with thirteenth-century Flanders,[2] or early Greece with contemporary New York City. Many schoolchildren, even, would feel — if but intuitively — that such societies differ in a fundamental manner, and that the same term might not properly designate both, though within each one might observe a certain use of *money,* even a considerable *exchange of commercial goods.* In fact, Plato's Athens and the England of today *are* qualitatively dissimilar, not only in language, culture, and religion, but in the very manner in which men relate to nature and each other and gain the necessities of life. The major point of differentiation, I think, must be sought in their variant levels of technology and the different economic classes and social psychologies which are so much the product of that technology. If it is reasonable to conclude from this that mankind has passed through certain distinct stages of historical development, then perhaps one should use terms like *slave society, feudalism,* and *capitalism* with precision and reserve.

Thus *capitalism* in this study refers to a society characterized by a definite relationship between technological capacity and social structure, a society which follows in time the dominance of the artisan workshop and is based upon new sources of power and methods of labor organization. This new technology first found expression in the "manufactory," a large-scale commodity-producing enterprise of the early capitalist period. The manufactory was different from artisan production in its use of power gained from water falling from the sluice of a dam onto a water wheel, the drive-shafts of which fed the energy thus captured into the machinery of an industrial enterprise. This power was so much greater than the brawn of the individual artisan that it made possible an enormous expansion in the size of tools and machinery and necessitated a certain concentration of both capital and workers (for the equipment was expensive and demanded a number of men to operate it) as well as a rudimentary but very real "division of labor."[3] The manufactory system which took shape in Western Europe after the fourteenth century was as striking an advance over the earlier form of artisan production as, in its turn, the factory system of the eighteenth century (based first on steam and then on electricity) was an improvement over the manufactory.*

Historically speaking, the widespread dissemination of this technology called forth new class relationships, for as a class appeared which was investing capital in new factory equipment another class was forming which was forced to seek work with the capitalist-entrepreneur. It was composed of former peasants and artisans whose traditional economic activities and life patterns had been made obsolete by technological developments. Clearly, this formulation of the essential features in the historical evolution of capitalism emphasizes that we are dealing with a system determined far more by the production of commodities than by their exchange. In fact, looking at the broad view of history one might conclude that commerce (looming so large in the judgments of Pirenne and Rostovtzeff) has actually had a rather small impact upon the technological level and social relationships of a society. As Maurice Dobb said of Western Europe, so too might one say of Russia that the appearance of a merchant class had no revolutionary significance in early modern society, because as mere intermediaries between producer and consumer such entrepreneurs found their fortunes to be bound up with existing technology and organization of production; their natural thought under such circumstances was to "muscle in" on the existing form of appropriating surplus labor rather than trying to change and improve—but also disturb—that form.[4]

What do Soviet historians have in mind when they speak of the "origins of capitalism" in Russia? Obviously a number of approaches to this classic historiographical problem have been attempted by different scholars at different times in the

---

*Despite the technical distinction noted above, for reasons of literary convenience "factory" and "manufactory" are used interchangeably in this book.

USSR – and it would be as fruitless to attempt to catalog them all here as it would be wrong to suggest that all Soviet writers have been of one "official" mind on the subject. But to clarify the intent and argument of this book I must isolate one influential contemporary school of thought and explain why I feel compelled to reject its theoretical premises. I have in mind those Soviet scholars who have viewed the "transition from feudalism to capitalism" in their country during the sixteenth and seventeenth centuries largely in terms of such internal dynamics of the economy as the differentiation and separation of agriculture and artisanry; the specialization of arti-san-masters within individual handicrafts (presaging a "division of labor" in later industry), with successful artisans and wholesale merchants gaining the capital of less successful masters and even hiring them as wage-workers; the general expansion of a money economy and a pronounced tendency for cash *obrok* to be preferred to *obrok* in kind; and so forth.*
Whatever the merits of this approach, its effect upon the work of those who have used it has been to de-emphasize such external factors as the integration of Russia into a network of international commerce, and all but to ignore the investment of foreign capital in Russian industry and trade, at least before Peter the Great. In thus taking the internal economic situation as the groundwork of his attention, I. V. Stepanov, for example, proved that even in the seventeenth century people who fled the central regions of Russia were used as laborers in fish and salt industries and in navigation on the Volga, whereas N. V. Ustiutov has demonstrated that peasants turned to wage-labor in the building and maintenance of ships along the northern water routes. V. G. Geiman, in a pioneering article on the birth of capitalistic relationships in seventeenth-century Russia, concluded that the poorest peasants in the Seregov area lost their "means of production" and turned to salt-making, an "industry of factory type using the wage labor

---

*Obrok, peasant rent payable in cash or kind, might be understood as the Russian equivalent of "quit-rent"; *barshchina,* the obligation of unpaid labor service, was the Russian equivalent of "corvée." See the Glossary at the back of the book for these and other unfamiliar Russian terms.

of free workers." K. N. Serbina has written an especially impressive book concerning the considerable economic differentiation which had occurred by the late seventeenth century among the iron artisans and other masters of Tikhvinskii *posad* (suburb), and V. I. Shunkov has established that at the same time refugees from European Russia were selling their labor power to monasteries and government factors in faraway Siberia.[5]

Although the research underlying these investigations is solidly empirical and of high professional quality, one may question the extent to which these and similar investigations have really touched the problem of the origins of capitalism in Russia. Specifically: in what sense do such developments as the growth of *obrok* in agriculture or the new use of wage-labor in an age-old activity such as salt-making represent the "origins of capitalism"? In the West the significance of such developments is clear: they formed a prelude to the growth of capitalism. Differentiation among merchants and artisans, dispossession of peasants and growth of quit-rent, and so forth—these were several of the economic tendencies which eventually broke down an earlier economic order based (largely) on the exchange of personal services and "natural" goods, and opened the way for industrial enterprises which could base themselves on a constantly expanding sector of the population with money to exchange for needed industrial commodities. But it was the manufactory which represented the real emergence of the tremendous productive powers of capitalism. It is perhaps not too much to say that the manufactory *was* capitalism.

Therefore, it seems that Soviet scholars who focus upon internal dynamics are studying not so much the substance of an emerging capitalistic system as its background—its prelude, to use an earlier characterization. The substance of the matter, as I conceive it, would be the real emergence of new productive forces, specifically the manufactory and industrial capital for the production of commodities on a new and expanded scale. And here we perceive a striking difference in the history of capitalism in Russia and in Western Europe. In the West the manufactory was an indigenous development, but in Russia it was introduced by foreign merchants who resided in the country and were always alert to the possibility of tapping increased profits through new economic activities. In Russia the transition from simple artisan production to the more advanced production of the capitalistic manufactory came not as a consequence of the "ripening" of capitalistic tendencies in artisanry, transport, fishing, and so forth, but rather as a result of the failure of a semi-medieval economy to move independently and with sufficient speed toward advanced technology on a capitalistic basis. To put it simply, the Russian government turned to foreign merchants for the construction of manufactories during the sixteenth and seventeenth centuries because pressing industrial demands (created above all by military needs) were not being met by existing productive forces. In this sense, therefore, manufacturing represented an "external force" which interacted during the sixteenth and seventeenth centuries with those internal dynamics of the Russian economy which have, as I suggested, been so thoroughly studied by Soviet historians.

I hope to make clear that in focusing upon manufacturing in this book I do not wish to condemn Soviet historiography, nor to add another chapter to the American critique of intellectual life in the USSR. Least of all am I attempting to dwell upon what some Western "historians" would have us think to be a Russian penchant for social or technological backwardness. In fact, the reader may well conclude that a considerable amount of industrial development occurred in Russia during the sixteenth and seventeenth centuries. Specifically, foreign entrepreneurs (and some Russians) at this time built no fewer than fifty-seven manufactories: twenty-eight iron works, two copper mills, five gunpowder factories, six paper plants, three glassworks, three sawmills, three rope walks, three textile factories, a tannery, and three silk shops. These manufactories have not been ignored in historical literature published in the Soviet Union. But they are dealt with mostly in articles written in the 1920's and 1930's, whereas books which treat these enterprises do so by individual industry (also characteristic of the articles) or in a few introductory pages to works which have as their main objective a more intensive study of later periods. In the absence of a single lengthy or systematic account of the beginnings of manufacturing in Russia, this book attempts to synthesize historical knowledge on the subject and to place manufacturing into the larger context of the origins of capitalism in Russia.[6]

Because artisan production sometimes appeared in fairly large-scale forms in Russia during the sixteenth and seventeenth centuries,* I found it necessary to set certain criteria for what constitutes a manufactory and was therefore suitable for extended treatment in this book. First is the question of technology. Forty-seven of the enterprises discussed in these pages—the iron, copper, gunpowder, paper, and glass works, plus the sawmills—used water power and may therefore without controversy be considered manufactories. The remaining ten enterprises—rope, textile, leather, and silk shops—did not use water as the source of their energy, but their equipment and methods were "modern" by foreign standards and unprecedented in terms of Russian industry. Hence I have called them manufactories, and they form an integral part of the entire study. Second, most of these enterprises were organized by foreign entrepreneurs and staffed, especially at the beginning, by foreign workers acquainted with the new technology. Third, most of these enterprises were in the hands of private individuals and operated to realize a profit from the sale of commodity output.

To be sure, the actual life of a given manufactory might differ in some respects from this basic schema. For example, the distinction between private and state ownership is not

---

*As examples of such large "artisan" enterprises one might cite the royal mint *(monetnyi dvor)* or Moscow's first large publishing house, the *pechatnyi dvor.* Both were state-owned, in no way related to commercial activity, and not based upon technology which was then "modern" by Western European standards. Much the same might be said of the *pushechnyi dvor* ("cannon yard"), which is briefly described in following pages in order to demonstrate the continuity between Russian iron artisanry and iron manufacturing.

always clear, for most manufactories received direct or in-direct subsidies from the tsar, a few were built by the state, and others went through intermittent periods of state ownership. But it would be unwise to force the life and variety of a complex historical process into impetuous conformity with a schematic set of "rules and regulations" — as if the ultimate significance of history were to provide material for the classification exercises of a bookish scholar. What is demanded of any one enterprise for inclusion in this study is a broad harmony with the three general criteria specified above. Feeling certain that the fifty-seven enterprises described in this book are individual constituents of a unified and coherent process which propelled the Russian economy in a new and definite direction, I leave the reader to judge whether or not my principles of treatment have resulted in a discussion too sweeping or poorly focused.

Justification of what is to be included and excluded in a history of manufacturing in Russia also forces us to consider the extent to which a book of this type should treat those activities of foreigners not directly related to manufacturing. This problem flows from the nature of the subject itself, for manufacturers such as Andrei Vinius, Peter Marselis, and John of Sweden were involved in a number of other projects ranging from the organization of a modern international post to the establishment of the first significant Russian fleet to the operation of artisan-type enterprises for processing pitch, resin, potash, and so forth. Hoping to broaden the appeal of my study, I decided to treat these and similar undertakings at some length. Having taken that step it also seemed fitting to develop the entire context within which the foreigner-capitalist acted in this period, and this demanded an explanation of how other foreigners came to work in Russia as soldiers, physicians, linguists, and diplomats, and sometimes to go so far as to convert to Eastern Orthodoxy and accept the Russian citizenship which had the effect of integrating them still more firmly into their new and (apparently) agreeable environment. Thus I have departed (in Chapters XI and XII) from what might otherwise have been a fairly narrow history of manufacturing in Russia during the sixteenth and seventeenth centuries, and it is this departure which both justifies and necessitates my subtitle: "Industry and *Progress* in the Sixteenth and Seventeenth Centuries."* Chapter X deals with industrial aspects of the mercantilist policy of the state in the same period, while the final chapter attempts an overall view of manufacturing, treating such analytical questions as the achievements of Russian industry before Peter the Great, its limitations, importance for the future, and so on.

Depending on the vantage point, the fifty-seven manufactories built in early modern Russia may be considered a relatively large achievement or a small one. The argument of this book is that these enterprises, appearing as they did in the context of a still rather backward feudal economy, represented a significant first step in the development of Russian capitalism.

---

*I occasionally use the term "early modern Russia" to refer to Russia during the sixteenth and seventeenth centuries.

1.

The Town Life, Artisanry, and Commerce of Early Modern Russia

STUDENTS OF RUSSIAN HISTORY have been surprisingly reluctant to assign the Mongols much influence in shaping modern Russian civilization. Perhaps this is due, in part, to the fact that the contrast between Russian society before and after 1237–1241 was so great that a "mere" external shock such as the Mongol invasion presents an explanation altogether too simple and convenient to appear also profound. Indeed, Michael Pokrovskii, writing just before the Bolshevik Revolution, was by no means unique among historians in seeing the decline of Kievan Russia as well under way by the time the Mongols came upon the scene. For the Marxist Pokrovskii, of course, the basic feature of the late 1100's was what he believed to be an economic deterioration unfolding in Russia because of "profound economic causes . . . , a shifting of world trade routes and exhaustion of the country through predatory methods of economy."[1] According to this analysis, the Tatars did little more than increase the tempo of shifting forces within Russian society itself.

There is evidence to support Pokrovskii's analysis. During the twelfth century Russia did experience severe problems in maintaining that once-vigorous trade with Byzantium that had long been the basis for Kiev's economic power and cultural glory. This development was due in part to nomadic raiders from the east who undermined the security of the southern trade routes.

Even more important was the fact that European commerce with Constantinople, once based upon the north-south Novgorod-Dnieper-Black Sea waterway, was then in the slow process of west-east reorientation as the Scandinavians entered the Mediterranean and gained control over key trade routes formerly monopolized by the Arabs and Greeks. Pokrovskii emphasized that the Viking merchant no longer needed the great Dnieper "detour" to obtain Byzantine goods for transit to the west, so naturally the economic significance of Russia steadily declined. The fall of Constantinople to the western Crusaders of 1204 deprived southern Russia, at least briefly, of her last access to Byzantine markets, while the Venetian and Genoese successors to Scandinavian merchants in this area at a later time reaffirmed the Dnieper's superflousness as a western trade route to the east.

With due respect to this ingenious explanation for Russia's supposed economic "decline" on the eve of the Mongol conquest, on balance Russia's economic decline was more apparent than real. Russian commercial losses in the south during this period were somewhat offset by gains elsewhere. Smolensk developed new overland routes to the west, while Novgorod and Pskov entered the Hanse and experienced tremendous commercial expansion. To be sure, during the twelfth century Kiev lost both economic and political hegemony over the Russian lands, thus inaugurating a long period of inter-princely disunity and strife. But by the 1230's the economic forces of Russian life were clearly regrouping themselves (along with the actual mass of the Russian population) in the northeast, in the vast and largely undeveloped area between the Oka and Volga rivers. Historians may speak of a contraction in foreign and domestic trade in these decades, for boyars began to invest more capital in land and this created a discernible shift in the former balance between agriculture and commerce. But even at that Pokrovskii is not justified in speaking of "exhaustion of the country through predatory methods of economy." B. A. Rybakov has shown that Russian handicrafts of the early 1200's were actually expanding in diversity, scale, and quality of production. He concludes:

> The very same broad road of further development stood before Russian artisanry of the early-thirteenth century as stood before the artisanry of the north Italian cities of the same period. The Mongol conquerors crushed and plundered this flowering culture at the moment of its highest development.[2]

The Tatars plunged Russia into backwardness—first through the very shock of their attack against the population centers standing in the path of the westward advance. They completely exterminated the populations of Riazan, Torzhok, Kozelsk, and Kiev; in other cities killing was extensive, while looting and destruction occurred everywhere on an incredible scale. Vernadsky estimates that 10 per cent of the entire Russian population was enslaved at the outset,[3] and a papal legate, Archbishop Plano Carpini, passing through the Kiev area on his way to Mongolia in 1245, observed that

> . . . when we passed through that land, we found lying in the field countless heads and bones of dead people; for this city had been extremely large and very populous, whereas now it has been reduced to nothing: barely two hundred houses stand there, and these people are held in the harshest slavery.[4]

The effect of all this upon Russian economic activity might well be imagined! Novgorod, Pskov, and Smolensk escaped destruction although not subjugation to the Golden Horde, but elsewhere handicrafts and commerce declined precipitously and in many areas town life all but died. Even during the next (fourteenth) century, Russian documents mention no more than seventy-nine cities, of which only four were new; during the fifteenth century such sources list seventy-eight towns in northeastern Russia—only nine of which were new—and 286 smaller "settlements" or *slobody*[5] in comparison with almost three hundred towns on the eve of the Mongol invasion. Even at that, Russia might have recovered sooner but for the Mongol practice of conscripting craftsmen on a scale sufficient to destroy many of the exquisite luxury trades which flourished in Kievan times.[6] Even Russian iron artisanry declined as a result of Tatar levies, and because foreign imports seldom passed beyond Novgorod the rural population was forced into a new dependency upon local craftsmen, many of whom were new to their calling and had little skill. Russian industrial recovery did not really begin until the late fourteenth century, at which time many artisans were no longer urban freemen but bondsmen to rural estates. Again the Mongols provide the explanation for this social development: from the outset monastery lands enjoyed taxation and conscription immunities which made them havens for craftsmen who consented to exchange "free status" for monastery protection. Princes and boyars who enjoyed good relations with the Tatars also managed to retain some of their artisans, while in other instances they were permitted to redeem (and then exploit) Russian masters already taken by the Golden Horde.

Russian economic recovery was also hindered by war and domestic strife. Before Ivan III (from 1237 to 1462), we know of forty-eight major wars between the Mongols and Russian princes, and in this period smaller Tatar raids were even more common. Not only did this destroy life, property, and normal economic activity; the price of Russian defeat was always the enslavement of entire populations for sale in the east, some of which might be ransomed but only at additional high cost. Between 1228 and 1462 Russia also suffered ninety inter-princely wars,[7] many fomented by the Mongols and all economically debilitating.[*] In the same period famine occurred, as did plague which struck both animals and people. As early as 1230 some 32,000 citizens of Smolensk died in

[*]One cannot always "blame" the Mongols for Russian wars with the West at this time: forty-one with Lithuania, thirty with the German Crusading orders of the northwest seaboard, forty-four with Sweden, Bulgaria, and so on (Blum, *Lord and Peasant,* pp. 59–60). But these conflicts, too, sapped Russian resources and brought little in the way of material rewards.

great epidemic. In the mid-1300's the Black Death fell terribly upon Russia, bringing to urban areas widespread death and incredible scenes of mass hysteria and despair. Supposedly in Smolensk in 1387 only five people survived a later attack; in 1390 the foreign traveler Kranets tells us that eighty thousand Novgorodites died of a plague. From broad and careful research in old Russian documents, S. M. Solov'ev was able to relate nearly thirty other instances of plague in Russia between 1308 and 1448, many of which affected broad areas and shattered economic activity for years.[8]

These, then, were the elements and causes of Russian "backwardness" vis-à-vis the modern West. An economic depression in Russia lasted a full 150 years at the very time when Western Europe of the High Middle Ages was experiencing a tremendous expansion of international commerce and urban culture. A certain Russian economic "recovery" began during the fifteenth century, when significant domestic commerce started anew, artisans improved their technique and scale of output, and Prince Dmitrii Donskoi of Moscow (1350-1389) resumed the minting of coins. But this was progress only in terms of the immediate Russian past, and represented a meager state of affairs compared not only with the contemporary West but even with the earlier Kievan period. In 1063 Henry I, king of France, and his Russian wife, Anna, daughter of the Kievan Prince Yaroslav the Wise, testified to the relative material and intellectual cultures of their respective lands when Henry signed a royal document with his mark, the queen with her signature. During the sixteenth century, by contrast, for all her progress Russia was still, in Western terms, a rude and barbarous kingdom. And so she was to remain.

A basic feature of Russian economic development during the sixteenth century was the new importance of money in agriculture. Growth of domestic commerce during the late 1400's soon affected agricultural relations as landlords came to prefer *obrok* in cash to *obrok* in kind,[9] and this forced a significant number of peasants into economic activities from which they could obtain money. At the end of the sixteenth century, for example, many peasants of the Kama basin discharged their obligations by selling furs, wax, and honey, or by working for wages in transportation, at salt works, and so forth. Even when peasant *obrok* continued to be rendered in kind, such payments might also be closely related to the new market conditions of the sixteenth century. Peasants often delivered raw wool, wool cloth, or linen to their nobles, who in turn offered those commodities for sale. The vigorous flax trade of the Novgorod-Pskov area rested upon noble exaction of such *obrok* in kind. The new importance of *obrok* in cash and in produce is relevant to a study of capitalist tendencies in the Russian economy of that time because the growing involvement of the peasant in such pursuits helped to create the forms of social wealth necessary for broad and profitable merchant and artisan activities.

The growth of urban centers also affected agriculture by presenting potential markets to those nobles who were able to undertake what might be called, for the time, large-scale "capitalistic" farming. And town life *was* growing throughout this entire period. Sources from the second half of the sixteenth century mention some fifty new towns.[10] Some of these were on the southern and southeastern frontiers and hence little more than military strongholds connected with agriculture. But as the frontier shifted from central Russia, even these towns usually lost their original character and became local centers of handicrafts and trade. Other new cities of the sixteenth century from the outset displayed a thoroughly economic character, especially those cities between Moscow and the White Sea created as a result of the foreign trade route discovered by the English during the 1550's. Archangel, founded in 1584, was the scene of a great international fair each August (extended from June through August after 1663), while Vologda, described by Thomas Randolph in 1568–1569 as "a town . . . of great traffic and many rich merchants," was also important for iron artisanry and leather trades.[11]

Exact information is not available concerning the size of Russian towns in this period. According to Herberstein in Moscow in 1511, "...the houses were counted by order of the prince [and] the number exceeded 41,500." Forty years later Richard Chancellor noted that "our men say that in bigness [Moscow] is as great as the city of London with the suburbs thereof." From this and other evidence, M. G. Rabinovich estimates (conservatively, I think) Moscow's population toward the end of the century at eighty thousand. In these years Kazan, a medium-sized city by Russian standards, had some fifteen thousand inhabitants, a figure which included a large garrison. Unusually reliable data for Kolomna and Tula, examples of smaller yet still significant towns, suggest populations during the 1570's of 3,000 and 2,500 to 3,000, respectively.[12]

Inhabitants of the early modern Russian town pursued diverse professions, not all of which were by any means connected with artisanry or trade. In fact, military and service people constituted the largest single element even of older towns, and they were followed by a heterogeneous group of rag-pickers, midwives, bleeders, apothecaries, clowns, songsters, coachmen, handymen, day-laborers, waggoners, and so forth. S. V. Bakhrushin maintains that if we disregard such vocations as these, sources nevertheless indicate an impressive total of 186 artisan trades, as well as thirty or more in food processing.[13] Of the latter the most prominent were bakers (of both plain and fancy *kalach* bread), distillers, beer brewers and hops raisers, makers of the sour milk beverage *kissel,* fish processors, and so forth. In towns like Pskov, Tula, and Kazan, this group of artisans constituted 30 to 40 per cent of the population, elsewhere as much as 50 per cent.[14]

Another large group of urban artisans, ranging from a third to a quarter of their total number, were clothing producers. These men often obtained flax and wool materials from masters who lived in the countryside, which left the urban artisans free to work as fullers, hatters, drapers, makers of sarafan. kaftan, and coarse *sertiaga* cloth, hosiers, tailors, and producers of mittens, pockets, or padded jackets known as *dushe-*

greiniki; also tanners, furriers, sheepskin processors, fur coat designers, and bootmakers. A different category of handicraftsmen made such household articles as candles, soap, resin, lantern fuel, needles, locks, tin items, and pans. A concrete example of such trades in a typical town of the period may be found in Medna, located in Novotorzhskii *uezd* (district) on the Tvertsa river, a tributary of the Volga. In the mid-1400's the town came under the ownership of the Troitse-Sergievskii monastery, at which time a census revealed seventy-two households *(dvory)*, fifty-six of which belonged to families not engaged in agriculture. Of this number there were nine shoemakers, eight tailors, eight bakers, four smiths, one hatter, sheepskin processor, clown, lantern fuel maker, and so on. The artisan population of Medna grew during the sixteenth century. The same is true of the northern town of Staraia Ladoga, to take yet another example. According to the census of 1500 only four of that town's 114 *dvory* belonged to artisans, but comparable records for 1586 mention thirty-six such masters, most of them engaged in food processing.[15] Elsewhere artisan communities were also becoming large enough to comprise 20 to 25 per cent of Russia's urban population. Internal warfare, Mongol raids, foreign invasions, heavy government taxation, and peasant flight and unrest led to severe economic dislocation and contraction during the 1560's and 1570's, and again in the early 1600's. But these crises were surmounted during the remainder of the seventeenth century, at which time the Russian economy resumed its growth. By 1638 Moscow had 2,367 artisans, Novgorod about 2,000, Serpukhov 331, and Kazan 318; at that time Kolomna's 159 artisans formed 22 per cent of the town's population, Mozhaisk's 224, 40 per cent. During the 1670's Iaroslavl' had over two thousand artisan households; Nizhnyi-Novgorod, Viatka, Kostroma, and Vologda each contained a thousand or more artisan *dvory*.[16]

The most important artisan industries in Russia at this time were iron-working, tanning, the making of leather goods, salt production, and fish processing. The latter activity was based upon the urban dweller's need for foodstuffs, a need so great that fishing became the most important economic activity in many northern regions, especially in Pomor'e, in the areas of lakes Il'men and Ladoga, on the Volkhov and Sheksna rivers, and near Beloozero.[17] Drying, salting, and packaging fish demanded a great many workers and a certain division of labor, and if in the central regions this work remained of supplementary importance to agriculture, in the north many found it so profitable that they abandoned farming to pursue fish processing as a full-time occupation. The growth of the industry can be traced through such typical towns as Dubno, situated on Lake Ladoga, which is on the Dubna river, a tributary of the Volga. The census book (*pistsovaia kniga*) of 1500 does not even mention a "fishermen's row" in Dubno, which suggests that if fishing occurred there at that time it was small-scale and involved few people. But in 1545 Dubno and three adjacent villages reported thirty-three fishermen households (*dvory*); in 1568 Dubno alone had forty such residences, plus two described as "empty." By then Dubno displayed a fishermen's row comprised of nineteen barns, some of which belonged to merchants at the town of Ladoga and one of which was the property of a Novgorodite who had another barn at Ladoga. Other Novgorod entrepreneurs were active in out of the way corners of this region, and fishermen in the tiniest places also came to Novgorod. An observer of the 1520's noted that "people who two years ago carried fish to market or were butchers, rag-pickers and gardners have been transformed into very wealthy merchants." Fishermen's rows appeared in other Russian cities during the early sixteenth century and grew dramatically in later decades.[18]

Quantities of salt were needed for fish as well as for the preservation of other foods. At Perm', Vychegda, Tot'ma, Kineshma, and on the Una and Nenoksa rivers, salt was mined from large natural deposits. This was also the case at Astrakhan, where Fletcher noted that sea water cast salt up into "great hills" which merchants "dug" and hauled away. Elsewhere, both inland and on the seas, salt was evaporated by ovens equipped with iron pans (*tsreny*) or copper cauldrons (*salgi*). These salt works demanded large capital investments and the employment of labor on a scale so great that only the tsar or some boyars and monasteries could finance the necessary operations. For this reason, although salt-making usually remained within the framework of the life of large estates, it was also one of the first areas of the Russian economy to experience capitalist technology and wage-labor relationships. And in the north, at least, smaller salt producers and traders were soon eclipsed by their large competitors. Agents of the Solovetskii monastery, for example, integrated the activities of peasant salt cooperatives (*arteli*) along the entire White Sea coast which were indebted to the monastery, transporting and selling their output to distant regions in the south. The Stroganovs began to develop their salt interests at Sol'vychegodsk during the last quarter of the fifteenth century. They gradually absorbed all competitors in the area, and by 1550 the tsar bestowed upon Anika Stroganov a monopoly on salt production in the region. At the time of his death (in 1570), a significant number of the Stroganovs' six thousand peasant wage-workers were employed in the family's ten large salt works.[19]

Russian artisan leather production underwent striking specialization during the sixteenth century. Tanning first separated itself from shoemaking, while within that field masters were becoming differentiated into heelmakers (*kabluchniki*), makers of soles (*podoshvenniki*) and boottops (*golenishchniki*), and so forth. Leather-working was especially strong throughout the northwest and in Novgorod, where at one point during the 1580's 458 men worked as tanners and another 806 cut and sewed finished leather goods.[20]

But even during Kievan times iron was the commodity which "formed the backbone of the material culture of the country, for both peace and war."[21] At first Russians smelted iron in pits filled with wood and ore, and covered with earth and tree branches after the fire was started. By the tenth century primitive iron furnaces were in use, and their design and operation were improved considerably during the next two centuries. The Russian smith (*kuznets*) of this period produced sickles, scythes, spades, picks, plowshares, axes, knives, frying pans, and kettles, and such weapons as swords, pikes, arrowheads, helmets, and cuirasses.[22]

As mining scarcely existed during the sixteenth century, Russian artisans depended upon ore easily obtained from bogs, swamps, meadows, and lakes. Furnaces usually huddled together around sources of this type. Ore was extracted during August and September, heated on bonfires during October, then brought in more concentrated form to smelting sites by sleigh. From January to April the artisans worked to produce higher quality iron through the so-called "two-stage process" (*syrodutnyi protsess*). This involved placing the ore above a charge of charcoal fuel while two leather bellows created a temperature of not less than 1350° C. to seperate slag from metal. The metal flowed to the bottom of the furnace in a spongelike mass called "blooms" (*kritsy*). This malleable "pig iron" (*chugun*) still contained many impurities, so masters took it hot to a forge (*gorn*) for the second stage and "fined" the iron through forging and reheating until the percentage of slag decreased and a higher-quality iron remained. The final product emerged as square- or round-cornered bars (*prutovoe zhelezo*) or strips (*lemeshnoe zhelezo*), which could then furnish material for swords, plowshares, axes, and so on.[23]

Ancient peasant iron furnaces were round or oval and possessed external diameters of 85 to 110 centimeters (about 33 to 43 inches), internal diameters of 60 to 77 centimeters (about 23 to 31 inches). In the late eighteenth century the Swedish traveller J. E. Norberg saw an old furnace in Ustiuzhna Zhelezopol'skaia which stood nine feet high and whose inner foundation was twenty-two by twenty-two inches. Its daily capacity was six blooms, each bloom weighing about one *pud* (thirty-six pounds). Such furnaces usually rested upon a base of cobblestones covered with clay. Although the technology of Russian iron artisanry improved steadily through the end of the twelfth century, iron handicrafts experienced few

other changes or innovations until the nineteenth century.[24]
We are not certain exactly when and by whom firearms were introduced into Russia, nor do we know the types of weapons used at the very beginning. But in 1382 Muscovites used arbalists and cannons to defend their city from a Mongol attack. The first indigenous Russian artillery pieces were iron strips bound into crude tubes by hoops, although by 1446 such Russian masters as Mikul Krechetnikov of Tver' were casting single-unit cannon. The preferred metal at this time was bronze, a material familiar to bell masters since Kievan times and often used by Krechetnikov and other cannon smiths. But copper and tin were then available in Russia only through import, which made the metals expensive and undependable in supply. For this reason most Russian cannon of the period were probably made of wrought iron.[25]

Although Russian artillery suffered from a lack of standardized calibers, the number of cannon and arquebuses grew steadily during the first two-thirds of the sixteenth century. The quality of these weapons was good even by Western norms, and in fact foreigners worked in the Muscovite state even during the fifteenth century. Rudolfo Fioravanti (the subject of further discussion in the next chapter) organized Moscow's famous "Cannon Yard" *(pushechnyi dvor* or *pushechnaia izba)* in 1479, and he was followed in Russia by Pierre du Bois and other foreigners. Baron Sigismund von Herberstein, Holy Roman Ambassador to Russia in 1517 and 1526, noted that the tsar "has now German and Italian cannonfounders, who cast cannon and other pieces of ordnance, and iron cannon balls such as our own princes use. . . ."Credit for this achievement, however, should by no means go to foreigners alone. By the sixteenth century, at the latest, Russia could boast of many skilled native metallurgists. The Moscow artisan "Peter," for example, smelted a large cannon in 1501 and two years later a bell weighing 350 *puds*. Bulgak Novgorodov cast an eighty-three-*pud* artillery piece in 1513, and around the same time the master Ignatii made the first Russian howitzer *(gaubitsa)*. From the 1550's there still exist eighteen cannon

signed by the "russkoi master Bogdan."[26] In 1586 Andrei
Chokhov cast the famous "king-cannon" *(tsar'-pushka)*,
which weighed forty tons and had a muzzle-bore of eighty-
nine centimeters.*

Although technological innovations in Russian iron artisanry for domestic uses were less impressive than in areas of
military production, the craft as a whole experienced a definite
division of labor by the sixteenth century. Sources during this
period mention "smiths" *(kuznetsy)* and "hammer-men" *(mo-
lotniki* or *molotoboetsy)* who assisted them at the forge; others
specialized in making nails, knives, saddles, muskets,
rifle-locks, plowshares, watches, brackets, and about ten other
individual items. During the thirteenth and fourteenth centuries these Russian iron handicrafts existed mainly in the
Novgorod area, which retained its importance through the
early seventeenth century. Incomplete records for Votskaia-
Piatina during the early 1500's disclose the operation there of
about two hundred smitheries, while the Izhorskaia region,
Pashskaia *volost'* (village), and Orekhovskii *uezd* (district)
were also scenes of considerable activity. Information for
1583-1586 indicates 230 Novgorod iron masters and at least
299 at a similar time in Ustiuzhna-Zhelezopol'skaia. By the
early seventeenth century the peasants of Karelia (near modern-day Finland) were energetically smelting iron for the entire
northeast. Iaroslavl', Tver', and Vologda were other centers of
iron artisanry, as was the Tula-Serpukhov area just south of
Moscow. In 1556 sixty-five iron masters lived in Serpukhov
alone, comprising over 10 per cent of the city's taxable population.[27]

K. N. Serbina's research into iron artisanry at Tikhvinsk
enables us to describe the situation there in some detail —
doubly fortunate because the evolution of the iron masters'

---

*The opinion has been expressed that this weapon was too large for combat
purposes, and that Chokov cast the piece as a tribute to his skill, or perhaps
to frighten the enemy! This admittedly arbitrary theory is criticized by N. I.
Fal'kovskii, *Moskva v istorii tekhniki* [Moscow in the history of technology]
(Moscow, 1949), pp. 63-64.

posad (suburb) of that city* seems representative of Russian development in other areas as well. By 1583 iron craftsmen already formed 13 per cent of the artisan population of Tikhvinsk, reaching 40 per cent by 1686. In 1678 seventy-four iron-smiths *(kuznetsy)* lived at Tikhvinskii *posad,* as did twenty-two other artisans connected with metallurgy. Besides this growth in the number of artisans, we also detect a growing "maturation" of their production process, indicated above all by increasing specialization. By the early 1600's, for example, the Tikhvinsk masters obtained pig iron largely from outside sources, which enabled them to concentrate on producing finished commodities. The artisans of this period specialized in making one or two items such as knives, agricultural tools, household items, nails, and horseshoes. Arquebuses *(pishchali)* and other armaments were made upon order of the Moscow government or the local nobility. Some of Tikhvinsk's smiths specialized in the production of *uklad,* a quality of metal between iron and steel and an impressive achievement by Russian standards.[28]

After the 1630's the iron artisans of Tikhvinskii *posad* lost direct contact with the market and became dependent on "middlemen" merchants *(skupshchiki)* to dispose of their goods. This too represented economic specialization and made possible the sale of Tikhvinsk iron goods over a large area which included Iaroslavl', Nizhnyi-Novgorod, and even faraway Moscow. In time the middlemen gained increasing control over the production process itself by issuing artisans money "in advance," the debtors mortgaging their premises *(dvory)* "with all blacksmith equipment" as security. (In such cases, evaluation occurred at a mere portion of true value.) In this way several artisans were forced into various sorts of work for their *skupshchik,* and sometimes, because they lost control

---

* Artisan iron works posed such a fire hazard to Russian towns of the period that iron masters lived and worked in *posady* (suburbs) just outside urban areas. Tikhvinsk was situated northeast of Pskov and northwest of White Lake (Beloe Ozero), quite near Olonets.

over their original equipment, they ended as nothing more than his hired workers. There was also growing differentiation among the Tikhvinsk iron masters themselves, with some through economic misfortune being forced to work for more fortunate colleagues, who in this way expanded the scope of their own activities.[29]

The distribution of Russian resources naturally predisposed the growing feudal economy toward a geographical division of labor. As we have seen, iron deposits accessible to existing peasant mining technology made certain northern regions important centers of iron artisanry. The Novgorod area was first in cultivation of flax and hemp, followed by Olonets, Smolensk, Iaroslavl' *oblast'*, and Mozhaisk. Hides were important in Kostroma, Vologda, Novgorod, and Mozhaisk. Viaz'ma was noted for dyes and cloth. Textiles were significant at Vologda, in Belozerskii *krai*, and in Mozhaisk *uezd*. The Troitse-Sergievskii monastery near Moscow was noted for especially high-quality fabrics.[30]

Regional differentiation of economic activity led naturally to a broad network of local markets, all of which grew (especially during the first two-thirds of the sixteenth century) as agriculture and handicrafts revived and expanded. Even the smallest towns and remotest areas had their commercial activities. In the middle of the century the German adventurer Heinrich von Staden noted of Pustozersk, in the far northeast just west of where the Pechora drains into the Barents Sea:

> The Samoyeds and the Russians gather to trade here. The Russians trade broad-cloth, kettles, bacon, butter, chain mail, and oat flour for the sables of the Samoyeds. Russian merchants come this far.

A document dating from 1589 reveals that the town of Eremeitsevo in Iaroslavl' *uezd* had a market each Saturday, when Muscovites and others would arrive with a great variety of trade items. The most insignificant villages supplemented their normal operations with trade fairs. Thus Mlevskoi *pogost* (in the area of the Msta, Tvertsa, and Volga rivers) had an annual two-week fair during the days of St. Peter; in 1551 "visiting merchants" *(priezzhie gosti)* set up 332 shops *(lavki)* there, "large," "medium," and "small," while local peasants "held forth with bread and all kinds of goods."[31] Russian cities and towns, of course, were scenes of continuous commercial activity. In 1586 Pskov had 1,230 shops in 35 "rows," each row specializing in a certain commodity — textiles, leather goods, copper products, iron wares, salt, fish, meat, and so forth. In 1583 Novgorod merchants operated in their city 1,800 shops in 42 rows; Kazan at the end of the century counted 368 shops and 240 smaller trade operations. Smaller towns with populations of from two thousand to five thousand people were also commercially energetic throughout the period. Toropets in 1540 had 94 shops and barns; during the late 1500's Pereiaslavl'-Zaraisk recorded 190 shops and barns plus 181 counters, shelves, and the like, while Mozhaisk registered 259 shops and barns, 72 benches and counters. Tula illustrates the dynamic commercial expansion of the period. Around the mid-1500's Tula contained 218 shops (72 sold meat, 31 salt, 10 copper goods, 10 fish, 4 butter, 4 malt, and so on), but by 1598–1599 city documents listed 280 shops plus 130 benches and huts.[32]

Moscow was Russia's most important commercial center during the sixteenth and seventeenth centuries. Almost one-third of the "fifth"-tax on commerce collected in Russia during 1634 came from Moscow alone.* With its needs and ser-

---

*This was a 20 per cent *ad valorem* tax which merchants paid on goods sold. During 1634 Moscow delivered 450,000 rubles in this tax to the treasury, followed by Kazan (140,000 rubles), Nizhnyi-Novgorod (50,000 rubles), Iaroslavl' (35,000 rubles), Pskov, and others. The men responsible for collecting this tax were the *gosti*, the wealthiest merchants of the land (see pp. 60–61, below). They almost certainly took advantage of their official positions to understate, and hence undertax, the volume of their own trade. We must not conclude, then, that 450,000 rubles was nearly as much as 20 per cent of the trade turnover for Moscow during 1634.

The date I give here as 1634 was actually by the Russian calendar the year 7142, which was, according to the Eastern Orthodox Church's calculation of time, the number of years which had elapsed since the creation of the earth.

vices, this city more than any other provided a focus for the economic life of the entire nation. In the early 1550's Richard Chancellor described trade between Moscow and Iaroslavl' (two hundred miles to the northeast) whereby in a single morning one might see seven to eight hundred sleds coming and going laden with grain and salt-fish. Yet Moscow exported grain through merchants who came a thousand miles from the north to exchange fish, furs, and hides for that product.[33] Boards, lard, wax, and other "semi-natural" goods were also brought to Moscow and then carried to other areas. Serpukov and Ustiuzhna-Zhelezopol'skaia sent, respectively, steel and iron to Moscow, where masters made axes, plowshares, kettles, scythes, houselocks, knives, and sidearms for sale throughout the nation.

Foreigners during the sixteenth and seventeenth centuries often commented upon the number of Moscow's commercial enterprises—ranging from shops to benches to pack-peddlers—as well as on the diversity of goods and their frequent high quality and low prices. Deception must have been the rule when Russians and foreigners met to do business. Herberstein noted that Muscovites offered goods usually available in Russia at a ducat for "five, eight, ten, and sometimes twenty ducats," while Europeans would fob off articles for ten or fifteen florins which were "scarcely worth one or two florins." Herberstein did not underestimate Russian business acumen; he warned his fellow foreigners:

> . . . in making bargains, if you happen to say or promise anything somewhat imprudently, they carefully remember it, and urge its performance; but if they themselves in their turn promise anything, they do not hold to it at all. Whenever, also, they begin to swear and protest, you may know for a certainty that there is some trick underneath, for they swear with the very intention of deceiving and overreaching.[34]

The Russian Eastern Orthodox new year begins on the first of September. Literally, then, the year "7142" in terms of the modern Western Gregorian calendar extends from September 1, 1633, through August 31, 1634. My methodology throughout this book has been to state Russian years in Gregorian terms, rounding them off to the Western year containing eight months rather than four — in this instance 1634.

No discussion of Russian commerce in this period would be complete without consideration of the role of the Church, which was also important as a landowner[35] and exploiter of artisan labor on monastery estates. Economically speaking, the most important monastery was probably the Troitse-Sergievskii monastery near Moscow, which Fletcher understood to have an annual income of 100,000 rubles during the late 1580's. By the end of the century the Troitse-Sergievskii monastery owned over 200,000 *desiatins** of arable land, traded salt and fish and "all goods whatsoever" as far away as Vologda, Kholmogory, and Novgorod, and even operated its own merchant vessels on the Volga, Northern Dvina, and Uga rivers, and on Lake Beloozero. During mid-century von Staden said of the Solovetskii monastery in the far north: "Six Russian princes have entered this monastery with all their money and property," and added that ". . . Suma is an unfortified settlement and belongs to that same Solovetskii monastery. It trades in many goods and boils train oil."[36] The Kirillo-Belozerskii monastery was another enterprising organization which owned almost twenty thousand *desiatins* of land by late century and hired artisans from surrounding areas to supplement the output of its "own" serf-handicraftsmen. The Kirillo-Belozerskii monastery operated throughout the entire kingdom, selling annually ten thousand *puds* in Dmitrov alone while buying bread and other goods in Rostov, Dmitrov, Iaroslavl', Kashin, and elsewhere for retail in other areas. The brothers of these and other monasteries benefited economically from the Church's exemption from taxes and trade duties.

By the middle of the fifteenth century the Russian government had already begun the attempt to bridge the economic and military gap existing between Muscovy and her immediate neighbors to the west. Above all, Russian statesmen tried to use diplomatic contacts with friendly European powers to

---

*A *desiatina* is 2.7 acres or 1.092 hectares; a *chetvert'* of land equals one-half a *desiatina*.

develop commercial relations, hire foreign artisans and engineers for service in Russia, and even, as we shall see, to encourage foreign entrepreneurs to establish "modern" industries in the Muscovite state. These problems are discussed elsewhere in this book, so there is no need at this point to study the fine details of the question of Russian foreign trade from the fifteenth to the seventeenth centuries. But a few notes on the nature of Russia's international commerce at this time will round out this survey of Russian economic development just before the introduction of capitalist manufacturing.

Furs were always of great importance among Russia's export items. A general rise in Europe's demand for furs (especially Russian furs) became apparent in Muscovy in the early 1500's and remained for a century and a half thereafter. The Muscovite state gained Siberian furs for export mainly through tribute from local tribes and a 10 per cent tax on Russian trappers in the area. Surviving records usually do not make clear the quantities of furs exported to the West, but in this period Dutch entrepreneurs often contracted squirrel and wildcat skins in lots of up to 100,000; wolves in lots of 5,000; martens in lots of 4,000; rabbits in lots of 1,000; and minks, ermines, weasels, and arctic foxes in lots of 100 to 500. The Dutch re-exported these skins to other European states. For example, in 1646 the Dutch shipped to France 675,000 louis in Russian furs, leather, and hides. Unusually good export figures for Archangel in 1653, when the Russian fur trade was at its height, show furs exported from that city worth 98,059 rubles. Other sources of export — such as overland through Poland, or through Astrakhan to the east — suggest that total fur exports for that year might have approached 300,000 rubles.[37]

Russian leather was an important export commodity during the sixteenth century, and became the most important export item after the late seventeenth-century decline of the fur trade. By 1653 leather accounted for one-third of the value of goods shipped from Archangel, averaging throughout the decade 75,000 rolls worth some 335,000 rubles. Fletcher noted the importance in Russian export of cow hides (about thirty thousand annually) and goat skins (in "great number"). But during the next century the inferior quality of these Russian animals led Russian leather merchants to buy many hides from Poland, the Ukraine, and Podolia for resale to the West.[38] Flax and hemp were also important throughout this period. Fletcher reported that when the Russians held the Baltic port Narva from 1558 through 1581, "a great part of a hundred [foreign] ships small and great yearly . . ." shipped hemp and flax to the West, but in the later 1580's the number leaving Archangel was "not past five" whereas the overland route through Poland was blocked altogether. The seventeenth century, however, saw a steady and marked revival in the export of these goods, not surprising if we consider the different price levels of these items between Russia and the West at this time. During the 1680's hemp sold in Russia at thirty-three kopecks per *pud*, in Holland for the equivalent of fifty kopecks, and in Spain for twice that amount, one ruble. Flax in Russia was valued at eighty-two and a half kopecks per *pud*, one ruble in Holland, and two in Spain. Wax was another key Russian export item, second only to furs in Fletcher's time, although it declined completely during the seventeenth century. Russian wax sold at two rubles, thirty-one kopecks per *pud* during the 1680's, three rubles in Holland, six rubles in Spain.[39]

As we shall see, by the 1620's a number of foreigners were interested in exporting grain to Europe, where the price levels were high enough to insure considerable profits to a foreigner trading in that product. On several occasions during the 1630's Dutch diplomats attempted to gain grain export monopolies for their Russian-based merchants, and even to break into large-scale grain farming in Russia. The Russians, however, were determined to keep grain export a tsarist monopoly, especially since such leading merchants (*gosti*) as Nadia Sveteshnikov shared their sovereign's profits by exporting their surpluses under the aegis of his "monopoly" and name. The Russian grain trade to the West never approached that of Prussia or Poland, but before the 1670's large shipments through Archangel were sometimes negotiated at a profit to the tsar and his *gosti* of 60 to 75 per cent.

Foreign shipments of other natural and semi-natural products in this period were also royal monopolies, notably salmon and isinglass, rhubarb (esteemed in Europe as a purge), train oil, walrus tusks, and tallow. Fletcher describes at length how Russian boats in the Bay of St. Nicholas hunted seals for train oil and the walrus for tusks. The latter served as a good substitute for ivory and were known to the Russians as "fish teeth," being

> . . . used both among [the Russians themselves] and the Persians and Bulgarians [of the Volga] that fetch it thence for beads, knives, and sword shafts of noblemen and gentlemen, and for divers other uses. Some use the powder of it against poison, as the unicorn's horn. The fish that weareth it is called a morzh [walrus] and is caught about Pechora. These fish teeth, some of them, are almost two feet of length and weigh eleven or twelve pounds apiece.

Fletcher also took note of tallow as an export commodity, the best of which came from Smolensk, Novgorod, Vologda, and Iaroslavl'. While Narva was a Russian port the Russians exported 100,000 *puds* of tallow each year; by the 1580's tallow was down to thirty thousand *puds* or less, and by the mid-seventeenth century was consumed entirely at home.[40]

Unlike their efforts to control the tsar's grain reserves, foreigners did succeed in gaining control over the caviar trade. During the sixteenth century French, Dutch, and English merchants carried this product in pressed form to Italy and other Catholic countries which demanded caviar during fast days. In the seventeenth century caviar export became the monopoly of a Dutch-Italian company (later purely Dutch), which from the 1650's to the 1670's sent through Archangel about twenty thousand *puds* of caviar yearly, paying one and a half rubles for the product during the earlier decade, two rubles during the latter.[41]

Western European merchants in this period were extremely anxious to gain access to Persian silk through Russian trade routes. Before the 1590's the English succeeded in organizing such expeditions, and von Staden once took note of an English river vessel in Russia returning from Persia "loaded with geniue silk cloth and spices." During the seventeenth century, however, the Russian government decided that Russians should serve (and profit) as middlemen in this trade, so foreign diplomats were rebuffed in their efforts to gain passage for their merchants from Persia through Russia. The English Ambassador John Merrick sought such an arrangement from 1614 to 1617; the French Ambassador in 1629; in 1630 the Dutch vainly offered an annual sum of fifteen thousand rubles for a Persian silk monopoly from Russia; Danish envoys opened negotiations soon after this on the same subject; Sweden renewed earlier efforts in 1650, as did the Dutch in 1675. Holstein came close to reaching an agreement with the tsar during the 1630's, and an Armenian silk company based in Persia actually gained permission in 1667 to sell directly to European buyers in Archangel. But the Holsteiners' negotiations collapsed when it became apparent that they lacked sufficient capital to buy the tsar's favor, and the Armenian project, too, never reached fruition. *De facto* Russian policy, then, was to forbid direct Persian-European silk commerce, retaining this monopoly for the tsar. And a profitable monopoly it was, to be sure. A *pud* of raw silk delivered at Archangel cost no more than thirty rubles, sold easily at forty-five rubles, allowing a profit of 50 per cent. But slow turnover in the silk trade kept sales volumes low: caravans arrived from Persia every three years, usually with about nine thousand *puds* of silk valued at some 405,000 rubles.[42]

In Russia's commerce with the East, Astrakhan played a role similar to that of Archangel and Novgorod in the west. During the sixteenth century the Eastern trade was probably more profitable to Russia than her commerce with the West. In contrast to the Western market, in the east Russian merchants appeared far from home and sold "manufactured" goods — metal wares, copper, textiles, leather goods, weapons, and armor, and even some Western products. Sables and valuable furs were also important exports to the East, the tsars proving more successful here than in the West in maintaining a royal monopoly. Although trade with India and China was sporadic and disappointing to more ambitious and farsighted Russian statesmen,[43] significant relations were established with Persia, the several khanates of Central Asia, and Greek merchants operating from the Ottoman empire. Of the latter a hundred or more arrived in Moscow each year with gold and silver, plates and cups, silk textiles and gold brocades, precious stones, jewelry, elegant riding gear, and raw silk. In addition to these "regular" merchants, Greek traders accompanied the ever-frequent delegations of Greek Orthodox clergymen to Moscow, gaining on those occasions relief from customs and dues and even official reimbursement for all travel expenses.[44]

In the khanates of Central Asia, Russians exchanged furs, walrus tusks, cloth (some of it European), leather, and other such goods for cotton, Calico fabrics, silk, and tiger and leopard skins. During the second half of the sixteenth century commerce between Russians and the merchants of Central Asia apparently averaged fifty thousand rubles on each side. The most significant trade between Russia and an Asiatic power, however, took place with Persia, commerce being eased through friendly diplomatic relations between shahs and tsars mutually fearful of the Ottoman Turks. Although direct trade with Persia began just after Ivan the Terrible's conquest of Kazan in 1555, not until the mid-1600's did a caravan go from Moscow to Persia or Astrakhan as often as once a year. Russo-Persian trade increased markedly during the second half of the century, but surviving records are too fragmentary to give an exact picture of its volume. Unusually complete records for 1663–1665, however, tell of a Russian caravan to Persia which sold goods valued at 76,749 rubles at a 7 per cent profit, returning with Persian goods valued at 73,586 rubles. These figures suggest considerable investments but small profits and a slow trade turnover because of great distances; we must also conclude that at this point Russia's Asian trade was no longer comparable to her commerce with the West. Besides raw and fabricated silk, Russians took from Persia fine leather (called "Morocco"), cotton goods, paper, and a few precious stones. [45]

2

First Steps Toward Industrial Modernization, 1470's–1590's

BY 1480 MOSCOW HAD overthrown the last remnants of more than two centuries of Mongol domination and was well on its way to building a unified Muscovite-Russian state by crushing the lingering independence of such neighboring principalities as Novgorod, Pskov, Rostov, and Tver'. Thus by the early 1500's Russia was no longer a divided land isolated from the West by the need to struggle against savage conquerors of the East. Russia was now a united country relatively free of attack from Asia and the South and sufficiently powerful to seek new victories in the area of the Baltic, Poland, Lithuania, and her "lost" lands of Belorussia and the Ukraine. Karl Marx forcefully stated the significance of these developments when he noted:

> Astonished Europe, at the commencement of Ivan's reign [1462-1505] hardly aware of the existence of Muscovy, hemmed in between the Tartar and the Lithuanian, was dazzled by the sudden appearance of an immense empire on its eastern confines, and Sultan Bajazet himself, before whom Europe trembled, heard for the first time the haughty language of the Muscovite.[1]

But opportunities in this new situation also posed problems for the Muscovite state, for any policy of involvement in the affairs of her immediate neighbors to the west and northwest brought Russia into competition with the relatively advanced armies and economies of Poland, Lithuania, and Sweden. Specifically, the problem for Russia was that her military and economic might was not yet the equal of her political consolidation and diplomatic ambitions. As we have seen, Russia experienced a certain revival of artisanry and trade after the late 1400's, but even at that the society's technological foundation remained traditional at a time when even Eastern Europe was undergoing a certain modernization of industry and army organization, training, and equipment. To meet the demands of this new age Russia needed an army of professional soldiers well supplied with modern weapons and military goods. In other words, Russia needed *capitalism* and the entire host of skills, attitudes, and levels of culture which seem to accompany the emergence of that economic system. But capitalism and the manufactory were quite absent in the Russia of the fifteenth and early sixteenth centuries, for neither the Russian merchant nor the Russian artisan was close to breaking that barrier of technology and understanding that separated the economy of the handicraftsman and small merchant from that of the manufacturer and large-scale merchant.

At the risk of belaboring the obvious, one might note that the inability of the Russian economy to meet its new economic needs no more dissipated the pressures which created those needs than it undermined the determination of Russian statesmen to partake of the technology and skills of Western Europe. And Muscovites were familiar with many of the West's resources from rather early times. Italian merchants penetrated the Black Sea and established trade networks there as early as the second half of the thirteenth century: around 1267 Mangu-Temir granted the Genoese special trade privileges in Kaffa (modern-day Feodosia), and in 1347 the Golden Horde concluded a commercial treaty with Venice. In 1356 chronicles note the presence in Moscow of "gosti of Surozh," traders from the Genoese colonies of the Crimea. When Tokh-tamysh attacked Moscow in 1382 the chronicle mentions a foreign "clothier" named Adam, probably an Italian, who was involved in the defense of the city.[2] European physicians appeared in Russia to serve Vasilii II (1425 – 1462), and at the same time a permanent colony of Italian merchants in Moscow exerted a certain influence on Russian life. Clearly it was an appreciation for Italian learning and talent which caused young Ivan III to make Gian Battista della Volpe director of the Royal Mint. In fact, Ivan hoped to use his modest contacts with Italy to attract more European talent, and in 1468 the tsar instructed della Volpe to send a party of foreign residents of the Russian capital to Italy to engage a number of technicians for service in the Muscovite state.[3]

Under normal circumstances della Volpe's agents would probably have accomplished their mission in a routine manner, sending back several craftsmen and artisans who would have had a modest impact on the material culture of Tsar Ivan's kingdom. As it was, when the Russian party arrived in Rome it was immediately enlisted in a diplomatic project of interest to Pope Paul II: the promotion of Roman Catholic influence in Russia and the recruitment of the Muscovite grand duke as an ally of the Vatican in a crusade against the Ottoman Turks. The instrument of this rapprochement was to be the niece of the last Byzantine emperor, Zoe Palaeologue, who after the fall of Constantinople in 1453 had grown up in Rome under the care and observation of the pontiff. In February 1469 the greater number of Ivan's party returned to Moscow with two Italian technicians and a letter from the Pope proposing mar-riage between the tsar and Zoe Palaeologue. Suggestion of a union between the fallen yet still memorable Byzantine Empire and the rising but scarcely recognized Muscovite dynasty was so flattering to Ivan III that a marriage was quickly negotiated and finally concluded in Moscow in November 1472. For our purposes, the most important result of this royal union was that it initiated the first considerable influx of Western masters into Russia, for Sof'ia Fominichna (Zoe's Russian name) was accompanied by a large number of foreign priests, artists, craftsmen, and scholars, and "it may have been at her instigation that further missions were sent to Italy to hire artisans, masons, architects, painters and even doctors and bring them back to Russia. . . ."[4]

In 1474 Ivan sent another mission to Italy headed by his trusty boyar Simen Tolbuzin to recruit the best available architects and engineers. Tolbuzin was so fortunate as to secure the services of the sexagenarian Rudolfo Fioravanti of Bologna, "who, like Leonardo da Vinci, was at once an architect, an engineer, and an expert in hydraulics, military fortifications, pyrotechnics, and metal casting."[5] While in Moscow, "Aristotle" Fioravanti (as the Russians called him) built the Cathedral of the Dormition (*Uspenskii Sobor*) and improved Russian metallurgy by establishing a new armory in 1479 in the very center of Moscow (on the Neglinnaia river), which became famous in Russian history as the "Cannon Yard" (*pushechnyi dvor*).

The rise of Muscovite power under Ivan III led to other relationships with the West. Diplomatic and economic ties with Venice, Naples, and Genoa were expanded, contact was established with Moldavia and Hungary, and, if the Pope's ambitions for certain agreements with Russia came to nought, the Hapsburgs became increasingly interested in using Russia as a counterweight against both Poland and the Turks. As for Western technical influence on Russia in the same period, it continued, though perhaps not at a level that the Russians found satisfactory. In 1482 Ivan asked the Hungarian king, Matthias Corvinus, to send him ore experts to help prospect for copper in Russia, but was refused. Eight years later, in 1490, a similar request was made of the German emperor through the Greek ambassador, Iurii Trakhaniot. There is evidence to indicate that this contact produced a prospecting mission in the far northwest and even copper works on the Tsil'ma river.[6]

The main obstacle to large-scale Russian adoption of Western technology and skills in this period was not so much geographic isolation or economic backwardness as a conscious policy on the part of Russia's Western neighbors to isolate and contain her. With the fall of Novgorod in the 1470's, Muscovy herself became a Baltic power, and in 1492 Ivan III, hoping to establish direct maritime contact with the commercially active powers of the far West, established Ivangorod on the eastern bank of the Narova river. But Ivangorod's harbor facilities were less satisfactory than those of the neighboring town, Narva, so ships continued to dock there or at other non-Russian Baltic ports. As for Russia's overland trade routes, these ran through Poland and Lithuania, which enabled either country to block Russian industrial-technological communication with Europe as a whole. The Poles carefully watched the few German traders who crossed the Lithuanian frontier, to be certain that no goods passed which might harm Polish interests. They also investigated "merchants" on their way to Moscow, since often the latter were artisans who had been secretly engaged for service in Russia and were attempting to deceive the Polish-Lithuanian authorities. The Hanse pursued a similar policy with regard to Russian commerce conducted through their towns on the Baltic seaboard. In 1506 we find an interesting case of the Hanse towns being warned of Dutchmen preparing to slip into Russia to learn the languages and, presumably, to establish more extensive commercial relations with the government in Moscow.[7]

The Russian dilemma is well illustrated by the first major effort of Ivan the Terrible (Ivan IV, 1547-1584) to establish intensified economic contact with the West. Ivan, knowing the weakness of his large empire vis-à-vis Sweden, Poland, and Lithuania, decided immediately after his coronation to renew and expand earlier Russian efforts to draw upon Western European technology. Before, Russian rulers had tried to develop ties with Charles V, Emperor of the Holy Roman Empire (1519–1556), by sending embassies to Spain as early as 1524 and 1527. Ivan knew that in 1547 Charles was still anxious to suppress the Protestant Reformation and restore the unity of Christendom. So in that year the tsar dispatched

Hans Schlitte, a German Protestant merchant and adventurer from the town of Goslar who had established himself in Moscow, to visit Charles and convince the emperor that Ivan was favorable to a restoration of Catholic-Orthodox unity. In fact, Ivan was interested only in raising a large party of craftsmen and technicians,* but this was suggested to Charles as a mere token of friendship and good will.[8]

With the permission of Charles, in the following year Schlitte raised 123 men for service under the tsar, a number which included doctors, bell-makers, masters of mining and gold work, architects, diamond-cutters, well-diggers, papermakers, typographers, scholars, masters of ancient and modern languages, and, perhaps most surprising, four theologians. But when the party reached Lübeck these plans came to grief, for Hanseatic ruling circles persuaded the fathers of that city that the tsar was not sincere in his proposals for religious unity, and that in any case the enlightenment of Muscovy was not in the best interests of the West. Soon thereafter Charles himself became convinced of the same thing, and he sent instructions not to admit any masters to Russia.[9]

Schlitte then turned to Rome, hoping to interest the Pope in Orthodox-Catholic reunification and a joint attack on the Turks. Here again, in 1553, he was exposed and discredited, finally ending up in Denmark, from where he wrote the tsar on March 5, 1555, requesting new instructions and a replenishment of finances.[10] The lesson was clear: "Cut off as she was from direct access to the sea, Russia [was bound] to feel once more the weakness of her position."[11]

As the Schlitte mission neared its final stages, Ivan might well have despaired of ever establishing direct and unhindered relations with those European nations which might provide

---

*Speaking of a slightly later period the German traveler Heinrich von Staden noted that "The Grand Prince [Ivan the Terrible] would like to, and is of the opinion that he ought to, maintain friendship with the [Holy] Roman Emperor until he acquires all kinds of craftsmen and so many thousands of [mercenary] soldiers that he can resist the Crimean Khan. He also thinks he might persuade the Roman Emperor to go to war with Poland." *Land and Government,* p. 61.

him military goods and skilled craftsmen. But on August 24, 1553, a small English ship, the 160-ton *Edward Bonaventure,* seeking a northern sea route to Cathay and India, arrived at the mouth of the Dvina, near the monastery of St. Nicholas. Local fishermen informed the captain of the ship, Richard Chancellor, that he was in the domain of the tsar of Muscovy.[12] While the English were spending the early part of the winter in this area, news of their arrival reached Moscow. The tsar was greatly excited by this new development, for although he had recently defeated and absorbed the kingdoms of Kazan and Astrakhan, he knew that future battles lay in the west where the enemy was stronger and better prepared. Hoping to establish commercial and diplomatic relations with England, in late 1553 Ivan ordered Chancellor and his companions to be taken to Moscow for a personal audience in the Kremlin.[13]

Chancellor spoke with Ivan and delivered an open letter from Edward VI, addressed in several languages to any and all rulers of the northern lands, requesting a favorable reception for his sailors. As for the tsar, he could not have been more gracious. He sent Edward (who had actually died on July 6, 1553) a friendly reply granting permission to English merchants to trade in Russia duty-free without any technicalities or delay. Chancellor left Russia in March 1554 and in London helped form a special company to trade with Russia.[14] By 1555 he had already returned to Russia as the English Ambassador, receiving a charter from the tsar on behalf of the Moscovy Company.[15] This document provided for a duty-free English monopoly of trade with Russia, granting the English the right to establish warehouses in Rozovyi Island, as well as in Vologda, Kholmogory, Iaroslavl', and Moscow. Justice, when necessary, was to be administered only in Moscow, thereby protecting the foreigners from the whims or prejudices of local authorities. In 1567 these privileges were expanded still further.[16]

From these negotiations the Russians began to obtain such English goods as cloth, paper, sugar, dishes, organs, copper, and sheet lead for roofing. But military equipment was what

Tsar Ivan most desired — saltpeter, gunpowder, lead, sulphur — and it was this possibility which most alarmed Russia's Western neighbors. Since Poland and Sweden were at war with Russia during the late 1550's, they tried to stop, through protests and negotiations with Queen Elizabeth of England, what they suspected was a secret traffic in military goods. Soon the Emperor of the Holy Roman Empire and the Senate of Hamburg were exerting similar pressure on the English sovereign, as did Frederick II of Denmark in 1565.[17] A revealing statement of the fear which Russia managed to instill in her neighbors to the west is contained in this excerpt from a letter of the Polish King Sigismund to Queen Elizabeth, dated December 6, 1569:

. . . as we have written afore, so now we write again to your majesty that we know and feel of a surety, the Muscovite, enemy to all liberty under the heavens, daily to grow mightier by the increase of such things as be brought to the Narva,* while not only wares but also weapons heretofore unknown to him, and artificers and arts be brought unto him: by means whereof he maketh himself strong to vanquish all others. Which things, as long as this voyage to Narva is used, cannot be stopped. And we perfectly know your majesty cannot be ignorant of how great the cruelty is of the said enemy, of what force he is, what tyranny he useth on his subjects, and in what servile sort they be under him. *We seemed hitherto to vanquish him only in this, that he was rude of arts and ignorant of policies. If so be that this navigation to the Narva continue, what shall be unknown to him?* Therefore we that know best and border upon him, do admonish other Christian princes in time, that they do not betray their dignity, liberty and life of them and their subjects to a most barbarous and cruel enemy, as we can no less do by the duty of a Christian prince. For now we do foresee, except other princes take this admonition, the Muscovite puffed up in pride with those things that be brought to the Narva, and made more perfect in warlike affairs with engines of war and ships, will make assault this way on Christendom, to slay or make bound all that shall withstand him: which God defend. With which our admonition divers princes already content

*The Russians captured Narva in 1558 during early phases of the Livonian War, but lost it to Sweden in the peace of 1581. Peter the Great permanently regained the city in 1704.

themselves, and abstain from the Narva. The others that will not abstain from said voyage shall be impeached by our navy and incur the danger of loss of life, liberty, wife and children.[18]

Actually there is no clear record of just how much military equipment was shipped to Russia during the war with Poland and Sweden. It is true that Anthony Jenkins, in November of 1567, informed Elizabeth of Ivan's expressed desire for artillery "and things necessaire for warre." But the Queen generally assured her fellow monarchs that no such commerce was being conducted by English merchants. This was widely disbelieved, however, and in the early 1560's many Western European observers attributed Russian successes in Livonia to the presumed influx of English goods into Russia.[19]

The study of commercial relations between Russia and the West in this period is a fascinating subject worthy of extensive treatment in its own right. For our purposes at least two aspects of the subject should be noted. First, the English did not succeed in maintaining their original monopoly on the Russian market. By 1567 the first Dutch ship had reached Lapland, and in 1578 the Dutch began to operate even on the Dvina. As early as the 1560's French and Dutch trade was brisk in Narva, and when Russia lost this Baltic outpost at the end of the Livonian War (1581), commodities from those countries continued to enter Russia through the White Sea. The English protested this infringement of their commercial prerogatives, but in vain. So by the 1580's Russia was developing relations with Western Europe as a whole and not alone with England.[20]

Second, these commercial contacts with Western Europe stimulated the drive toward industrial modernization in early modern Russia which is our main subject. Russia's expanded foreign commerce did not actually affect internal forces or methods of production, of course, although imports of military equipment and luxury goods probably alleviated some of the harshest shortages which existed before the 1550's. But such products were expensive and their availability was at best limited and precarious. Perhaps this explains why Russian statesmen toward the end of the sixteenth century continued their long-standing desire to reconstitute – to the greatest extent possible – the foundations of the domestic economy along Western European lines. This meant bringing Western masters to Russia, establishing new industrial enterprises and even fields of industry not yet known in the country – using, all the while, foreign craftsmen as instructors of Russian apprentices who could then exercise their new talents solely for the benefit of Russia. Although this aspect of "Westernization" before Peter the Great reached its high point in the last two-thirds of the seventeenth century, there were, as we shall see, significant elements of it during the sixteenth century as well.

The Livonian War of 1558–1583 so intensified the desire of the Russian government to obtain technological aid from the outside world that Ivan IV engaged ore experts from his enemy, Sweden, and at one point went to the extreme of ordering a search for metallurgists among those taken prisoner during the fighting. The main bearer of industrial progress for Russia in this period, however, was England. In addition to his diplomatic activities, Osip Nepeia, the first Russian Ambassador to England (1556–1557), was ordered to engage English masters for service in Russia, and he returned to Moscow with a doctor, a pharmacist, two coopers, seven rope masters, furriers and foresters, some copper smiths and ten apprentices. In 1567 Ivan asked Queen Elizabeth to send him an architect "which can make castells, towers and palaces – a Doctor and a potycary, and other masters suche as are coming to seke ought [sic] gold and silver." Though she had her reservations about the wisdom of aiding Russia's capacity to wage war, Elizabeth did send some architects who built fortifications for the Muscovites, and they were accompanied by approximately a dozen other craftsmen.[21]

The first capitalistic industrial enterprises in Russia were organized by the English Muscovy Company,* which with the

*The *pushechnyi dvor* which Fioravanti organized in 1479 was state-owned and hence not "capitalistic"; moreover, its technology was of artisan

permission of the tsar sent a trade director, Richard Grey, and seven London rope masters to build a rope walk in the northeastern town of Kholmogory in 1557. This factory was so successful (producing over 1,200 tons of rope as early as 1558) that soon thereafter a second rope works was established in nearby Vologda. After several years a hundred or more men were working at Vologda alone, of whom no more than twenty were English. As the wages of Englishmen were higher than those of the natives, Russian masters were employed in increasing numbers as they became more proficient in their work, and by 1584 scarcely any Englishmen were engaged at Vologda. By that time, according to Madame Mildred Wretts-Smith, the Vologda rope walk was "a busy settlement, for many hundreds of 'ends' were sent yearly to England, from small ropes of one inch in thickness, through every grade up to great cables of fourteen and sixteen inches." These two English enterprises provided most of the cordage for the English fleet which defeated the Great Armada of 1588, and their product was of such high quality that its reputation rivaled that of Danzig, which enjoyed such high esteem for rope manufacturing in this period. It appears, however, for reasons unknown today, that the Kholmogory and Vologda rope walks were closed by the beginning of the seventeenth century.[22]

Russian contacts with the Muscovy Company produced other entrepreneurial projects. While the English rope walks flourished at Kholmogory and Vologda, a flax-spinning enterprise also operated in the former city. At the end of the century both Dutch and English ships hunted the whale and walrus for blubber oil in Russia's northern waters, and the English cut the trees on the shores of this area for ship masts.[23] England also served Russian naval ambitions in this period, for if Elizabeth was reluctant to meet Ivan's request of 1567 for shipwrights to build ships and mariners to sail them, enough English craftsmen did appear in Russia at this time to

---

rather than manufactory type. The copper enterprise mentioned earlier in this chapter is of uncertain nature, but I have not considered it capitalistic.

construct galleys and brigantines at Narva and Vologda, and a small Russian fleet of some sort existed at Ivangorod while it was in Muscovite hands. The importance of the English in these Russian efforts has been well described:

> At Narva the English not only built ships, but were given command of them and their crews by the Tsar. They became captains and master gunners and were given good wages, with "fifteen pence a day for meat and drink and every man a house at the Emperor's charge." "Mariners," said a merchant in 1572, "bear all the sway now."[24]

Most of these ships were lost through the unfavorable conclusion of the Livonian War in the early 1580's, but in 1585 the English built another twenty vessels at Vologda and were preparing to construct twenty more. In this period the English also finished a number of ships in Iaroslavl'.[25]

Foreigners helped to establish other industrial enterprises in sixteenth-century Russia, though surviving information on these efforts is often so fragmentary that one can scarcely estimate their nature. For example, we have an account of a terrible explosion at a powder works near Moscow in 1531 which is said to have killed more than two hundred workers. So many casualties might indicate either a large manufactory or a great exaggeration. The French master Aleviz who is mentioned in connection with this establishment might have been a private capitalist entrepreneur or the organizer and manager of a large state artisan works. Sources also indicate the existence of a paper mill during the sixteenth century. Rafael Barberini, an Italian visitor to Moscow in 1564, noted that as a consequence of the recent introduction of the printing press the Russians "also ventured to introduce the making of paper, and they still make it, but are unable to make use of it because they have not brought that art to perfection. . . ." The paper manufactory to which Barberini referred was located on the Utsa river, near Kannino-Vanteevo, thirty *versts* from Moscow. The founder of this first known Russian paper mill, which by 1567 was no longer operating, was a feudal landowner, a *pomeshchik* by the name of Fedor Savinov.[26]

An early attempt to introduce silk manufacturing into Russia came at the beginning of the sixteenth century, when a native of Constantinople established a shop in Moscow for the production of clerical brocades. Around 1593 the Venetian master Marco Chinopi came to Moscow upon Tsar Fedor's invitation to make damask, velvet, and silk brocades. Chinopi organized a shop in the Kremlin, near the church bell tower called "Ivan the Great," but this enterprise lasted no more than two or three years. At the same time, in line with his desire to free Russia from dependence on imports or foreign masters, Tsar Boris Godunov (1598–1605) tried to introduce the factory production of cloth into Russia, and he commissioned the German Beckman to engage woolen masters for this purpose in Lübeck. We do not know how this project ended, but it seems that no manufactory resulted from efforts expended in this direction.[27]

The most ambitious English plan for the building of new industries in Russia was the Muscovy Company's project for iron manufacturing in the northeastern part of the country. The company's discussion of the matter with the Russian government began as early as 1557, though it was not until a decade later, on April 18, 1567, that the company's chief agent in Russia, Anthony Jenkinson, was instructed to obtain the necessary license for iron smelting from the tsar. This project was incorporated as a privilege in the company's charter of 1569. A contemporary translation of the passage concerning this point reads as follows.

> Also we have of our goodness given and granted to the English merchants, leave to buy them a house at *Witchida* [valley of the Vychegda river], and there to search out mines of iron. And where they shall happily find it, there to set up houses for the making of the said iron, and to make the same, and of our goodness have granted them woods, five or six miles in compass about the said houses, to the making of their iron, and not to exceed those bounds and limits: And where they shall cut the said wood, not to set up any village or farm there; bringing the artificers for making of their iron out of their own Country and to learn our people that art, and so freely to occupy the said iron in these our Dominions, transporting also of the same home into

England, allowing for every pud weight one den'ga, or Moscow penny.

And if any of the said iron shall be needful for our works, then we [are] to take of the said iron to our works, upon agreement of price, paying money out of our Treasury for the same.[28]

Because diplomatic relations between Russia and England began to worsen soon after the charter was granted, construction of the projected iron factory never began, although the English shipped iron ore from the Vychegda to London for smelting at home. It is interesting to note, however, that the English presence in Russia did lead to the creation of an enterprise which may have borne some resemblance to their original plans. This was an iron manufactory built by the Stroganov family in the area of Sol'vychegodsk, some eight hundred kilometers northeast of Moscow.

Some historians have regarded the Stroganov iron enterprise as a result of specifically Russian innovation and experience,[29] but deeper and more recent research indicates that it was probably a product of English influence and technology. The English arrived in the Sol'vychegodsk area in the 1560's and, as we have seen, obtained a charter from the tsar in 1569 to prospect and build factories on the Vychegda river. On August 8, 1570, a royal *ukaz* was issued ordering the Stroganovs (who had considerable economic interests in this area) to observe English activities to make certain the English did not exceed the privileges Ivan IV had set forth in his charter. Although the English did not build iron manufactories in Russia at this time, it seems possible that the Stroganovs, in their government-imposed role of supervising the English merchants and entrepreneurs, got the idea of establishing the same kind of enterprise, as well as the technical information on how to do it.[30]

In any event, the Stroganovs soon organized expeditions to find ore sites and good factory locations; they discovered "iron ore in unused swamps" in Sodrolinskaia *volost'* on the Vaga river and on the Lakhoma river near Sol'vychegodsk. A charter dated May 18, 1577, gave Iakov Stroganov the right to build iron factories and use local forest resources, with an *obrok* of *polupoltina* (twenty-five kopecks) to be paid on each blasting furnace. By 1583 an iron manufactory was in operation near Sol'vychegodsk and the Lakhoma river. In time Stroganov's iron activities also embraced the part of his estate at Tsyvozero.[31]

During the seventeenth century we no longer find references to mining and iron manufacturing in the Pomor'e area, which suggests that the Stroganov iron works operated for no more than two decades. But artisan iron and copper production on a fairly large scale was established in the family's properties at Perm (which is on the Kama river, some 600 kilometers southeast of Sol'vychegodsk) sometime before 1625, and this continued well into the nineteenth century. The Stroganovs were also interested in gold, silver, and lead in this area.

Iakov Stroganov's Sol'vychegodsk-Lakhoma iron works was clearly a capitalistic manufactory and is an interesting example of the influence of foreign technology upon the economic life of early modern Russia. Yet it had little significance for the industrial development of the country as a whole, perhaps because of its short life and geographical isolation in the northeast. The output of this factory influenced the lives of Russians in Siberia, but the broad and consistent application of the water-wheel technology upon which it was based came only after the construction of the Tula iron enterprises of the 1630's, an event we shall describe in the following chapter.

3

Andrei Vinius and the Beginnings
of Iron Manufacturing

A MAJOR RUSSIAN OBJECTIVE during the
Livonian War—the gaining of access to the Baltic—was lost
as Russia was defeated decisively by Poland and Sweden. The
next significant Russian confrontation with the West was the
Smuta, or *Smutnoe vremia,* the "Time of Troubles." It began
as a dynastic and agrarian crisis in the reign of Boris Godunov,
led to a Polish-inspired *coup d'état* in 1604–1605, and then to
a Polish-Swedish invasion of Russian lands. Not only did
Russia suffer considerable destruction during these years; the
very character of the government was called into question by
Polish occupation of the capital and interference in the most
basic affairs of state. The invaders were driven from Moscow
only by the winter of 1612. In the following year the first
Romanov, Michael Fedorovich, began his reign.

The Stolbovo peace treaty of February 1617 initiated a
lengthy period of peace with Sweden, but Russia was not so
fortunate in her relations with Poland. Russian statesmen
concluded a fourteen-and-a-half year truce with Poland at

Deulino in December 1618, but the parties understood that this signalled nothing more than a breathing spell during which the two nations could prepare for renewed warfare. The Poles continued to uphold the pretensions of Prince Wladyslaw to the Russian throne, and to occupy large areas of Russia, including Smolensk, the Seversk area, and the road to Podneprov'e. The return of Tsar Michael's powerful and single-minded father, Filaret, from Polish captivity in 1619 merely reinforced an existing attitude,[1] for at the time of Filaret's arrival in Moscow the general mood "was one of aggrieved nationalism and religious exclusiveness; memories of the intervention were still fresh, and Poland was commonly seen as the vanguard of militant Catholicism."[2]

This being the situation, the Russian government acted to improve its military equipment by mobilizing artisans to produce goods needed for war. In this the problem, of course, was the destruction still lying in the wake of the Time of Troubles. The *Pushechnyi dvor* iron works, for example, had greatly declined by 1613, and was not to enjoy full capacity again until the 1630's. Most of the craftsmen once employed at the *Oruzheinaia palata** fled to the provinces, where in fact smaller artisan shops at Zhelezopol'skaia, Ustiug, Vologda, Novgorod, Pskov, and elsewhere had also ceased to function in a normal manner. But in time recovery did come. Many foreign masters returned to Russian service (or entered it for the first time), and Russian artisans took up their duties again. By 1637 thirty-five iron masters and sixty-six apprentices worked at the *Pushechnyi dvor,* which was considerably expanded in the next decade. The fact that over two hundred masters were registered at the *Oruzheinaia palata* in 1681[3] suggests that it had a comparable work force in earlier years, too. During the 1630's some 350 iron masters were active in ten areas outside Moscow,[4] and this was by no means the full extent of Russia's iron artisan capacity in more sparsely populated areas.

---

*The *Oruzheinaia palata* ("armaments palace") was a large armory organized in Moscow during the early sixteenth century.

To speed preparation for war with Poland ("scheduled," according to the agreed duration of the Deulino armistice, for mid-1633), the government ordered the registration in 1629 of all blacksmith forges in the Russian empire, and early the following year certain obligatory work "for the sovereign" (*na gosudaria*) was levied against each smith.[5] The regular orders which followed this government action were often quite large. For example, on December 16, 1632, the tsar ordered the *voevoda* (governor) of Ustiuzhna-Zhelezopol'skaia to have local artisans make 100,000 projectiles 3 *grivni** in weight and 2,000 projectiles ¾ *grivna* in weight. The government ordered 314,500 projectiles the next year. Other artisan crafts were involved in the tsar's war mobilization efforts. Great quantities of knee socks were required for newly organized regiments in Moscow during the autumn of 1633. When local markets could not meet the demand, orders were sent to Vladimirskaia and Galitskaia *chetverty* (districts) for the purchase or manufacture of such socks from local masters. [6]

Despite great efforts and high hopes, the government found that its artisan resources came nowhere near meeting the demands placed upon them. Even when profitable, iron artisans found their work burdensome, and many began to flee their registered domiciles. To check this form of resistance, entire populations of towns and villages were made responsible for the presence of their smiths, and if a metallurgist succeeded in escaping "punishments which the sovereign commands" could be levied against his guarantors. It was also common practice at this time for the tsar to order iron masters in the provinces and smaller cities to come to Moscow to ply their trade, especially if the work of a particular area was poor or slight.[7] Even at that, iron artisanry was undistinguished, being far more subject to the vicissitudes of men and nature than manufacturing. The projectile order to the blacksmiths of Ustiuzhna-Zhelezopol'skaia, for example, was not actually filled. Heavy rains fell in the area during the summer and fall of 1632, and for this reason the necessary charcoal and ore were

*One *grivna* = approximately one *funt* (14.4 ounces avdp.).

not prepared. Nor were there enough hammer-masters on hand, and the smiths who were available forced the government to raise the price of what could be delivered by two *altyn** per *pud* of projectiles.[8] Thus in the twenty years or so preceding 1633, Tsar Michael's government tried to supplement its own productive resources by working to restore and intensify the economic and diplomatic contacts with the West which had been broken during the *Smuta*. Here the objective was to supply the Russian army with superior European equipment† and to gain, if possible, military alliances and diplomatic support for the coming war with Poland.

Although Russians welcomed merchants of all nationalities even during the Time of Troubles, the tsar's officials after

---

*One *altyn* = 6 *den'gi;* 200 *den'gi* = 1 ruble. See Appendix I on Russian money of the sixteenth and seventeenth centuries.

† It is surprisingly difficult to estimate the worth of Russian artillery at this time. Russian ordinance frequently failed to perform well in battle with the armies of Russia's Western neighbors, and the Muscovites themselves were dissatisfied with its quality — one reason they were so anxious to import guns from Europe or obtain Western gunsmiths to work in Russia and instruct native apprentices. But Muscovite artillery earned frequent praises from foreign observers. Kobentsel, the Ambassador to Russia of Maximilian II (1564–1576), reported that the Russian artillery service had no fewer than two thousand weapons and was, in his opinion, the finest in the world. That this is not an isolated opinion is illustrated by the writings of Raphael Barberini in 1565, an anonymous Englishman of the same period, and the Italian writer Guardini toward the end of the century. (Guardini praised Russian smiths, saying they had learned their skills from German, Italian, and Lithuanian masters.) Even Giles Fletcher esteemed Russian weapons: "It is thought that no Prince of Christendome hath better stoare of munition, than the *Russe* Emperour. And it may partly appeare by the Artillerie house [*Pushechnyi dvor?*] at *Mosko,* where all sortes of great ordinance, all brasse pieces, very faire, to an exceeding great number." [9]

Herberstein also had a high opinion of the quality of Russian artillery; its failures came, he believed, because gunners of the period were poorly trained. "I mean to say that they do not know when they ought to use the larger kind of cannon which are intended for destroying walls, or the smaller for breaking the force of an enemy's attack." He reports the amusement of a German bombardier who overheard a Russian officer during a Mongol campaign against Moscow order his men to place ". . . one of the largest cannon . . . under the gate of a fortress, where it could scarcely be brought in the space of three days, and with only one discharge of it he would have blown the gate to pieces." Herberstein also claimed that Russian artillerists were poorly prepared and never ready to use their weapons upon short notice.[10]

1613 initially looked to England as their main source of outside support. As early as 1617 the Russian government was
encouraging the English to renew both commercial and industrial activity in Russia. A letter of that year from Tsar Michael
expressed the hope that English merchants would "freely bring
[to Russia] all manner of Comodityse that is needfull and re-
quisit for the warrs, as Leade, powther, or ordinance, copper
and other mettall, and munitione for ordinance and all other
warlike munitiones and weopens. . . ." Another letter of the
same year from the tsar to James I tells us that the Russians
"granted unto your merchants of the sayd [Muscovy] Company in our domynions to search for Iron mynes upon the
River [Sukhona] and other Rivers, and upon barren Grownd-
es where they can fynde yt with libertie to worke the same
into Iron."[11]

At first the English moved to exploit their opportunities in
Russia. While John Water led a prospective expedition to
Perm in 1618, the government of James I was hoping to gain
exclusive trade rights for its merchants in Russia through
diplomatic support of the tsar against Poland.[12] But as in the
case of the Muscovy Company a half-century before, the
projected English iron factories of the early 1600's were never
built. In both instances the failure of England's industrial
ambitions stemmed from a deterioration of diplomatic relations between London and Moscow, for in this period commerce, industry, and diplomacy were closely interconnected
and no development occurred in one area without affecting the
others. In fact, despite the apparent intimacy of Russia and
England in 1617, the decline of England's diplomatic position
with Muscovy appears to have begun as early as the following
year. And as in the previous century, so now too it was
Holland which benefited from England's misfortune — despite
a certain disadvantage. Dutch prestige in Russia had slipped
during the Russo-Swedish peace negotiations of 1617, for
while England was helpful to the Russians at that time, the
Dutch played no useful role in the conferences at Stolbovo,
and even withdrew before the conclusion of a treaty. So Isaak

Massa, Ambassador of the Dutch General States, arrived in Archangel on August 22, 1618, to improve his government's relations with the tsar. And events could scarcely have moved in a direction more favorable to Massa's cause, for at almost the very moment of his arrival the English Ambassador, Sir Dudley Diggs, fled Archangel suddenly and without clear reason. Perhaps Diggs suddenly became skeptical of Russian ability to withstand the Polish armies then pressing into Russia (on what soon proved to be a last offensive before conclusion of the truce at Deulino in December), and decided to save himself and the English loan money in his possession.[13] Whatever his motives, Sir Dudley did not tarry long enough to explain them to his Russian hosts. As a result,

> . . . the Russians did not disguise their indignation at Diggs's conduct, and ostentatiously flattered the Dutch, who had arrived simultaneously with a "subsidy" for the Tsar from the States General. . . . From this moment, it would appear, the fortunes of the English began to change; the Dutchmen on Russian soil began to gain more and more ascendancy over them. . . .[14]

The English might yet have regained their diplomatic position after 1618 had they been willing to accept the "Perpetuall League of Alliance, Defensive and Offensive" for which the Russians had pressed in 1569, 1617–1618, and then finally in 1623. But the English estimation of Russia's diplomatic importance to them at this time was limited. For England, Russia "was merely a convenient trademart for the barter of English wares, [a country] whence could be received the raw materials, necessary to the maintenance of English industry."[15] Thus James I was unwilling to meet Tsar Michael's alliance proposals, and diplomatic ties between the two countries cooled steadily during the remainder of the seventeenth century.*

---

*The nadir point in this decline surely came when James's court began to discuss the subjugation and colonization of northeast Russia. Such possibilities were discussed as late as 1631, although at no time did the Russians then appear to have been aware of such a threat from England. This is an interesting commentary, incidentally, on the dangers posed at that time to a backward country playing the game of power politics with technologically advanced nations of the West. Consult Inna Lubimenko, "A Project for the

Despite the importance of these diplomatic developments, Dutch ascendancy over England in Russia at this time was even more the product of economic realities. When the English arrived in Russia during the mid-sixteenth century, Ivan the Terrible was so overjoyed at the possibility of unhindered trade with the West that he thought little about the terms under which that trade would occur. The tsar was only too happy, for example, to grant the Muscovy Company duty-free trade rights. By the 1620's, however, merchants of other nationalities had arrived in Russia, and the customs dues they paid on their commercial activity were of no small benefit to the state treasury.* The English, by contrast, maintained their original free-trade privileges, and the Russian government — long recovered from its original burst of gratitude and generosity — now found that what once appeared to be a just courtesy was nothing more than an outrageous and unprofitable immunity. During the seventeenth century the Netherlands was, moreover, clearly the leading European power in shipping, commerce, and finance.[16] As in similar cases, the Dutch in Russia based their commercial position on the quick turnover of goods which were cheaper, of wider variety, and available in greater quantities than those obtainable through English competitors. Although the quality of Dutch-imported commodities was usually low, they were satisfactory to a nation like Russia, which was not only poor and backward but struggling with the aftermath of war and invasion.[17] Finally, to make the situation still worse for England, the Muscovy Com-

---

Acquisition of Russia by James I," *E.H.R.*, XXIX (1914), 246–256; S. Konovalov, "Thomas Chamberlayne's Description of Russia, 1631," *O.S.P.*, V (1954), 107–111.

*The significance of foreign commerce as a source of state revenue may be most easily understood by studying the customs records of Archangel, whose trade turnover by the mid-seventeenth century represented some 75 per cent of all Russian foreign trade. The amount of revenue gathered there during the first half of the century varied between 26,000 and 40,000 rubles, and in 1675–1676 reached a figure of 82,180 rubles. Annual collections remained high during the 1680's, 82,600 rubles in 1687–1688 being the highest sum for this period. *Ocherki istorii SSSR, period feodalizma xvii v* [Studies in the history of the USSR, feudal period, seventeenth century] (Moscow, 1955), pp. 131, 132.

pany was a monopoly suffering from insufficient capital. This meant that English goods entering the Russian market emanated from a single, noncompetitive source, and were by virtue of this fact alone overpriced.[18]

This is not to suggest that England disappeared as a factor in Russian economic relationships with the West during the 1620's and 1630's. In 1621 John Water resumed prospecting efforts at Perm, and in 1626 the English engineer Bulmer conducted an ore expedition along the Northern Dvina and Pechora rivers. In 1624 Sir John Merrick, English Ambassador to the tsar, actually engaged foreign iron masters to work in the Russian northeast, and in 1625 the English renewed their inquiries into the possibility of iron manufacturing in Russia. But English entrepreneurs, accustomed as they were to easy profits in Russia from duty-free trade, had neither the means nor the desire to assume industrial development of the country.[19]

In the realm of commerce the English were forced to give ground to the Dutch, whose volume of imports into Russia soon reached great quantities. Thomas de Swaen, for example, served the tsar as an intermediary for military purchases in Holland in 1630, 1632, and 1634, and in 1633 he personally sold the tsar ten thousand *puds* of iron, fifteen thousand *puds* of cannon balls, three thousand sabre blades, and a quantity of gunpowder. Elias Trip was another Dutch merchant who profited from Russian military needs at this time; in 1630 he delivered ten cannon, and in the next few years filled orders for five thousand rifles, two hundred partizans, four hundred halberds, and two hundred pistols. Paul de Willem and Jan van Lier Abmachungen sold a huge amount of military equipment to the tsarist agent Colonel Alexander Lesly in Amsterdam in the fall of 1631 to equip the mercenaries Lesly had just raised in Germany.[20] Hendrik van Ringen, David Ruts, and Karl du Moulin were other Dutch merchants who obtained large quantities of military goods for Russia.[21] A certain amount of equipment also came from Hamburg, Schleswig-Holstein, Sweden, and elsewhere.[22]

Even in this period some Russian commercial orders were placed in England, and in this connection personal favors might well be exchanged between the rulers of the two countries.[23] But the final blow to English fortunes came in 1649, when Tsar Aleksei Mikhailovich responded to the execution of Charles I with an outraged and philosophical defense of monarchical rights; more to the point, he also expelled English merchants from all Russian cities except Archangel, and revoked their duty-free trade rights. As for the Dutch, their already commanding position in the Russian economy was strengthened still more by the fate of their English competitors.[24] Even if the English managed to re-enter the Russian interior soon after 1649, it was not until the very end of the seventeenth century that England would again play a significant role in the economic relationships between Russia and Western Europe.[25]

Among the foreigners living in Moscow at this time was a man who was in time to play a large part in the beginnings of iron manufacturing in Russia, a merchant whom the Russians called Andrei Denis'evich Vinius. Born in Amsterdam in 1605 in the prominant merchant family of Dionysius Tjercksz Winius, Andries Denijsz came to Russia in search of his fortune in 1627, married Geertruyd van Rijns, daughter of another Dutch merchant active in Russia, and, as it happened, settled permanently in his new home.[26]

Soon after his arrival in Moscow Andrei Vinius hoped to break into the grain trade between Russia and Western Europe. In these years the price of grain was 15 to 20 per cent higher in the West than in Russia, which meant that tremendous profits were available to merchants who could convince the tsar (who claimed exclusive export of the product) to sell them grain from his own rather limited surplus. Naturally, intense competition raged between England, Sweden, and Holland for control of the Russian bread market, and as early as 1608 and 1618 the Netherlands was trying to secure an export monopoly on the product. In 1630–1631 Dutch envoys opened negotiations in Moscow to obtain a monopoly on the purchase and export of Russian grain and saltpeter. And in this very period (January 1631) Vinius gained an extraordinary privilege: the right to purchase from Michael Romanov's personal storehouses 100,000 to 120,000 *chetverti* of grain at a price of one ruble, forty kopecks (2.75 Joachimsthalers) per *chetvert'*.* No fewer than fifteen ships were required to take Vinius' produce to Holland, and in later years he was to assert that the price of this order, together with export duties, gained the tsar a profit of more than 100,000 rubles.[27]

By now Vinius must have been one of the wealthiest foreigners in Russia, for Michael soon granted him the title of *gost'*,† and the charter which gave him the right to buy and ship his enormous purchase of grain also permitted him to travel throughout Russia and obtain goods on a duty-free basis, "as [were] of yore his brother Dutch gosti. . . ." Vinius had the right to import goods duty free into Archangel and sell them in such towns as Ustiug Velikii, Vologda, Iaroslavl', and Moscow. On March 31, 1633, the tsar issued Vinius a still more favorable trade charter, permitting him to build a house in any Russian city he needed to visit in connection with his commercial activities. Except for affairs connected with murder or theft, he and his employees were to receive justice in Moscow at the *Posol'skii Prikaz* (foreign office), and in civil cases his

---

*One *chetvert'* = 209 liters or about 8 bushels. Concerning the Joachimsthaler, consult the Glossary under its Russian designation *Efimok*.

†The *gosti* were the most privileged merchants of the Russian state. They conducted trade for the tsar, as well as for themselves, and administered various key offices in the state economy. Kotoshikhin tells us that in 1650 there were about thirty *gosti*, and in the future their number remained small. Some foreigners were *gosti*, such as Klinck Bernhardt and Vogeler in Amsterdam and Thomas Kellermann in Moscow. Consult O'Brien, *Russia Under Two Tsars*, pp. 71-72. B. G. Kurts, *Sochinenie Kil'burgera o russkoi torgovle v tsarstvovanie Alekseia Mikhailovicha* [Account of Kilburger on Russian trade during the reign of Aleksei Mikhailovich] (Kiev, 1915), pp. 164, 238, 443-449. Grigorii Kotoshikhin, *O Rossii v tsarstvovanie Alekseia Mikhailovicha* [Concerning Russia during the reign of Aleksei Mikhailovich] (St. Petersburg, 1884), pp. 157-159. Lyashchenko, *History of National Economy*, pp. 224-225.

word would be accepted simply by his kissing the cross. Vinius
was also to have the unqualified right of departure and entrance into the Muscovite state. Little wonder, then, that the
skill which earned Vinius favor at the Russian court likewise
won him the enmity of other foreign entrepreneurs — an enmity
which was ultimately to help bring about his downfall.[28]

The moment favorable to a Russian attack against Poland
presented itself rather suddenly when King Sigismund died
unexpectedly on April 30, 1632. There began a period of such
political instability within Poland that boyar M. B. Shein soon
initiated his ill-fated campaign against Smolensk. The Russian
government's armaments program now became an even more
urgent problem than before. Having noted the high prices
Russians paid for Western military equipment, Andrei Vinius
began to think of undertaking Russian manufacture of the
same type of commodities. This would not only provide the
tsar's armies with a regular and dependable source of military
supplies; modern iron factories within the Russian state would
check the flight of Russian bullion through foreign trade. And
by eliminating transportation costs home manufacturers would
reduce the government's armaments expenses.

Although the advantages of Russian iron manufacturing
were probably well understood among Russian statesmen of
this time, we do not know the exact manner in which Vinius
went about approaching court circles with his project.* He
may have worked through important Russian friends who were

---

*There is no reason, however, to assume that the government would have
been particularly hesitant about giving Vinius the necessary permission and
assistance in establishing his suggested factories. This basic issue had already
been resolved in 1617, when English merchants were inquiring about the same
sort of privileges. At that time court boyars consulted leading Russian merchants on the question of foreigners undertaking manufacturing in Russia,
and they answered in the following terms: "If only the sovereign will command
the English to look for iron ore in unutilized areas, there will be no loss to the
sovereign or to any Russian merchants. . . . And if the English find anything,
then Russians will obtain a living from it, and iron will become cheaper because [now] no iron goes overseas from the sovereign's dominions, but iron
comes to the sovereign's dominions from overseas. But if they find iron flowing like copper, that will be a remarkable achievement [*dikovina*] for the Muscovite state." Cited in Solov'ev, *Istoriia, ix*, 93–94.

close to Tsar Michael and his father, the Patriarch. In any event, on February 29, 1632, Andrei Vinius and two partners, his brother, Abraham, and the Dutch merchant Julius Willeken, received a charter granting them permission to build Russia's first important water-powered iron manufactories. These enterprises were to be located near Tula, on three rivers, the Voshana, Skniga, and Vorona, and were to operate tax free for the ten-year duration of the charter. The foreigners were "to make freely cannon and projectiles . . . and plank iron and various sorts of rod-iron and all types of iron work. . . ." The tsar granted exemption from trade duties *(poshlina)* and promised to order such quantities of the factory's output as needed at 23 *altyn,* 2 *den'gi* per *pud* for cannon, 26 *altyn,* 4 *den'gi* per *pud* for plank iron, and 13 *altyn,* 2 *den'gi* for rod-iron and cannon balls. After four years, however, if the prices of these commodities on the open market were less than the prices stated above, the factory owners were to make deliveries to the state at market prices "with such reduction as is possible" *(s ubavkoiu kak mochno).*[29]

As we see, the Russian government did not promise to order a certain amount of iron equipment from the Tula factories in any given year. For this reason, though he was a man of considerable wealth, Vinius was unwilling to assume the risk of establishing large modern iron works without insuring himself of various kinds of support. First, the tsar agreed to grant Vinius a monopoly to guarantee that other foreigners would not manufacture iron in Russia during the ten-year period of his charter privileges. Moreover, each year Vinius could receive an advance from the state of three thousand rubles as partial payment for the goods he would deliver in that year, and on at least two occasions during the 1630's he requested and received loans of three thousands rubles. Vinius' charter also specified that goods not purchased by the state could either be sold on the open market in Russia or, with permission of the tsar, be exported abroad. Significantly, the charter specified that if goods accepted by the state in the course of a year fell short of three thousand rubles, the Russian money advanced for that year would be repaid in *efimki* (Joachimsthalers) according to the current exchange rate, the assumption evidently being that in such a case Vinius would export surplus commodities produced in that period and thus obtain foreign coin which could be exchanged at the royal treasury.[30] Finally, to minimize his own risk Vinius sought partners among other foreign merchants then active in Russia. Peter Marselis and Thomas de Swaen joined the original group of investors in the very first year of their undertaking, in 1632.

We know little about Andrei Vinius' brother, Abraham, who is in any case no longer mentioned in connection with the iron works after 1637. More information is available concerning Thomas de Swaen (called Foma Romanov by the Russians), who arrived in Russia from Holland sometime before 1630, served the tsar as factor and merchant during the early 1630's, and remained active in Moscow as late as 1651. After 1638, however, de Swaen was no longer a partner in the Tula works. Julius Willeken also withdrew from the partnership at an early date, possibly due to involvement with other business ventures. In 1636 Willeken received a charter for the resin *(smola)* trade at Archangel and was active there at least until 1644.[31]

This breakup in the original group of investors led Vinius to seek partners in addition to Peter Marselis so that sufficient capital could be raised to insure early completion of the Tula iron factories. It was probably at this time that Boris Morozov, a great Russian boyar-merchant and a statesman close to the young heir to the throne, Aleksei Mikhailovich, was taken into the partnership, this being the first known case of a Russian participating as a silent partner in a foreign business undertaking. In the late 1630's Thielemann Lus Akkema also became a partner, and in 1639 a new charter was obtained to reflect these changes in the ownership of the Tula works.

The family from which Peter Marselis came was surely one of the most remarkable entrepreneur families of the entire seventeenth century. They began as religious refugees from the Netherlands who found asylum in the free Protestant city of Hamburg during the second half of the sixteenth century. The head of the family, Gabriel, soon established himself in the commercial life of that city and went on to develop business interests in foreign lands, including Muscovy. Gavrilo, as the Russians renamed him, appeared in Russia at the time of Boris Godunov and traded there for more than thirty years. The importance of Gavrilo's Russian commerce may be judged from the fact that his Moscow agent, Isaac Alin, obtained one of the first charters after the Time of Troubles (in 1614) re-establishing free entrance and duty-free commerce in Archangel, and within a few years the Russian branch of the Marselis family was paying annual trade duties of one thousand to fifteen hundred rubles. His economic activities also gained Gavrilo Marselis political influence with the Russian government, and in 1619 he earned the undying gratitude of Mikhail Romanov by using the Hamburg company's connections in Poland to secure the release of the tsar's father from Polish captivity.[32]

Peter Marselis was born in Rotterdam in 1605 and arrived in Moscow in 1629 to carry on the trade interests of his father.[33] The remaining forty-three years of his life (all of which were spent in Russia) mark Peter as an energetic and indomitable — if unscrupulous — man, a veritable master of the arts of intrigue and deception. Enemies and setbacks which would have easily destroyed a man of lesser fiber did not keep Peter from defending and expanding his family's position in Russia, drawing all the while on the backing of his kin as well as on his own connections in Denmark, Holland, and the German states. As a merchant Marselis dealt in grain, tar, potash, fish oil, shipbuilding materials, and especially in armaments — all of which necessitated the maintenance of warehouses in Kola, Archangel, Kholmogory, Vologda, Iaroslavl', and Moscow. Peter Marselis also served as representative in Russia for King Christian of Denmark (who elevated him to the Danish nobility on September 17, 1643) and the Duke of Holstein, for whom he once attempted unsuccessfully to gain control of the Persian trade routes running east and west through Russia. As we shall see later, these relations with foreign monarchs by no means detracted from Peter's standing in Russia. Quite the contrary, in this age of international entrepreneurial activity Marselis' political and economic contacts in the West made him all the more valuable to the Russian government, and he was frequently sent abroad on diplomatic missions. In 1638, in recognition of his many services, Marselis received the title *gost' s gostinnym imenem,* an honor which placed him in the highest and most privileged circle of Russian and foreign merchants.[34]

In 1636 Peter Marselis married Dorothea, daughter of the Muscovite English merchant John Barnesly. After Dorothea's death in 1650, Marselis married Anna Akkema in 1655, thus becoming the son-in-law of his partner and friend, Thielemann Akkema. Marselis was contented in both marriages and rewarded with four sons and two daughters. A staunch leader of the foreign Protestant community in Moscow, he never accepted Orthodoxy and the Russian citizenship which went with conversion, though Russia was his permanent home for his entire adult life.

Fewer words need be said about Thielemann Lus Akkema, whose career was less marked by extremes of success and failure than that of his partner, Peter Marselis. Filimon Filimon'ich Akema was born in Harlingen, in the Dutch province of Friesland. Before settling permanently in Russia Akema came often to Archangel and Moscow as an agent of the Amsterdam merchant Ioann Bernars, whose ancestors had traded with Russia. Akema served Colonel Lesly in 1631–1632 when he went to Amsterdam to purchase military equipment for the tsar. In 1633 he received a royal charter for trade in Russia and joined the Vinius-Marselis-Morozov partnership in 1639. Akema had been born into an Anabaptist *(Taufgesinnte)* family, and though he remained in Russia until his death around 1676,[35] like Peter Marselis Akema remained a Protestant and a "foreigner."[36]

Although Russia was abundantly provided with the natural resources needed to develop iron manufacturing, seventeenth-century technology interacted with the country's negligible transportation facilities to limit the areas in which an iron factory could be located. Specifically, what was needed was a geographical convergence of the various materials used in an iron enterprise, in quantities sufficient to assure an entrepreneur a long period of production. First, abundant iron ore had to be available and fairly accessible, for primitive Russian mining techniques precluded the exploitation of deep or irregularly shaped deposits. The ore beds had to be fairly close to the smelter; high-grade ore was rare, land transport slow and difficult, and it was wasteful to cart large amounts of slag over long distances. Second, forests were needed to supply construction materials for the factory buildings and charcoal for production. Third, a navigable river was indispensable both for shipping finished products to their destination and for delivering raw materials to the iron works. In addition to a large river, an iron factory at this time required a small, fast-flowing stream, since large quantities of water were used to wash the ore and in various smelting operations as well. This stream also had to offer favorable locations for dam sites to provide the hydro-power for the plant's machinery. Finally, there had to be nearby villages of peasants who could be made available to transport raw materials and finished commodities to their respective destinations.

Tula and its environs presented an obvious location for iron manufactories because of abundant forest and ore supplies, as well as such materials for iron smelting as limestone, galina, and sand. Tula also had the advantage of being close to Moscow and linked to it by an excellent water route beginning with the Upa river, leading to the Oka, and thence to Moscow via the Moskva.[37] Rivulets and streams in the area provided water power for factory machinery. Vinius finally decided to build his four factories on the Bol'shaia Tulitsa river (now called the Sine-Tulitsa),* a fortunate location since the Tulitsa,

---

* In this period an "iron enterprise" was not the huge and unified structure of later years, but rather a *group* of workshops separated by the need for each stage of the operation (blasting, forging, boring, etc.) to have its own

flowing through mountainous terrain, had a significant "fall" at this point, and its high banks made it a convenient place upon which to build factory dams.[38] The first of the four dams and factories was near the hamlet of Slobodka-Gorodishche; the second dam was four hundred *sazhens* (about 2,800 feet) further down the Tulitsa; the third workshop was three hundred *sazhens* from the second dam and located at Torkhov, quite near Tula. The first manufactory was fifteen kilometers from Tula, the fourth twelve kilometers from the same city.[39]

The main blast furnace was located at the second workshop, a similar furnace in the third factory being used only in emergencies. The second and third enterprises had annexes where specialists made cannon and projectile molds; all but the third were provided with shops where cannon were bored, polished, and finished. The first factory had a hammer shop, the fourth no less than three. Although less information is available concerning the activities of the third Tula works (and it probably passed through periods of idleness), it appears that weapons were manufactured there as well.[40]

Because Russian craftsmen of the 1630's were not prepared to work the metallurgical equipment of the seventeenth-century manufactory, Vinius depended on foreign masters to operate the blast furnaces, forges, boring mechanisms, and other equipment of his iron works. But we do not know who actually built the factories. S. G. Strumilin, believing that the first twenty foreign workers arrived in Tula "no earlier than the fall of 1637, when the factory was already finished," feels that "it is clear that even if the specifications and features [of the enterprises] were Dutch, this first Russian iron-smelting factory was built by the hands of Russian masters." In fact, foreign workers were present at Tula before

---

water wheel. On the other hand, these workshops were unified by the role each played in terms of the others in the production process as a whole. The factory which smelted pig iron from ore with a blast furnace was known in Russian as the *domennyi zavod;* enterprises which refined that product into a higher-quality iron were called *zhelezodelatel'nye* or *zhelezoobrabatyvaiushchye zavody.* In this book the more generic term "iron factory" embraces both types of iron enterprises.

1637, and it seems reasonable to conclude that they were brought there to supervise construction of the enterprise. Vinius tried to hire twelve Dutch masters for employment in Russia as early as 1632, and if the results of these efforts are uncertain we do know that his father signed agreements for his son with a number of qualified workers in Amsterdam in 1635. In early February 1636 Vinius petitioned the tsar to admit twenty iron masters from Holland into Russia, and soon thereafter the factory manager, Jan Dani, brought the men to Tula by way of Novgorod. Another four workers (with nine dependents) arrived in Novgorod on August 28, 1637, and at least nine more masters entered Russia for employment at Tula between February 1636 and February 1641.[41]

If foreign masters arrived at Tula by mid-1636 it is likely that construction of the enterprise also began at that time. Iosif' Gamel' discovered that Vinius made his first deliveries to the state in 1636,[42] but this does not prove that the factory was then in full operation. (These iron goods might have been samples prepared in hand forges by artisan methods if the blast furnace was not yet completed.) In later years Akema and Marselis claimed the factory's blast furnace was not completed until 1640, but this contention should probably be discounted in favor of the date then alleged by the government, 1637.[43] Significantly, Vinius did not request ascription of the peasants of nearby Solomenskaia *volost'* until 1638,[44] suggesting that before that time they were not needed for transport and menial labor.

In comparison with artisan production, the iron manufactory represented advanced technology. Water wheels of a manufactory caught the energy of water falling from dam sluices and channeled it into the factory machinery. In the second Tula works this power was used primarily to drive the huge bellows of the blast furnace; in the other three workshops (and in certain operations of the second factory), the force of the water operated the forging hammers as well as horizontal boring and polishing devices for cannons and smaller firearms. Water power made possible a break with the old tiny leather hand-driven bellows of the artisan. The new and larger wooden bellows created a more powerful blast, higher temperatures, and therefore made possible large furnaces. Hydro-powered hammers provided greater impact for the forging of higher-quality iron, while horizontal drilling devices using the same source of energy could finish more pieces in a given unit of time.

The high blast furnaces of this period (German models even by 1340 had reached a height of thirty feet with internal diameters of ten feet) received ore at the top and produced liquefied metal to be regularly tapped at the bottom. Some products, such as cannons, projectiles, and grenades, were cast from the comparatively low-quality pig iron produced in this initial stage.[45] Their molds (made either of clay or copper) were placed in earthen pits before the blast furnaces, the finished articles being removed with the help of oak beams and iron pulleys.[46]

If a higher-quality iron was desired, pig iron was taken from the furnace of the blasting factory in blooms weighing seven or eight *puds* and then "fined." This occurred in hammering shops containing large hearths — usually two — served by leather hand-bellows. The water-powered hammers here weighed seventeen, twenty, or even twenty-one *puds* (756 pounds). To sustain blows of such magnitude, the anvils were held and stabilized by a tier of sturdy oak beams, each beam being almost three meters long and a meter wide.[47]

This fining process was in the charge of a team usually consisting of two masters, two submasters, and a number of unskilled assistants. As repeated heating at the hearth and hammering at the anvil progressively freed the metallic mass of much of its slag content, the bloom could be drawn into rods or iron bars,[48] or into angle-iron for use in the construction of stone buildings. Small iron articles, rifle barrels and locks, armor, and various sidearms would be made in other shops which had hearths but no water-driven hammers. Rifle barrels were produced from iron sheets "rolled up" under a hand hammer and welded in hearths. For finishing the barrels were taken to still another shop furnished with water-driven spits, machine tools which bored the barrels, and ordinary grindstones for their polishing. Other shops bored and finished cannons.[49]

The blast furnaces at Tula were seven *sazhens* (forty-nine feet) long, four *sazhens* wide, and four *sazhens* high. They were lined with white, porous Miachkovskii stone, and each was equipped with two powerful wooden bellows no less than 8.75 *arshins* (about twenty feet) in length. Using two hundred *puds* of ore and three hundred carts of fuel, such a furnace would produce from 100 to 120 *puds* (3,600 to 4,320 pounds, or 1,600 to 1,920 kilograms) of pig iron in a twenty-four-hour period, or a maximum of 3,600 *puds* (about sixty-five tons) in a month and 36,000 *puds* (over 650 tons)[50] in a working year of three hundred days.[51]

The technology of these furnaces was based upon that current in the southern Netherlands, but under Russian conditions Vinius and his partners developed it to an extraordinarily high degree. Not a single blast furnace in seventeenth-century Western Europe had a twenty-four-hour capacity of 100 to 120 *puds*. At this time the best German and Swedish blast furnaces produced six hundred to nine hundred kilograms (thirty-seven to fifty-five *puds*) per twenty-four hours. In 1700 the finest iron works in Western Europe had an annual capacity of 750 short tons, which was — if more than the Tula enterprises of the mid-seventeenth century* — achieved only by the use of two furnaces, as compared to one furnace at Tula.

The productivity of these Russian factories was also outstanding. The Tula works used two hundred *puds* of ore and three hundred carts of fuel each twenty-four hours, which meant the furnace required two tons of ore and three tons of fuel to make a ton of pig iron. Swedish furnaces in the early eighteenth century required about four tons of fuel for a ton of pig iron, and some German models took six. The very size of

---

*Even figuring a "working year" as three hundred days, the comparable figure for the Tula works (at 100–120 *puds* per day) would be 545–655 short tons per year.

the blast furnaces at Tula indicates an advanced technology: the best German and Swedish furnaces of the seventeenth century were no higher than five or six meters (sixteen to nineteen feet), and even during the eighteenth century a great English furnace in Sussex was 8.5 meters high (providing 97.5 *puds* of pig iron per day). Yet in backward Russia a full century earlier the Dutch-designed Tula furnaces were 7.5 meters high and gave one hundred or more *puds* of pig iron daily.[52]

How did the productivity of the Tula manufactories compare with Russian iron artisanry of the same period? Since the Tula blast furnace produced 100 to 120 *puds* of pig iron every twenty-four hours, and since it was serviced by two shifts, each involving a master, two submasters, and seven less skilled assistants — a total of twenty men per day — we conclude that the productivity level for casting was not less than five or six *puds* per man each day. By contrast, small hand-operated artisan furnaces with two workers gave from 24 to 36 *funts* in twenty-four hours. Larger artisan furnaces in the Rakitianskii enterprise of the 1670's provided 4.5 *puds* of pig-iron daily, which represented an average of perhaps one *pud* per man per day. It is clear therefore that at the very least the Tula furnaces were five times more productive than artisan furnaces. Furthermore, records dating from 1706 indicate it took a Russian artisan at least twelve days to make a musket, not counting the time for preparation of the material (e.g., smelting the iron, and so forth). At Marselis' Chentsovskii iron factory[53] it took three days, four at an absolute maximum, and the output of muskets per worker was much greater as well. For the period one might even assert that the Tula factories approached "quantity production." One master in twenty-four hours could cast either two or three large cannon balls, five or six small ones, one hundred large and small grenades, or fifteen to twenty iron sheets one-half *arshin* in length. A team of one master and two workers could produce two cannon in twenty-four hours. In another Tula factory three groups composed of one master and two workers per group could bore twelve muskets each day, or 3,600 musket barrels in a working year of three hundred days. Three other teams of one master and three workers each could do eighteen per day, or 5,400 in a working year of three hundred days. A single hearth in a Tula hammering shop in the same period produced no less than thirty *sazhens* of rod-iron in twenty-four hours, or nine thousand *sazhens* (about seven thousand yards) of rod-iron in a working year—a truly impressive figure for this time.[54]

A word is in order concerning the "division of labor" in these manufactories. One team of masters was responsible for the operation and fueling of the blast furnace; another group was occupied at the forge, producing iron from pig iron. Other teams made swords and firearm barrels, or labored in the boring shops, or assembled the wooden and metal parts of the rifles into finished products. In fact, there were no fewer than thirty specialties among the masters and submasters of the Tula works.[55] Although this separation and allotment of function represented a genuine advance over peasant artisan practice and was one factor in the achievement of a higher rate of labor productivity, it does not follow that the division of labor in seventeenth-century European manufactories had attained a high point of development. At various times the same master usually engaged in totally different operations, so that a particular craftsman from the blasting shop might follow the product of his labor into the hammering shop, or even participate in the finishing of arms, cauldrons, and door plates.[56] Production, even at Tula, had by no means yet attained the disciplined and continuous quality of the modern-day "assembly line," characterized as it is by the intensive application of both consecutive *and* simultaneous operations.

As we have seen, from the very beginning skilled masters and submasters came from abroad. At least thirty-three such men arrived at Tula between February 1636 and February 1641. On February 9, 1642, Andrei Vinius petitioned the tsar to admit into Russia still more foreign masters for work in Tula. Peter Marselis also served the factory in this respect, helping to obtain at least four Swedish iron masters in 1640 and 1641 alone. Christian Schimler, Marselis' secretary, used visits to Sweden in 1643 and 1645 to engage needed masters for the factory.[57] Personnel records of the factory indicate that the largest number of foreigners at Tula in this period were Walloons, masters from the southern, French-speaking part of the Netherlands. There were also a number of Swedes and a few Germans. Foreign workers and their dependents were brought from abroad at the expense of their employers, and as such specialists were scarce even in Western Europe at this time, they were paid excellent wages.* In some cases masters were unable to exercise their favorite skills at Vinius' factory, so it was unusual for a master to remain at Tula for long. (One also suspects that life in Russia may have been idealized by factory recruiters abroad, and that a harsher reality caused some foreigners to become dissatisfied.) Indeed, it was not uncommon for a master to leave before expiration of his prearranged work period. Only in later years were Marselis and Akema able to create a solid core of workers, many of whom became Russian citizens and never returned home.[58]

A few Russians worked as submasters, and a still larger number were engaged as apprentices. These Russians, it appears, were usually free men who sold their labor power to the foreigner-capitalists in exchange for wages; but there is some question as to whether or not this relationship was voluntary or based upon the ascriptive powers which the tsar at that time exercised even over those of his subjects who were not serfs. In any event, the Russian government wanted Russians to

*In 1647 the highest wages were paid to a smelting master, Christian Wilde, who received 150 rubles per year. Other specialties were paid less, according to the established differentials of the seventeenth century. The cannon and projectile master Andreian Kerkoven and his brother, Fatden, each received one hundred rubles per year; Pieter Fillison, an apprentice, was given fifty rubles. While copper money was in circulation in Russia, foreigners too were paid in that coin, which could be exchanged for precious metal at the time of departure for home. *Real wages* for all masters and apprentices were significantly increased by free housing plus daily *korm* (feeding) allowances of several *altyn*. *K.m.,* I, xxvii, 12–13, 24, 31.

learn thoroughly all aspects of modern metallurgy, and the obligation to instruct Russians and conceal nothing from them was written into the original factory charter of 1632. As we shall see, however, both the foreign capitalists and their non-Russian workers sought to evade this obligation in every possible way, and thus maintain their indispensability to the Russian state. During the first two decades of iron manufacturing in the Tula factories, Russian submasters and apprentices were the students and understudies of these foreigners and were unable to participate in advanced work without them.[59]

We do not have much information on the life of a skilled worker at the Tula enterprises during the seventeenth century. From the material available, one might conclude that masters and submasters, both Russian and foreign, were paid enough in wages and maintenance to insure a satisfactory standard of living for the times. Skilled workers and their apprentices lived in special *izby* (cottages, huts) at the factory, the degree of comfort of a particular worker's accommodations depending upon the value attached to his work in the factory.[60]

Had Vinius so desired, he could have recruited a labor force devoted to the menial and less skilled aspects of factory work as voluntary wage-workers. But it was more profitable for him to utilize the feudal practices of seventeenth-century Russia to gain control over a number of workers who could then be exploited in a less limited and conditional manner. In 1638 Vinius received, in answer to his petition of that year, the nearby royal Solomenskaia *volost'*, which had 250 households and 347 men. The peasants of Solomenskaia *volost'* traditionally paid the tsar 470 rubles annually in *obrok* (quit-rent) and taxes. After 1638 this was paid to the factory owners, who delivered to the tsar equivalent value "in bread and military equipment."[61]

The peasants worked for the capitalists on the basis of "agreement documents" *(dogovornye zapisi)* which were one-sided in favor of the foreigners. Every year the peasants were to prepare nine hundred *sazhens* of fuel wood for the factory, bring three thousand carts of ore from the mines at Dedilov to the factory ("by winter route," "because during the summer it is impossible to bring ore over the steppe"), carry pig iron from the blast furnace at the second factory to the various hammerships, cut wood for factory construction and repair needs, and load barges on the Oka and Moskva with finished commodities. Each peasant was to present himself at the factory to serve for the duration of every sixth week. The work schedule was arranged so that half of the available peasants for a given week came with their horses (these men were paid from three to four and a half kopecks per day), while the other half of the labor force—those without horses—owed a week and a half of service (and were paid from two to three kopecks per day).[62]

The ascription of the peasants of Solomenskaia *volost'* to the Tula works was important for the profitable operation of the enterprise as a whole. Strumilin estimated that such labor on the free market would have cost the capitalists 627 rubles annually, but Vinius paid less than a quarter of this amount thanks to the compulsory conditions under which his unskilled men worked. The peasants involved in these obligations found the situation both unprofitable and disruptive of their normal pursuits.[63] A small number responded in a manner so characteristic of the oppressed in Russia during this time: they ran away. Available documents indicate that in 1647 there should have been 281 households and 488 males in Solomenskaia *volost'*, but when we figure the number of families who fled from the "many exactions of the foreigners," the actual number was 276 households and 469 male inhabitants.[64]

Miners also played a role in the life of the Tula manufactories. Vinius obtained iron ore from a site forty kilometers south of the Tula works and ten kilometers southwest of the town of Dedilov. Ore was mined there in the winter from the first of December to the first of March, because such heavy loads could be brought to the factory only by sleigh. The ore in this area was from swamp deposits, of low quality, and it lay in shallow beds from three to seven feet deep and from forty-two to ninety-four feet wide. The miners *(rudokopy)* came from the Cossacks and *strel'tsy* of Dedilovskii *uezd,* who were ordered by the tsar to provide a continual number of fifty men; these workers were divided into five groups of equal size, each group having a foreman and working in "shifts." Four miners worked at a single pit, and each man produced one cartload (twenty-five *puds*) of ore per day. As part of their feudal obligations to the tsar, each of these teams had to provide one hundred carts of ore without pay, or a total of 1,250 carts per year. Another 1,750 carts were to be provided by "the Cossacks and other free people at a free price." In addition to obtaining the ore, the miners also performed the first stage of ore cleaning *(obogash-chenie),* which involved separating the ore from stones and debris. Although mining had been a well-developed industry in Germany, Hungary, and other parts of Europe for two centuries or more, when one ore site at Dedilov was exhausted or flooded with water, no attempt was made at deeper or more extensive exploitation; rather, the miners simply moved on to a new location.[65]

B. B. Kafengauz noted that working conditions at the mines were so disagreeable that "duty and compulsion found itself combined with wage payment and agreement." At times the miners petitioned the tsar to supplement their numbers with other recruits. The pay was so poor and irregular that strikes developed as, for example, in December 1669, when thirty-seven miners refused to go to work. (They were punished with the knout and returned to their jobs by force.) But it was impossible to expect these men to take interest in mining, considering that it was not only compulsory but seasonal and secondary to their regular pursuits. Difficulty was also caused by the fact that the local *voevoda* (governor) did not hesitate to move the miners to some other area of work as the need arose, causing a delay in factory work until a petition to the tsar from the factory owners would bring the men back to the pits.[66]

In contrast to mining or transport work, fuel-making at Tula was carried on by wage-workers completely independent of compulsory or ascribed labor, for this was skilled work and demanded true specialists. The wood was obtained from forests bought from three different landowners, located five, seven, and fifteen *versts* from the factory. The charcoal was prepared in special pits six *versts* away, under the supervision of foreign masters, five of whom in 1647 received annual wages of ninety or one hundred rubles. Russian workers cut the wood, transported it, and tended the fires, and they were each paid wages varying from ten *den'gi* to two *altyn* per day. The peasants of Solomenskaia *volost'* were obligated to provide nine hundred *sazhens* of fuel-wood per year.[67]

When the Swedish traveler Kilburger visited the Pavlovskii, Porotovskii, and Tula iron factories during the 1670's,* he reported that birch, linden, aspen, and spruce were variously used as base material for the charcoal, although birch was considered most desirable. At this time wood was brought by peasants from the province of Galich (over five hundred kilometers northeast of Tula) during the summer and sold to the factories in hundreds of baskets. A pile of wood measured three and a half *arshins* (about ninety-eight inches) and cost from eleven to fourteen kopecks. According to Kilburger, the blast-furnace operators used much more charcoal than was really necessary for their work.[68]

The life of a large iron enterprise such as the one established by Vinius also demanded a number of auxiliary masters who produced various commodities required by the factory, or who saw to the maintenance and repair of its facilities. Carpenters and sawyers, for example, were charged with tending the dams, waterwheels, and the many buildings, large and small. Special smiths forged iron objects and tools required for the machinery of the Tula works; other masters made molds and bellows. The skilled work of these men was of obvious importance for the total functioning of Vinius' manufactory, and it must be said that most of these artisans were Russians, probably free men voluntarily selling their labor power to the factory. Their wages, by Russian standards, were high.[69]

*The Pavlovskii and Porotovskii enterprises were built after the Tula works, and are described below on pp. 94–95, 97–98.

The Tula iron works produced cannon in large quantities, and in 1646 the partners exported six hundred cannon to Holland, to be followed by 360 the next year. These cannon fired four to eight *funt* projectiles and weighed from thirty to sixty-one *puds*. Projectiles from two to twelve *grivni* in weight were smelted in large numbers, and some went up to twenty-five *grivni*. Grenades were usually one, one and a half, or two *grivni,* though larger models were not uncommon. The Tula factories manufactured angle-, rod-, and bar-iron, but sheet-iron and wire were not often produced. A document from this period tells us that "Andrei Vinius and his comrades did make musket and carbine and pistol barrels and armor and spiked helmets, but they have [now] abandoned these activities and sent [those] masters abroad. . . ." Since the cannons were cast directly from pig iron and not from higher-quality forged iron, it seems that the cost to the purchaser (at seventy kopecks per *pud*) was also lower.[70]

Delivery records indicate that the Tula works operated on an intensive basis. In April 1641, for example, the *Pushkarskii Prikaz* accepted 1,853 cannon balls from Andrei Vinius, and in May 1641 the *Prikaz Bol'shoi Kazni* bought 684 cannon balls from the factory. In 1647 the factory was producing over five thousand *puds* of joint-iron per year, which demanded as much as ten thousand *puds* of pig iron. Probably at least twenty thousand *puds* of cannons and cannon balls were also produced each year, and Strumilin estimates the value of all 25,000 *puds* to have been ten thousand rubles or more.[71]

Orders of this size made it possible for the factory owners, producing goods at perhaps one-tenth the cost of artisan technology, to reap profits which may have reached 200 per cent. The actual cost of the Tula works to its owners can only be estimated, but it probably did not exceed five thousand rubles.[72] And yet Vinius was constantly in debt during the construction of these enterprises, and was forced at all times to operate with co-investors. This might indicate that his expenses were quite high, although the return of this investment seems to have been sufficient to make the ownership of these iron factories a highly desired privilege, and one which, as we shall see, was to be the object of fierce and ruthless competition among the partners from almost the very start of their manufacturing activity at Tula.

4

The Downfall of Andrei Vinius

BY THE EARLY 1640's certain tensions and disagreements threatened the future of the profitable partnership Andrei Vinius had established with Peter Marselis and
Filimon Akema. The cause is not clear from evidence available today. Akema and Marselis may have been dissatisfied
with some aspect of Vinius' management of the Tula iron
works. Or, as staunch Protestants, perhaps they were offended at Vinius' announced intention to convert to the Russian
Orthodox Church, and in this way become a Russian citizen
and enjoy economic advantages not available to "foreigners."
It is even conceivable that Marselis and Akema saw the possibility of establishing other iron enterprises and simply wished
to eliminate a threefold division of profits in the new manufactories; or possibly Vinius was willing to participate in new
projects but encountered difficulties in doing so. Whatever
their reasons or motives, in 1643 Marselis and Akema petitioned for the right to build, without Vinius, new iron factories
far from Tula, on the Vaga, Kostroma, and Sheksna rivers. In

this petition Marselis and Akema asserted that Vinius was a person of "poor character" *(malomochen)* and did not wish to be their partner in the new enterprises. When the *Prikaz Bol'shoi Kazny* questioned Vinius on the matter, he replied that he wished to continue operating the Tula works, but was unable to build new factories at the time. This being the case, the tsar granted Marselis and Akema a charter (dated April 5, 1644) giving them the right to build iron enterprises on the requested sites, "and where henceforth in our Russian state such [favorable] places will be discovered. . . ."[1]

The charter was issued for twenty years. During this time the partners were to have the right of duty-free export "to other lands which are in council and friendship with ourselves, the great sovereign. . . ." The factories were to operate without payment of *obrok* (tax) or *poshlina* (trade duty) for the entire twenty-year period, after which an annual *obrok* of one hundred rubles would be collected on each blast furnace, and *poshlina* would be levied according to the tsar's *ukaz*. The goods of the Vaga factory were to be accepted by the state at the following prices:

cannon	20 *altyn* (60 kopecks) per *pud*
cannon balls	10 *altyn* per *pud*
musket and carbine barrels	20 *altyn* apiece
rod-iron	13 *altyn*, 2 *den'gi* per *pud*
sheet-iron	26 *altyn*, 4 *den'gi* per *pud*

— unless at a given time market prices were lower than these figures, in which case the market rate with a discount would prevail. Marselis and Akema could hire Russian workers, but were not allowed to buy serfs. They promised to instruct Russians in all aspects of the factory's operation and to conceal nothing from them.[2]

Vinius' factory charter of 1632 had guaranteed him a ten-year iron-manufacturing monopoly in the Russian state. As the Tula factory did not begin to function until 1637, by granting Marselis and Akema their charter in 1643 the tsar was breaking his original agreement with Vinius. Apparently this reversal of policy is to be explained by the fact that Peter

Marselis became useful to the government in connection with a delicate diplomatic problem. From 1640 until 1643 the tsar used Marselis as the chief representative in an ultimately unsuccessful attempt to arrange a marriage between his daughter Irina and Waldemar, prince of Denmark.* We know that in 1642 Marselis demanded various concessions for his services, including twenty-year privileges in the iron industry;[3] these privileges must have been related to his intention, announced later, to establish iron factories on the Vaga river.

Vinius finally managed in some way to have himself included in the new partnership, and a written agreement was concluded among the three partners stating the terms of their new relationship.[4] But Vinius' success on this issue did not diminish his personal hostility toward Akema and Marselis, though he was forced to bide his time until a shift in the political forces at the royal court would strengthen his own position and weaken that of Marselis.

Vinius did not have to wait long. On the night of July 13, 1645, Tsar Michael Romanov died. Since the heir to the throne, Aleksei Mikhailovich, was then a lad of sixteen, he would obviously be dependent for a time on the guidance of men who were more experienced than he in affairs of state. The nature of political life in Russia at this time was such that the reign of a minor always initiated a struggle among prominent members of the ruling class to determine who would

*This episode well illustrates Peter Marselis' diplomatic skill and lack of scruple in attaining his objectives. The Danes were concerned over reports that the Russians had recently destroyed Protestant churches in their country. Marselis minimized the truth of these allegations, blamed the Orthodox clergy for what he was forced to concede had happened, and asserted that tsarist policy was to maintain considerable freedom for Protestants in Russia. In May 1643 Marselis transmitted to Michael a statement of marriage conditions from Christian IV which demanded, above all, liberty of faith for Waldemar and his companions and a place in Moscow to build a Lutheran church. Marselis returned from another trip to Denmark in December 1643. By early 1645 Marselis' negotiations ended in failure, which may have encouraged the Russian government to betray him by confiscating his factories on November 30, 1647, as described below. On Marselis' role in the Waldemar episode, see Amburger, *Die Familie Marselis*, pp. 85–91; Tsvetaev, *Protestanstvo*, pp. 74–75, 78–80, 483–490, and *passim;* Solov'ev, *Istoriia*, IX, 229–248, 460.

"advise" the tsar and thus play the leading role in shaping government policy. The person who now emerged as the royal favorite was Boris Morozov, a silent partner in the Tula iron works and a close personal friend of Andrei Vinius. In fact, from 1645 until sometime during 1647 Vinius was himself a present and powerful figure in the Russian government — probably the first person of Western European origin to play such a unique role in the government. He was adviser to Morozov, close to Nazarii Chistyi, the secretary of the Duma (*dumnyi d'iak*), and friendly with other statesmen in the Kremlin.[5] With his position thus secure, Vinius decided to take revenge against his faithless associates.

Apparently Vinius knew that a number of people in the Russian government were dissatisfied with the performance of the Tula iron factories, and decided that by shifting the blame for this onto the shoulders of Marselis and Akema they could be eliminated from the partnership, leaving him to enjoy the undivided profits of the enterprise. In the spring of 1646 Vinius submitted a denunciation of Marselis' and Akema's operation of the Tula factories to the *Prikaz Bol'shoi Kaznyi*. In this document Vinius charged that his partners had violated such provisions of their factory charter as the requirement that Russian apprentices be instructed in the skills of iron manufacturing. Vinius also claimed that the cannon delivered by the factory were inferior and the iron goods often overpriced.[6] But Vinius would correct these and other abuses if the iron works were given to him as absolute owner.

Marselis and Akema learned of Vinius' attack by accident. While at Akema's residence Vinius lost a copy of his report, and it fell into Akema's hands. After this Akema and Marselis reviled Vinius more than ever, insulting him to his face as well as behind his back. In the spring of 1646 Vinius turned to the tsar with a petition in which he defended himself against his partners and requested that his misplaced document be returned and that Marselis and Akema appear in court to show upon what basis they had slandered his good name. Vinius claimed that such an inquiry would clear him from public disgrace.[7]

On June 8, 1646, the government opened an investigation of the dispute. Akema and Marselis were summoned to answer Vinius' charges. Akema denied cursing Vinius, but Marselis admitted it, saying that among foreigners "they do not call [a liar] a good person, nor do they esteem him nor speak good words about him." Vinius maintained that both his partners called him a "soulless person and a rascal" *(bezdushnik i shel'ma)*. He charged that Akema and Marselis had said "I wanted to be baptized, and for this reason [they] did not wish to drink or eat with me; I call as witness all the Dutch merchants that they, Peter and Filimon, lied and dishonored me, called me a rogue and a heartless person and said such words about the baptism." Although the charge of slandering Orthodoxy was probably true, the Russian state was so passionate in its defense of the Eastern faith that Marselis and Akema denied Vinius' allegation and requested (as did Vinius) that the government interrogate the other Dutchmen living in Moscow concerning the truth of the matter.[8]

The fourteen witnesses listed by Vinius were questioned by the Russian authorities, but they refused to indict their fellow Protestants and foreigners by admitting that statements hostile to the Orthodox Church had come from Marselis and Akema. This would have compromised the entire foreign community of Moscow, merely to help a single Dutchman who had turned his back on his original faith, nationality, and countrymen. The witnesses Vinius named agreed he had been insulted by Akema and Marselis, but they denied any knowledge of slander in connection with his intended conversion to Orthodoxy. Since their number included such respected Dutch merchants as David Ruts and Akema's brother, Gillis, this testimony dealt a substantial blow to Vinius' case.[9]

On June 12, 1646, government investigators visited the Tula factories in order to determine the extent to which the terms of the factory charter had been violated by the foreigners, and who was to blame for such violations. Two major conclusions emerged from this inquiry: the Tula factories were not producing all of the commodities desired by the government, and

Russians were not being instructed in the more skilled aspects of iron manufacturing. Marselis and Akema rationalized the failure to manufacture sheet-iron, armor, and the like by claiming a lack of qualified workers; they maintained that the quality of the cannon delivered to the Russian government was good, even by international standards. Failure to teach Russians the advanced skills of iron manufacturing, however, could not be so easily explained. State inspectors even learned that a Russian workman who had tried to take the dimensions of a blast furnace was surprised by the foreign master Christian Wilde and beaten for his display of curiosity.[10]

As the judicial proceedings were coming to a close, the Russian government sent *stol'nik* Il'ia Danilovich Miloslavskii and Ivan Baibakov on a diplomatic mission to Holland. Among their other duties, the Russian ambassadors were instructed to protest the misconduct of Akema and Marselis in handling the iron factories at Tula. On December 29, 1646, Miloslavskii complained to the Dutch States concerning "the many unjust things" done by Akema and Marselis, claiming they had not fulfilled the terms of the contract concluded with the tsar. The foreigners were said to have taken others into their partnership without permission of the tsar; they had not instructed Russians in metallurgy, as agreed, but had ordered the foreign masters to keep their skills a secret from Russian apprentices. The output of the factory was also unsatisfactory: rifle barrels, wire, and white tin had not been made at all, and what was produced was often not delivered on time. Akema and Marselis were charged with delivering low-quality cannon to the Russian government while selling the best of their output to foreign countries.[11]

The Dutch representatives rejected responsibility for any such offenses committed against the Russian government. Miloslavskii was told that Marselis was from Hamburg, and as for Akema, no one in Holland even knew his birthplace or where he had lived or was now living. No Dutchmen, in fact, had any relations of any sort with him. This being the case, was it not clear that the Prince of Orange could scarcely be held accountable for anything Akema or Marselis might have done?[12]

The fact that Vinius' name was not included in Miloslavskii's diplomatic protest indicates that Vinius remained in good standing with the Russian government as late as December 1646. In the long run, however, the controversy triggered by Vinius' denunciations discredited *all* the foreigners engaged in iron manufacturing at Tula. In retrospect this development seems all but inevitable, for in the process of accusing Akema and Marselis of malfeasance Vinius compromised his own integrity. He was, after all, one of the partners in the Tula factories; and while Marselis and Akema had used foreign managers as their personal representatives at Tula, it was actually Vinius who directed the day-to-day operations of the iron works.[13] If the case of the Tula ironworks proved anything at all it was that no foreign capitalist would subordinate his own interests to those of the Russian state.

The next development in this story was therefore quite logical — though apparently not expected by Vinius, Marselis, or Akema. On November 30, 1647, the government seized the Tula factories and announced its intention to operate them as state enterprises.[14] Boyar Grigorii Pushkin of the *Prikaz Stol'nogo Dela* was put in charge of the works, and Iurii Telepnev was made director of the manufactory. As if to drive home the new realities of the situation, on December 2 Telepnev left Moscow to assume control of the Tula ironworks.[15]

As soon as they lost their factories, Vinius, Marselis, and Akema took many of the masters from Tula and sent them to their new enterprise on the Vaga river.[16] Then Akema and Marselis began a struggle to recover the Tula enterprises, but without taking Vinius back into the partnership. While turning to their powerful *boyar* friends at the Russian court,[17] Marselis and Akema also sought intervention of the Dutch and Danish governments. Akema's interests were handled at The Hague by his merchant friend Isaac Bernart, who continually appeared before the General States on his colleague's behalf. On July 15, 1647, Bernart finally succeded in gaining recognition for both Akema and Marselis as Dutch citizens, which resulted in three letters to the tsar on their behalf from the Dutch General States between July 1647 and April 1648. At one point Akema himself went to Holland and returned to Moscow in December 1648 with official correspondence supporting his position. Meanwhile, the king of Denmark had not forgotten his old friend Marselis, and a personal note from Christian IV to Aleksei Mikhailovich begged the tsar to act favorably in Marselis' case.[18]

The tsar reiterated his complaints against Marselis and Akema in a document answering the three letters of the Dutch authorities. It was delivered at the *Posol'skii Prikaz* on June 20, 1648, to Konrad Burgh, the Dutch envoy in Moscow. A month later Burgh replied that Vinius simply wanted to eliminate Akema and Marselis from the Tula factories, and that the tsar, far from being angry at Marselis and Akema, should actually be grateful to them, for without their services the Tula enterprises could scarcely have succeeded. Upon this occasion, in the words of the pre-revolutionary historian A. S. Muliukin,

> . . .our prikaz officials, in a language delicate to the highest degree, but at the same time not without irony, chided [*vysmeivali*] the foreign governments for their lack of principle concerning questions of citizenship.[19]

Considering the pressure suddenly mobilized from abroad on behalf of two men once scarcely known to exist (in Holland, at least), it is perhaps remarkable that the Russian government held to its position as long as it did. Even at that, the tsar's officials did not reverse their earlier actions for diplomatic reasons alone. Specifically, while mobilizing political pressure from Holland and Denmark Marselis and Akema were wise enough to try another method of regaining their lost factories: they volunteered a series of concessions in the suggested future management of the Tula ironworks. For example, on April 19, 1648, Marselis offered to deliver goods to the state at prices lower than those stated in the charter of 1632. This step, combined with the intervention of Denmark and the Netherlands, won a royal decree dated April 27, 1648, restoring the Tula manufactory to Marselis and Akema.[20]

Andrei Vinius responded to this turn of events with another petition (July 17) in which he reminded Aleksei Mikhailovich of his loyal service to the tsar's father, starting with the grain purchases of 1631 and culminating in his adoption of the Orthodox faith and Russian citizenship. Vinius argued that his original charter of 1632 stipulated that even after the expiration of his duty-free years the factory would remain under his ownership. He continued to slander his old partners, Akema and Marselis, but, more to the point, he promised the tsar that if the Tula factories were returned to his ownership he would deliver iron goods to the state at prices still lower than those upon which Marselis and Akema had just won their new charter.[21]

Marselis and Akema replied immediately with a counter-offer which underbid Vinius, and he met it with a second reduction on August 2. Seven days later Vinius' competitors lowered their prices for a third time. But this proved to be the last move in this vicious price war, for Vinius was evidently in a weaker economic position than Akema and Marselis and unable to respond further to their price initiatives. On August 28 Marselis and Akema learned that the issue had finally been decided in their favor. They received a new and definitive factory charter (dated September 1, 1648) stating they were to operate the iron works for twenty years without payment of taxes or duties, during which time the factories could be inherited by the heirs of any deceased partner. The tsar granted the owners right of export and required them to teach Russian apprentices the advanced skills of their trade.[22]

Despite the low prices stated in the factory charter of 1648, Marselis and Akema had won a great victory. As Strumilin noted,

> This cruel competition with its finale is very instructive. It
> shows how favorable conditions were in the seventeenth centu-

ry for the development of large-scale capitalistic production in Russia. It is not accidental that the owners so recklessly lowered the prices of state deliveries, if only to retain their monopoly on large-scale production.

In fact, Marselis and Akema did not overestimate the value of the monopoly which they gained, for having been delivered from a price war with Vinius they were in a position to regain lost ground in coming years. Again Akema brought political pressure from the Netherlands to achieve his economic objective: in 1651 the Dutch diplomat Alexander Hoist arrived in Moscow and intervened with the tsar on behalf of Akema, saying that he and Marselis were suffering unjustly as a result of their price competition with Andrei Vinius. These discussions produced a new price agreement in 1652, whereby commodities were to be accepted by the state at prices which were the highest in the entire history of the Tula iron factories![23]

Although defeated in his attempt to gain exclusive control over the Tula enterprises, Andrei Denis'evich Vinius remained active in Russia for many years. He continued the merchant activity which in fact he had not abandoned even while acting as an iron manufacturer.[24] In 1649 Vinius obtained a six-year privilege for making, purchasing, and exporting pitch (*smola*) at Archangel, with a provision that English merchants desiring to export this item could buy it only from him. Vinius failed, however, to gain a settlement of four hundred rubles from Peter Marselis through litigation conducted in the *Posol'skii Prikaz* in January 1651, nor did he succeed in later efforts to recover his lost factories.[25]

In these years Vinius began again to serve the Russian government. In 1653 he traveled to Holland and Denmark to purchase military supplies for the army, and later he occupied various offices in the *prikazy* (chancelleries) for affairs pertaining to communications, artillery, pharmaceutics, Siberia, and, in particular, diplomacy.[26] Vinius died in Moscow in 1662 or 1663, at the age of fifty-seven or fifty-eight.[27]

Although Vinius ceased to play a role in iron manufacturing after 1648, the years of his service as an industrialist left an unmistakable imprint on the economic life of seventeenth-century Russia. Excessive ambition and an ultimately unrealistic sense of the possible led to the loss of his industrial holdings. Nonetheless, Vinius was a man of unusual talent, well endowed with qualities of energy, originality, and persistence. Above all, he possessed an adaptable spirit and the ability to meet new challenges and grow in response to them. Vinius' very adjustment to life in Russia is an illustration of this feature of his personality, and it was precisely his synthesis of Western and Russian elements which permitted him to render so many distinctive services to his new homeland. It is possible, however, that Vinius' great contribution to Russian history was his illustrious son, Andrei Andreevich Vinius, who attained fame as a friend and co-worker of Peter the Great.

5

Surging Ahead: Russian Iron Manufacturing, 1648–1662

DURING THE SECOND HALF of the seventeenth century the military needs of the state and the growth of domestic demand for such iron commodities as door plates, axes, hammers, and construction iron created a favorable situation for the growth of iron manufacturing in Russia. The increasing difficulty of importing Swedish iron provoked an intensified search for native ore deposits as Russian manufacturers and government figures moved in a modest but definite manner toward a broader and more consistent use of the country's iron resources. The years 1648–1662 mark a time in which the Russian iron industry registered particularly striking gains: during those fourteen years eight important iron manufactories were established in the central regions of the country alone.* Most of these enterprises belonged to the

*This excludes iron factories built in the far north, of which the Vaga river enterprise was the first. Iron development in this remote area is treated separately from iron manufacturing in the central part of Russia, in Chapter 7.

rapidly expanding Marselis-Akema industrial empire, and were located in the Tula-Moscow area. By the most stringent criteria they indicate a significant development of Russian capitalism during the mid-seventeenth century.

Before Marselis and Akema could build new iron manufactories after 1648 they had to reactivate their Tula enterprises. By the time they regained ownership of these workshops in September of that year, the factories were no longer in operation — scarcely surprising when we consider that from the very beginning of Pushkin's responsibility for the Tula works (in the winter of 1647), he faced great problems in securing their steady and efficient activity. Vinius, Marselis, and Akema not only withdrew their own managerial experience from the Tula factories; they transferred their most skilled workers to the Vaga river enterprise which remained under their control. Pushkin and Telepnev carried on in some fashion for the state, but then in the summer of 1648 a new difficulty arose. Pushkin, being a member of Morozov's circle, fell from power as a result of a popular uprising in Moscow in July. After Pushkin fled the capital, the iron works came to a halt and the foreign masters, now idle, left for Moscow.[1]

This was a time of real crisis for the young Russian iron industry, for in the absence of work the foreign masters from Tula naturally thought of leaving Russia. Now international intrigue also entered the picture. Karl Pommerening, a Swedish agent in Moscow, saw an opportunity to exploit the unsettled situation to destroy Russian iron manufacturing and thus gain greater markets for Sweden's international iron trade. Pommerening placed his residence (always protected by a *strel'tsy* guard) at the disposal of any iron master from Tula who claimed to be Swedish, gave his guests food and other necessities, and obtained for them their back pay. But Pommerening's real objective was to remove the men from Russia altogether. For this he was only too happy to use his influence to obtain exit passes for a large detachment of masters and their families which left for Sweden in the summer of 1648.

Pommerening encouraged the remaining workers to leave Russia too, but a large number chose to stay, hoping the Tula factories would soon resume operation. The sly Swede even resorted to a form of sabotage, as he reported to his sovereign on October 18, 1648 (evidently referring to the Vaga works): ". . . I obtained for Peter Marselis an inferior blacksmith from [the Tula factories of] Andrei Denis [Vinius]. . . ." Commenting upon Pommerening's actions, Erik Amburger observes that "these events clearly show how jealously Sweden observed the rise of an indigenous Russian iron industry, and how she attempted to sabotage it upon any opportunity."[2]

Although reports from Pommerening as late as January 1649 indicate that "The Tula and Viatskie [Vaga?] iron factories . . . for the most part lie in idleness," the Tula works were soon repaired, reactivated, and even expanded.[3] Probably the Vaga cannon manufactory was closed in this period or shortly thereafter, for after regaining the Tula enterprises Akema and Marselis were most interested in restoring them to maximum production, especially since the great distance of the Vaga factory from the center of the Russian empire would have made its continued supervision difficult.[4]

The second iron factory established in the 1640's was a state enterprise, and probably developed as a result of the Russian authorities' intention of conducting iron manufacturing with their own resources. While in Holland, Miloslavskii had engaged the iron master Hendrik van Aken for service in Russia. Van Aken was presented to the tsar on November 1, 1647, worked for a time in the *Stvol'nyi Prikaz,* and on October 11, 1648, concluded an agreement with the *Posol'skii Prikaz,* under the terms of which the next year he built a water-powered blasting factory on the Iauza river just north of Moscow. According to the agreement van Aken and his four sons would make musket and carbine barrels for ten years to government order. They were to be assisted by ten Russian apprentices and ten ordinary workers.[5] Van Aken's charter reflects the profound desire of the Russian government to establish an indigenous iron industry, for it stipulated that

Russian apprentices were to learn all aspects of weapon manufacturing—even how to build furnaces, hearths, forging hammers, boring mechanisms, and the like. The desire of the
government to have skilled native workers was also expressed
in the arrangement of van Aken's salary. At first the master
and his sons were to receive ten rubles per month, but when
the Russians had perfected the skills of their craft this was to
be increased to twenty rubles per month. Presumably this
would give the Dutchmen an incentive to carry out their
instructional obligations, and shows that Russians were coming to understand better the psychology of self-seeking foreigners.[6]

Unfortunately Hendrik van Aken died on April 19, 1650.
His wife and two of his sons evidently hoped to remain in
Russia, because the sons informed the government that although they could not continue manufacturing weapons alone,
since they were young and inexperienced, should the tsar
permit Romashka, the eldest, to go abroad, "he will bring to
the tsar the same sort of barrel master as his father was." In
1651, however, the van Aken family returned to Holland, and
nothing more is heard of the Iauza iron factory.[7]

Soon after leaving the Vinius-Akema-Marselis partnership
in 1647, Boris Morozov began to think of developing iron
manufacturing on his feudal estates. His correspondence indicates that he was familiar with the iron artisanry of his serf
population and the profits which were to be had from that type
of activity,[8] and he assiduously cultivated and encouraged the
work of his artisan metallurgists to increase his own income.
By 1651 Morozov had an iron mill with a blast furnace built at
his village of Pavlovskoe, forty kilometers from Moscow, on
the Beliania, a tributary of the Istra river. This enterprise was
probably inspired by the acquaintance Morozov gained with
the iron industry through his friend Vinius.[9]

In 1651 twenty Polish masters hired by Morozov to build
and operate his iron works arrived in the town of Pavlovskoe.
For some reason these workers remained idle for a time,
though they continually asked to be permitted to exercise their

craft. Perhaps there was some kind of labor disagreement between them and Morozov, since the Poles suggested they retain and market the fruits of their labor in return for a yearly *obrok* payable to Morozov. However that might be, factory activity in this area was under way by the autumn of 1652, although certain difficulties curtailed production for that winter.[10]

We know almost nothing of Morozov's ironworks from the documents preserved today. When he died in 1661 the Pavlovskoe factory was inherited by his widow, Anna Il'inichna, and upon her death in 1668 it was taken by the tsar in escheat and placed under the jurisdiction of the *Tainyi Prikaz*. [11] When the Swedish merchant Kilburger visited the enterprise in 1674 the Pavlovskoe manufactory was still operating successfully, although Kilburger noted that the quality of the iron was low, probably because in this area iron ore came from marshes and swamps.[12]

Marselis and Akema expanded their iron manufacturing activities most significantly in 1653, with the construction of four new iron factories located in Kashirskii *uezd*, about forty kilometers to the north and slightly to the west of the Tula group. The upper factory, called the Vedmenskii works, was on the Skniga river, near its point of confluence with the Solomenka. Its dam was 140 *sazhens* (about 980 feet) long, fourteen *sazhens* wide, and seven *sazhens* high, and the power generated by the water was used to operate two forging hammers for the preparation of musket and carbine barrels, nails, plowshares, handmills, and, when required, halberds, spades, small axes, picks, hoes, and shovels. The second manufactory was located near the village of Salamykova, also on the Skniga river, and was known as the Salamykovskii works. This dam was also equipped with a forging shop which produced iron plates for armor and doors.[13]

The third and largest factory in the *Kashira* group was the Chentsovskii enterprise, built on the Skniga river at the town of Chentsova. Like the other three establishments, this "factory" was a complex of buildings, each performing a particular function. First, there was a forge with two hammers, where the iron strips for musket and carbine barrels and steel swords were made. In a second building masters converted the iron strips into gun barrels; in a third shop the barrels were bored and polished with two "spits" (drills). The second structure was especially large (twenty-four *sazhens* long and six *sazhens* wide) and contained four large furnaces equipped with bellows, served by four masters. There were three smaller furnaces for making nails and small iron objects, parts of the gun barrels, and various tools used by the masters. A section of the building was used for finishing the firearm barrels, "and in the same *izba* [hut] are vizes, saws and all sorts of equipment useful for barrel finishing." Opposite this large building were six interconnected huts *(izbi)* with six furnaces for the manufacture of armor. Finally, the Chentsovskii factory was provided with a fuel shed, three storage barns, and several *izbi* used as homes for the masters.

The fourth factory, the Elkinskii, was also on the Skniga river. There was a forge shop here with two large furnaces and a "large hammer." The same enterprise had two other forges, as well as a barn with eight drills for musket barrels powered by a single water wheel. The Elkinskii dam was small, being of normal width and height but only seventy *sazhens* (about 490 feet) in length.[14]

The Kashira enterprises were forging and boring shops; they had no furnace for smelting pig iron. Before the construction of the Vepreiskii factory in the same area in 1668, they obtained pig iron solely from the second Tula works, refined the product at their forges, and then made the commodities described above. After 1668 the Vepreiskii factory also shipped pig iron to the Kashirskie enterprises. A considerable number of masters, apprentices, and workers were engaged at the Kashirskie group, and the output was quite large for the time. In 1662 a government inspector estimated that eight masters and their assistants at the Chentsovskii factory could turn out 7,200 musket barrels in a working year of three hundred days. In a single week two masters at the same plant could produce eight suits of cavalry armor, complete with sword and decorations. A considerable quantity of consumer goods also came from Kashira as, for example, in 1668 when the government ordered 1,003 plows with double-bladed plowshares and one thousand plowblades *(obrezi)*. Fragmentary evidence suggests that the masters at the Kashirskie factories were paid higher wages than at Tula. [15]

Marselis and Akema acquired two other iron factories during the 1650's, both of which were situated in the Tula-Kashira area, approximately one hundred kilometers southwest of Moscow. The first of these, the Porotovskii works (so named from its location on the Porotva river), was in Maloiaroslavskii *uezd*. It was built by boyar Il'ia Danilovich Miloslavskii, who for some reason immediately tired of his investment and leased it to Akema and Marselis for fifteen years, beginning on February 5, 1656.* According to their agreement, the lease-holders were to pay Miloslavskii an annual *obrok* of three hundred rubles and one hundred *puds* of angle-iron. Marselis and Akema also took from Miloslavskii for the duration of the lease three Polish metallurgists whom he had engaged, as well as "my peasant, the fuel master, Pan'ka," paying Miloslavskii ten rubles per worker per year, and giving each master annual wages of twenty-five rubles. In January 1657, however, Marselis and Akema bought the Porotovskii factory outright for the sum of one thousand rubles. The second enterprise in this area was built by Marselis and Akema in 1659 on the Ugodka river, four *versts* northeast of the Porotovskii works. [16]

The Porotovskii and Ugodskii factories were smaller than the Tula and Kashirskie enterprises. In 1662 the Porotovskii was equipped with seven water wheels, a double-blast furnace, and a forge shop with five hearths and two large hammers. At the same time the Ugodskii enterprise functioned with two

---

*The reader will recall that as Russian Ambassador to Amsterdam in 1646–1647, Miloslavskii had delivered a biting criticism of Marselis' and Akema's entrepreneurial activity. It appears, however, that after ten years Miloslavskii and the "unscrupulous" foreigners found no difficulty in doing business to their mutual advantage.

water wheels and two forge shops containing three large
hearths and two hammers.[17] Apparently it obtained its pig
iron from the Porotovskii blast furnace and was probably built
in order to provide the Porotovskii manufactory with more
forges and thus maximize total output.

The Ugodskii and Porotovskii factories had the obligation
during the 1660's to deliver fifteen thousand *puds* of iron to the
state each year. Their commodities consisted of cannon, projectiles, grenades, cannister shot, floor plates, and angle-iron,
all in great quantities. Arquebuses, swords, armor, and spiked
helmets were also made at times. The tsar ascribed Vyshegorodskaia *volost'* in Vereiskii *uezd* (consisting of 170 households) to Akema and Marselis to provide unskilled labor for
the Porotovskii and Ugodskii enterprises.[18]

Between 1648 and 1662 no fewer than eight new manufactories were established in the Moscow-Tula area of the Russian empire. Of these, one was a state enterprise, two were
the property of great boyar-entrepreneurs, and five were constructed by Marselis and Akema. As we have seen, by 1662
the state factory had closed and only one of the original
"feudalist" enterprises remained in noble hands (that of Anna
Il'inichna Morozova). The fact that Marselis and Akema built
five of the eight factories established between 1648 and 1662,
and ended by owning six of the seven of these factories still
operating in 1662, shows the tendency for foreigners to gain an
increasingly large share of the industrial market even in this
early period. And Marselis and Akema continued, of course,
to operate the four other iron enterprises at Tula throughout
the entire period 1648–1662, giving them a total of ten modern
iron manufactories by 1662.

6

Crisis in the Affairs
of Peter Marselis

PETER MARSELIS WAS MORE than an ambitious and successful merchant and iron manufacturer who dabbled in diplomacy and the political affairs of Russia and Denmark. He was also an unscrupulous entrepreneur willing to use dishonest methods to supplement the building of his family's fortune. Doubtless we shall never know the full extent of his shady operations, but the exposure of one aspect of Marselis' illegal activities in 1662 brought about the greatest crisis of his life and raised the question of his continued presence in Russia. To understand this episode in Marselis' career we must recall that the fiscal problems of the Russian government during the 1650's and 1660's led to an extreme inflationary step, the substitution of copper coin for precious metal. This produced a sharp rise in prices and enabled Marselis and Akema to secure increases of fifty kopecks per *pud* on iron goods delivered to the state. Marselis, however, sought to profit from the existing situation by more unprincipled means. Counterfeiting and other forms of corruption were quite common at this time, and it seems that Marselis could not resist the temptation to become involved in the illicit dealings going on about him. As partner in a scheme devised by a coinage official at Moscow, Marselis smuggled fifteen thousand copper rubles from the mint into his house and was rewarded with three thousand of these rubles for his services. All might have gone well but for the discovery by honest authorities (on June 16, 1662) of the theft. An investigation which followed implicated Marselis. When arrested and interrogated by the tsar himself, he confessed everything. The scandal finally encompassed some six hundred people, including the entire mints of Novgorod and Pskov.[1]

On August 21, 1662, "execution" of the convicted embezzlers took place in Moscow, meaning in this instance that the left hand of each prisoner was hacked off as punishment for his criminal deed. Like a seventeenth-century precursor of Dostoevskii, Marselis was taken to the bloody spot and the usual sentence read. But then it was announced that instead of suffering physical mutilation, Marselis, as a foreigner and a Danish citizen, would simply forfeit his entire fortune to the tsar. Whereas other culprits were exiled to Siberia or similarly removed places, Marselis was to be expelled from the country. His house was occupied by *strel'tsy* and Marselis himself temporarily reimprisoned.[2]

After Marselis' fortune was seized in June 1662, the state became Akema's new business partner. *Stol'nik* Afanasii Denis'evich Fonvizin, a foreigner, was sent from Moscow to help run the enterprises and represent the interests of the state. The new situation seems to have bothered Akema in various ways. For one thing, Marselis' fate was quickly known in Holland, and this made it difficult to recruit new workers from abroad to replace those returning home, all the more so as the Russian government, the "oppressive" force which had wronged the hapless Marselis (as Dutchmen understood the matter), was now more deeply involved than ever in the affairs of the iron industry. And Russian artisans were continually being sent from Moscow to learn the advanced skills of modern iron manufacturing. We have seen that foreigner-capitalists resisted elevating native talent to high positions in their enterprises, for this would, at a certain point, eclipse their own once indispensable services to the Russian state. With the state as a partner, however, Akema no longer had any control over factory labor policies, and foreign masters who refused to educate their Russian apprentices were now being hindered in their desire to return home after completion of their contracts in the Muscovite state. [3]

From Akema's point of view, the obvious solution to this conflict of interest lay in a division of the iron enterprises so that a certain number would belong to him outright and the remainder would be state property. On May 21, 1663, after a year of strained partnership with the government, Akema petitioned for such an arrangement. According to his suggestion, the tsar would retain the Porotovskii and Ugodskii factories (including Karamyshevo village and the surrounding forestry resources), and Akema would receive the Tula-Kashirskie factories, along with Solomenskaia *volost'*, which had been ascribed to these enterprises. But in view of the fact that "those factories are larger and better than the Porotovskii and Ugodskii and the ore is [more] dependable," Akema would pay the government compensation of five thousand rubles at the rate of one thousand rubles per year. [4]

On June 3, 1663, the *Oruzheinaia palata* ordered Fonvizin to inspect and evaluate the factories to determine if the division suggested by Akema would be profitable for the tsar. Among other things, Fonvizin was to report the monthly output of the various plants. The results of this investigation[5] revealed that two of the four Tula dams had been destroyed by floods, and as of 1662–1663 some of the workshops had been standing idle for several years. The blast furnace at Tula, however, continued to work, as did one of the forging enterprises, and these combined with the large and active Kashirskie manufactories to make this complex the most serious achievement of Russian metallurgy at this time. For this reason the government decided to act in a manner quite different than that hoped for by Filimon Akema. On December 1, 1663, the tsar announced that Akema would receive the Porotovskii and Ugodskii factories and that the state would retain the Tula-Kashira enterprises. As compensation for receiving the smaller part of the bargain, Akema was to be the one to receive the sum of five thousand rubles, payable at one thousand rubles per year.[6]

Akema was unable to run the Porotovskii-Ugodskii factories on his own resources, so he took as partners his nephew Thielemann, who had earlier gained experience in administering the Salamykovskii and Vedmenskii factories at Kashira, and Richard Andrews, a *prikaz* official and son of Thomas Andrews, the former manager of the Tula works about 1662–1663. Akema and his associates received a new charter (dated December 25, 1665) granting them entrepreneurial rights over the Ugodskii and Porotovskii factories and the royal Vyshegorodskaia *volost'* containing twenty-one "vacant plots" *(pustoshi)* for firewood and 646 male peasants. The term of tax-free ownership was set at twenty years, beginning on December 1, 1663, after which time the owners or their heirs would pay *obrok* of one hundred rubles per year per blast furnace, as well as such trade duty as the tsar would decree. Should factory activity be halted through damage from water, fire, and so forth, the time lost in making state deliveries would not be counted as part of the twenty-year exemption period.[7]

By the fall of 1662 Peter Marselis' star seemed in complete eclipse. He had lost his house, his industrial and commercial interests, and now was waiting in prison for the final blow: deportation. Yet even now Marselis, out of prison, was struggling to regain his lost position. His first problem, of course, was simply to remain in Moscow, a feat which he managed to accomplish. This achievement behind him, Marselis followed a dual strategy to recover his factories. On the one hand, he brought to bear all possible pressure upon the Russian government from abroad; on the other, Marselis strove to re-establish himself as a figure useful to the tsar and his leading statesmen, thinking in this way to redevelop the goodwill and influence necessary to secure reinstatement of his economic interests.

Peter's powerful brother, Gabriel Marselis, had been of service to the Russian-based branch of the family when Filimon Akema and Peter Marselis lost the Tula factories in 1647. From far-off Amsterdam Gabriel again sprang to the aid of his brother, seeking for Peter either the return of his enterprises or compensation for the losses he suffered. Gabriel secured the intervention of the king of Denmark, who wrote the tsar no less than three times between March 1663 and November 1664 requesting pardon for Peter Marselis. Meanwhile, Peter was making use of his own Swedish connections, and in July 1663 he sent his son Leonhard to Sweden to rally influential people to their cause. Success must have still seemed remote, however, for as an alternative to regaining their position in Russia Leonhard explored the possibility of his family immigrating to Sweden. But within a year the tide had begun to turn: Peter Marselis and his family were not only still in Moscow — they had even recovered their house, probably due to the efforts of Swedish friends. The English may also have been helpful, for in search of aid Leonhard even went to England, where he secured the friendship of Charles Howard, the Earl of Carlisle, who arrived in Moscow in 1664 as the English Ambassador to the tsar.[8]

Marselis' diplomatic services to the Russian state during this time arose in connection with the Russo-Polish War of 1654. After Poland ended her war with Sweden in 1660, she turned on her Russian enemy with such force and determination that within a year the Muscovites were routed at Zeromsk and driven from nearly all the eastern provinces then under contention — so that when a peace conference opened at Durovicha in 1664, Poland's chances for a favorable treaty with Russia seemed bright indeed. At this point Peter Marselis entered the picture. Not only did he travel in 1665 to the Elector of Brandenburg, the rulers of several German states, and Frederick III of Denmark requesting intervention for terms favorable to Russia. At the very moment when Poland needed all possible strength to sustain her diplomacy, Marselis opened secret negotiations with the great magnate Prince Lubomirsky, which significantly contributed to his raising a major rebellion and civil war against the Polish King, John II Casimir. This dramatically shifted the balance of power in Russia's direction and forced the Poles — after protracted negotiations at Andrussovo — virtually to accept the terms of the Muscovites. Marselis had served the Russian cause brilliantly, and it brought him all the more closely into friendship with the bright and rising Russian statesman of this period, Afanasii Lavrent'evich Ordin-Nashchokin.[9]

Marselis served Ordin-Nashchokin as economic adviser and participated in discussions which finally produced a new commercial code reforming Russia's conduct of foreign trade. Although Marselis' ideas were rejected because of the concern he displayed for the position of Western European merchants in Russia, it was clear that by 1667 the attitude of the Russian authorities had shifted in his favor. This being the case, on April 20, 1667, Marselis submitted a petition to the tsar, recalling the devotion of his father and himself to the Russian state, and requesting the return of the Tula and Kashira iron enterprises. On May 8, 1667, the day following the proclamation of the *Novotorgovyi ustav* (the New Commercial Code), the tsar issued an edict restoring these iron factories to the Marselis family in the light of Peter's "many small services and for all sorts of zeal. . . ."[10]

Aleksei Mikhailovich's edict returned the Tula-Kashirskie factories for a period of twenty years. But for several reasons Marselis was never again to enjoy the unrestrained and majestic position in Russian economic life that had been characteristic of Andrei Vinius before 1647, or himself and Akema in the period 1648–1662. First of all, after 1667 Marselis and his sons no longer enjoyed a monopoly over the iron industry, for they now faced competition from Akema and his heirs and from other entrepreneurs and even the state itself, all of whom were building various enterprises. Second, as we shall see, in the future the state was much more exacting in securing from Marselis his obligations, for during the second half of the seventeenth century the commercial and industrial base of Russia was broadly enough developed that any single foreigner-entrepreneur could be eliminated without causing a major setback to the national economy. This meant that foreign merchants and capitalists could no longer count on the official benevolence which had once permitted them to exploit and abuse their economic positions. In the case of Marselis, the government was willing to lend him money, assure him profits, even help him to expand — but it was also more demanding in the fulfillment of contracts and agreements, far less permissive with regard to the repayment of debts, and, in fact, not above bringing additional claims against Marselis on extremely arbitrary grounds.

When Marselis returned to assume control over his iron factories, he found that the Tula works had declined during their period of state ownership and control, and at least one historian has suggested that this was the reason for Ordin-Nashchokin's decision to return them to Peter.[11] We have already noted the dilapidated state of these enterprises in 1662, and it appears they were equally in need of repair five years later. In general, the Tula-Kashirskie manufactories were suffering from deforestation, the flight of some of the peasants of Solomenskaia *volost'*, and exhaustion of several vital stores at the factory. Extensive reconstruction was also needed, particularly at Tula, which was largely idle by 1667.[12]

After Marselis recovered his factories, he obtained a loan of one thousand rubles from the *Pushkarskii Prikaz,* which was soon being repaid with iron goods from the factory. The question of Marselis' debts, however, did not end there, for from the very beginning various state departments and officials descended upon the unfortunate man with the most demanding claims. The state decided that Marselis should pay some 1,314 rubles for "all sorts of stores, ores, fire-wood, fuel, cast-iron and other supplies" at the Tula-Kashirskie factories at the time of their reinstatement to him in 1667. Marselis maintained that the records upon which this debt was calculated exaggerated the value of these supplies twofold, but these objections gained him no concessions. Other officials brought claims based upon Marselis' alleged failure to settle all of his obligations concerning Solomenskaia *volost'* before 1662, and Marselis was informed that from 1669 he would not be excused from payment of *obrok* but would pay annually 286 rubles plus specified quantities of various natural products from the peasants of the village.[13]

Most extravagant, perhaps, was the demand that Marselis reimburse the government for the five thousand rubles it had paid to Akema as compensation for not receiving the more valuable Tula and Kashirskie iron works![14] Marselis grew particularly angry at this exaction and simply refused to pay. In a statement of November 30, 1668, he pointed out that the factories had been built with his money, and that the awarding of five thousand rubles to Akema was none of his doing. For that matter, during the five years of his absence the various enterprises had been in the tsar's hands, "and from the factories there were profits of many thousands" of rubles. Finally, Marselis asserted that the works which had been returned to him had greatly decreased in value. The factories were "ruined and broken down" *(razoreny i rospalis'),* and the number of peasants there had grown few in number *(oskudali)*. Marselis pointed out that he would have to make extensive and costly repairs, and even suggested that the iron enterprises might be abandoned soon because of their poor condition.[15]

The outcome of this controversy over the extent of Marselis' indebtedness is not clear. In 1670 the state maintained that his debts totaled 6,319 rubles, not counting the natural products also being demanded of him.[16] A document dated April 6, 1669, indicates that Marselis was actually paying some of his debts, but we also know that in 1671 he continued adamantly to reject at least some of the state claims.[17] Apparently he hoped to receive more favorable treatment by having jurisdiction over his factories transferred to the *Posol'skii*

Prikaz (accomplished on September 18, 1667), where his friend A. L. Ordin-Nashchokin was chancellor of foreign affairs. Interested as he was in the development of modern industry in Russia, Ordin-Nashchokin tried to help Marselis secure loans, and even favored rescinding the low prices demanded by the government for iron goods produced by the mills.[18] But evidently Ordin-Nashchokin was unable to curb the government's exactions against Marselis, and in any case he fell from power in February 1671. Thereafter Marselis' relations with the authorities continued to be strained.

At first Marselis had difficulty in operating his iron factories. Since the state had placed no orders with him when the factories were returned in May 1667, he hesitated to hire more workers or to do work of any sort, so the factories stood idle for a time. In 1668 he made extensive deliveries to the *Pushkarskii Prikaz* and two other government departments, but except for the sum of one thousand rubles (which actually seems to have been a loan) he was not paid for these goods. Unable to pay his workers' wages, Marselis claimed that work at the factory had halted and that he was suffering "great ruin and large losses." As late as early 1669 Marselis still had not been reimbursed for his earlier work, and state goods valued at 3,690 rubles sat in his factory storehouses undelivered. Finally Tsar Aleksei Mikhailovich ordered the chancellery of Novgorod affairs to pay Marselis 2,690 rubles (the amount of the government's debts, minus the original one-thousand-ruble loan) from its "incomes."[19]

In 1668 Marselis claimed that the absence of qualified masters rendered him unable to make cannon from forged iron, or pots, nails, and the like.[20] But finally, in April of that year, Marselis was ordered to deliver the following goods for that and every succeeding year:

20,000 *puds* of rod- and angle-iron	@ 16 *altyn*, 4 *den'gi* (50 kopecks) per *pud*
5,000 *puds* of sheet-iron for city gates and for roofing	@ 30 *altyn* per *pud*
twenty cannon (of standard caliber)	@ 10 *altyn* per *pud*

6,000 cannon balls weighing ½ *grivna*, ¾ *g.*, 1 *g.*, 1-½ *g.*, 2 *g.*	@ 8 *altyn, 2 den'gi* per *pud*
10,000 grenades weighing four and five *grivni*, as well as of medium and large size	@ 10 *altyn* per *pud* (for large grenades)
100 iron hand-mills for grinding flour	@ 5 rubles apiece
1,000 *tuyères* (see Glossary) ⎫ 50 iron ingots ⎪ 50 (hand) grinding mortars ⎬ 100,000 assorted nails [21] ⎭	prices not listed

As one document dating from 1668 points out, the cost to the state of the full inventory listed above would have been no less than 18,020 rubles for a single year.[22] In practice the full roster of commodities and quantities was never delivered, though orders were usually large. During the year from September 1, 1673 to August 31, 1674, for example, the Tula-Kashirskie factories delivered 13,675 *puds* of angle-, rod-, latticed-, and strip-iron, plus 3,580 *puds* of sheet-iron, and this was priced at 10,077 rubles, 18 *altyn, 3 den'gi*. On August 31, 1668, the *Pushkarskii Prikaz* requested a price reduction on the goods of the Tula-Kashira factories. Marselis made various counter-proposals to this demand. The final compromise was that the old prices would remain in effect but that Marselis would deliver annually at no cost one thousand grenades and pay the sum of five hundred rubles. This meant, in effect, that he had lost his freedom from taxation and trade duty. Although there is evidence that Marselis sometimes evaded these obligations, on May 1, 1673, his sons petitioned for relief from this burden, and on January 4, 1674, Aleksei Mikhailovich formally acceded to their request.[23]

The history of iron manufacturing in Russia involves the questions of what specific commodities were produced, at what price and quality, and with what influence on the material culture of Russian society during the seventeenth century. As early as the 1650's construction materials formed an important part of the output of the Tula-Kashirskie iron works. A foreign visitor to Moscow at this time, Paul of Aleppo, said of the iron manufactured at Tula:

> This iron is quite inexpensive, and for this reason all the doors of stone houses, palaces, churches, warehouses, basements, and shops in the city of Moscow, as are all the windows, are in large part made of pure iron. We marveled more than a little at the hugeness of church doors, of fort and palace gates.[24]

During the late 1660's and early 1670's it was common for Marselis to deliver rod-, bar-, and sheet-iron for public buildings in Smolensk and Vologda[25]—or even Archangel[26]—as well as for Moscow,[27] Kiev, and other Ukrainian cities.[28]

Much useful information on the work of the Akema and Marselis iron factories is provided by a Swedish merchant, Johann Philipp Kilburger, who traveled throughout Russia and wrote a book in German immediately after his return home entitled *A Brief Account of Russian Trade, how it was Conducted with Exported and Imported Goods throughout all Russia during the Year 1674*.[29] Peter Marselis and his sons, Leonhard and Gabriel, had all passed away before Kilburger's Russian tour. The "Peter Marselis" with whom Kilburger spoke was the youngest son from Marselis' first marriage, and to distinguish him from his father we shall call him, in Russian fashion, "Petr Petrovich Marselis."[30] Kilburger tells us that under Petr Petrovich the enterprises had three blast furnaces (two of them at the second Tula works), and ten water-hammers, each with a double hearth,[31] from which we conclude that between 1667 and 1674 the Marselis family had expanded the production facilities of the Tula-Kashirskie factories.

According to Kilburger, Petr Petrovich Marselis made rod-iron for construction purposes in thick, thin, and medium sizes, the latter two in lengths of sixteen feet. Thick iron was less often used, and then only for wall reinforcements in churches, monasteries, and homes. Door frames and window fittings were made from thin rod-iron.

> ... And since now with every day they are building more and more stone houses, a considerable amount is spent on rod and

sheet iron, since, due to frequent fires, all the external doors and openable windows are made of iron.[32]

At this time four iron rods would form a window frame, the windows being made either of glass or of white and colored mica in various sorts of grid patterns. Rod-iron was also used for clamps *(skrepy)* in window frames and in other parts of a building as needed.[33] Sheet-iron was also an important construction material in this period, and Kilburger notes that among other things the Marselis brothers made large and thick iron slabs which were placed before the thresholds of large stone houses.[34]

Cannon were cast in various calibers and lengths,[35] the largest of which weighed 7,200 *funts*. (According to Petr Marselis, in the near future they would be producing cannon weighing as much as 9,600 *funts*.) Although the bores of these cannon were found to be very smooth on the inside, Kilburger doubted their quality. He related that earlier a number of such cannon had been exported to Holland, where they had exploded during trial. According to Kilburger,

> . . . it is true that Marselis does not have red-short iron *(krasnolomkoe zhelezo)*, but, on the contrary, cold-short iron *(kholodnolomkoe zhelezo)*, from which it may be easily concluded that his cannon could not be the very best.[36]

It appears that previously there were means of strengthening lower-quality cannon:

> Several years ago the foreigner died who was well capable of binding the above-mentioned cannon [which burst on trial] with hoops. Of those I saw, there were still several among the Strel'tsy artillery which were bound by 18 hoops. But now there is no one else in the country who possesses such ability.[37]

Kilburger's strongest words of praise were reserved for Filimon Akema's Porotovskii factory.[38] Kilburger observed that the output of Akema's plant, based on two blast furnaces and four hammers, was better than that of Marselis because Akema paid a *grivna* per pud more for his iron ore. [39] This being the case, the retail prices of Akema's iron goods on *zhe-*

leznyi riad* were correspondingly higher, as indicated by the following figures given by Kilburger, dated May 30, 1674:

Rod iron of "crude sort":
   Marselis, 5, 5-½ *grivni* (50-55 *kopecks*) per *pud*
   Akema, 6, 6-½ *grivni* per *pud*
Rod iron of good quality:
   Akema, 7 *grivni* per *pud*
Window shutters and door fittings:
   Marselis, 1 ruble per *pud*
   Akema, 1 ruble 10 kopecks per *pud*
Thin double sheet-iron *(dvoinye tonkie doski)*:
   1 ruble 20 kopecks per *pud* (factory source not specified) [40]

The fact that iron commodities of different quality were competing with each other on a retail basis indicated that a well-developed market for iron goods existed by 1674. The ever-increasing use of brick and stone for construction combined with the growing use of money in the society as a whole to make this possible. The Marselis family in these years was orienting its iron output more and more toward the domestic market, a tendency even more pronounced in the case of Akema, who actually abandoned the production of military goods after he obtained the Ugodskii and Porotovskii factories in 1663, turning to the open market as the source of his profits.[41] Besides sheet- and rod-iron ("which is especially beautiful, soft, and malleable, so that each bar may easily be bent in a circle"), the Porotovskii factory produced anchors, many of which were four-pronged and weighed seven or eight *puds*. Kilburger noted that none of the three iron factories he visited made steel, nails, awls for bast shoes (called *kochedyki*), ordinary shoe awls *(sapozhnye shili)*, or other such small items. This was because peasant iron artisanry was able to produce these goods more cheaply, though in the case of nails the ore was of poor quality and completely "cold-short"

---

*Literally "the iron row," which refers to a row of shops in Moscow where iron fittings for windows and doors, large cauldrons, frying pans and kitchen utensils, etc., could be purchased (Kurts, *Sochinenie Kil'burgera*, pp. 468-469).

(kholodnolomkoe), "so that the nails if struck by an unbalanced blow, shatter like glass. . . ."[42] Kilburger's observation indicates the limitations of large-scale iron manufacturing during the seventeenth century, and explains how it was possible for the peasant metallurgist, despite the low quality of his output, to continue his activity, or even to increase it in order to keep pace with a constantly expanding market demand.

The high point in the building of stone churches, government offices, and noble palaces of the seventeenth century came a decade after Kilburger's visit, during the 1680's. A major reason was Prince V. V. Golitsyn's determination to combat the danger of fires in Moscow (which suffered terrible conflagrations in 1611 and 1671) by rebuilding much of the city and its bridges in stone. Thus between 1684 and 1685 the Tula-Kashira iron works furnished the government over 2,700 sheets of cast iron for repairs in the Kremlin, plus one thousand corrugated sheets and two hundred *puds* of bar-iron for new roofing on the *Granovitaia palata*. During the 1680's some three thousand stone buildings were erected in Moscow, and, according to C. Bickford O'Brien:

> A palace for foreign ambassadors erected in stone and Golitsyn's own palace built of stone with heavy brass sheet roofing served as models for the wealthy nobility. According to contemporary accounts, the Golitsyn palace was "one of the most magnificent in Europe" and more like "the palace of an Italian prince." Its interior was ornamented with wood carvings and murals. Costly mirrors filled the space between windows, interspersed with German maps in heavy gilt frames.

Considering the production of Russian iron manufactories during the second half of the seventeenth century, it does not seem exaggerated to conclude that "the flowering of noble and church architecture" at this time could not possibly have occurred without the pioneering work of Andrei Vinius, Filimon Akema, and Peter Marselis.[43]

Important as iron manufacturing was to Russia's economic and military situation, not much progress was made in expanding the industry during this period 1662-1674. Certainly the government displayed a keen interest in ferrous metallurgy (and state officials organized numerous ore-prospecting expeditions during the third quarter of the seventeenth century),[44] but only three new iron manufactories were established in central and western Russia between 1662 and 1674.* Peter Marselis built the first of these during the late 1660's in partnership with Thomas Kellermann. The enterprise was located on the Vepreia river in Aleksinskii *uezd,* twelve kilometers southwest of the Kashira works. As the twenty-year privileges granted to the owners by the *Posol'skii Prikaz* dated from June 1, 1671, it would appear that the Vepreiskii (or Aleksinskii) factory began operation at that time. It specialized in cannon, projectiles, and grenades, and drew the ore for its blast furnace from the same source as the Tula-Kashira group. In fact, the Aleksinskii works was a part of that industrial complex, and when its furnace was temporarily out of order it obtained pig iron from Tula.[45]

Boris Morozov's iron manufactory, on his estates near Pavlovskoe, was seized by Tsar Aleksei in escheat upon the death of Morozov's widow, Anna Il'inichna, in 1668. It was placed under the direction of the *Prikaz Tainykh Del,* which then decided to expand state iron manufacturing in this area, using the Pavlovskii works as a foundation. On September 21, 1668, "the newly-baptized [foreign master] Dementei Ivanov, son of Budi, was sent with his son [from Marselis' Tula works] for the examination of iron ores" in Zvenigorodskii *uezd,* near the old Pavlovskii enterprise. By October 1668 work on the new factory (variously called the Borodnikovskii, Borodinskii, and Briazginskii works) was far advanced, firewood was being prepared, and seventeen soldiers were mining ore in a nearby field. In the following month carpenters and blacksmiths were working in the area, and in all probability the Borodnikovskii factory was in full operation by early 1669. Three years later, in 1672, state workmen built a third iron works in this area, the

---

*Activity in the far north at this time will be discussed in the following chapter; Siberian developments are treated in Chapter 8.

Obushkovskii (Abushkovskii) factory, located on the Beliana river, as were its two predecessors, the Pavlovskii and Borodnikovskii enterprises.[46]

When Tsar Aleksei Mikhailovich died in 1676, the *Prikaz Tainykh Del* was dissolved, and the Zvenigorodskie factories (as the three state iron works in this area were called collectively) were transferred by decree of February 18, 1676, to the jurisdiction of the *Prikaz Bol'shogo Dvortsa*. At this time the authorities assembled information about the Zvenigorodskie enterprises which provides a rounded picture of the works. There were only twenty-eight skilled workers at all three plants: two blast-furnace masters, six hammer masters, four fuel masters, five submasters of various specialties, six unskilled workers ascribed *(poddatnye)* by the tsar, four smiths, and one "miller" *(mel'nik)*. The entire factory complex drew its pig iron from the blast furnace of the Pavlovskii enterprise, although the poor quality of the local soil (which had also been noted by Kilburger when he visited this factory in 1674) caused the management to resort on occasion to the use of fine imported Swedish iron.[47]

The output of the Zvenigorodskie factories was solely for the army, state construction projects, and the economic needs of various royal artisan workshops and estates. Nothing from these manufactories was sold on the domestic market. The Borodnikovskii enterprise turned out sheet- and rod-iron, and — after the arrival in 1672 of several workers formerly with Marselis — cannon. The Pavlovskii factory, by far the largest of the three, smelted pig iron from ore, and in its hammer shop forged such items as sheet-, rod-, and angle-iron, shovels, axes, and nails. In addition to the above items, the Obushkovskii workshop manufactured iron salt pans for use in state salt mills, which gave the Obushkovskii enterprise special significance in the overall functioning of the tsar's economic enterprises.[48]

Sixteen iron manufactories appeared in Russia between the 1630's and 1674: three state enterprises, two iron works built by Russian nobles (Morozov and Miloslavskii), and eleven by

Marselis and Akema (five of these factories in partnership with Andrei Vinius). By 1674 two of these manufactories had been closed,* leaving fourteen still in operation. Three of these were state enterprises, while two belonged to Filimon Akema and the remaining nine were property of the Marselis family.† The establishment of fourteen successful iron manufactories in forty years in a backward country such as Russia at this time not only was a great achievement, it was the prologue to one of the most fascinating episodes in early Russian economic history: the effort to establish modern metallurgy in a frozen, snowbound area more than one thousand kilometers north of Moscow and the Russian heartland.

---

*These were the state-built Iauza river enterprise of 1649–1651 and the Vaga river works of 1648. The latter manufactory, it is true, was scarcely in the "central part of the country," but it was discussed (see pp. 80–81, 97–98, above) in connection with that area of industrial development, so I have included it in this summary.

†These were the state-owned Zvenigorodskie iron manufactories (Pavlovskii, Borodnikovskii, and Obushkovskii works); Akema's Ugodskii and Porotovskii enterprises; and Marselis' four Tula and four Kashira factories plus the Vepreiskii (Aleksinskii) manufactory jointly owned with Thomas Kellermann. The Pavlovskii and Porotovskii works were originally built by the Russian nobles Morozov and Miloslavskii, respectively.

7

Iron Manufacturing
in the Far Northwest

COPPER AND IRON SMELTING in the Olonets area* dated from Kievan times and was carried on by the local Russian, Karelian, and Lopard peoples as a supplement to their agricultural activities. During the last third of the seventeenth century iron manufacturing was established even in this remote part of the country, though it differed in some aspects from the process already under way elsewhere. Factories located in the center of Russia were inevitably more bound up with serfdom than the manufactories at Olonets, where serf relationships were far from being socially dominant at this time. The great distance of Olonets from the capital combined with climatic conditions to produce other unique characteristics of the region: industrial development was more difficult to set in motion, it occurred at a later time, the extent of the development was more limited, and, most interesting perhaps,

---

*Olonets was a medieval town in the southern part of the northeastern province of Karelia, situated between Lake Lagoda on the west and Lake Onega on the east, and quite near the present-day city of Petrozavodsk.

extensive labor disturbances broke out as a result of the effort to build manufactories and exploit peasant wage-labor.

Serious attempts to utilize the mineral resources of the far northeast were not made until the Novgorod *gost'* Semen Gavrilov was sent by the *Novgorodskii Prikaz* in March 1666 to Tolvuiskaia *volost'* of Olonetskii *uezd* to look for copper ore. Gavrilov was accompanied by three foreigners: Denis Joris, a Dutch prospector, Doctor Nils Andersen, a physician and assayer, and Lorenz Anderson, an interpreter. The party was paid 260 rubles and given 247 rubles for equipment and materials, as well as the right to cover expenses beyond that figure with grants from the treasury house of the Olonets *prikaz,* and from the customs office and state-owned taverns *(kabaki)* of that city. These provisions for funds indicate that officials in Moscow expected Gavrilov and his friends to organize copper smelting as soon as deposits were located. Joris found copper ore in Foimogubskaia *volost',* and in the next year, 1667, Gavrilov took preliminary steps to organize foundries in this area, joining together small lakes and widening a river bed to supply water and wood to the factory site. Fields were cleared and haystacks formed to feed animals needed for transportation. By this time Gavrilov was receiving hundreds of rubles and considerable amounts of equipment from local government authorities.[1]

Although copper mining and some artisan smelting began here as early as October 1669, large-scale copper manufacturing at Olonets went slowly. In 1673 the water-powered factory was not yet finished. A report of Gavrilov (dated September 8, 1673) tells us that Joris was still prospecting, and that although the Dutchman believed he would discover better deposits of copper ore, he could not be certain. [2] A year later, in 1674, Kilburger reported that copper had at last been located near the Olonets-Kolonets river, not far from Lake Onega. Kilburger's information on this subject is not altogether clear, but he writes that at that time the mines were not being used and that this project "was operated by the tsar himself at a great loss." It is amusing to note that in the midst of this financial disaster Dr. Andersen had set up a laboratory in which he was examining various ore samples, apparently trying, as an amateur alchemist, to change their properties—an effort which was gloomily symbolic of the entire enterprise.[3]

Gavrilov's eight years of activity in the Onega-Olonets area failed to live up to the expectations of the Moscow authorities, and by 1674 the Russian government was about to discontinue its metallurgical efforts in this part of the country. At this point private enterprise stepped into the picture to carry the Gavrilov project in a more fruitful direction. The entrepreneurs responsible for this chapter of the story were none other than the redoubtable Marselises, though they too were plagued by difficulties which delayed ultimate success.

When Semen Gavrilov began his expedition in 1666, Leonhard Marselis was doing his own prospecting in the Russian far north. Peter Marselis was still in disgrace in this period, and young Leonhard hoped to contribute to his father's reinstatement by his own efforts and ingenuity. Indeed, Leonhard was so fortunate as to find copper deposits on the Tsyl'ma, a tributary of the Pechora.* Leonhard trekked over thirteen hundred kilometers back to Moscow to present the tsar with a sample of this ore. Aleksei Mikhailovich was pleased with the discovery, but would neither issue a letter of pardon for the father nor honor the son's request for a miner's claim and manufacturing privileges.[4]

After Peter Marselis' iron factories were returned in May 1667, he began to use his renewed influence at court to obtain the rights previously requested by his son on the Tsyl'ma. He also asked for privileges in the Olonets-Onega region. In a petition submitted to the tsar in 1669, Peter Marselis noted that Leonhard had found copper on the Tsyl'ma and in Olonetskii *uezd,* and gave assurance that if he (Peter) were granted

---

*This was the exact region where the foreign masters "Ivan and Viktor" sought copper and silver under orders of Ivan III. Is it possible that Leonhard knew of this successful expedition and that it guided him in his own efforts?

the necessary permission he would seriously develop these regions. Marselis noted that this would benefit the Russian state, for instead of buying copper from abroad the tsar would now have it within his own realm, whence it could be exported to obtain foreign "gold and efimki." Marselis promised to undertake northern metallurgy on his own resources, but requested a charter guaranteeing him and his heirs privileges for ten, twenty, or even thirty years. It would be a long time, he pointed out, before profits could be realized on these new investments. In 1669 the Marselis family received the requested charter for thirty years; Peter Marselis even obtained a loan of six hundred rubles for his projected copper works at Olonets.[5]

A series of deaths in the Marselis family at this time kept it from making immediate use of these factory concessions in the far north. Leonhard, the member of the family for whom this area was intended, died in Moscow in 1670 at thirty-two; on July 10, 1672, Peter Marselis followed his son to the grave. Three of Peter's sons were now alive: two from his first marriage with Dorothea Barnesly (d. 1650) — Gabriel, an officer in the Russian army, and Petr Petrovich, who was interested in the entrepreneurial and commercial pursuits of his father; from his second marriage with Anna Akema survived a son called "Peter the Younger."[6]

On December 10, 1672, the "poor and defenseless and helpless" sons of Peter Marselis petitioned Aleksei Mikhailovich for the same rights over the family iron factories as had been enjoyed by their late father.[7] The tsar issued an *ukaz* on January 8, 1673, giving the three young men full rights of inheritance to their father's iron enterprises. At this point Petr Petrovich worked out an agreement with his stepmother and brothers whereby he assumed direct ownership and control of the Marselis iron enterprises. On August 22, 1674, the tsar granted Petr a new charter,[8] recognizing him as sole owner and specifying that in case of his death the iron factories would pass to Petr Petrovich's "wife and children and heirs."[9] Petr was preparing to activate his family's copper interests at Lake

Onega[10] when a third calamity struck the Marselis house. On August 7, 1675, Petr Petrovich Marselis died at the age of thirty-five.

Fearing the worst, on July 27, 1675, Petr Petrovich had dictated his will to his factory manager, Jakob Schammer. Marselis provided that if his wife, Margreta Bekerfendendinovaia [sic!], remarried she would be granted five thousand rubles from what remained of his estate. Otherwise his infant son, Christian, was to receive all the "iron and copper factories and [all] that belongs to them. . . ." A guardianship was set up for Christian until the boy reached the age of twenty-five, the guardians being Petr Petrovich's partner, Harmen van der Gaten, and Heinrich Butenant von Rosenbusch, a prominent Danish merchant who engaged in such lucrative pursuits as the export of potash, salmon, and trees for shipmasts.[11]

Since Christian Marselis was barely a year old at the time of his father's death and no remaining member of the family was qualified to supervise the iron factories, it was inevitable that the guardians appointed by Petr Petrovich would become the real guiding force in the northern branch of the Marselis industries. Butenant von Rosenbusch quickly emerged as the true master of Christian Marselis' industrial empire.[12] In the new charter[13] for the Olonets manufactories issued in 1678, Butenant appears for the first time not as guardian but rather as a full-fledged partner of Christian Marselis. Although Amburger is correct in terming this a "contravention" ("*eine Missachtung*") of Petr Petrovich's will of 1675,[14] it must be remembered that at this time Christian was still a child of four, and that the entire responsibility for operating and expanding his industrial empire fell on Butenant. Butenant was the one who would actually build Christian Marselis' factories in Olonetskie *uezd,* and apparently he felt justified in obtaining part-ownership of those enterprises (which passed fully to him and his family after Christian's death). It does not appear that Butenant made further divisions of his ward's properties or otherwise abused his position; and, as we shall see, Butenant von Rosenbusch more than earned whatever money came his way as Christian Marselis' partner at Olonets.

There is still confusion as to how many copper and iron factories were built in the Olonets-Onega area, and in which years.* Apparently Butenant established at least one copper works in Foimogubskaia *volost'* by 1676, but it proved impossible to produce copper in large quantities there so the coppersmiths were dismissed, and on January 25, 1681, Butenant began making iron. The Foimogubskaia iron factory (or factories) apparently ceased operation in the early 1680's, at which time Butenant organized two new iron manufactories in the same vicinity: a blasting enterprise (called the Ust' factory, from the river upon which it was located) and a forging shop (Spirovskii works). Butenant's activities must have been successful, for we know that from 1683 to 1685 he exported almost ten thousand *puds* of iron through Archangel. After a few years Butenant expanded the scope of his work by building two more forging plants in the same area: the Lizhemskii factory in 1689 and the Kedrozerskii a little later.[15]

When Christian Marselis died in 1690, Major Olimpei Iurenev compiled a description of the iron works in this area. According to this report, Butenant's manufacturing complex included the following buildings:

1 blasting factory with two smelting furnaces
3 hammer factories
2 smitheries
3 fuel barns
6 storage barns
2 courts *(dvory)* for *prikaz* officials
1 *dvor* for masters
23 huts *(izby)* for masters, submasters, and local government officials
2 brick buildings
1 barn "where the iron ore is cast" (?)
2 *izby* where factory bellows were made[16]

From this description one may conclude that Butenant's once-

---

*Since existing documents and the books and articles based upon them contain numerous contradictions on this matter, the reader should follow the explanation contained in these pages with appropriate reservations.

modest iron works at Olonets had become a medium-sized iron manufactory. Production was expanded still more during the last decade of the seventeenth century.

The charter privileges of the Butenant-Christian Marselis Olonets iron works dated from January 25, 1681, when the smelting of iron ore began in this area. According to this agreement, Butenant was to deliver rod- and angle-iron and other items to the state at prices which had been fixed by earlier *ukazy*. Goods not taken by the government could either be sold within Russia or exported through Archangel, in which case foreign specie gained would be exchanged at the tsar's treasury at fifty kopecks per *efimok*. After twenty years the entrepreneurs would pay *obrok* of one hundred rubles per blast furnace, as well as duty *(poshlina)* on iron placed on the market. A unique provision of this charter was that Russian or foreign masters and submasters employed at Olonets could not be accepted for work at another iron factory within the Russian state without a *pis'mennyi otpusk* ("written leave") from the employers at Olonets.[17] This was evidently designed to protect Butenant from losing the investments he might make in bringing iron workers from abroad, unless it was mutually agreeable for a particular master to leave Butenant's employment.

As we have seen, Russian iron manufactories were usually served by skilled foreign workers and unskilled workers from nearby "ascribed" villages. Neither case was true at the Olonets-Onega factories. To be sure, Butenant's copper masters were foreigners, but the first iron masters were Russian and Karelian artisans drawn from the local population.[18] Since most of the peasants of this region were not serfs, the tsar granted Butenant rights only over the "land, forests, and waters" of the area, leaving Butenant to hire workers for mining, firewood-cutting, fuel preparation, transport, and similar duties. Workers comprising this section of the labor force were free peasants *(chernye krestian'e)*, plus a few serfs from private estates and from the Tikhvinskii and Viazhitskii monasteries.[19]

The iron mines were located one and a half *versts* from the factory smelters. Mine work was constantly threatened by flooding, and a special team of six men worked with tubs and vats every evening and on Sundays to remove water from the shafts. (Windlasses and pumps were also used for this purpose.) Night work, and probably day work too, was performed under the illumination of special lamps called *luchiny*. Special beams were brought to the mines and used to crumble the rock formations which blocked convenient gathering of the iron ore. In contrast to the Dedilov mines, Butenant's iron pits operated through the summer.[20]

An upper and lower dam provided the water power to operate the bellows serving the two blast furnaces as well as the hammers and several hearths in the forging shops. Unfortunately there is little information about the workers involved in the production of pig iron and iron commodities at the Olonets iron factories. There were other skilled workers in Butenant's factories, notably carpenters, bellows masters, hemp-cord weavers, and makers of tubs and barrels. Factory blacksmiths made picks, hammers, and other tools for the enterprise, and repaired instruments. At times they used Swedish iron and iron bought from local Lapp artisans. Unskilled laborers brought stones, clay, sand, and lime for construction and maintenance of the blast furnaces. Firewood was cut and placed in charcoal pits, where it was converted into fuel for the furnaces under the supervision of a "fuel master" (*ugol'nyi* master). Molds were usually made of clay.[21]

Understandably, the location of the Olonets factories on territory previously occupied by free peasants produced tense relationships between the factory management (which was also foreign) and the local population. Available sources indicate that private capital was far more energetic in exploiting its legal rights than was the case with Gavrilov, another factor which could have scarcely endeared these intruders to the peasant settlers of the Olonets-Onega area. In a revealing petition of 1684, Butenant complained to the tsar that the peasants surrounding his enterprises were plowing and cutting hay on factory land and poaching from the factory forest. Butenant also indicated that since he arrived in this area, the peasants had resisted him by not meeting their obligations in damming rivers or helping with the construction of the mills and factories. [22]

On January 8, 1684, peasant-capitalist antagonisms at Olonets reached the first of several high points. According to a report Butenant submitted describing these events, on that day Konstantin Semenovich Popov, the elder *(starosta)* of Kizhskii *pogost,* led a large armed crowd of his people to the Ust' river factory. The mob confronted the foreigners and abused them verbally. They chased the masters and workers and beat the *prikaz* representative, Andrei Kastrop (a foreigner), and the fuel master, Ivashka Venediev (evidently a Russian), the latter so badly that several weeks later he still lay near death. The rebels then turned on the carters, beat them, and destroyed their wagons after throwing the ore contents into the water. This so frightened the unskilled factory hands that they fled and refused to return to work. Police officers came from Olonets, but they were repulsed by Konstantin's men, after which the local authorities would — perhaps could — do nothing. Butenant complained of his financial losses and factory inactivity, and petitioned that Konstantin Popov and other leaders of the insurrection be brought to Moscow and punished. In February 1684, a few days after receiving Butenant's petition, the *Pushkarskii Prikaz* (cannon office) issued an order to the *voevoda* of Olonets ordering him to deliver Konstantin to the *prikaz* in Moscow by March of the same year, to stand trial before Prince V.V. Golitsyn. But we are not certain this was done. [23]

These stormy events indicate how difficult it was for Butenant von Rosenbusch and his foreign assistants to assume all the rights granted them by law. Local authorities were not really successful in protecting the factories or in guaranteeing the privileges of the owners, though throughout the entire period peasants were exiled because they had "caused injuries" and were responsible for "many continuous threats

and destruction and fire and many other losses at the factory."
But the chief government figure of this period, Prince Vasilii
Golitsyn, was sufficiently concerned over the question of
Russian industrial development to support Butenant whenever
possible, and in May 1684 Golitsyn secured a royal decree
clarifying the property situation at the Olonets factories in
Butenant's favor.[24]

Neither local punishments nor edicts issued in Moscow
halted the disorders. Another "rebellion" broke out early the
following year, in 1685, which might be termed a "labor
disturbance" rooted in the nature of the production process
itself. The peasants of Khutynskii monastery had been quarry-
ing and transporting limestone to the Olonets factories, when
other "volunteers" *(okhochye liudi)* offered to do the same
work at a lower price. This suggestion was pleasing to the
management, but the Khutynskii peasants were outraged, beat
their competitors unmercifully, and would not permit them to
work. The earlier pattern of events was repeated: factory
operations came to a halt and Butenant submitted a petition
complaining about "great losses" and asking the tsars* to
intervene on behalf of a "free price" for this labor operation.
On April 13, 1685, the *Pushkarskii Prikaz* decided the dispute in favor of the capitalists, and the local town crier, upon
orders of the *voevoda,* was "to cry during trade days" that
people were being hired at the Olonets enterprises freely and
without hindrance.[25]

In the summer of 1687 new conflicts arose as the peasants of
Foimogubskaia *volost'* clashed with Butenant over use of
Shil'ta field, which the government had allotted to the Olonets
factories. By August 1687 local inhabitants were not only
mowing hay on this land but were menacing the factory as

*From 1682 until 1689, Russia was theoretically ruled by the "co-tsars"
Ivan V and Peter I, sons of Aleksei Mikhailovich by his first wife (Maria
Miloslavskaia) and second wife (Natalia Naryshkina), respectively. The real
power in the government at this time, however, was Ivan's full sister, Sof'ia
Alekseevna, who was regent, and Prince V. V. Golitsyn, her first minister and
lover. Petitions in this period were formally addressed to "tsars" Ivan and
Peter.

well. Some eleven of the people involved in this trouble were rounded up and sent to Olonets for trial. *Pod'iachii* Ivan Burakov then tried to recover the disputed lands from the rebels, who were led by such men as *d'iachek* (junior clerk) Fed'ka Iakimov and Khariton Manoilov, the village priest. But Evsegneiko Afanas'ev, "with comrades . . . did not give ground and stood firmly with each other. . . " Armed with rifles, axes, lances, and stakes, they shouted to the approaching government authorities, ". . . Don't come near us or there'll be trouble and we won't let you live!" Even a reading of orders from the tsar did not change the hostile mood of the crowd, which then cried, ". . . We won't let you live, even if there are still more of those Strel'tsy with you!!"[26]

The revolt ended with the arrest of the leaders. On August 31, 1687, Evsegnei Afanas'ev petitioned for release from prison in Olonets, though he must not have had much faith in the tsar's mercy, for less than two months later he escaped from prison and disappeared. But the disorders over Shil'ta field continued in October 1687, and at the same time peasants were still gathering hay on Rimbozerskii field. In October local peasants interfered with factory activity by threatening some of the iron enterprise's masters and workers. A government report dated January 21, 1688, describes how *strel'tsy* and cannon were sent from Olonets to Foimogubskaia *volost'*, where Evsegnei Afanas'ev was again acting as the peasants' leader in defense of their use of the Shil'ta lands. If foreigners occupied this area, the rebels promised "to beat them all to death."[27]

As before, the rebellion collapsed, and Evsegnei was taken prisoner and jailed in the *prikaz* headquarters at Olonets. He escaped again, was recaptured, beaten savagely, and returned to prison. In February 1688 government authorities came to Foimogubskaia *volost'* from Olonets, rounded up the rebellious peasants, and knouted them "mercilessly." Some ran away; others tried, but failed. A few, instead of being knouted, were severely thrashed with wooden branches.[28]

When the seventeen-year-old Christian Marselis died in 1690 a chapter ended in the history of iron manufacturing i Russia. The only members of the Marselis family still alive were Christian's mother (née Margarethe Bocker von Delden) and his uncle, Peter the Younger, the youngest brother of Christian's father, Petr Petrovich. Although the mother and uncle pressed for their inheritance rights, the Marselis family was by then decadent, represented as it was by a woman and a man who was a merchant rather than a manufacturer. Because of their relative weakness, the Marselises were outmaneuvered at court by L. K. Naryshkin, a prominent boyar, uncle of the young Tsar Peter I, and, at that time, a most influential government figure. A decree issued in the name of the tsar excluded the Marselises as heirs to the Tula-Kashira-Aleksinskii factories and passed them on to Naryshkin as his own private property.

What of the Olonets factories? Here the death of Christian Marselis made his heirs half-partners with Heinrich Butenant von Rosenbusch, though a dispute over future ownership seems to have caused the enterprise to lie idle for a period. The Olonets manufactories were eventually declared the full property of Butenant, and in fact the two families eventually reached a rather complicated agreement[29] which insured that no further arguments over title would impede the operation of the iron works.[30]

In 1694 another issue arose which caused further inactivity at the Butenant iron works. On this occasion the challenge to continued operation of the factories came from "below," from the unskilled workers. A dispute resulted from the management's efforts to impress local peasants into serfdom so as to gain a stable and disciplined labor force free of noncooperation and indifference. In light of the Rosenbusch family's debts, financial difficulties, and labor problems, the tsar issued an *ukaz* in 1694 ascribing Kizhskii *pogost,* with its peasants and forests, to the Olonets iron factories. This meant that the 1,197 households *(dvory)* of that village owed labor service to the owner of the iron works. The peasants, however, resented this infringement upon their personal freedom, and refused to discharge their new obligations to the iron enterprises. A colonel, a *pod'iachii,* and 335 *strel'tsy* were sent to break this strike. As soon as the soldiers arrived at the village, the bell of the local church sounded an alarm, and the peasants assembled, ready to fight for their freedom, though armed with nothing more than clubs and stakes.[31]

The outcome of this clash is unrecorded, but the impact of the affair on factory activity is clear: one report, in speaking of the peasants' obstinacy, remarks that "due to their disobedience, the factories stood without activity for nearly two years," and for this reason the foreign masters returned home.[32]

In the mid-1690's the Olonets iron works resumed operation. Peter's military preparations were now driving Russian metallurgy toward new heights of productivity, and this included Andrei Butenant's enterprises, which in a twelve-month period during 1701-1702 produced 34,000 *puds* of pig iron with two small blast furnaces. The facilities here were so pressed by government orders that in 1701 Andrei Butenant requested (and received) permission to build a third furnace. This, combined with the importation of several foreign masters, placed Butenant deeply in debt, but his initiative was appreciated by the tsar. In 1703 Andrei Butenant abandoned his iron works, probably in part because of continuing labor difficulties. The Olonets iron factories were then taken over by the state, and, according to N. N. Stoskova, in reconstructed form they continued to operate into the nineteenth century, for well over a hundred years.[33]

8

Expansion and Russification, 1675-1690's

DURING THE LAST QUARTER of the seventeenth century the fledgling Russian iron industry registered modest but genuine gains. Although two of the old Tula factories were not working toward the end of this period, activity in the Tula-Kashira-Vepreia complex as a whole was pronounced, and if the Porotovksii and Zvenigorodskie enterprises closed during the 1670's and 1680's, they were replaced by enlarged iron works which operated with profit and success. Moreover, private entrepreneurs after 1689 built a small iron manufactory and four large ones on the Dugna, Vora, and Tulitsa rivers and in Romanovskii *uezd*. Perhaps none of this was equal to the phenomenal growth of Russian industry during the Petrine period, stemming as that did from the tremendous forces set in motion by the Great Northern War of 1701-1724. But the achievements of the earlier age were important in laying the foundations for later intensified development, and for this reason alone the 1670's-1690's merit careful attention. The last decade is especially interesting because at that time foreigners — both as entrepreneurs and skilled masters — lost much of their earlier importance in the Russian iron industry, and in other areas of the national economy as well. This fact suggests that manufacturing attained a profound integration with the Russian economy before the eighteenth century, and was of greater significance than historians of early modern Russia have often supposed.

After Andrei Vinius died in 1663 and Peter Marselis followed his old partner to the grave in 1672, Filimon Akema became the last of the original founders of Russian iron manufacturing to pass away. At the time of his death in 1675, Akema was operating only one iron factory, the Ugodskii, the Porotovskii enterprise being finally closed in 1673 because its sandy soil and poorly disposed lower bank caused flooding almost every spring. A double blast furnace was then built at Ugodka, and in this reconstructed and expanded form the manufactory continued to function.[1]

Evidently Richard Andrews had died by the time of Akema's death, so that the Ugodskii factory went to the third partner, Akema's nephew Thielmann. But on February 2, 1676, Thielmann Akema also died. At this point the Ugodskii works (along with factory debts of eleven thousand rubles) were inherited by Thielmann's heirs: his widow, Anna Dekroo, and his young son, Johann Akema. For a short while the Akema manufactory was actually supervised and directed by Heinrich Butenant von Rosenbusch. By 1678, however, Anna married the prominent foreign merchant Werner Müller, and he personally assumed direction of the Ugodskii enterprise.[2] Müller immediately set about expanding his family's iron interests by obtaining a charter (dated July 14, 1678) to build a second iron factory on the Ist'ia river in Borovskii *uezd*, less than eight kilometers from the defunct Ugodskii works. Müller brought cannon and grenade masters from Austria for the new enterprise, which, combined with his expenditures on renting land for the Istenskii enterprise, brought the family heavy debts. Nevertheless the Istenskii iron works was in full operation by 1680.[3]

When Johann Akema died in Moscow on December 4, 1693, his stepfather, Werner Müller, was already deceased, so the Ugodskii and Istenskii manufactories went to Anna Müller and her two sons by the second marriage, Werner and Peter Müller.[4] The financial situation of the family was difficult at the time of Johann's death, for "after him there remained to be paid many thousands of rubles in factory debt. . . ." Furthermore, in 1693, the time had come to begin paying *obrok* (tax) and *poshlina* (trade duty) on the Ugodskii enterprise, though it had actually stood idle since 1690 as a result of difficulties with ore supply, factory dams, and the river level. The state was grateful to the foreigners for establishing this iron works, however, and saw to it that the Müllers' debts and expenditures for factory repairs in 1695 did not prove disastrous. Government authorities agreed to take fifteen thousand *puds* bar- and angle-iron per year, at a price of fifteen *altyn* per *pud*. (Filimon Akema had produced only for the open market.)

Werner and Peter Müller operated the Ugodskii and Istenskii iron factories through the entire first half of the eighteenth century, until the death of Peter in 1748 and Werner in 1750. In the next year, 1751, the Ugodskii and Istenskii enterprises were given to a powerful figure at the Russian court, Count Aleksandr Ivanovich Shuvalov, who had earlier received the Tula, Kashirskie, and Aleksinskii iron factories.[5] (In later years Anna Müller also demonstrated entrepreneurial abilities. In 1705, when the Swedish and Turkish wars created a need for increased artillery supply, she established another blasting factory in Obolenskii *uezd* on the Nechaika river.)[6]

One of the new iron entrepreneurs of the last quarter of the seventeenth century was *gost'* Vladimir Voronin, a wealthy Russian merchant who was simultaneously a grain wholesaler, shipowner, army contractor, and the owner of thirty stores selling wool cloth and other goods. Voronin's projects and enterprises were far-flung and diverse, and he conducted large-scale trade with both the East and Western Europe. He probably became interested in the iron industry through his partner, the Dutch *gost'* Thomas Kellermann, who in previous years had participated in the capitalistic activities of his relative, Peter Marselis.[7]

In 1681 the *Prikaz Bol'shogo Dvortsa* leased the three Zvenigorodskie factories to Voronin for twenty-five years for an annual payment of 125 rubles. His partner in these enterprises was Semen Vikulin Kiprianov, who about 1686 closed the old Pavlovskii, Borodnikovskii, and Obushkovskii workshops and established two larger manufactories, the Sorokinskii and Kezminskii in the same area, in Zvenigorodskii *uezd.* The difference in the scale of metallurgical activity at the new and old Zvenigorodskie factories* may be judged from the fact that whereas in 1686 there were thirty masters involved in iron-working here, in 1695 the number had grown to fifty or more. Under Voronin the output of the Zvenigorodskie enterprises found its way solely to the domestic Russian market. He received no orders from the state. When Vladimir Voronin died in 1696, his widow continued to operate the iron factories until around 1701, when it appears that the Zvenigorodskie enterprises were no longer producing iron. In 1703 the factories were given to Boldwin Andrews, who died in 1705, at which time the Zvenigorodskie works may have closed.[8]

In 1689 a new iron factory was built (evidently by Heinrich Butenant in the name of the Marselis family) in Aleksinskii *uezd,* some fifty-two kilometers northwest of Tula. These works were located on the Dugna river, on land rented from the Begichevyi *pomeshchik* family for sixty-five rubles and one *pud* of iron per year. But construction of the Dugna iron works seems to have lagged behind the expectations of government authorities, and in 1690 the Dugna factory was included in the transfer of iron factories into Naryshkin's hands. In 1690 a forging shop and other structures were built at this site. The

---

*The Sorokinskii and Kezminskii factories were collectively still called the "Zvenigorodskie," and sometimes even the "Pavlovskie," iron works.

last reference to the Dugna iron factories in contemporary documents was in 1751, when it was reported as belonging to the peasant entrepreneur Nikita Demidov.[9]

When Christian Marselis died in February 1690, his factories in the Moscow-Tula area immediately fell under the control of the *Pushkarskii Prikaz*. A *prikaz* official made a complete description and inventory of the Tula, Kashira, and Vepreiskii enterprises, submitting the material to boyar Lev Kirilovich Naryshkin. As head of the *Posol'skii Prikaz* and uncle of young Tsar Peter, Naryshkin gained these iron works simply by "petitioning" Peter for their ownership.[10]

Although the Vepreiskii enterprise and the four Kashira works were in good condition at the time, only two of the Tula factories were working by 1690.[11] Yet the report of that year suggests that considerable production was achieved at the seven manufactories which were in operation. Seventy-two workers were then employed in the seven enterprises, mostly in the hammer shops and at the forges. (There were also a number of doctors, tailors, administrators, and other supporting workers.) Of the fifty-four foreign masters and submasters, there were Frenchmen, Swedes, Germans, Saxons, Hamburgites, Dutchmen, one Irishman, a Pole with his son, and others listed simply as "foreigners" without specification of nationality. Russian wage-workers were excluded from the items "granted" boyar Naryshkin, indicating the "free" nature of such labor.[12]

Having used his influence at court to obtain ownership of the iron factories of the Tula area, Naryshkin then sought to obtain other advantages to insure profitable operation of his industrial interests. On January 29, 1692, he secured a royal *ukaz* instructing all army regiments to buy their iron solely from his enterprises. Furthermore, according to this decree, all stone *prikaz* buildings, regimental warehouses, and the like, were to obtain iron materials only from Naryshkin. Although the government once paid iron entrepreneurs at a rate lower than prevailing price levels, Naryshkin was to receive "actual trade price," payment being in the iron coin then in circulation.

Naryshkin ran his eight iron manufactories (including the Dugnenskii iron works, which he received in 1690) together with his sons Aleksandr and Ivan. All these enterprises were almost certainly still in existence in 1720, and in time ended in the hands of count A. I. Shuvalov. Naryshkin's iron factories seem to have closed sometime in the mid-eighteenth century.[13]

The only foreigner to build an iron works during the 1690's was Evert Isbrants, called Elizar Izbrant by the Russians. During this decade he established a blasting factory on the Vora river, thirty *versts* northeast of Moscow. Little information seems to be available concerning this enterprise, but according to Kafengauz, at the time "Izbrant's armaments factory was so famous that masters and government officials were sent there to study the factory's specifications and operation and calculate the productivity ratios." In 1698 Izbrants had a gun-powder manufactory in this same area.[14]

In 1693 a large new iron factory was built in Romanovskii *uezd* on the Belyi Kolodets, a tributary of the Voronezh river, about 280 kilometers south of Tula. This works was established by Nikita Grigor'evich Aristov, a merchant of the *gostinaia sotnia,* and K. Borin, a cloth merchant of the *sukonnaia sotnia,* a *d'iak* in the *Kazennyi Prikaz* (state treasury), *Prikaz Bol'shoi Kazny,* and later in the *Prikaz Rudokopnykh Del* (office of ore-smelting affairs). This manufactory was equipped with a blast furnace and other workshops. The output of the Aristov-Borin enterprise was large for the time; in 1704, for example, no less than 256 cannon were smelted at the Romanovskii works. In 1720 this factory went to the state and is still mentioned in documents in 1725.[15]

Another Russian commoner entered his country's iron industry in this period—not a merchant but a state peasant and artisan-gunsmith of Tula. This was Nikita Demidov (1656–1725), who was to found an industrial empire in the Urals and become the greatest Russian capitalist before the nineteenth century. By 1697 Demidov had finished his first iron factory, a large enterprise located on the Tulitsa river, just south of Tula. Demidov established this factory on his own resources, without government help. In 1700 he presented six of his cannon to the tsar, at which point Peter took a liking to Demidov and began to help him in his industrial ambitions.[16] Demidov's Tula factory was operated by his heirs, and finally closed in 1754.[17]

Up to now we have dealt with largely successful efforts to establish iron manufactories in the central, northern, and northwestern parts of the Russian empire during the seventeenth century. But other parts of the country were less successful in attempts to develop ferrous metallurgy of manufacturing type. In the Smolensk region (near the Polish border), for example, a copper works was set up in the 1630's, but it led a troubled existence and was finally abandoned in 1648. When Russia regained Smolensk under the Peace of Andrussovo (1667), a decision was made to organize iron production on the spot and thus eliminate the problems connected with transporting armaments from Tula or Moscow. In 1670 *voevoda* A. I. Khovanskii built a smelter with a productivity of three *puds* per day. Greatly encouraged by his first effort, Khovanskii ordered a second shop constructed. Despite the abundance of iron ore, however, the finished products were of poor quality, and although Moscow officials ordered further attempts at prospecting, in 1674 the new *voevoda* of Smolensk, Prince M. A. Golitsyn, informed his superiors of his failure to find a better grade ore. The *Smolenskii Prikaz* then farmed out the two iron enterprises to local entrepreneurs, and no further experiments in iron manufacturing were undertaken here for several decades.[18]

The most important of the "underdeveloped" areas was Siberia. Even before the seventeenth century the Russian government had been aware of Siberia's great wealth in gold, silver, copper, tin, iron, and lead, but serious efforts to locate and develop the region's natural resources did not begin until after the Time of Troubles. After the 1630's there were so many metallurgical explorations in the far east that it would be fruitless to catalog them all here. It is indicative of the Russian authorities' great ambitions, however, that as early as 1661 Vasilii Shpilkin was sent as far as the Kanin peninsula (70° longitude) to search for silver.[19]

From early times Siberia was the scene of peasant artisanry, and during the sixteenth and seventeenth centuries it reached a highly developed stage. During the seventeenth century the Russian government tried to organize copper and iron production in Siberia on a larger scale, hoping in this way that Siberia would be able to keep pace with its own growing metallurgical needs, and perhaps even produce a surplus for central regions of the empire.[20]

The first Siberian cannon were cast by artisan methods in 1625 from iron ore discovered two years earlier by the smith Fedor Eremeev.[21] Another significant event in the history of Siberian metallurgy came in 1628 when Ivan Shul'gin found iron deposits in the Nitsa river area (below the Irbit) in the Urals. Soon thereafter, in 1630, government authorities were building a "large" iron enterprise in this region which began to operate in 1631. For many years this Nitsynskii works was characterized as the first Russian iron manufactory, but later research has proved it to be a large artisan shop which produced wrought iron in four furnaces with hand-driven bellows and forges. In a working year of 180 to 200 days, the sixteen artisan families working here could produce four hundred *puds* (7.3 tons) of iron. This iron enterprise burned down on March 18, 1637, but was immediately rebuilt and continued to operate for a half-century or more.[22]

The 1630's also saw the establishment of the first copper works in the Urals. In 1633 an expedition composed of *stol'nik* Streshnev, *gost'* Nedei Sveteshnikov (one of the leading merchants of his time), and *d'iak* Vasilii Sergeev was sent northeast of Kazan, where copper was discovered on the Iaiva, a tributary of the Kama. Two years later Sveteshnikov returned here with the Saxon ore specialist Ernst Petzold and a number of Russian and foreign copper masters. The party finally discovered a favorable location for copper production on the

Kamkarka, on the western slope of the Urals, near Solikamsk. In 1642 both foreign and Russian masters were working here, at the Pyskorskii works, along with a number of convicts. After some two decades of operation the state leased this enterprise to master Aleksandr Tumashev. In 1656 the Pyskorskii artisan shop exhausted its local copper supply, but seems to have been relocated, for it continued to produce copper until the 1660's.[23]

Dmitrii Tumashev, son of Aleksandr Tumashev, had learned copper-smelting from his father, and was a competent artisan and ore expert. In 1666 he received government permission to prospect beyond the ' Urals, in Verkhoturskii *uezd*. Tumashev discovered large deposits of iron ore just above the Neiva river, "on an unused field thirty versts and more from people," in the vicinity of modern-day Sverdlovsk. On December 21, 1668, he obtained a state charter giving him the right to establish an iron works and sell goods duty-free, although he was to depend solely on his own resources and was obliged to deliver ten per cent of his output to local government authorities at his own expense.[24]

By late 1669 or early 1670 Tumashev built a large iron artisan works composed of a shop with a blast furnace and three hearths, and a forge with two hearths, two anvils, and six large and small hammers. Dmitrii and his three brothers, Petr, Ivan, and Vasilii, provided the skilled labor for the enterprise, and about fifteen or seventeen freely hired local peasants worked at unskilled tasks. Although Dmitrii was the most experienced of the workmen, it is interesting to note that all of the Tumashev brothers were literate. The productivity of their workshops must have been fairly high, since from September to December 1671 they turned out 223 *puds* of pig iron. On this basis A. A. Preobrazhenskii estimates the annual output of the Tumashev enterprise to have been at least eleven hundred to twelve hundred *puds* of pig iron per year. Three mines, one-half to one and a half *versts* from the smelting site provided ore for the blast furnace.[25]

In 1671 the rebellious Bashkirs of this area attacked the Tumashev works and halted factory activity. As a result of this and other dangers, Tsar Aleksei Mikhailovich acted favorably on a petition from Dmitrii Tumashev to ascribe the peasants of Krasnopolskii to the enterprise both for labor and defense.[26] And yet the Tumashev brothers (who were the first Russian commoners to build a large iron enterprise—even of an artisan nature—in Siberia) never succeeded in developing iron *manufacturing* in Siberia. Dmitrii Tumashev is significant to our study only because he might "have been able to organize large-scale iron production, but the government did not support him; on the contrary, it constantly ordered him to search for precious stones, copper, and silver ore."[27] The Tumashev artisan works probably ceased operation in the 1690's.[28]

There were a few other (rather insignificant) efforts at organized iron and copper production in Siberia and the Urals during the seventeenth century. The Dalmatova and Solovetskii monasteries both had small artisan smelters in this period, and there was a short-lived copper works at Kazan. The Krasnobarskii iron "factory" was established in Cherdynskii *uezd,* southwest of the town of Cherdynia during the 1660's, but it had nothing more than two hand-operated furnaces, and only one of them functioned without interruption. The Krasnobarskii enterprise existed only a brief time.[29]

The copper and iron works built in Siberia during the seventeenth century were significant mainly as forerunners of the development which was to occur in following centuries. In the words of B. B. Kafengauz:

These factories, introduced during the seventeenth century in the Urals, were small and primitive enterprises, but slightly distinguished from peasant blacksmith shops; they were not water-powered and proved to be short-lived. Some of them, as the Pyskorskii and Kamenskii, were revived under Peter I, or, to be more accurate, they were then built anew. Their significance evidently consisted in the fact that they helped locate favorable places for the large future Petrine factories. Their establishment at particular places indicated the availability of ore and other favorable conditions.*

This is not to say, however, that such efforts had no impact on the metallurgical needs of seventeenth-century Siberia. A. A. Kuzin correctly noted that, despite all difficulties, the efforts of the Russian government

. . . progressively opened up more and more new ore deposits which not only guaranteed local needs, but even made possible the sending of a certain quantity of metal from Siberia to the European part of the country at the end of the seventeenth century.[30]

During the 1680's and 1690's a certain amount of Siberian resources in mica, dyes, and precious metals were also exploited for the first time.[31]

During the last two-thirds of the seventeenth century no fewer than twenty-seven modern iron manufactories were established in Russia.† At least eighteen of these were large or medium-sized enterprises, and of the total number no less than twelve were equipped with blast furnaces. The final chapter of this study will discuss the nature of the capital invested in these iron works and deal with such analytical problems as monopolistic tendencies within seventeenth-century Russian iron manufacturing and a comparison of Russian and Western European achievements in ferrous metallurgy in this century. Here it is only necessary to note that between 1637 and 1697 the Russian iron industry made considerable progress in the construction of factories and in the development of a stable labor force trained in manufacturing technology. With the

---

*The above-mentioned Kamenskii factory was one of the first large state-owned iron manufactories of the eighteenth century. It was located on the former site of the Dalmatova monastery's tiny iron works. See Kafengauz, *Istoriia,* pp. 24, 50.

†Consult the listing and classification of these enterprises given in Appendix III to this study. The figure of twenty-eight iron manufactories is derived from a rigorous application of the definition of a "manufactory" (see pp. 9–10) and excludes such marginal or doubtful establishments as the Neiva river works, the two Smolensk smelters of 1670–1672, etc.

passage of time, increasing numbers of Russians entered the various categories of skilled work as masters and submasters, a development which suggests that the iron industry was (even in the seventeenth century) an indigenous phenomenon well rooted in the overall pattern of Russian industry and handicrafts. The shift of factory ownership from foreign to Russian hands during the seventeenth century is a further indication of the extent to which iron manufacturing in Russia was becoming part of the basic structure of the entire national economy. Whereas at the end of the first half of the period (1630's–1660's), ten of the eleven existing iron manufactories were owned by foreigners, with the death of Christian Marselis in 1690 the "Russification" of factory ownership reached a high point. Only seven of the nineteen iron enterprises functioning in the following decade were in foreign hands.

The iron industry was not an isolated or confined development in Russian economic life. The same tendencies which led to the creation of twenty-seven iron manufactories simultaneously affected other branches of national industry. In particular, the production of gunpowder, rope, paper, glass, silk, leather, cloth, and sawmill products all felt in different ways and to varying extents the impact of foreign industrial knowledge and methods during the seventeenth century. This development is the subject of the next chapter.

9

Other Russian Manufactures of the Seventeenth Century

A WORD OF CLARIFICATION should precede a survey of other "modern" industries introduced into seventeenth-century Russia. Our basis of distinguishing iron artisanry from iron manufacturing has been the use by the latter of water wheels to provide power for blast furnaces, forge hammers, boring mechanisms, and other equipment. Foreigners in Russia established such other water-powered enterprises as paper mills, glass factories, and sawmills, and these too are clearly manufactories. Yet some industries new to Russia at this time were not based on the water wheel, even in Western Europe (for example, cloth, leather, and silk). But contemporary documents and historical literature also commonly refer to these enterprises as "manufactories." They are included in this chapter, however, for more than semantic reasons. Foreigners played the same role in building cloth mills and leatherworks as paper mills and iron factories—and the technology of all was equally unprecedented in terms of Russian history. Russian manufacture of these consumer products forms a noteworthy chapter in the economic history of Russia because it shows that the development of capitalism in this period was by no means limited to the iron industry or dependent upon military necessity. The Russian state played an active role in introducing and fostering Western consumer industries, though the extent of that concern was more limited than in the case of metallurgy. This aspect of early Russian industry is all the more interesting because of the characters involved: the Hamburg silkmaster Arent Paulsen, the Dutch cloth manufacturer Egidius Tabbert, the Swedish glass miller Julius Coyet, and, above all, that ambitious entrepreneur, John of Sweden.

Iron manufacturing, as we have seen, developed in Russia as a result of contacts established through foreign trade, the government being especially interested in the purchase and production of armaments. To understand the growth of other manufactures one must remember that throughout the sixteenth and seventeenth centuries — and in particular after the 1620's — there was also a steady influx into Russia of nonmilitary commodities, from luxury items to raw materials to simple market goods, all of which enjoyed a wide territorial distribution. Few of these goods reached the average peasant or townsman, but more cosmopolitan members of the upper classes bought Western furniture and mirrors and rugs, watches and clocks (N.I. Romanov had nine clocks, Prince Golitsyn eighteen), and a variety of musical instruments. Tin for the construction of elegant doors was imported from England and Holland, and paintings, portraits, maps, and sketches were collected by such eminents as Golitsyn, Nikita Romanov, and A.S. Matveev. Some Russians bought books, cloth (notably lace and silk), German beaver skins and hats, chamois, yufts of leather, weapons, silver and gold wire, and copper, mercury, and lead. Especially popular were diamonds and other stones, precious coins, ivory, turquois and pearls, indigo, and toilet cases and personal chests. Exquisite glassware also was in great demand, as were dishes of porcelain, crystal, and stone, and such lesser items as beads, tinsel, knives, needles, tobacco (the American product being superior to that of the Ukraine), medical supplies, spice roots, dried and candied fruit, pepper, almonds, anise, millet, sugar, salted fish, wine, songbirds and other fowls, horses with special harnesses, coaches, and, at the time of Aleksei Mikhailovich, many esoteric items relevant to the tastes and interests of the tsar.[1]

The government was also a customer for nonmilitary commodities. The tsar's agents bought Dutch cloth for people in state service, spyglasses, and a large number of books on military affairs, engineering, metallurgy, and associated subjects. German locks were widely used in government buildings, as was foreign glass for the windows. Paper was needed for royal clerks, state printing presses, and the church.[2]

Russians, then, were buying a wide variety of Western goods after the Time of Troubles, and it was not uncommon for thirty or more ships to arrive at Archangel in a single year. Despite the rising curve of imports, however, the demand usually exceeded the supply, and the prices of imports remained high. Thus it is not surprising that the Russian government continued those efforts it had begun in the sixteenth century to establish home manufacturing of certain nonmilitary products. From the beginning, Russian statesmen understood that this would cut national expenditures for such goods. And after the 1620's another thought was more strongly injected into the formation of economic policy, the idea that successful Russian manufacturing of paper, glass, silk, and the like might open up new items of export to the West.[3] Thus Russian gold reserves would be replenished, not depleted, through trade with Western Europe.

While Andrei Vinius was establishing his iron works at Tula, the government was also taking steps to organize glass manufacturing in Russia. The foundation for glass production (in terms of previous artisan activity), however, was more barren than was the case with iron. For whereas iron handicrafts were well established by the sixteenth century, at the same time the lower classes had no knowledge of glass but used dishes made of wood, clay, or metal, while fish bladders and animal skins covered windows. The government buildings and the houses of wealthier people employed mica for window screens, and Russian masters had learned to mount pieces of this material into multicolored designs. This craft was by no means crude or insignificant, for Paul of Aleppo reported that quality mica "does not break, but is pliable like paper," and Giles Fletcher found that Russian mica passed more light than European glass of the same time.[4]

During the seventeenth century, however, glass panes were introduced to the elements of Russian society then imitating the life of Western Europe. A.S. Matveev's country home had glass windows, as did the palace, country cottages, and other residences of Prince Golitsyn. Such government buildings as the *Posol'skii Prikaz,* the *Prikaz* for Ukrainian affairs, and the *dvorets* at Izmailovo, and a few wealthy churches (the Kirillo-Belozerskii monastery, for example) also had glass. Glass dishes likewise became increasingly popular with the Russian aristocracy throughout the seventeenth century. Although not a single glass item was listed in the inventory of dishes remaining after the death of Maksim Stroganov in 1627, by the end of the century glass dishes are often to be found in the property inventories of important people. Golitsyn had several "Venetian" goblets, mugs, glasses, and dishes, while *stol'nik* A.I. Bezobrazov owned over three hundred glass objects.[5]

The first Russian glass factory was established by Julius Coyet, member of a Protestant family from the Brabant which fled religious persecution to Sweden early in the seventeenth century. Julius' father was a goldsmith by trade, and the son worked in the royal mint from 1614 to 1630, at which time he arrived in Russia with Colonel Lesly to smelt cannon at Moscow. Coyet initially intended to stay in Russia for only a short time, but the tsar's officials were determined to keep him in their sovereign's service. Michael Romanov presented Julius a silver ladle weighing two *funts,* several lengths of the highest quality London cloth (as well as velvet, taffeta, and silk), forty precious sables, thirty-five rubles in money, and a splendid horse with saddle and bridle. Then, as if this were not enough, "for knowledgeable service" Coyet received a large house *(dvor)* in Moscow. Quite overcome with such generosity, Coyet decided to settle in Moscow, and in 1631 his wife, two daughters, and three of his five sons (Otto, Petrus, and Julius) left Sweden to join Julius in their new homeland.[6]

By this time Coyet was already discussing with court officials the possibility of establishing glass manufacturing in Russia, and in 1632 the Swedish glass master Paul Kunkel joined Coyet in Moscow to help select a location for a factory. They finally decided on an area in Moscow *uezd,* and in 1633 petitioned Tsar Mikhail and his father, Patriarch Filaret, for permission to build a glass manufactory there. On May 31, 1634, Julius received a royal charter granting him a monopoly on glass manufacturing in the Muscovite state and designating sixteen unused fields upon which he might base his industrial activities. Starting in 1634 Coyet could import materials (salt, ash, sand, bricks, clay, and so forth) for five years duty free, and for fifteen years (until 1649) the factory was to operate tax free. The factory was to belong to Julius and his heirs for as long as they lived in Moscow, but the Coyet family could not sell, mortgage, or forgo the factory in favor of another person. Should Coyet leave Russia, the glass works would become the property of the tsar.[7]

The Coyet family moved quickly to take advantage of their new privileges. Kunkel returned to Sweden in 1633 to hire twenty glass masters while the Coyets were building the glass factory on Dukhanino field, forty *versts* from Moscow. Even the misfortune of Julius Coyet's death (on July 23, 1634) did not delay construction of the works, for title to the uncompleted enterprise immediately fell to the eldest of his sons, Otto Coyet. At this point, however, Hans Falck, otherwise famous as a cannon and bell caster, became the most important figure at Dukhanino because of his technical knowledge and experience. In 1637 Falck even purchased half-interest in Otto Coyet's glass works, presumably with permission of the tsar.[8]

The first years were difficult for the Dukhanino factory. Although the glass works was "fully established" by 1639, it was long plagued by deaths and departures among the foreign workers, and on several occasions it was necessary to search for masters in Denmark, Holstein, and Danzig. When a new charter updating the factory's privileged years from 1641 was issued on November 1, 1643, the glass manufactory had not operated for some time, and a continuation of the Coyet family's financial difficulties led Otto to mortgage his remaining half of the factory to Falck for the sum of one thousand rubles.[9]

Although departure of workers and the seeking of replacements abroad continued to be a major difficulty throughout the 1640's, after that time the Dukhanino factory operated in a satisfactory manner. Otto Coyet died around 1660, leaving his part of the glass factory to his wife, Maria, and son, Peter. Hans Falck had also passed away by this time, and his heir was his father-in-law, David Bacheracht, a foreign merchant and industrialist who had traveled to Germany during the 1640's to recruit workers for his son-in-law's glass works. After Bacheracht's death in 1671, Maria and Peter Coyet shared ownership of the factory with David's widow, Jacomina Bacheracht, agreeing that neither party would sell the products of the manufactory without knowledge of the other. The Bacheracht family soon disappeared from connection with the Dukhanino factory, however, and in the 1690's the merchant Heinrich Münter appeared as a partner of the Coyet family. Peter Coyet was involved in the affairs of the glass works as late as 1696, but by 1701 his knowledge of the German, Swedish, Danish, and Dutch languages gained him a well-paid interpreter's post in the *Posol'skii Prikaz*. Peter's activities at this time did not include the Dukhanino glass manufactory, which seems to have continued operating as a state enterprise for a few years.[10]

In the 1660's the tsar decided to use the Coyet glass works to organize a similiar enterprise in the nearby town of Izmailovo. Aleksei Mikhailovich was the leading merchant and entrepreneur of his kingdom, and, possessing an imaginative and experimental spirit, he was interested in using the new arts and crafts of Western Europe for the profit of his own private activities. As early as 1656 Aleksei commissioned John Hebdon, the English merchant and Russian agent, to buy materials and hire masters to establish a modern glass manufactory in Russia. An entire decade passed before the tsar devoted sufficient attention and resources to glass manufacturing for his dreams to achieve fruition, but finally a state glass works was established in the town of Izmailovo, * on the Serebrianka river no more than a mile from the Foreign Quarter (*Nemetskaia sloboda*). The new enterprise was modeled on the Coyet family's Dukhanino factory, and workers from that enterprise were commandeered both for construction (between late 1668 and February 1669) and operation of the new manufactory.[11]

The Izmailovo factory was initially staffed by the foreign glass master Ivan Martynov, the Russian masters Boris Ivanov and Grishka Vasil'ev, and five other skilled Russian workers—all of whom, apparently, came from the Dukhanino enterprise. Whatever the quality of glass may have been at the tsar's factory to begin with, the addition of eight or more "Venetian" masters (actually foreign workers, many of them Dutch, trained in the technique of Venetian glass-blowing) in 1670 and 1674 caused a more refined and exquisite product to emerge from the glass furnaces of Izmailovo. And the account books of Izmailovo for 1676-1677 indicate that by this time a great variety of glassware was being produced there: bottles one *chetvert'* (about eight bushels) in size, large Venetian bottles, bottles measuring "one bucket," a half- and a quar-

---

*Izmailovo, a town on the outskirts of Moscow, was an important center of the royal economy during the seventeenth century. Besides fishing and agriculture, orchards and vast pastures were located here, and these aspects of the tsar's economic activities provided the basis for animal husbandry, kitchen-gardening, and experimentation with various plants. Workers from all parts of the Russian empire and abroad were employed at Izmailovo, and by mid-century their number reached seven hundred. Besides a glass factory, a Morocco tannery (pp. 161–162, below) and a large salt works were also established here during the 1660's. Pankratova, *Formirovanie*, pp. 177–183.

ter-bucket, glass jugs large and small, general table tureens, mugs, cups, goblets with and without covers, wine glasses, large glasses, small high-rimmed glasses, flat glasses, flasks, dishes of many sorts, plates, saucers, iron lamps, candlesticks, ink pots, and, in particular, a diversity of pharmaceutical bottles and dishes. The skill of the Izmailovo glass masters is indicated by the complex shapes of their work (one report describes glasses which were "high, flat, smooth, scaly, twisted, and with hoops") and by the sophisticated use of dyes to produce colored patterns and effects.[12] Presumably the largest Izmailovo glass piece was a monster "wine glass of one sazhen" (a *sazhen* equals about seven feet) which Zaozerskii characterizes as the glass counterpart of the *tsar-kolokol*.*

The best glass from the Izmailovo factory went to satisfy the needs of the tsar and his court, or at times as presents for favorite boyars and government figures. Pharmaceutical items, of course, were sent to the *Aptekarskii Prikaz*. Izmailovo products were also sold on the open market at Moscow in a special state shop at the *gostinyi bol'shoi dvor*. In this store the glassware was displayed on shelves, and in 1687 there were no fewer than 535 dishes of various types available for purchase here. Izmailovo glass was of fine quality, and was even exported to Persia in exchange for raw silk. Glasswork of the Coyet Dukhanino factory, by contrast, was of lower quality; in fact, it appears that the Izmailovo works was established to meet the rising standards of the Russian aristocracy in glassware. Peter Coyet's production was primarily for the *Aptekarskii Prikaz* (which in July 1670 placed a typically large order for 2,720 assorted phials), although window panes, dishes, and bottles were also made and placed on the market not only in Moscow but in the provinces. The scale of production was considerable at both factories, and Kilburger speaks of the Coyets sending eighty to ninety thousand bottles to Moscow each year. [13]

*The *tsar-kolokol* was literally the sovereign of bells, weighing no less than eight thousand *puds* (over 130 tons). Cast by Russian artisans in Moscow in 1654, the bell was mounted with great difficulty only in 1668; in 1701 a fire caused the bell to fall and break. The *tsar-kolokol* may be observed today by visitors to the Kremlin. Danilevskii, *Russkaia tekhnika*, pp. 123–124.

Although the Dukhanino factory began operation with raw materials imported from abroad, by the time of Kilburger's visit in 1674 both the Dukhanino and Izmailovo works were being provided with high-quality sand, fireclay, and brick galina from the Moscow area. Ash for the glass furnaces came from local birch wood, five hundred to six hundred *sazhens* of which was cut in the summer for each factory by peasants who lived in the vicinity of the factories. The peasants then burned the wood and delivered it to the manufactories at twelve kopecks per ton. Kilburger noted that the cold Moscow climate permitted the two glass enterprises to work only twenty-five or thirty weeks each year. Since no more than ten masters were engaged at one time at either the Izmailovo or Dukhanino factories, they should not be characterized as "large" manufactories. They were, however, successful and long-lived, and we know that the Izmailovo works was in operation as late as 1706. [14]

A third glass factory was in operation at this time, located in the town of Voskresensk, in Chernogolovskaia *volost'*, quite near the Izmailovskii and Dukhaninskii works. Although equipped with two furnaces (one for melting glass and another for glazing), the Chernogolovskii enterprise was probably small in comparison with its two predecessors. Baklanova concludes that since Kilburger does not mention this factory, its activities were insignificant and little noted, [15] but it seems more likely that the Chernogolovskii works was built after Kilburger's visit of 1674. Concerning the question of significance, Baklanova herself gives evidence indicating it may have been considerable, for inventories of 1687 disclose 5,147 glass objects at Chernogolovsk and only 2,512 at Izmailovo. Since the Chernogolovskii factory was located near the Izmailovskii enterprise, and since both were state owned, it is possible that the former was organized as a supplement of some sort to the activities of the latter.

An unsuccessful effort was begun in 1691 to organize a fourth glass works in the Moscow area. Iakov Romanov, a merchant of the *gostinaia sotnia,* was ordered to establish a new glass factory on the banks of the Moskva, at the Tainitskii gates, for which he was given two hundred rubles from the *Prikaz Bol'shoi Kazny*. Romanov actually completed the construction of a glass-smelting enterprise, but he searched throughout Russia in vain for the necessary masters. After two years he turned to the Ukraine for skilled glass workers, but the years dragged by and production at this manufactory was never actually realized. [16] Iakov Romanov's glass works is interesting simply as an unsuccessful concluding note to the development of an industry which would appear to have been very successful during the seventeenth century. [17]

A certain amount of manufacturing of rope, gunpowder, and paper occurred in sixteenth-century Russia. Surviving evidence suggests that seventeenth-century development in these areas represented at least a modest continuation of promising beginnings. For example, it appears that rope manufacturing in Russia did not come to an end after the English closed their enterprises at Vologda and Kholmogory. Certainly in 1617 a group of prominent Moscow merchants who advised the tsar on state economic policy expressed their belief that English rope manufacturing had benefited Russia, and that many Russians had learned the trade. We know that in Archangel in 1618 the Russians Sorokin and Busin had a "rope machine," and in 1627 government records from Vologda mention "spinners" *(priadil'shchiki,* rope makers). During the mid-seventeenth century Aleksei Mikhailovich built a large rope walk to give employment to the needy from all parts of his kingdom, and during the 1690's Vologda and Nizhnyi-Novgorod were active centers of an indigenous Russian rope industry. Although the technology of rope making was rather simple (which was also the case in Western Europe at that time), the number of workers involved in these enterprises was considerable (ten, twenty, and more), so that these workshops might be included in the category of "large" factories. [18]

Apparently foreign capital was no longer active in rope manufacturing in Russia during the seventeenth century. It is true that Kilburger advised his fellow Western European entrepreneurs in 1674 that "without a doubt, hemp and workers in Russia are so cheap that one could establish rope factories or rope production there to good advantage," but the only clear instance of such activity was the rope factory of the Dutch *gost'* Karp Demulin, which was yearly producing one thousand *puds* "and more" of rope at Kholmogory in 1623.[19]

Gunpowder was made in Russia by artisans from early times, but during the second half of the sixteenth century it became such a highly prized foreign import that in 1588 the Russian government threatened to export wax to the British Isles (wax was then a scarce and valuable commodity in England) only in exchange for saltpeter, gunpowder, brimstone, and lead. A number of gunpowder manufactories were built in Russia during the seventeenth century. By 1626 a powder mill had been organized on the Iauza river near Moscow, and in 1637 the Dutch *gost'* Andrei Fanringen received a charter for a saltpeter enterprise in the Novgorod area. In 1650 the foreign merchant David Bacheracht built a powder works of Western European design just outside Moscow. When Marselis and Akema threatened him with competition in this industry in 1653 (Marselis had already opened a non-water-powered artisan powder shop in 1644), Bacheracht petitioned the state for help in establishing another large gunpowder manufactory in the vicinity of the original Iauza enterprise of 1626 (not in operation at this time). In 1655 the state decided to support Bacheracht's proposal, and the "new" Iauza factory near Moscow which materialized from his ambitions functioned successfully until its founder's death in 1671.[20]

In 1671 the state assumed ownership of Bacheracht's factory and converted it into a paper mill. In this form, title to the enterprise passed to Hermann Löfken in 1676, who re-established gunpowder production six years later, in 1682. Löfken's widow, Maria Ivanovna, continued to operate her husband's factory after his death in 1685; in 1693 the gunpowder privileges passed to the Löfken's son-in-law, Rudolf Meyer, a Dutch merchant. By this time similar enterprises had been established by other foreigners in the Muscovite state. The iron entrepreneur Evert Izbrants had a powder factory in the area of his Vora river iron works (thirty *versts* northeast of Moscow) in 1698, and this manufactory existed until around 1711.[21]

While it is true that Russian gunpowder manufactories of Western European type were important sources of that commodity during the seventeenth century,* they were not the sole internal Russian sources of gunpowder production in this period. During the mid-seventeenth century, gunpowder and related products were produced in fairly large quantities in the artisan economies of great feudalists such as Aleksei Mikhailovich and Boris Morozov. Speaking of the year 1674, Kilburger tells us that "although there are only a very few powder mills operated by water power in this kingdom, there are, on the other hand, many more hand mills." According to Kilburger, gunpowder was produced in places other than Moscow; the masters, he says, were both foreign and Russian, but ordinary workers were Russian. The same source indicates that saltpeter sold in Moscow at two to two and a quarter rubles per *pud,* and "the best powder" brought as much as four rubles on the same market.[22]

Gunpowder factories not indicated in surviving documentary material may have existed in Russia in the sixteenth century. The same conclusion might be drawn for the seventeenth century, for whereas the above quotation from Kilburger suggests the existence of at least "a very few powder mills operated by water power in this [Russian] kingdom," other sources on gunpowder manufacturing examined for this study give no indication that a single gunpowder *manufactory* existed in 1674, the year of Kilburger's visit to Russia. Perhaps there are gaps in original sources which prevent the modern historian from doing justice to this aspect of Russian industrial development during the early modern period.

In Kievan times Russians used parchment, birchbark, and

*Löfken's Iauza works, for example, delivered nine thousand *puds* of powder to the state in a single year during the 1680's.

bast *(lub)* for writing material. Paper was introduced into Russia (possibly by the Mongols) during the first half of the fourteenth century, and by the fifteenth century Italian paper was used in both the northern and southern parts of the Muscovite state. During the sixteenth and seventeenth centuries French, German, and Dutch paper was most popular in Russia, the main purchaser of this product being the government.* With the expansion of the tsar's bureaucracy, paper imports steadily rose, and in a single day (on July 30, 1621), 1,831 reams were unloaded at Archangel. [23]

Unsuccessful efforts were made during the sixteenth century to introduce paper manufacturing into Russia. Apparently the next effort in this direction did not come until the late 1630's when the Russian technician Vasilii Burtsev built a paper workshop to which he invited the Prussian master Frum "to instruct Russian apprentice people in paper crafts." But for some reason Frum soon asked permission of the tsar to return home, and when he left in 1641 the paper mill was probably closed. Patriarch Nikon decided to build a special paper factory for the state publishing house *(pechatnyi dvor)*, and before the spring of 1665 Vasilii Burtsev had directed the construction of such an enterprise on the Pakhra river, near *Zelenaia sloboda*, not far from Moscow. Apparently there were only six masters involved in the actual production process of this manufactory. After a year and a half Luk'ian Shpil'kin, who had succeeded Burtsev as factory supervisor, delivered seventy-five reams of paper to the *pechatnyi dvor*, but the paper was "black" and fit only for the binding of books.[24] Then, on March 16, 1667, spring floods damaged the paper factory so severely that government authorities decided that the four hundred rubles spent on their paper mill had been wasted, and the enterprise was closed.[25]

The next Russian paper manufactory was built by Johann van Sweeden. John of Sweden (as his English name would

---

*Ink was made in Russia from oak-galls (nutgalls), to which vitriol was added for a higher-quality product. Nutgalls were grown in Russia and also imported from east and west; vitriol was obtained from Western Europe. Baklanova, "Privoznye tovary," p. 111.

read) began his career in Muscovy as a merchant, but was far too ambitious and energetic to limit himself to commercial activities. Actually of Dutch origin, John often used his foreign connections to serve the tsar as factor, as, for example, when he traveled to Hamburg and Holland in 1660 to purchase firearms, military equipment, and clothing for the armed forces. As we shall see later, van Sweeden was to organize the first modern international post, and he played a leading role in the construction of the *Orel,* Russia's first important warship. In the mid-1660's he also conceived an impressive scheme which might have resulted — but for his unexpected death — in the importation of English and Spanish sheep and the establishment of large-scale cloth, paper, and glass manufacturing in Russia.

To fulfill his industrial plans, John needed both the permission and financial support of the tsar; this led him to write a long letter to Aleksei Mikhailovich, the contents of which suggest that John of Sweden was a pragmatic economist of ability. He pointed out that Russians would work in the proposed factories under the direction of foreigners, and in this way would themselves learn new industrial skills. Moreover, the money which Russians would eventually pay John for glass, paper, and cloth

> will also go for peace and remain in the Russian state, and not go beyond the seas as money once [did] for these goods, and Russian goods will go beyond the seas, and at that place for the purchase of Russian goods they will begin to send from beyond the seas gold and efimki and different foreign goods, and from that the Russian state will become rich.

In return for establishing these factories, John of Sweden asked to be freed from *obrok* for thirty years, after which he would pay state taxes on condition that "until then those factories will remain and not be given to anyone save ourselves and our heirs."[26]

When he sent his petition to the tsar in 1668, John of Sweden had already taken various steps to build his industrial complex. As early as 1666 he had brought "ship, and cloth,

and paper, and crystal, and Venetian glass and all other masters" to Russia in connection with his various entrepreneurial
projects. In 1667 he had received the ruins of the Pakhra river
works,* promising to restore paper production on this site by
employment of

> . . . the very best masters from Foreign lands, and to teach
> Russians the same craft, so that henceforth there will be Rus-
> sians able to carry on the same craft even without Foreign
> masters, and henceforth paper-making will not halt, and the
> great sovereign will henceforth have profit in that papermak-
> ing.[27]

Van Sweeden's factory charter, issued in the mid-1660's,
ignored his proposed glass- and cloth-making activities, recognizing only his right to build a paper factory. According to this
agreement, after ten years of duty-free factory operation John
would pay the tsar a yearly *obrok* of one hundred reams "of the
very best paper of Foreign type." In 1667 John went to
Amsterdam in connection with his commercial activities and
had his agents engage nine masters for the projected factory.
All of these men received "wage-money according to agreement," but only five actually came to Russia. In addition, in
Essen John contracted the services of the Ottendal brothers,
Berent and Johann, both of whom were to serve "in the paper
factories" four years. For this they "will be given wages in a
year: to Johann 110 efimki, to Berent 60 efimki above what
they eat and drink at Ivanovo." The Ottendal brothers were
especially instrumental in re-establishing paper manufacturing
on the Pakhra river.[28]

John of Sweden's industrial ambitions were abruptly halted
by his death in 1668. He had constructed only the one paper
mill, but his wife Maria now suggested to the *Posol'skii Prikaz*
that she be allowed to carry out her husband's industrial
project. Maria requested a loan of three thousand rubles to
complete John's glass factory (which was evidently in an
advanced stage of construction) and to hire additional masters,

---

*This was the paper manufactory built by Vasilii Burtsev in 1665 and
abandoned after March 1667. See p. 153, above.

for which she promised to deliver to the state in following years, at reduced price, "200 sheets of Hamburg glass, 2000 reams of writing paper, crystal-cut glass ware: wine-glasses, glasses and all sorts of different wonders and fine Venetian caskets according to choice at 500 rubles."[29]

Had Maria van Sweeden received the necessary state support she might have further expanded Russian industry and emerged as a lady capitalist of distinction. But for some reason the Russian government was unwilling to back her plans to complete the glass manufactory,[30] and van Sweeden's widow had to content herself with a state loan of six hundred rubles, for the paper factory already in operation, plus a five year monopoly on the manufacture of paper.[31]

The Pakhra river paper mill functioned well under Maria van Sweeden's management. Then, on May 9, 1676, the *Prikaz Bol'shogo Dvortsa* took John's enterprise from his widow and placed it under the direction of Herman Löfken, a Dutchman and nephew of John of Sweden.[32] Berent and Johann Ottendal continued to serve under Löfken.[33]

In 1673 the Russian government used the resources of Maria van Sweeden's paper mill to convert its gunpowder works on the Iauza river to a paper-making enterprise. By royal *ukaz* of May 19, 1673, the Ottendal brothers, against their will, were taken temporarily from the Pakhra river factory and sent to the Iauza, Johann being master of "paper affairs" and Berent master of "carpentry affairs." Karp Fedorov and Ivan Gordeev served the factory continuously as highly skilled carpenters, along with five Russian *trepishniki,* or "ragmen," who sorted and processed the rags. Artamon Matveev, then a leading official of the *Posol'skii Prikaz,* was coordinator and director of factory construction and activity. From Kilburger, we know that the factory was finished by 1674, "but they are still doing little work there."[34]

At the same time that Herman Löfken received Maria van Sweeden's Pakhra river paper mill, the state awarded him the Iauza river paper manufactory. Löfken's career as a paper manufacturer, however, did not last long. In 1682 he converted the Iauza factory into a gunpowder works;[35] by the time of his death in 1685 the Pakhra enterprise is no longer mentioned in documents, which indicates it had ceased to function.[36]

Although their achievements must not be exaggerated, foreign entrepreneurs and the Russian government tried to establish sericulture and silk weaving, cloth manufacturing, and Western forms of leather-working in Russia during the seventeenth century. In fact, as early as 1605 Tsar Boris Godunov commissioned the German Beckman to engage woolen masters in Lübeck and introduce the factory production of cloth into Russia.[37] And at a later time, as we have seen, John of Sweden explained to the tsar his desire

> . . . to have Spanish, English, and Pomor'e sheep, with people who know the shepherding of such sheep and who are able to instruct the subjects of his royal majesty, so that henceforth great flocks will be established in such places as are now empty and not receiving profit from them.[38]

Presumably the raising of sheep was related to John's other plans to organize a woolen factory in Russia * — plans he took quite seriously, for on a trip to the West in June 1667 he hired eight millers, four wool spinners, and eleven cloth makers for his projected enterprise. Apparently fifteen of these twenty-three men actually arrived in Russia and were settled by their employer in Medynia, near Moscow. John then asked the *Posol'skii Prikaz* to ascribe nearby Ivankovskaia *volost'*, where he would establish a cloth manufactory. Van Sweeden explained that at this time he had taken "from beyond the seas many cloth masters, and they are living in Moscow without work." The Russian government granted John of Sweden's requests, and even extended him loans for the construction of

---

* These sheep pastures, if successful, would have been no less revolutionary for the Russian economy than the factory which they were to serve. Foreign visitors such as Fletcher, Kilburger, and Perry all remarked on the poor quality of Russian sheep, and although Aleksei Mikhailovich made several efforts to import superior Persian breeds, in each case the exotic animals died under Russian conditions. Kilburger saw a number of Persian sheep belonging to Artamon Matveev and various foreign merchants. Zaozerskaia, *Razvitie*, p. 41; Kurts, *Sochinenie Kil'burgera*, pp. 475–476, 171.

a cloth works, but in the same year, 1668, he died before work on the factory had even begun. After this, all of John's masters save one returned to Western Europe, and on November 30, 1674, Ivankovskaia *volost'* was returned to the *Prikaz Bol'shogo Dvortsa*.[39]

The first successful Russian textile manufactory appeared soon after this as a result of the efforts of the Dutch merchant Egidius Tabbert (called by the Russians Il'ia Il'in Tarbet), who petitioned the tsar in February 1683 for the right to build cloth factories in Moscow *gubernaia*. Tarbet glowingly outlined the potential for cloth manufacturing in Russia, praised his own talents and abilities, and asked for a twenty-year monopoly on cloth production in the entire Russian kingdom. He requested the right to duty-free import of wool, sheepskins, and other necessary materials from abroad, and the option to market the products of his factory within Russia or export them through Archangel. But Tarbet's charter (dated April 9, 1684) bestowed manufacturing privileges for only ten years, and nothing was said about a national monopoly or the right of export.[40] To protect Tarbet's investments in bringing foreign masters to Russia, it was specified that they could not leave his enterprise to work elsewhere without his permission.[41]

In July 1683 Egidius Tarbet's brother Matthäus returned to Novgorod from Holland with six masters and one apprentice, and such a quantity of dyes and other materials that twenty-five carts were needed to transport the entire shipment to Moscow. The factory was built near Moscow soon after that time. We have no exact picture of the technology of Tarbet's cloth works, but it must have been fairly primitive, for "modern" wool-spinning machinery had still not been invented even in Western Europe, where spinning wheels of the sort developed by Leonardo da Vinci were still in use. The factory produced various sorts of woolens and serges, using dyes prepared at the factory. In 1687 Matthäus returned from Germany with two more masters and two apprentices. The most skilled worker at the enterprise was the dye master, who received annual wages of forty-five rubles plus free lodging and firewood; other masters received lower wages according to the value of their labor.[42]

Tarbet's cloth factory apparently ceased operation around 1688. Perhaps the cloth works closed because of Egidius Tarbet's death in 1689 (although one wonders why Matthäus Tarbet, or even the state, could not have continued its operation); or the fall of the industry-minded Sof'ia-Golitsyn government in September 1689 may have had an adverse impact on the future of Tarbet's enterprise. (Such — as we shall see — was clearly the case with silk manufacturing.)[43] But the short life of the Tarbet enterprise does not detract from the fact that it was, in the words of E. I. Zaozerskaia,

> . . . a small, but genuine manufactory. At its head stood a merchant-capitalist; a division of labor existed at the enterprise, there being weavers, cloth shearers, and dyers. It was a centralized manufactory with regard to the structure of its organization; all stages of production were unified under one roof and evidently everyone even lived and ate together.

In evaluating the impact of Tarbet's manufactory on Russian economic development, we should note that some of his masters remained in Moscow in connection with other types of textile work. The apprentice Ivan Parfienov, for example, was given raw silk, dyes, and other materials by the government in April 1689, and ordered to produce silk for the court.[44]

The last attempt to establish European-type textiles in seventeenth-century Russia which lies within the scope of this study was by Franz Timmermann, a friend and tutor of young Peter I. In 1692 Timmermann received a twenty-year monopoly on sailcloth manufacturing in Russia, and by February 1693 had constructed a sailcloth works and wharf in Archangel. Timmermann brought sixteen cloth masters from Western Europe to work in his mill, which seems to have closed around 1697. The artisan *Kadashevyi dvor* in Moscow also produced sailcloth in 1693. [45]

When we turn to silk and leather manufacturing in Russia during the seventeenth century, we cannot but note some striking similarities of development. Both silk and leather played a role in Russian trade with the West — the former being imported from the East, the latter produced by native artisans — so that with the expansion of international commerce after the 1620's the Russian government began to think of reaping increased profits by making silk at home while placing the production of leather on a broader, more modern basis. Although attempts in these directions preceded and followed his reign, such efforts were especially pronounced under Aleksei Mikhailovich (1645-1676), and resulted in the operation of two successful enterprises: the Vorontsovo leather manufactory (after 1666) and the Moscow silk works of Arent Paulsen (after 1683). Both state-owned industries were liquidated by economy-minded regimes after their original state sponsors passed from the scene, the leather factory with the death of Aleksei in 1676, the silk enterprise as a result of the fall of Sof'ia and Golitsyn in 1689. One of the most striking features of these manufactories was their labor force. As before, the state relied heavily on Western European masters, but in this case we see two unique features of development. First, Armenian workers were also important; second, at the end both the silk and leather works operated solely through the efforts of Russians who had learned their trade from foreigners.

Leather-making was known in Russia since antiquity and is noted in the earliest Russian chronicles. During the Muscovite period a large number of artisans produced finished goods from the leather provided by Russia's many tanning centers. Novgorod was especially important for leather-making, and in the 1580's no fewer than 458 men were engaged in cutting and sewing various commodities (shoes, purses, scabbards, and the like) which were then distributed to Novgorodites and other Russians through some 314 leather shops and trading enterprises. Leather was also an important item in Russia's foreign trade, with Russia importing Persian morocco from the East and exporting her own less valuable skins to Western Europe. Kilburger reported that twenty years before his visit Russia annually sent 225,000 pairs of yufts to Europe, and that in 1674 the quantity was still greater.[46] Besides ordinary cattle hide, horse leather was popular with foreign purchasers, as were, to a lesser extent, ox and goat.[47]

The high price of leather during the seventeenth century gave a special incentive for leather-making. It was not unusual for Russian merchants at this time to own leather works whose products were designed especially for export. The first known attempt at the penetration of foreign capital in this area, however, did not come until 1634, when the foreign velvet master Efim Fimbrant received a charter for the establishment of a chamois factory of Western European type. Fimbrant obtained the right to make leather and sell or export it duty free for ten years, and he was to be the only foreigner with tanning privileges in Russia during that period. Fimbrant went to Sweden to engage masters for the construction and operation of his leather shop, but there is no indication that his enterprise was actually organized. [48]

A "large-scale" Russian tannery was finally established during the mid-1660's, when the *Prikaz Tainykh Del* bought a *dvor* (court) on the Iauza river, quite near Moscow, from Mikhail Bechevin, a cloth merchant. The intention of the *Prikaz* was to initiate morocco leather production at this location, and in March 1666 government authorities began building a factory and acquiring goods for its activity. Within a month significant progress had been made in construction, and on April 1, 1666, the tsar ordered the Armenian master Arabit Martynov to serve at the leather works, along with the "newly-baptized" foreign interpreter Boris Ivanov and an apprentice named Ardeik Chukaev. The Russian government soon realized, however, that the Iauza river works was so poorly placed that it would be necessary to build an entirely new enterprise if leather production were to continue. So from September 1669 to April 1670 the tsar's carpenters and masters built—at the cost of some 158 rubles—a new leather factory in the nearby state village of Chasnikov, also in Moscow *uezd*. [49]

The Chasnikov enterprise was not destined to function even as long as its predecessor, for on September 20, 1670, a fire destroyed it. Because of a shortage of spring water at the existing location, the factory was moved a second time, now a short distance to Vorontsovo field, where two large barns, a pond, and a drainage system into the Iauza for water used in the tanning process were organized at an expenditure of 250 rubles. The tannery worked well at this site and was further expanded in August 1672. The enterprise remained small, however, no more than ten masters being involved in the tanning process. Foreign workers were no less indispensable to the operation of this workshop than to most of the manufactories previously described in this study, though in the case of the leather industry they came from Armenia rather than Western Europe. Arabit, the Armenian master who initially directed leather production at the Iauza river location, soon died, and on May 8, 1667, a royal *ukaz* was issued ordering that the interpreter, Boris Ivanov, "be taken into the mastership [of leather workers] . . . due to the fact that Arabit died." But the results of this appointment were not very satisfactory. For if Ivanov served Arabit as an interpreter, the Russian had not—contrary to the expectations of the state officials who promoted him—learned enough about leather-working to direct tanning operations on his own. After three years, on August 20, 1670, the unfortunate Ivanov was beaten with sticks and expelled from his mastership and the affairs of the leather factory. His successor, the Armenian master Martynov Mard'iasov (assisted by ten "apprentices"), also ruined a large number of skins, but he was simply dismissed without disgrace or punishment.[50] Presumably later workers were more talented than Ivanov and Mard'iasov!

Leather-making at Vorontsovo came to a halt with the death of Aleksei Mikhailovich in 1676. Many royal enterprises which had failed to operate at a profit were closed; at that time imported leather could be had in Russia which was both cheaper and of better quality than the Vorontsovo product. The manufactory had been sustained all by government purchases, Aleksei's policy being in effect to subsidize new manufactures even if they were more expensive at first than foreign competitors, with the expectation that in the long run the increasing rationalization of native manufacturing would cut production costs — at which point an overall profit on the entire investment would begin to materialize. [51]

By the time the factory closed in 1676, Russians were apparently in complete control of the production process. In contrast to the silk factory of Arent Paulsen, workers at the Iauza-Chasnikovo-Vorontsovo leather works did not receive high wages. Russian apprentices were paid a mere fifty kopecks per month, and Arabit Martynov drew only three rubles per month. After 1676 the premises of the former Vorontsovo leather works were used for royal artisan cloth production.[52] The leather workers displaced by this change do not appear to have suffered from it, for many of them went to small leather shops in Moscow. [53]

Russians were familiar with the silks of Byzantium and the Orient as early as the time of Oleg (873-912), and by the sixteenth century the import of Eastern silk had become a basic feature of the commercial life of the Muscovite state. As we have seen, during the seventeenth century various European countries hoped to gain access to the Persian silk market via overland trade routes through Russian territory, but the tsars were usually inclined to refuse such trade agreements. While importing silks from Italy and Holland, Russia continued to serve as the connecting link between India, Persia, and Western Europe, Armenian merchants often functioning as the middlemen in this process.[54]

Foreign masters made at least two efforts to establish silk-weaving enterprises in Russia during the sixteenth century. Similar attempts occurred during the early seventeenth century, but in the absence of a trained cadre or artisan tradition in this specialty, these ventures failed. In 1624, for example, the Dutch velvet master Kaspar l' Hermite arrived in Russia to build a silk works, but lacking the means to bring the necessary workers and equipment from Europe and finding none of them in Russia, he soon returned home. L' Hermite's parting advice to the tsar was to abandon the idea of establishing silk manufacturing in Russia, for even if the necessary masters were brought from abroad, in the absence of silk "the work would stop; but they [the masters] would want to have their payment for each day, although they do nothing, for in this way they live."[55]

A "velvet court" *(barkhatnyi dvor)* was actually established in Moscow during the 1630's. In 1632 no fewer than twenty-eight Russian apprentices were at the *dvor,* and by 1635 the number had reached thirty-five. Work here was conducted within the premises of a single enterprise, and a division of labor clearly existed. A group was responsible for only one step in the entire production process: unwinding the silk thread, binding it together, spinning and drying the thread, weaving the silk cloth, and so forth. And yet, though of considerable size the silk shop was not a success, probably because of the amateurish labor of the apprentices. By the 1650's the *dvor* was used as a storage place for armaments.[56]

Tsar Aleksei Mikhailovich established a second velvet works in 1652 (also without success) and took new measures to develop silk production. *Stol'nik* Rakov sent an order to *voevoda* Dashkov in Simbirsk on October 21, 1664, specifying that

> he [Dashkov] will grow mulberry trees in bushes, and from him 100 bushes will be sent to Moscow, and grafts will be cut from these trees, as many as possible. And Dmitrii will be sent from Simbirsk in iam wagons with all these trees so as to convey them and to transplant them in Moscow before the first autumn frosts.[57]

We do not know what happened to these plans, but early in the following year, 1665, the Armenian silk master Larion L'gov did arrive in Moscow to set up a silk factory. In January he traveled to Astrakhan to obtain "sea plants and silk worms and cotton seeds"; at the same time other men were sent with orders for thirty thousand mulberry bushes to be sent from Smolensk and twenty thousand from Kiev. It appears that state supervisors in Moscow were not satisfied with L'gov's efforts, but far from abandoning sericulture, by 1672 the tsar was planning to re-establish it on a still larger scale. In line with this desire, Aleksei issued orders

> to seek in Astrakhan or in Terki or abroad in order to summon the very best gardeners of mulberry gardens who would be able both to establish a mulberry garden in Moscow and to produce seeds of the mulberry tree and silk worms.[58]

Other masters were involved in futile attempts during the 1660's and early 1670's to establish mulberry gardening and silk manufacturing in Russia, and in 1667 a "royal silk factory" seems to have been set up in Astrakhan. But the first clear success in the silk industry for Russia was not to come until the 1680's, when the Hamburg velvet master Arent Paulsen (known to the Russians as Zakharii Pavlov) decided to establish a silk shop in Moscow. In July 1681 Paulsen received a charter and a loan of two thousand rubles from Tsar Fedor to set up a "factory" for the manufacture of velvet, moire, atlas (a smooth and glossy type of silk cloth), *kamka* silk, and brocades *(baiberek)* of the best Italian and Chinese sort. According to this agreement, at the outset Paulsen could import silk, dye, and other equipment and supplies to organize his enterprise; but after that he could buy materials (duty free) only from Armenian and Indian merchants. Paulsen had the right to sell his factory output "at a free price" and duty free anywhere in Russia for a ten-year period, although the tsar's agents were to have the right of first refusal at prevailing shop prices on all of Paulsen's silk goods. His cloth could be exported by paying duties specified in the New Commercial Code of 1667. Paulsen was to teach his skills to as many Russian artisans as the tsar desired, and a repayment schedule was provided whereby the entire two-thousand-ruble loan would be liquidated by the termination date of Paulsen's ten-year charter privileges.[59]

On December 12, 1681, Paulsen arrived in Novgorod with eighteen masters hired in "The Holy Roman Empire, in Hamburg and in Holland and the Spanish Netherlands," along with twelve carts of factory supplies purchased in Hamburg for three hundred rubles. On the very day he arrived in Moscow he set to work unloading and sorting his equipment, and within a short time Paulsen had organized silk manufacturing at the old *barkhatnyi dvor*. But space here soon proved so insufficient that he built another enterprise which was functioning in the Foreign Quarter by February 1683.[60]

From the very beginning failure haunted the best of Arent Paulsen's efforts. His manufactory was large and well equipped; it began its activities with a large staff of competent masters and a generous state order for silk goods valued at more than seven hundred rubles. But Paulsen was faced with a situation which would have been difficult for any entrepreneur. Bringing the masters from Western Europe cost him more than three thousand rubles, and the construction of his second factory required another 650 rubles. Apparently Paulsen turned to other foreigners in Russia (perhaps even to Butenant von Rosenbusch) for loans in order to keep his investment operating, but the only real solution to the problem was the profitable operation of the silk factory. And this is precisely what did *not* happen. After the death of Fedor in 1682, the government entered into a turbulent and unsettled situation, and the authorities left Paulsen to shift for himself. Also, for no apparent reason, orders placed in the name of the tsar were often not accepted, and at times Paulsen was not even certain which government offices he should be working for. Nor did he succeed in integrating his enterprise with the Moscow market; the reason, he said, was that the Russian merchants were jealous of him and would not accept his goods. In 1682 Paulsen requested permission to open a store of his own in the Polish section of the Moscow cloth market, but even if this were done it did not resolve his financial difficulties. [61]

Paulsen also had constant trouble with his masters. He often complained to the state of his inability to pay them their wages (which were as high as 130 and 150 rubles per year), and this may explain why many of them began to go home! Within a year (by December 1682) only eight of the original eighteen European workers remained at the silk factory. Paulsen also suffered personal conflicts with some of his employees, as, for example, on January 25, 1683, when he came to the cabin of Hans Jacob Starck, cursed and beat him, pulled his hair, and called him a thief, so that "all of the masters who lived on the dvor saw them." The final chapter in Paulsen's relations with his European masters came early in 1684, when, "with tears" in his eyes, he told his remaining men that he was helpless, that there was no work to be done, and that he was not even able to hold on to his factory any longer. Paulsen arranged for a government *ukaz* (issued June 8, 1684) permitting the masters to return home by sea. [62]

These events brought the young Russian silk industry to a crisis. In December 1684 Paulsen asked the government either to allow him to leave Russia and confiscate the factory equipment for his remaining debts, or to assume ownership of the enterprise, in which case he would remain in Moscow to weave silk and instruct Russian apprentices so that the work might continue after his eventual departure. [63] On January 13, 1685, by decree of Princess Sof'ia and Tsars Ivan and Peter, the state took control of the silk works and placed it under the jurisdiction of the *Posol'skii Prikaz,* then headed by the industry-conscious Prince Golitsyn. According to this arrangement, Paulsen was to remain at the manufactory and receive yearly wages of three hundred rubles (after a year, he would begin repaying a reduced debt of five hundred rubles) in return for making velvets, satins, and silks. He was given eight boys of humble class origins, ranging in age from twelve to fourteen, who were to help him in his work and learn the silk master's art. (Later their number was raised to twelve.) Some of these apprentices were paid as much as twenty rubles per year. A number of women were employed to unwind silk at fifty rubles per year for the entire group. [64]

The affairs of the silk factory were quite satisfactory under state ownership. Paulsen did splendid work, diligently instructed his apprentices, and seems to have efficiently managed the finances and supply of the factory. Neither he nor his helpers now found themselves in idleness! Between February 9, 1685, and February 9, 1686, the silk enterprise turned out no less than four hundred *arshins* (over 930 feet) of silk brocades. Through 1688 the demand for Paulsen's silk was so great that government institutions were hard put to supply him with enough raw material to keep pace with state orders.[65] Silk cloth from the enterprise was used by the royal court and was given to favorite *d'iaki, pod'iachie,* officers, envoys of the hetman of the Ukraine, and others. The Likhudy brothers received silk cloth for their sermons and clerical activities, as did Patriarch Ioakim, the artist Karp Zolotarev, the monk Kiril Filimov ("for his labors"), and the Novodevichii monastery. This and other evidence suggests that quality silk was produced in Moscow during these years.[66]

In September 1688 Arent Paulsen asked permission to leave Russia and return to Hamburg, asserting that his apprentices had learned their work well enough to continue manufacturing silk without him. Despite certain gaps in the knowledge of any one apprentice (five were able only to spin and dry silk), they agreed with their master's evaluation of their collective ability, though they asked that Paulsen's books in French, German, and Dutch be purchased and translated to aid them. A demonstration of the apprentices' skill in the *Posol'skii Prikaz* before Golitsyn himself convinced the prince that Paulsen could be allowed to depart, which he did by December 1689.

Now ensued the most interesting period in the history of the silk factory. The question was, could the Russians, in the absence of foreign supervision, produce a delicate commodity like silk cloth? In fact, they could. Between April 17 and October 3, 1689, Paulsen's "apprentices" wove 122 *arshins* of quality brocade. The Russian silk industry was finally indigenous and self-sustaining.[67]

Silk weaving had been established in Russia, but its cost was higher than equivalent material from the East (see p. 327, below). Just as Aleksei Mikhailovich once sponsored leather manufacturing, so the Sof'ia-Golitsyn government had been willing to pay a premium to establish a valuable new industry in Russia, the rationale for this being—again—that in the long run the costs of native production would fall to a "normal" level, at which point the national economy would begin to reap the benefits of a more diversified and highly developed industrial foundation. But in September 1689 Sof'ia was toppled from the regency, Golitsyn was exiled, and a new and more narrow economic policy was initiated by the Naryshkin family, the temporary power behind the thrones of the young co-tsars, Peter I and Ivan V. After the fall of Sof'ia's government, the Moscow silk works was promptly closed, this step occurring, to quote P. G. Liumbomirov, "in the over-all situation of the reaction against the undertakings of Sof'ia as ruler." Zaozerskaia thinks this action was shortsighted and mistaken, and she is probably correct. In any event, Russia had to wait another quarter-century for the reintroduction of silk manufacturing. Silk production began again only in 1714, as part of the industrial program of Peter the Great.[68]

When foreign merchants arrived in Russia over the northern sea route in the mid-sixteenth century, they soon realized that great profits could be made from exploitation of the country's natural resources. Foreign entrepreneurs were particularly struck by the vast forests of the Russian north, and from an early time the English sent a number of old coniferous trees home as ship masts. The Dutch were also involved in this activity, and during the 1660's a group of Russians and Amsterdamites formed a joint-stock company for the export of Russian ship-mast timber to the Netherlands, receiving from the tsar the use of forests at Sukhona for this purpose.[69]

Dutch entrepreneurs also saw an opportunity to establish sawmills in Russia and ship finished boards to the markets of Western Europe.[70] When the Dutch diplomat Massa was in Moscow in 1624, he acted as intermediary to the Russian government for three of his countrymen who asked permission to build a water-powered sawmill on the Dvina, in an area where the tsar had many forests. According to the project submitted by Jansen, Pad, and Adrians (all of whom had engaged in commerce in Russia for twenty years or more), ten Dutch masters would work at the mill and would instruct

Russian apprentices who could then use their skills to organize Russian-owned enterprises. The prospective entrepreneurs offered to pay export duty, and Massa pointed out that the Russian government could also tax future sawmills the Russians might build. In the summer of 1625 Massa promised to communicate still more information on this project to the *Posol'skii Prikaz,* but even if he did it appears that no sawmill was organized at this time.[71] Some time after this it seems that Aleksei Mikhailovich considered setting up a royal sawmill, for a report from Colonel Gustav van Kampen (dated June 25, 1666) tells of his trip to Archangel on behalf of the tsar in search of ore, mica, salt solutions, and, among other things, "a river upon which to build saw-mills for sawing wood upon the forest places themselves." But again it seems that nothing materialized from these ambitions.[72]

The first evidence of actual sawmill activity in Russia comes only during the last decade of the seventeenth century. In 1691 at least three sawmills were operating near Archangel, one of which belonged to Butenant von Rosenbusch and his two Russian partners. The charter for this mill permitted it to operate *obrok* free for an unspecified period, but duty was collected on the purchase of trees and the sale of boards according to the rates of the New Commercial *Ustav* of 1667. The partners had the right of export upon payment of twenty-six *altyn,* four *den'gi* per one hundred boards. The *gost'* Vasilii Grudtsyn also had a sawmill in the Archangel area, but its exact location is unknown and apparently it worked for only a short while. A more impressive venture was undertaken (also near Archangel) in the 1690's by the Bazhenin brothers, Osip and Fedor, whose family owned a large trading-industrial firm in the Russian north. This sawmill was organized on a "foreign model" but "without the foreign people themselves." Its scale of operation may be estimated from the fact that in 1703 the brothers obtained permission to buy and cut down four thousand trees each year, and of this number Liubomirov estimates that no fewer than 2,500 to 3,000 trees were cut into boards for export to Europe. (The remainder were probably used in the Bazhenins' ship-yard.) By any criteria, this was a large and productive sawmill.[73]

A further development in the history of water-powered sawing in Russia occurred during the 1690's in the Voronezh region, in connection with Peter's construction at Azov of the first large Russian fleet. To examine this project would carry us too far from the subject of industrial growth in the pre-Petrine period. It should be noted, however, that Peter the Great was interested in supporting sawmill technology, and even before his trip to Western Europe he invited Dutch masters to come to Russia to build and operate such enterprises and instruct Russians in the same skill. These efforts and the mills described above indicate the extent to which Russians succeeded in adopting manufacturing technique in the sawing industry during the seventeenth century.[74]

10

The Russian State's Industrial Policy

RUSSIAN MERCANTILISM DERIVED ITS specific features from those economic problems which existed after the final liquidation of Mongol rule in the late fifteenth century. From that time the state was anxious to encourage international commerce, for not only did foreign trade bring needed and otherwise unavailable goods to Russia, it often provided revenues of gold and silver from customs dues.[1] Although it was not true (as sometimes supposed) that Russian trade with the West in this period consisted solely of raw materials from Muscovy exchanged for finished products,[2] Russians did expend considerable sums on manufactured goods—especially military equipment.

While Russian statesmen accepted the necessity of such purchases, they realized that considerable amounts of precious metal left Russia to pay for them. Dissatisfaction with this situation had much to do with the consistent effort after the 1630's to encourage construction of manufactories within the country. The tsar and his officials realized that Russian indus-

172

trial enterprises of European type would provide weapons, construction materials, and luxury goods at a cheaper price and in more dependable supply than was possible through foreign trade alone. Had Russia continued to buy from the West without pursuing a parallel policy of developing home manufactures, the state's ability to wage war would have depended completely upon maintaining good relations with the more advanced nations of Western Europe. But it would have been intolerable for a large and ambitious nation such as Russia to place such a fundamental aspect of its security in the hands of forces outside its borders and far from its control. Sweden provides a good illustration of the limitations inherent in that approach: Sweden and Muscovy enjoyed cordial relations after their treaty of 1618, and Russians purchased large quantities of Swedish weapons and iron thereafter. By mid-century, however, Sweden was alarmed by Russian successes in the Ukraine, for Russia was clearly becoming a major power and threatening to upset the political equilibrium in Northern and Eastern Europe. For this reason the Swedes ceased to supply arms and ammunition ordered earlier by the Russian government, and by the fall of 1654 Charles X was even considering a "defensive" war against the Muscovites.[3] Although in such an event Holland and the German states might have been willing to continue selling military goods to the Russians, a long and destructive war might have disrupted trade routes and probably would have made large-scale commerce difficult or impossible. Recurring problems of this type made the Russian government anxious to establish domestic iron manufactories.

Also important in gaining government support for native manufactures was what proved to be largely a chimerical hope that these industries would quickly provide Russians with goods which they could then export to the West to increase the amount of silver and gold gained for Russia through foreign trade. John of Sweden used these arguments to obtain state support for his plans to establish paper, glass, and cloth manufacturing in Russia,[4] and Arent Paulsen insisted that the output of his proposed silk factory could serve as exports to Western Europe to expand the influx of precious coin into Russia.[5] The same approach was used to obtain charters and state aid by Efim Fimbrant (for a chamois factory in 1634)[6] and Egidius Tabbert (for a cloth manufactory in February 1683), and in the latter case a government report subsequently expressed pride over the fact that a new industry had been successfully established in Russia.[7] Similarly, a discussion of the development of the Russian copper industry prepared for Tsar Fedor Alekseevich by the *Posol'skii Prikaz* (dated March 26, 1677) exclaims enthusiastically, "There will be glory unto the great sovereign and the Muscovite state, in that copper factories are being built, of which earlier there were none." This document is cognizant of the job-creating character of industry, and observes that, in previous years, cannon, projectiles, grenades, "and all other sorts of military supplies" were obtained from abroad, and at a high price. "But now all this originates in the Russian lands, and the money remains for peace." For all these reasons, the author of the memorandum urged the tsar to support the development of iron and copper works, noting that "other states are enriched by metallurgical factories."[8]

Russian mercantilism was not, however, the product of a clearly defined or consistently applied economic theory, for Russian statesmen in this period operated in a pragmatic, sometimes contradictory manner, and J. L. H. Keep has noted that an "unwillingness to consider broader issues and to take decisions on matters of principle"[9] was particularly characteristic of Muscovite officialdom throughout the seventeenth century. But the industrial policy which did develop throughout the sixteenth and seventeenth centuries may best be understood by studying the factory charters of this period. These documents not only state the rights of entrepreneurs and the expectations of the government, they also provide clues as to why the tsar and his officials acted in certain ways when faced with certain problems.

Here a word of warning is in order, for students of Russian

factory charters of this period should not interpret the "rights" they set forth in a rigid manner. The essential feature of Russian absolutism at this time was that no person possessed rights *against* the sovereign. The "rights" specified in factory charters actually represented little more than a general understanding of probable duties and privileges of a manufacturer before the Russian state. The realization of any charter always depended upon final agreement of the sovereign. For example, even though Julius Coyet's charter gave him the right to go abroad for glass workers (and the government wanted him to do this), when an occasion for such a trip actually arose Coyet was forced to petition the tsar (May 4, 1639) for permission to set out. In another instance Coyet had to obtain formal leave of the sovereign to bring from Pskov to Moscow men engaged on a journey abroad.[10] Similarly, on August 24, 1675, Petr Marselis asked Aleksei Mikhailovich to allow him to export a shipment of iron goods through Archangel,[11] though the Marselises' right to do this was clearly set forth in every charter they had ever received from any tsar. Despite complaints over the inconveniences and delays caused by this kind of bureaucratic control,[12] the system of issuing travel passes and export permits only through special petition of the interested entrepreneur continued to the end of the seventeenth century.[13]

Charters permitting the establishment of manufactories were granted to those who had approached the court with petitions embodying—and justifying—specific proposals. These would-be capitalists were generally foreign merchants, although in a few cases masters such as Julius Coyet and Arent Paulsen requested and obtained state approval for manufacturing. The Russian government was much more reluctant to support the entrepreneurial ambitions of nonaristocratic Russians during the seventeenth century, perhaps because these men did not have much personal influence at court.

One of the first issues to be settled between the government and a prospective entrepreneur was the location of the suggested enterprise. According to Russian law of the sixteenth and seventeenth centuries, "unbaptized foreigners" had no right to own land. But foreigners could rent land according to agreement with individual nobles, and in other cases the state provided sites for the location and raw-material needs of manufactories (specific land grants might even be listed in factory charters). Such lands were, in effect, *pomestia:* given for the duration of factory tenure and operation. When and if the original connection between the manufacturer and the enterprise ceased, all the land in question unconditionally returned to the original owner.[14]

The rights of the foreign capitalist to the machinery and buildings of the factory presented a different legal problem, for these parts of the enterprise directly embodied the entrepreneur's own personal investment and thus gained a certain respect from government authorities. For example, although Julius Coyet's charter (dated May 31, 1634) specified that if he left Russia the land of his glass works would revert to the tsar, the state also assured him that in such a case he would be reimbursed for buildings and equipment at the valuation of a *prikaz* inspector whom the tsar would appoint at that time.[15] This sort of guarantee was most common in the iron industry. A state document of 1665 promised Filimon Akema that in case of the dissolution of his iron mill he and his heirs would be paid for all iron goods, factory buildings, and machinery.[16] A similar provision was made in a charter of March 15, 1674, issued to the male heirs of Peter Marselis.[17] Nevertheless, property "rights" were never absolute in early modern Russia. Earlier we have noted dramatic—and sometimes arbitrary—confiscations of manufactories. Limitations on the use of some enterprises were actually spelled out in their charters. Often manufacturers could not sell or mortgage their interests or create new partnerships without special permission of the tsar. Paulsen's charter provided that he could not sell or destroy his *dvor* without prior agreement of the sovereign.[18]

The Russian manufacturer of the seventeenth century used political influence, whenever possible, to obtain monopoly rights. Manufacturing in Russia was still a new and largely undeveloped form of economic activity, the size of the exchange market and the needs of the government sometimes small and always uncertain, skilled workers few, the productivity of labor low, and vital raw materials might become unavailable at any time. For these and other reasons it was natural for such pioneering capitalists as Andrei Vinius, Akema, and Marselis to strive to eliminate competition and attain a degree of stability which would produce a profitable and long life for the enterprises they built with such considerable expenditures of time, labor, and capital.

The factory charter obtained by Andrei Vinius in 1632 granted him and his partners a ten-year monopoly on this type of iron production for the entire Russian empire. The exclusiveness of this type of monopoly, however, was broken in 1644 when Marselis and Akema also obtained the right to manufacture iron on the Vaga river. After this, iron manufactory charters were usually issued for twenty years or more, but they no longer guaranteed their holders absolute national "monopolies." To the extent that the word appeared in later charters, it seems to have reserved such manufacturing privileges to the factory owner only in the particular area in which his enterprise was to be located. Thus a charter granted by Aleksei Mikhailovich in 1676 stated:

> And wherever such [iron] ores will be found on any sort of votchina and otchina and monastery lands, agreements [may be concluded] freely with the owners for obrok. All sorts of factories may be constructed without hindrance. And wherever [your] factories will be established, no others may construct [iron] ore factories in those uezdy.[19]

Likewise, although Julius Coyet received a fifteen-year monopoly on glass manufacturing during the 1630's throughout Russia, by mid-century it was no longer government practice to issue such exclusive rights to a single entrepreneur. Therefore, when Egidius Tarbet requested a twenty-year monopoly on cloth production in the Muscovite state, his charter of 1684 provided only ten years of tax-free factory activity with no reference to his desire for monopoly rights.

The discrepancy between Tarbet's petition and the privileges granted him also reveals an interesting and consistent difference in the government's attitude toward metallurgical and nonmetallurgical industries. Iron manufacturers, though not blessed with privileges of absolute monopoly, were consistently treated in a more generous way than the organizers of "light" industries. In 1669 Marselis requested and received thirty-year metallurgical privileges on the Tsyl'ma river and in Olonetskii *uezd;* in 1681 the *Prikaz Bol'shogo Dvortsa* leased the three Zvenigorodskie iron factories to Vladimir Voronin for no less than twenty-five years. By contrast, John of Sweden petitioned in 1668 for thirty years of *obrok*-free paper production; provision was made only for a ten-year period. Butenant von Rosenbusch's sawmill of the 1690's, it is true, was to operate *obrok*-free for an unlimited period, but unlike iron manufacturers he had to pay *poshlina* (trade duty) both on materials purchased and products sold, charges being levied according to the New Commercial Code of 1667:

The most standard feature of a seventeenth-century Russian factory charter was provision for a period of industrial activity free of tax *(obrok)* and trade duty *(poshlina)*. The length of those periods for iron manufactories ran from seven to thirty years, twenty years being more or less the average figure after mid-century; charters for paper, cloth, silk, and glass factories usually granted ten years of tax- and duty-free activity.[20] Many factory charters also promised royal forbearance in the event of natural calamities. Privileges given on March 15, 1674, to Peter Marselis' sons specified, for example, a reduction of delivery obligations in case the iron factories fell victim to fire, breaking of dams, or exhaustion of local ore supply. The 1681 charter of the Olonets iron mill also reflected such policy. Butenant and his partners were promised that periods of factory inactivity caused by fire, flood, or difficulties in ore supply would not be counted as part of the time in which their iron factories were to be exempt from payment of *obrok* and *poshlina*.[21]

Besides relief from taxes and trade duties, the Russian state during the seventeenth century provided entrepreneurs with subsidies and loans. Andrei Vinius once received an annual advance of three thousand rubles for his iron factories at Tula (and another three thousand rubles when Marselis and Akema came into the partnership), with the understanding that he would repay the government during the coming year either with factory products or *efimki* gained through the export of iron commodities to Western Europe. On one occasion, in 1667, Peter Marselis received a loan as large as five thousand rubles for the expansion of his factory. Small loans were still more common. On December 21, 1683, Butenant and Christian Marselis obtained one thousand rubles from the local state finances of Olonets.[22] When John of Sweden died in 1668 he left behind him an accumulation of debts to the state which reached 2,948 rubles. The case of van Sweeden suggests that the Russian government in this period was far more willing to make loans to iron entrepreneurs (whose activities strengthened the armed forces) than to capitalists involved in light industry: Maria van Sweeden's request for a three-thousand-ruble loan to finish her late husband's projected paper, cloth, and glass factories was rejected by Aleksei Mikhailovich, who loaned John's widow a paltry six hundred rubles for completion of the paper factory alone.

Some entrepreneurs found the government offices and *prikazy* slow in settling their debts for goods they ordered. On many occasions Peter Marselis had to ask the tsar to instruct the officials whose orders Marselis filled to pay him the money they owed (once the sum reached 1,360 rubles).[23] Sometimes in these petitions Marselis would even hint at possible delays in factory work if money was not soon available to pay his workers and maintain and repair the factories.[24] The tardy payment policy of the government certainly had much to do with the fact that just before he lost his iron works in 1662, Marselis relied increasingly upon export, though this created another problem between him and the government: he stalled on royal commissions, filled them in part or not at all — much to the dissatisfaction of the government.[25] But in fact Marselis was well within his rights. Most factory charters of this period gave their holders the option of exporting their goods to any country enjoying good relations with the tsar, a privilege theoretically contingent upon the particular manufactory fully satisfying government orders for that calendar year. The low cost of production in Russia meant that, through export, capitalists could sometimes gain higher profits than by placing goods on the Russian market with its relatively modest price levels. And since foreign coin gained through international commerce had to be exchanged at the Russian mint for Muscovite currency, the export of Russian-manufactured products was usually satisfactory from the point of view of Russian mercantilists.

The Russian iron industry gained at least some profits through foreign trade. As early as 1646-1647 the Tula works shipped 960 cannon to Dutch markets. On August 24, 1675, Petr Petrovich Marselis requested permission to export a large inventory of military equipment which included 116 cannon weighing nearly 2,000 *puds,* 20,614 cannon balls weighing 3,456 *puds,* 2,934 hand grenades, 2,456 musket barrels, 2,700 sword blades, 9,614 *puds* of rod-iron, and seventy-two *puds* of "thin iron for chains." Butenant von Rosenbusch exported almost 10,000 *puds* of iron commodities through Archangel in 1683 – 1685. The scale of this international commerce was great enough to attract the attention of a cleric-traveler such as Paul of Aleppo, who observed:

> They transport a great number of cannon in the winter on sleds and take them a distance of 1,700 versts in the course of about 40 days to the port of Archangel, where there is the sea, the ocean, and they sell [these cannon] to foreigners, who take them them to their country.[26]

Since both foreign masters and Russian workers were needed for the construction and operation of manufactories, Russian law (as reaffirmed in Article 70 of the Law Code of 1649) permitted foreigners to employ the labor of people "of all different faiths."[27] The expense of bringing workers from abroad was so great, however, that more positive forms of government assistance were often extended to capitalists for this purpose, ranging from special loans to pay the masters' wage-advances and travel expenses to providing carts and horses for the foreigners and their families.* A state document of March 15, 1674, even refers to a system of labor control whereby a master, submaster, or worker at the Marselis Tula-Kashirskie-Aleksinskii iron factories could not be hired at Akema's Porotovskii-Ugodskii iron works (or vice versa) "without written leave" from the original employer. (This provision was also valid "for new factories which will be [constructed].") The government report which discusses this policy implies that it was related to the extreme cost and effort of bringing workers from abroad; the most powerful capitalists did not wish to see their valuable masters and apprentices lured away to another enterprise by some rival who, not having made the large investment in bringing workers to Russia, could then offer them higher wages and better working conditions. "Anti-enticing away" regulations based upon the desire for stable factory labor forces were applied to Butenant's Olonets manufactories in 1678 and 1681, and to other iron enterprises during the last third of the seventeenth century.[28]

The state provided workmen to build and aid in the operation of new manufactories as another aspect of its industrial policy.[29] This type of assistance included manpower for initial construction, ascribing peasants for unskilled labor once the enterprise began to function, and assigning state artisans on a temporary basis to assist in orders of particular concern to the government, especially if the factory proved incapable of filling that order with its normal staff. An illustration of the first type of aid is the charter issued for the Olonets iron works by the *Posol'skii Prikaz* to van der Gaten and Petr Petrovich

---

*In 1661 the tsar permitted Peter Marselis to spend 2,000 *Joachimsthalers* in Holland to recruit iron masters, a very large sum for that time (Kuzin, *Istoriia otkrytii*, p. 25). This demonstrates not only the tremendous cost of importing labor into Russia; the willingness of the Russian government to lose such a large amount of foreign specie indicates the extent to which they wished to develop home manufacturing. The money belonged to Marselis, of course, but he nonetheless needed royal permission for such an expenditure of bullion outside Russia.

Marselis (dated August 5, 1675), in which the partners were promised "*strel'tsy* and cannon-smiths and ore-prospectors, as many as would be advantageous," for the construction of iron manufactories. According to this agreement, the state would also supply cavalry and foot soldiers "for protection from thievish people," along with river craft, rowers, helmsmen, and guides—in all cases as many as needed. On January 14, 1676, van der Gaten petitioned for the use of state *iam* carts in order to transport equipment and supplies from Moscow to the ore sites of the far northeast; ten days later this request was also granted.[30]

From the 1630's to the 1690's the Russian government often ascribed villages of state peasants to nearby factories to assure these enterprises of fuel supply, transport, and so forth. According to Russian law, however, no unbaptized foreigner could actually own serfs,[31] so that peasants involved in factory work of this sort remained under legal jurisdiction of the original owner, whether it was the tsar or a local monastery or nobleman who had reached an agreement with a foreigner-capitalist whereby the manufacturer assumed control over a certain number of peasants. In such situations the foreigner could claim the labor power of "his" serfs only for the duration of his factory charter.[32]

The tsar also sent his own artisans to foreign-owned factories in need of extra labor. As we have seen, Arent Paulsen gradually lost his foreign masters, and after January 1685 was assisted only by twelve young Russian apprentices. This "command" system was even more common in the iron industry. On one occasion in 1674 Aleksei Mikhailovich commanded Petr Petrovich Marselis to make halberds and "sapping equipment" "quickly," and in September Marselis petitioned the tsar to help him with the order by providing—as in the past for rush orders—ironsmiths and equipment from Tula and other Russian cities. Specifically, Marselis asked the tsar to instruct the local *voevoda* to send "to the Tula and Kashirskie iron factories 20 iron smiths with bellows and with complete iron smiths' equipment," promising, as earlier, to feed the men at the factory. The tsar dispatched the artisans as requested. At another time in 1680 five rifle-lock masters with apprentices were dispatched from the Dvina to Tula because the factories there had failed to meet their production quotas.[33]

Almost all factory charters of the sixteenth and seventeenth centuries specified that the owners must use their foreign masters to instruct Russian apprentices in all the skills of iron manufacturing, glass-blowing, silk weaving, or whatever. (In fact, foreigners who petitioned the tsar for permission to build a manufactory commonly held out the assurance of such training as an example of how their enterprises would strengthen the country.) Russian statesmen saw clearly that the knowledge monopoly of these ambitious foreigners made them indispensable to the technologically advanced forms of production they had created, so factory owners were able to demand high profits and force concessions such as tax and trade-duty exemptions, and subsidies — all of which made capitalist development more costly for the state than it might otherwise have been. The long-term objective of the tsars was to establish factories owned by Russians and operated by Russian workmen. For this reason the foreigner, both as a capitalist and as a master, was viewed as a means by which this "industrialization" process could be set in motion.

In some industries (rope and silk, for example) the foreign entrepreneurs seemed quite willing to educate their Russian apprentices, and even to put their enterprises entirely in the hands of native workers.[34] But this was not always the case, least of all with iron manufacturing. Here foreigners recognized the need to defend the esoteric nature of their craft lest an already precarious position be altogether lost. The high wages of Western masters and the profits of their employers dictated a mutual interest in excluding Russian apprentices from the more complex and demanding phases of the production process. In this sense the struggle for ultimate control over Russian manufacturing was waged between the foreign capitalist and the Russian state through the masters of the former and the apprentices of the latter. In some cases Russians learned the skills involved in the industries to which they were assigned, but it was far more common for European craftsmen to occupy their Russian understudies with subsidiary tasks, thus assuring that a monopoly of true skills would remain in their hands. Thus it is no surprise to learn that a famous metallurgist like Hans Falk sent Russians from the scene whenever he came to the most important parts of his work, and the same practice was pursued by masters working for Vinius, Akema, Marselis, and the other iron entrepreneurs of seventeenth-century Russia. Surely the natural ability and ingenuity of the Russian craftsman (a "national trait" much commented upon by such foreign travelers as Herberstein, Barberini, Olearius, and Christopher Manstein) made secrecy all the more imperative from the point of view of foreign workers and capitalists.*

One of the strongest indications of the importance attached by the Russian government to the development of manufacturing is the extent to which royal legislation consistently defended the economic interests of factory owners against all who caused them difficulty — whether ascribed peasants, local officials, or uncooperative provincial nobles. And there were

---

*I admit to being puzzled by a certain contradiction in this historical question. If Russian artisans and apprentices attached to the iron manufactories were unable to use manufactory technology, then why did the Marselis family sometimes petition (in the manner just described above) for the loan of Russian artisan-masters to help them handle rush orders, large orders, etc.? Perhaps the secret of manufactory technology was not really so great. Perhaps an observant and experienced Russian artisan could have learned Western techniques in a matter of weeks. We have instances, in fact, of Russians being trained by Vinius and Marselis, though their number does not appear to have been great.

Another explanation is always possible: perhaps Russian artisans *could* work the manufactories, but not as well as trained European masters. Heinrich Butenant von Rosenbusch's Olonets factories suggest this, since he began iron manufacturing with local men but steadily replaced them with workers engaged in the West. But if this explanation is valid, then why were the foreigners so hesitant to instruct Russian understudies? It seems to me that sufficient evidence is not available to solve all the aspects of this problem.

frequent arguments and conflicts of class interest between various manufacturers (especially the Marselis family) and all these groups of people. The best example is perhaps the protracted and savage conflicts between foreign entrepreneurs and the peasants of Foimogubskaia *volost'* in the far north, each of whom claimed the land and its resources as their own. Despite repeated affirmations by the tsar and his officials of the rights of the foreigners in the area, throughout the late 1670's and 1680's the peasants refused to surrender "their" land and to stop harassing the factory and its workers. They swore to defend to the death what they felt to be theirs,[35] and on one occasion even concluded among themselves a written pledge "to not betray each other, to stand firmly by each other," a fine of thirty rubles being specified for anyone breaking the agreement![36] Soldiers intervened on various occasions, but conflict recurred during the 1690's, and it appears that the iron manufactories of this area never operated in an orderly or continuous manner.

Trouble between peasants and the Marselises occurred even in the Tula area, though here disputes did not revolve around the question of land ownership so much as around issues related to work at the factory itself. Royal serfs ascribed to the Tula iron works found their work difficult and unpleasant and their pay low, and by the early 1670's their dissatisfactions began to show. On September 3, 1672, the Marselis family submitted a petition to the tsar stating that the dam of the Vedmenskii factory had been damaged, and that when the peasants of Solomenskaia *volost'* were summoned to fulfill their obligations and repair it, the "old insurgents" *(buntovshchiki)* "Lar'ka Osipov of Alekseevaia village and Vaska Titov, nicknamed the mutt [*kobel'*], of Bogatkovaia village and Ivashka Mikheev of Zolotikha village" induced the peasants not to go to work, "so that our factories will be destroyed." Captain Dmitrii Bitiagovskii arrived in Solomenskaia six days later, on September 9, with orders to convince the peasants to work, or failing that to mete out "cruel punishment." He actually persuaded the peasants to carry out the foreigners' instructions, but trouble soon broke out again and the peasants refused to serve the factory and even petitioned the tsar (unsuccessfully) for a relief of their burdens. Thus began a stormy "strike" period in which the peasantry stopped transporting fuel and ore, the factory stood idle, and the Marselis family "suffered great losses because the masters were not [able to work] but during the idle days the foreigners took money according to their contracts." Apparently this dispute lasted through the winter of 1672–1673. We also have reports of "disobedient" miners at Tula and Kashira in 1657 refusing to work until orders were reissued by the tsar.[37]

Skilled factory workers did not participate in the disorders at Solomenskaia *volost'* but appear in contemporary accounts of these events only as witnesses.[38] This is probably because the position of masters and even apprentices in iron manufactories was good for the age, certainly better than that of ascribed peasants. Marselis paid the supervisor of his factory three hundred rubles annually,[39] while foreign masters received as much as 280 rubles. Even Russians inside the enterprise were free men who earned from 60 to 120 rubles a year plus free dwellings and regular bread and salt allotments.[40] Thus factory workers were likely to be more satisfied than ascribed serfs, though even the latter did not flock (as one might expect) to join the great peasant uprising of 1667 when Stenka Razin's lieutenant, Vasilii Us, passed through the Tula area[41] — indicating, perhaps, that for all their dissatisfactions factory serfs were not as badly off as others in the area.

Theoretically, local government officials such as *prikaz* clerks and *voevody* were available — in line with the tsar's policy of encouraging industrialization — to help manufactory owners in their areas. Many iron factory charters stated that it was the duty of the local *voevoda* to protect the enterprises, not levy taxes or duties or "carry out injuries to them," not hinder the masters or workers at the factories, nor fasten other obligations upon factory personnel.[42] In order to guarantee the inviolability of iron enterprises from the whims or hostility of local officials, such factory charters gave *voevody* the right to try the factory owners and their employees only for minor disorderly conduct. More serious charges against capitalists or their masters and peasants would be heard in the *Posol'skii Prikaz*,[43] where the defendants would not only be assured fair-minded and qualified judges, but where statesmen appreciating the importance of European industries to national development could be expected to give foreign capitalists a broad latitude of action.

Despite the theoretical obligations of local *voevody,* the Marselis family had trouble with government officials who apparently did not consider factory work to be as important as other seemingly insignificant activities. For example, a petition submitted on December 9, 1668, tells us that *voevoda* Skryptsyn of Dedilov took the fifty miners working for Akema and Marselis from their pits and sent them to the *voevoda* of nearby Bogoroditskoe to assist in bread-making. Traditionally these men did alternate between iron mining and agricultural work, but they were always occupied with the former between December 1 and March 1 "because to carry [ore] through the steppe for several measures by spring route is impossible." For some reason in this case the Bogoroditskoe *voevoda* needed help early and gained assistance from his fellow *voevoda* at Dedilov—all of which, of course, brought factory work at Tula to a sudden halt and triggered a series of shrill petitions from Peter Marselis begging the tsar to order his *voevody* to send the workers back to the mines. Interestingly enough, the tsar sent repeated instructions to that effect, but local officials resisted his commands for at least two months. Five years later a similar problem arose for Marselis when the *voevoda* of Dedilov sent the fifty miners of the iron factories (along with 380 other local people) to Voronezh for shipbuilding. A petition of January 31, 1674, brought the men back to digging ore.[44]

Local officials also bothered the Marselises by trying to collect trade duties despite their charter exemptions from *poshlina*. This happened to Peter Marselis in 1669, and in 1674 the three *gosti* responsible for collecting these levies attempted to exact from his sons no fewer than 1,075 rubles, which they claimed was the unpaid total owed for all years since 1668. In each case a royal *ukaz* defended the Marselises' free-trade privileges. Customs officials at Archangel also made efforts to assess duties on the Marselises' iron exports in October 1683 and the fall of 1684 – but again Moscow reaffirmed their charter rights to free export.[45]

Although the government was able to coerce peasants and local officials into supporting the operation of manufactories, it was less successful in forcing provincial nobles to cooperate with the industrialization effort. Not that efforts were lacking to expand the metallurgical base of the country by ordering all "prikaz officials, priests, village elders and tseloval'niki" to bring pieces of ore and even "unfamiliar stones" to their provincial or urban *voevody*. Those finding ores were promised rewards, just as landowners who concealed deposits on their holdings were threatened with severe punishment. But landlords in seventeenth-century Russia actively opposed prospecting, for it appears that royal assurances to the contrary notwithstanding, it was generally believed that the tsar would simply confiscate land which proved valuable for industrial work. Thus, although there exist numerous accounts of ordinary peasants reporting discoveries of mica and metals in response to the decrees and incentives coming from Moscow, there are also instances of nobles murdering peasants who cooperated with the tsar's prospectors.[46]

In fact, Russian statesmen at this time *were* quite willing to sacrifice *pomeshchik* interests to assure industrial progress. The Marselis-van der Gaten charter of 1675, for example, not only permitted the foreigners to seek the assistance of serfs in the areas in which they prospected, but warned that anyone hindering this work would be "in disgrace and fined and under severe punishments. . . ." The capitalists also had the right of eminent domain over ore-bearing lands, so that agreements for iron mining and manufacturing would be concluded quickly and "without any kind of arguments. . . ."[47] Similar government support to Heinrich Butenant von Rosenbusch in 1681 gave him permission to go through *pomeshchik* and *votchinik* lands surrounding the Olonets iron works to transport iron or wood to the factories.[48] Apparently the reaction of those landlords suffering from Butenant's transportation routes was of no concern to Tsar Fedor or his advisers! In other situations, however, government officials were less generous in their land allotment policy. The Müller charter of April 29, 1695, for example, stated that the Müller family could not build new factories in areas that would block long-established and well-traveled roads or rivers with heavy river traffic.[49]

An important aspect of the *prikaz* system of state administration was the management of the various economic enterprises belonging to the tsar.* The *Prikaz Bol'shogo Dvortsa* managed the tsar's personal economic enterprises and estates.

* The *prikazy* began to function in the late fifteenth century and operated until most were replaced by "colleges" at the time of Peter the Great. Many *prikazy* were characterized by a combination of judicial, administrative, and financial functions. Some governed specific areas of the Russian state (*e.g., Galitskii p.*, operating from the 1570's–1680, responsible for governing twenty-two or twenty-five cities with their *uezdy:* Galich, Beloozero, Shuia, etc.; *Novgorodskii p.*, 1560's–1720; *Sibirskii p.*, 1637–1763; etc.). Some *prikazy* were responsible for administering definite activities of interest to the state (*Aptekarskii p.*, 1594–1714; *p. gorodskogo dela*, 1638–1644; *Inozemskii p.*, 1624–1701; *Posol'skii p.*, 1549–1720 — responsible, respectively, for medical-pharmaceutical institutions and their staffs; construction of fortifications in the south; engaging, supervising, and paying foreigners in state service; and foreign affairs. Many *prikazy* collected various taxes, trade dues, special levies, etc. (*p. bol'shogo prikhoda*, 1554-1699; *p. bol'shoi kazni*, 1621–1718); other *prikazy* had mainly judicial functions (*sudnyi dvortsovyi p.*, 1664–1709, handled judicial affairs of state servants at the palace, etc.). Such *prikazy* as *p. sbora streletskogo khleba* (1672–1697) and *p. sbora ratnykh liudei* (1637–1654) had distinct military responsibilities.

Despite numerous reorganizations and attempts to unify several *prikazy* under the directorship of a particularly talented statesman, the *prikazy* never worked efficiently — probably because their powers and responsibilities were poorly defined and their lines of authority overlapped considerably in many cases. *Prikazy* were under the direct authority of the tsar and the Boyar Duma. *Boyars* or *okol'nichie* usually headed *prikazy*, though most of the real work was carried on by *d'iaki* and *pod'iachie* (clerks and subclerks), whose number varied from three to 400 according to the importance of the individual *prikaz*. At the end of the sixteenth century there were twenty-two *prikazy;* by the mid-1600's the number of permanent and temporary *prikazy* had grown to eighty.

It was especially important at the time of Michael Romanov, but as the royal economy expanded in later years Aleksei Mikhailovich became so dissatisfied with the heavy bureaucracy and overall inefficiency of the *Bol'shogo Dvortsa* that after 1663 he handed the responsibility for many economic enterprises over to another administrative institution, the *Prikaz Tainykh Del,* a "privy chancellery" which had been created in 1654 to improve (through the exercise of extraordinary powers) the functioning of leading government political institutions in Moscow.[50] The *Tainyi Prikaz* was especially interested in the affairs of the state-owned Zvenigorodskie iron works, and on many occasions *pod'iachie* from the *prikaz* would stay at the factories to be certain they operated well and filled government orders on time. Every month the iron enterprises sent a certain inventory of iron goods to the *Tainyi Prikaz,* which in turn distributed these products to royal estates and artisan workshops, as needed.[51] In other instances the *Tainyi Prikaz* simply ordered the Zvenigorodskie manufactories to dispatch equipment to specified destinations, as we can see, for example, from a *prikaz* order of February 15, 1663, to send to

Skopkin and Romanov:	250 plows [*sokhi*], 50 heavy plows,[52] 300 axes, 300 scythes
Pakhra:	300 plows, 300 heavy plows, 1,800 axes, 1,400 scythes, 1,000 trail spades [*soshniki*]
Izmailovo:	100 plows, 200 heavy plows, 400 axes, 600 scythes, 600 trail spades
Chashnikovo:	100 plows, 200 heavy plows, 400 axes, 600 scythes, 200 trail spades[53]

The *Prikaz Tainykh Del* also used the Zvenigorodskie factories to provide one hundred curved iron boards for supporting corner beams in cathedrals at Moscow; rod-iron for royal salt factories at Pereiaslavl' and Rostov (one hundred *puds*) and a potash works at Semenovskoe (five *puds*); three hundred *puds* of rod-iron to boyar Ivan Miloslavskii; and so forth. The *Tainyi Prikaz* supplied the Zvenigorodskie enterprises with equipment they needed—such as twenty barrels of lime "on loan" from the Savinskoi monastery or two thousand roofing boards from the *Pushkarskii Prikaz*. Wages and operating expenses were obtained by the *prikaz* official in charge of the Zvenigorodskie factories (himself paid two hundred rubles a year) from the funds of the *Tainyi Prikaz*.[54]

The *prikaz* system was also relevant to the activity of privately owned factories that did work for the government. State orders originated from a particular *prikaz* which needed equipment from a certain factory. Since the *Pushkarskii Prikaz* was the department to distribute artillery and other weapons from the iron works to the Russian Army, it often "supervised" the operation of these manufactories to be certain they filled orders properly and functioned in the interests of the state. Transfers of enterprises from one *prikaz* to another were common, sometimes because leading statesmen decided another *prikaz* needed the factory output or could administer its affairs in a more efficient manner,[55] sometimes because the entrepreneurs themselves petitioned for a change, thinking their interests would be better served by another *prikaz*. Thus at various times the Tula-Kashira iron works (to cite only one example) were "directed" by the *Bol'shoi Kazny, Tainyi Prikaz, Oruzheinaia palata, Bol'shoi dvor, Pushkarskii Prikaz, and Posol'skii Prikaz*.[56] Iron works and other enterprises were often under the jurisdiction of the *Posol'skii Prikaz,* because such heads of that chancellery as Ordin-Nashchokin, Matveev, Golitsyn, and Naryshkin (the latter for reasons of personal aggrandizement) saw the relationship between foreign trade and military production and international diplomacy and were personally desirous of using their power to foster Russia's industrial development. Foreigners also liked to be under the *Posol'skii Prikaz* because the officials there understood Western norms and favored the activity of European entrepreneurs.

The local *voevoda* was an important element in linking the affairs of the iron factories with the *prikazy* in Moscow.

Sometimes (as in the case of six light cannon and two hundred projectiles for the ship *Orel* on April 24, 1668), it was actually the *voevoda* at Tula who, on instructions from the capital, placed an order at the iron works and was responsible for providing necessary transport facilities to the specified destination. Even when factory orders originated in Moscow, however, the *voevody* were usually responsible for transportation of finished commodities from the enterprises, as well as for transport of raw materials to the factory, operation of the iron ore miners, and the like. Arguments often occurred between *prikaz* officials and Peter Marselis over who should bear the expense of factory deliveries, and sometimes (for example, a dispute involving two thousand carts in the winter of 1669–1670) goods were not moved until carts were finally provided on terms demanded by Marselis.[57]

11

Activities of the Foreigner in Early Modern Russia

THE ROLE OF THE foreigner in Russia during the sixteenth and seventeenth centuries involved activities which ranged from medicine to warfare, from shipbuilding to the organization of a modern international post. While this subject bears its own intrinsic interest and importance, it is also relevant to the origins of capitalism because many men then prominent as manufacturers were engaged in entrepreneurial pursuits not strictly related to manufacturing. As we shall see, the "foreigner" in Russia at this time was typically an agent who sought his fortune by providing a variety of skills and services to patrons who needed them all so badly that irresistible pressures were generated for those who could do so to transcend the narrow horizons of specialization. Thus in seventeenth-century Russia we often observe a diversity of function which in Western Europe was even then rapidly becoming the charming aspect of a bygone age.

There is a striking parallel between the problems of the

Russian army and the state economy during the sixteenth and seventeenth centuries. New diplomatic opportunities in this period put pressures on the existing artisan system which could not be resolved within the traditional technological framework. Similarly, the Russian army — backward in organization and haphazard in training* — was unable to withstand the forces of Poland, Lithuania, and Sweden, which were fewer in numbers but trained and equipped for precise maneuvering and concentrated attack on the battlefield. Therefore, just as the Russians turned to the Western maritime powers for military equipment, so the tsars attempted to strengthen their armies by recruiting mercenary regiments capable of meeting Russia's enemies on their own level of military proficiency. Possibly the first Muscovite ruler to use foreign troops in this way was Vasilii III (1505-1533), who employed some fifteen hundred Lithuanians and "foreign riff-raff" *(vsiakii prishlyi sbrod)* against the Tatars in units which, according to Kliuchevskii, "clearly . . . had a character quite distinct from infantry formations used up until this time, [so

---

*Russian army units at this time were raised, trained, and equipped through the feudal relationships which existed between noblemen and the tsar, on the one hand, and noblemen and their peasants, on the other. For this reason, when estate holders presented themselves for campaign with "horses, men, and arms," their armed hosts resembled mobs or brigand armies rather than disciplined military formations. This system also produced shirking of duty, for many nobles were late in preparing for action and some might not appear until the end of the fighting. The only professional regiments of Russian nationality in the early seventeenth century were the *strel'tsy* (musketeers), who numbered between 20,000 and 26,000 around the 1630's, including some 2,500 or 3,000 cavalry. But the *strel'tsy* scarcely produced a transformation of Russia's fighting power, so Fletcher was being harsh but not unfair in saying that "The Russe trusteth rather to his number, than to the value of his souldiers, or good ordering of his forces." And sometimes even that would not be sufficient to carry the day, as for example in 1563, when four thousand Poles defeated Prince Kurbskii and his army of fifteen thousand men. N. Ustrialov, *Istoriia tsarstvovaniia Petra Velikago* [History of the reign of Peter the Great] (St. Petersburg, 1863), I, 176; Carl B. O'Brien, "Agriculture in Russian War Economy in the Later Seventeenth Century," *American Slavic and East European Review,* VIII (1949), 170; Berry, *English Works of Giles Fletcher,* p. 241 (see also p. 183); Fletcher's statements are similar to observations on the same subject by Herberstein, *Notes upon Russia,* I, 97, 98.

much so that one might think that with these regiments] the basis was laid for the formation of a permanent infantry in the Muscovite army." Giles Fletcher noted almost 4,300 foreign mercenaries in Russia in the late 1580's, of whom 4,000 were Ukrainian Cossacks, 150 Dutch and Scots, and *"Greeks, Turks, Danes and Sweadens,* all in one band, and 100. or thereabouts." Boris Godunov had a German company as his personal bodyguard (still larger units were also used by later tsars of the seventeenth century), and these men remained loyal to him to the very end of his unfortunate reign. The false Dmitrii and Vasilii Shuiskii made use of foreign units during the Time of Troubles, and in 1610 the Russians employed six thousand mercenaries originally in Swedish service to good effect against the Poles in the Nizhnyi-Novgorod area.[1]

Mikhail Romanov came to the throne at a propitious time for the hiring of mercenaries. The Thirty Years' War (1618–1648) unsettled the life-pattern of Central Europe and provoked many men to seek livelihood and adventure beyond the borders of their own countries. Hoards of soldiers moved across Germany seeking employment wherever and from whomever it might be advantageous — not excepting the tsar of distant Muscovy. And the Russians did not hesitate to take advantage of opportunities presented by this situation. The tsar ordered Colonel Alexander Lesly, an English soldier in the tsar's service, on January 25, 1631, to travel abroad and hire five thousand "good" soldiers, two or three colonels, and the necessary captains to command such a force. Lesly recruited at least 2,200 men in northern Germany, while another colonel in Russian service, van Dama, raised a regiment of 1,760 men in Western Europe.[2]

But just as the Russians proved unable to rely on the import of foreign commodities to solve their industrial problems, so too they found mercenary regiments to be an unsatisfactory means of coping with their military shortcomings. The five thousand mercenaries raised by Lesly, van Dama, and others were competent soldiers, but during the siege of Smolensk in

1634—to cite only one example—some of the foreigners crossed over to the Poles while others introduced insubordination and disorder in the Russian ranks. And after the battle some of these foreigners pillaged the local population so badly that even after their departure, as Olearius passed through the area, a number of peasants fled from the approach of his diplomatic party, doubtless because the villagers assumed these foreigners were also mercenaries bent upon looting and murder. Little surprise, then, that as the Russian government was encouraging foreign merchants to augment Western commerce with manufactories located in Russia—manufactories which could supply quality goods at lower prices than imports, while training Russian apprentices in new skills—a similar policy was adopted in military affairs. Mercenary units were largely discarded in favor of Russian regiments organized by foreign officers along Western lines, with Russian nobles serving the European commanders as understudies to emerge in time as commanders in their own right. The tsar's statesmen were encouraged to pursue this policy by the fact that in that very Smolensk campaign of 1632-1634 there were already 6,118 Russians in six infantry regiments, one cavalry regiment, and a regiment of dragoons, all organized, trained, and commanded by 105 foreign officers. These men performed with far greater bravery and distinction than other Russian units, and without the unsatisfactory qualities of the mercenary regiments. So in the future the Russian government recruited foreign colonels, captains, lieutenants, army ensigns *(praporshchiki)*, and corporals to instruct and command Russian troops.[3]

At this time the tsar's generosity to foreign officers became so well known throughout Western Europe that hundreds of (usually) qualified men came to Russia—sometimes without invitation or prior agreement and often with families—to enter the service of the Muscovite state. We are unable to say precisely how many instructor-commanders were engaged in this manner during the seventeenth century; a German ambassador to Russia in 1661 spoke of an "endless multitude" of foreign officers in Russia, of whom he personally knew a hundred generals and colonels. In fact in that year alone at least forty-seven senior officers, thirty-eight lieutenants, and more than one hundred ensigns, corporals, and "cavalrymen" arrived from various countries for employment in Russia, and S. F. Platonov estimated that two years later, in 1663, 2,422 foreign officers commanded 55,714 Russian rank-and-file soldiers. The entire Russian army had by this time grown from 100,000 men before the 1630's to perhaps 300,000 men in the late 1660's, and to about 260,000 by 1681.[4]

To what extent did this foreign training and leadership bring the Russian army toward parity with the regiments of Poland, Sweden, or the West? Kliuchevskii believed that despite changes in organization, Russian battle tactics remained unchanged until the very end of the seventeenth century; but even if this negative estimate is valid, one should not conclude that there was no improvement in the *fighting power* of the Russian soldier. After the 1630's Russian artillerymen began to grasp the concept of coordinating cannonfire with infantry and horse, cavalry were equipped with the pistol and carbine, and there is reason to think that the Russian victory over Poland in 1654-1667 was at least partially due to the fact that by that time Muscovite soldiers were armed with lighter weapons such as muskets and flintlock carbines.[5]

A curious aspect of Russian military "modernization" in this period also indicates the extent to which progressive Russians had become enthralled by the mysterious technological powers of the West. This was the desire to gain control over what we now call "secret" weapons, many of which surely existed only in the form of rumor or imagination.* For example, Aleksei

*Some weapons in this category really existed, of course. Thus a Russian agent in Lübeck was treated to a "secret" demonstration of what he described as "high explosive musket shells" with a range of eighty *sazhens* (about 560 ft.), though without an immediate government order for the product he was unable to bring "samples" back to Moscow. Rockets were known in Russia from the early 1600's, but were not actually used until the time of Peter the Great. Baklanova, "Privoznye tovary," p. 21; Gamel', *Opisanie*, pp. 30–31 (documents); A. A. Shternfel'd, "Rakety v Rossii nachala xvii veka" [Rockets

Mikhailovich instructed his agent Hebdon to obtain in the West "a glass such as may be placed under a city, so that everything in the city may be seen." In the same vein, the tsar expressed a desire to take into Russian service "the very best sappers, who would be able to carry out sapping under a river, and under a lake, and through stone mountains, and upwards through a mountain and through water" by using "such sapping equipment as to enable a man to go two *sazhens* [about fourteen feet] in the strongest places, and 10 sazhens in twenty-four hours in easy places." In other respects, however, Tsar Aleksei had a very sound understanding of what Western engineers could do to strengthen Russian knowledge of fortification and siegecraft. He was extremely anxious to use foreign engineers to improve the defense of Russian cities, as instructions issued to an English agent in the tsar's own hand eloquently demonstrate. In fact, after the Time of Troubles Germans and Dutchmen began to erect stone walls around cities once protected only by wood, and a government document of 1631 expressed a desire to hire workers in Holland who could also build roads, bridges, and buildings. During the 1630's the Dutch engineer Cornelius Klaus constructed large forts in Rostov and at Terki, and there were probably other instances of such activity in the same period.[6] The flight of the Huguenots from France after 1685 spurred further the building of fortifications in Russia, for some specialists in that field came to Russia. Among other things they completed a line in the south which decreased the traditional Russian vulnerability to nomadic attacks from that direction. Perhaps the most ambitious fortification project of the period was designed to prevent secret passage of foreign ships into the mouth of the Dvina. This plan called for the building of a stone tower to support a great chain at Berzovskii, where the river was "not wider than 200 sazhens." The results of this scheme, if any, are apparently unknown.[7]

---

in Russia from the beginning of the seventeenth century], *Artilleriiskii zhurnal* [Artillery journal], No. 3 (March 1950), pp. 33–35.

Peter Marselis was also involved in the architectural affairs of Russia. After the terrible fire in Archangel in 1667 he and the Dutchman William Sharf were commissioned to sketch shop rows and stone parts of the city (which now included the walls of the city). At this time Muscovy was still quite backward in the art of "gorodskoe delo," as Russians then called the planning and building of towns. In all of his travels in Russia, von Staden saw only one small stone bridge (over Moscow's Neglinna river), and the apparent rarity of the object in Russia at this time may explain why Solov'ev regarded the building of another such bridge by a Swedish stonemaster in Moscow in 1634 as an innovation sufficiently important to be included in his multi-volume *History of Russia*. The foundations and many of the buildings of Vologda were built of stone during the mid-1500's, but throughout most of the seventeenth century the majority of Russian churches and nearly all palaces and fine homes were made of wood. By the time of Sof'ia, in the 1680's, however, foreign influence had stimulated extensive stone construction in Moscow (notably the new *Posol'skii Prikaz*), and a French visitor to Moscow in 1689 reported that in the few previous years Russians had built some 3,000 stone houses in the city.[8]

In this same period, Russians sometimes had cause to hope that foreigners would build canals which would have been extremely useful for trade. As early as 1556 two English sailors, Thomas Soutem and John Spark, inspected what is today the route of the White Sea-Baltic canal with a view to joining these bodies of water. This project did not come to fruition, however, nor did a proposal of the 1660's to dig a canal to link the White Sea with Moscow by the way of the Volga.[9] The first Russian canals were built only in the early eighteenth century.

Russian contact with foreigners also produced efforts to construct a seagoing fleet. Not that Russians completely lacked a shipbuilding tradition, for a significant amount of internal water transport existed on the Moskva, Oka, Volga, and other rivers, and sometimes during the fifteenth century, or even earlier, Russians are reported (though somewhat enigmatically) as sailing the Baltic Sea to Livonian ports, Danzig, and Lübeck. Such instances were not numerous, however, and it is clear that Ivan the Terrible was really breaking new ground when he used English help after 1567 to build ships at Narva, Ivangorod, Vologda, and Iaroslavl'. But Russian failure at this time to gain new access to the Baltic also retarded her development of a navy, so that establishment of a Russian fleet was still an unresolved question by the early seventeenth century. The next beginnings of a breakthrough did not come until the 1630's, when an embassy of Holstein diplomats negotiated an agreement to build ten ships in Russia for trade with Persia. The terms of the arrangement were typical of Russian hopes concerning Western innovation and technology: the German shipwrights were to employ Russian carpenters who would learn all aspects of shipbuilding—a provision which suggests even then the Russians might have been thinking of building their own ships in the future. The first of the ten vessels was built at Nizhnyi-Novgorod by Swedes, Holsteiners, Hans Berck (a "Muscovite foreigner merchant"), and a number of Russian masters. It was 120 feet long and flat-bottomed, with three masts and twenty-four oars. The ship was completed in June 1636, and on November 11 the same year it was wrecked at Nizibad, on the shore of the Dagestan river. Since the Holsteiners subsequently failed to negotiate a commercial agreement with Persia, the other nine ships were not built.[10]

The failure of the Holstein project by no means destroyed the Russian desire to create her own fleet. The preface to the *Voennyi Ustav* (military code) of 1647 promised publication of a book on the science of war vessels, and while Ordin-Nashchokin was governing the Russian-held part of Livonia he established on the Western Dvina a small naval squadron which was later destroyed under terms of the Kardisskii peace of 1661. In this period Aleksei Mikhailovich asked the Duke of Kurland to obtain for him several fully equipped ships, but without success. In 1651 the Frenchman

Jean de Gron submitted a project for the construction of ships in Russia,[11] suggesting they be sold abroad to obtain precious metal for the royal treasury. Although de Gron claimed the Russians would receive an enormous income of sixty barrels of gold per year, his plan was not adopted by the government. Yet it is clear from the above evidence that by the mid-seventeenth century Russians were thinking seriously of establishing a navy and were only awaiting a favorable opportunity to act. Peter Marselis, who was certainly well informed as to government intentions, sent his eldest son, Petr Petrovich, to become acquainted with naval science in Western Europe, the young man returning to Russia in 1669 with the rank of captain.[12]

Finally the government moved to build a modern navy. Under the guidance of Ordin-Nashchokin and in response to a specific proposal of the Dutch Muscovite merchant David Buthler, on June 9, 1667, Aleksei Mikhailovich ordered a ship *(korabl')*, a yacht *(iakhta),* and three smaller craft (a *shniak* and two *boty*) built in Kolomenskii *uezd,* at the town of Dedilov on the Oka river. These ships were to be based at Astrakhan, whence they would operate against the "thievish Cossacks." The Russians were motivated in this project by commercial considerations, for Armenian merchants had just negotiated a trade agreement with the Persian Shah Abbas II, and, according to Patrick Gordon, the Russian government wished to establish a fleet capable of navigating the entire course of the Caspian Sea in order "to draw the Persian and Armenian Traffique through this Countrey. . . ."[13] In building ships of sail type, however, the tsar rejected the advice of Andrei Vinius (son of the iron manufacturer and by now a rising statesman in his own right), who favored an oar-powered fleet as better suited for the Caspian than large ships, reminding the tsar that "as the Holstein diplomats in recent years sailed on a ship to Persia their ship was destroyed on the sea."[14]

John of Sweden was involved in construction of the Dedilov fleet. He went abroad at this time in connection with his own commercial and industrial interests, and Aleksei Mikhailovich instructed him to engage men to build and operate the ships then under consideration by the government. On June 19, 1667, John of Sweden presented the shipwright Lambert Holt and three comrades at the *Posol'skii Prikaz.* These masters went directly to Dedilov and began to organize the construction of the projected fleet; a year and a half later, on November 20, 1668, they were joined by fourteen Dutch masters and sailors led by David Buthler, who was to serve as captain on the largest of the ships, the *Orel.** The arrival of this group was likewise arranged by John of Sweden.[15]

Peter Marselis played a role in building these ships for the Caspian Sea. On September 9, 1667, he was instructed to make cauldrons, pots, buckets, pulley-blocks and hoists,

> . . . and if [these items] are not already made, you are ordered to make them quickly, and, having finished them, to send them to [the ship-builders] immediately, so that the ship-building will not be interrupted for any reason at all.

The Marselis iron factories, however, failed to provide most of the desired commodities, which were obtained finally through artisans or by searching the towns of the Russian empire. Marselis did send thirty-one *puds* of construction iron, and within a month he filled a request for six light cannon and two hundred projectiles for the *Orel.*[16]

The Russian government spent a total of 9,021 rubles on the *Orel.* By early 1670 it and its sister ships were finished and taken to Astrakhan, where they were formally launched. But the pleasure of the Russian government at the successful—if costly—completion of this project soon came to an end, for within a few months the violent uprising of Stenka Razin reached Astrakhan, the city was captured, and th *Orel* burned to a skeleton by the rebels.[17] This disaster, combined with the failure of the Armenian merchants to exploit their commercial

---

*"Orel" is the Russian word for "eagle." At this time the two-headed eagle was the symbol of the Russian monarchy.

agreement with the Persians (due to internal differences within the company and the death of Abbas II), caused the Russians to abandon their efforts to create a military and merchant fleet.[18] The expenditure of so much time, money, and effort had produced the desired ships, but a cruel turn of history had destroyed the fruits of this labor. Russians continued to build small vessels for inland transport,[19] but the country had to wait another quarter-century, until Peter I's Azov campaign, for construction of a permanent oceangoing navy.

A number of physicians were active in Early Modern Russia. They must have appeared at an early time, for we know that Vasilii III loved to converse with doctors and Ivan the Terrible had in his service at various times Robert Jacob, physician-in-ordinary to Queen Elizabeth (sent to Moscow as a token of friendship to the tsar), and an Italian known to the Russians as "Linzei." Boris brought doctors from Germany. They seem to have left Russia during the Time of Troubles, but as early as 1615 the Dutch Ambassador Massa brought his countryman Polidanus to attend the tsar. By 1621 Polidanus had been discharged and replaced by one of the most talented foreigners in Russia, the Englishman Arthur Dee, born in 1569 and educated at Oxford and in London. Dee, noted for his friendship with the tsar, came and went from Russia on several occasions, departing for the last time in 1634 to serve the English king Charles I (1625 – 49). In Moscow Dee was occupied with alchemy and astronomy and wrote a learned treatise entitled *Fasciculus chimicus, abstrusae Hermeticae scientiae ingressum, progressum, coroniden explicans,* published in Paris and later translated into English.[20]

There were perhaps twenty doctors and "subdoctors"* in Russia at the time of Michael Romanov, as well as four pharmacists and three alchemists and oculists. The fact that

---

*The *doktor* or *vrach* (such as Dee) ". . . gives his counsel and commands, but does not act himself; the *lekar'* ["subdoctor"] applies and treats with medicine, but is not learned himself; the apteker [pharmacist] is assistant to them both." From a contemporary document cited in Liubimenko, "Trud inozemtsev," p. 59. (The distinction drawn by Platonov, at least for the time of Tsar Michael, was that the *doktor* dealt with internal diseases, the *lekar'* with

even Jews were accepted into Muscovite service as doctors indicates the extent to which the profession was esteemed in Russia, as does the fact that physicians and pharmacies were normally available solely for the sovereign and his immediate family.* Leading nobles gained their services before the 1670's only through special permission of the tsar.[21] By then other significant changes had occurred in the practice of medicine in Russia, not the least of which was an increase in the number of specialists, some forty physicians and *lekari* accepting Alexsei Mikhailovich's invitation to come to Russia. Moreover, at this time a certain "Russification" occurred in the medical profession, for beginning with the approach of warfare with Poland in 1653 the Russian government took steps to provide the army with native *lekari*. (Foreign doctors were expensive and usually did not have a good knowledge of Russian.) Late in 1653 a royal *ukaz* instructed the *Aptekarskii Prikaz* to open a school to train Russian *lekari*.[22] Using several foreign doctors as instructors, four interpreters, and a library of published books and handwritten manuscripts, the *Prikaz* began its program of instruction in its offices in the Kremlin in Moscow with thirty children of *strel'tsy* origin as students. Without a doubt the school was a success. Twenty-five Russian *lekari* joined the regiments during the early fighting and by 1660 thirty men had completed their education at this first Russian medical college.

---

external disorders; *Moskva i Zapad*, p. 132.) Neither of these men performed surgery, this being the task of the lowly *khirurg* (surgeon), of whom there was at least one in Moscow in 1674 (Kurts, *Sochinenie Kil'burgera*, pp. 180–181). In practice, of course, these distinctions were not always maintained.

*The tsar displayed proper caution, however, in exposing himself to Western medical arts. Thirty, forty, or more boyars sampled Aleksei Mikhailovich's medicine before the tsar took it; in 1674 a pharmacist erred in mixing medicine prescribed for the tsarina by Dr. Rosenberg, so that the boyarina who tasted the potion became quite ill. According to B. G. Kurts, "Rosenberg got out of this mess only with the greatest difficulty" (*Sochinenie Kil'burgera*, p. 544). Two of the first European physicians in Russia were actually executed when their royal patients died, and in 1602 a self-educated doctor from northern Germany was briefly in disgrace with Boris Godunov after failing to save the life of Duke Johann of Denmark, who was betrothed to the tsar's daughter (see Olearius, *Travels*, pp. 147–148).

By 1655 the *Aptekarskii Prikaz* organized a second institute to supplement the work of the original school. This institution graduated *kostopravy-khirurgi*—literally "surgeons who repair bones"—these men being of doctor's rank but inferior in professional standing to *lekari*. One government document states that when another war for the Baltic opened with Sweden in 1656, twenty-eight men of both categories were dispatched to the new front.[23]

The first Russian physician to be educated in the West was Petr Vasil'evich Postnikov, who received his degree in Vienna in 1694. But the needs of the Russian government for men with Postnikov's education and cosmopolitan experience were such that he never actually practiced medicine at home. This should not lead us to conclude, however, that the medical profession as such was not significant in Russia by that time. In 1682 the *Aptekarskii Prikaz* had forty-four *lekari* and apprentices under its authority, and in Moscow alone six doctors, nineteen *lekari,* and thirty-six physicians of lower standing were practicing their skills. Fourteen foreign and seven Russian *lekari* attended the Russian regiments campaigning at Azov in 1695.[24] The humble elements of the population, of course, continued to rely on folk remedies and practitioners, and in Moscow people still purchased "medicines" in the shops of *Zeleinye riady.**

There were not many representatives of "pure science" in Russia during this period. The Italian physician Linzei mentioned above was also a mathematician and the author of a treatise on geometry, and an invitation to take service under the tsar was issued to Dr. Arthur Dee's father, John Dee, a mathematician, but he refused it. Tradeskont, a specialist in botany and horticulture, studied the flora of the far north of Russia and transported several Russian plants to his botanical garden; but he spent only a few months in Russia and was not under government employment.[25] Other highly educated Western Europeans traveled and worked in Russia during the

---

*A "zeleinik" is a *lekar'* ". . . who provides treatment and charms with grasses, earths and roots." Dal', *Tol'kovyi slovar'*, I, 677.

sixteenth and seventeenth centuries, [26] though apparently they did nothing to stimulate a deep interest in biology, chemistry, physics, or similar pursuits.

Because of the influx of Western commodities during the sixteenth and seventeenth centuries, the tsar and his court developed a taste for luxury goods of more exquisite design than those provided by Russian craftsmen. So a continual effort was made to obtain the services of foreign cloth masters, jewelers, metalsmiths, furniture makers, and others. During the seventeenth century available records prove that at least twenty-seven foreign goldsmiths and twenty-six silversmiths were active in Russia. (In these professions the English continued to be of great importance even after their overall role in the Russian economy declined.) It would appear that foreign artisans exerted a certain influence on Russian enamel work, decoration and design patterns, and *motifs*. Clocks with bells appeared in Russia as early as 1404, and were installed on the walls of the Kremlin after the Time of Troubles. A large, English-built clock was placed over the *Spasskaia vorota* ("Gate of the Savior") of the Kremlin in 1625, and by 1645 the German Hans Kezel was boasting that he had been the first successfully to teach Russians the art of clock-making.[27]

During the sixteenth century, foreigners were interested in the great wealth of Russia's forests. Both the Dutch and English exported shipmasts, and Russian bird-cherry trees were sent to England to make hoops for bending casts. After the Time of Troubles, Western Europeans also entrenched themselves as entrepreneurs in industries based upon traditional Russian (nonmanufacturing) technology which extracted commercial products from forest resources. Under Tsar Michael, the Dutch merchant Elisei Ul'ianov obtained permission to build a resin factory near Archangel. In 1630 the Dutch *gost'* Karp Demulin (who held a commercial charter dating from 1614) was allowed to burn ash in the forests of Sukhona; later he made potash in Totemskii and Ustiuzhskii *uezdy*, at the town of Viatka on the Volga, and near Novgorod for a period of ten years. In 1643 Simon Digby, an agent of the English Muscovy Company, was granted a charter for ten-year duty-free ash production in Iaroslavl' and in Vologda and Totemskii *uezdy;* when Digby died in 1644, his ash-burning privileges were transferred to his wife, Daria, and her three partners. In this same period Colonel Alexander Crawford engaged in similar projects at Muromsk. Apparently investments and profits in these factories were considerable. We know, for example, that the Englishman Osborn spent over two thousand rubles on equipment after receiving a ten-year charter in 1649 to make potash on his *pomest'e* (fief) at Arzamasskii.[28]

With the expulsion of English merchants from the Russian interior in 1649, Dutchmen replaced at least some English potash-tar entrepreneurs. In that year Andrei Vinius obtained a six-year concession to make and export pitch at Archangel, and Englishmen who wished to export this product could buy it only from him. In the 1660's a mixed group of Russians and Amsterdamites received the use of state forests at Sukhona to export shipmasts, though apparently the company was not very active. In 1670 the Dutch merchant Werner Müller worked out a similar arrangement with the tsar for a period of ten years.[29]

For lack of evidence to the contrary, we must assume that when Western Europeans took control of estates *(pomestia)* they made no significant alteration in crops, methods of cultivation, etc. But there are some instances of foreigners entertaining or undertaking innovations in Russian agriculture at this time. Colonel Alexander Crawford, for example, received an eight-year monopoly in 1651 to sow imported seeds from which he hoped to derive vegetable butter. These plans probably failed, but Crawford did grow asparagus, lettuce, roses, and other flowers. Aleksei Mikhailovich considered the use of foreign agricultural and husbandry techniques on his various estates, and his new Izmailovo gardens just outside Moscow contained herbs and flowers of Western origin. Since foreign workers are found in "pharmaceutical gardens" during the seventeenth century and since Russian medicines of that time were prepared according to Western European prescriptions, it seems likely that some new grasses, herbs, and plants were introduced into Russia in this manner. Efforts were made to acclimatize grapes and tobacco from the East to Moscow, but without much success.[30] On the whole, the achievements of foreigners in agriculture in Russia at this time were not considerable.

One of the most important activities of foreigners in Russia during the sixteenth and seventeenth centuries was service to the tsar as diplomats, commercial agents, and policy advisers. Men who served in these capacities had the great advantage over Russians of understanding the prices, problems, and mentalities of both Russia and the West, and in most cases an important European entrepreneur would have a host of contacts who could help him achieve assigned objectives. As early as the late 1400's Ivan III used as personal representatives on various occasions such knowledgeable Italians as Gian Battista della Volpe, and later della Volpe's nephew, Antonio Gislardi. Early in the next century an Italian banker with international connections, Paolo Centurione, was active in Moscow, and served Vasilii III as agent. During the seventeenth century many foreigners went to the West on behalf of the Russian government, for example, the Dutch goldsmith Julius van Eksel in 1628 to hire jewelers and experienced craftsmen; Colonel Alexander Lesly for officers and military equipment; the felt master Fimbrant to engage artisans in 1630;[31] the Englishman Hebdon on a mission similar to Lesly's in 1658.[32]

Russians usually accompanied foreigners on missions for the tsar, for the Russian government had reason to distrust its Western European agents with money and goods. The government employed long-time residents called "Muscovite foreign merchants" (*moskovskie torgovye inozemtsy*) who were well known to the tsar and possessed interests in Russia too great to be risked for the gains of a single dishonest enterprise. The

Russians also made use of a few men like the Dutch merchant Jan van Horn, who became a *gost'* in Russia and returned to the West, remaining available to help other Muscovite-foreigners fulfill assignments of the tsar.[33] Important boyars like Il'ia Miloslavskii also went abroad to hire officers and artisans for service in Russia, as did talented men of lesser rank such as the cloth artisan *(kadashevets)* Fedor Salin, who visited van Horn in Holland in 1670 to obtain cloth for *strel'tsy* in Moscow.[34]

Foreigners other than Marselis and Vinius acted as diplomats and policy consultants for the tsar. Lesly gave military advice concerning the Smolensk campaign of the early 1630's, and Paul Menesius, a Scotch major in the Russian army, traveled to Vienna, Rome, Venice, and Brandenburg in 1672 to convince the Emperor, Pope, doge, and kurfürst that only common action with Russia could save Poland from a threatened conquest by the Turkish sultan.[35]

Important remaining areas of foreign activity in Russia in this period involved translation work, the import of European newspapers, and the organization of an efficient international postal service. Translators were especially important for Russia as she strengthened her relations with the West, for the few Russians who bothered to learn foreign languages at this time were eminent statesmen who could scarcely be bothered with routine interpreting and translating. But if a foreigner settled in Russia and learned Russian, he could begin to work as a translator. The foreign office *(Posol'skii Prikaz)* in Moscow was the most important center of this activity, and according to Grigorii Kotoshikhin there were no fewer than 120 translators working there during the early 1660's. [36] These men were paid high wages and by the very nature of their work were privy to the highest state secrets. Thus they were trusted officials of surprisingly good character who sometimes also went abroad to hire masters, buy goods, or deliver personal letters from the tsar.

Russia's first postal system dated from the late thirteenth

century and seems to have been established by the Tatars. Known as the *iamskaia gon'ba* (or *"iam"*), it was continued by the Russian princes after the expulsion of the Mongols and raised to a level of some efficiency by Ivan III (1462–1505) and his successors.[37] Heinrich von Staden noted that under Ivan the Terrible the towns and countryside of Russia were divided into districts known as *sokhi,* one town *sokha* being comprised of a hundred houses. The inhabitants of each *sokha* paid a special tax to maintain the horses, sleighs, and river craft, etc., of its particular *iam* station. *Iam* outposts were apparently located at intervals of twenty to fifty *versts* (Jenkinson reports fourteen stations over the 420 *versts* between Moscow and Vologda). According to Olearius, during the 1630's *iam* station-keepers were obliged to maintain "40, 50, or more horses so that . . . they may quickly harness up the horses and speed [authorized travelers and royal couriers] on their way." For this service each station master received thirty rubles a year plus land "free of any levies and other obligations," payment sufficiently "advantageous to the peasants [that] many strive to become coachmen."[38]

The *iam* provided quick transportation. Von Staden tells us it took him six days to travel two hundred miles from Dorpat to Moscow, and added, ". . . A person can go from Moscow in six days to a neighboring frontier or from the frontier to Moscow." Communication between Novgorod and Moscow (a distance of six hundred *versts*) normally required five days during the winter, seven or eight days during the summer — although on one occasion a servant of Herberstein made the latter trip in seventy-two hours. Russian merchants could rent *iam* horses for low fees, and under Boris Godunov such privileges were even extended to foreigners. But by the mid-seventeenth century the old method of communication was no longer considered adequate for national needs. In part this was because *iam* messengers were often slower than the impressive but usually theoretical schedules cited above. For example, a report of 1669 concerning the *iamskaia gon'ba* reveals that on one occasion couriers took three weeks to reach Vil'no from Moscow, and in another case a trip from Moscow to the border which should have lasted no more than four days actually required sixteen.[39] By this time trade in Russia had become so intricate and highly developed that such slowness and inefficiency was unsatisfactory to those involved in commercial activities. Also, by the mid-seventeenth century Russian diplomacy was so integrated with that of Poland and other countries that it was essential for Russian statesmen to be continually in touch with policy and events abroad. Finally, the *iam* roads covered only some parts of the empire, but Russia's new commercial, political, and diplomatic life demanded a broader communications network within the country, as well as a more regular and efficient linking of Russia with foreign states. Serviceable as the *iam* system might have once been, by the mid-seventeenth century it had to be at least supplemented by new and more efficient lines of service.[40]

In line with growing sentiment for more effective postal service, in 1663 John of Sweden organized a delivery system from Moscow to Vil'no and Riga which left and arrived in the capital twice a week. Two years later, in May 1665, the government moved to take advantage of John's messenger project by concluding an agreement with him whereby he would "bring all news letters of the Austrian, Spanish, French, Polish, Swedish, Danish, English, Italian, Hollander and Netherlandish lands from the capital cities every two weeks, from the Turkish, from the Kizyl'bash [Ukrainian] kingdoms and on occassion from India," for which he was to receive twelve hundred rubles per year.* John's mail carriers departed

---

*Russians first gathered information from foreign newspapers at the time of Ivan the Terrible. After the early 1600's the *Posol'skii Prikaz* prepared reports consisting of excerpts from the foreign press supplemented with information from Russian diplomats and agents abroad. In 1631 the *Prikaz* began to subscribe to foreign newspapers (which numbered forty-three by the end of the century), though previous to van Sweeden's post its own news bulletins appeared irregularly. After 1665, however, the *Posol'skii Prikaz* issued two of these reports in two copies each month (one for the tsar and leading statesmen, the other for the *Prikaz* itself), surveying political developments abroad, as well as what the foreign press was saying about Russia. This information was treated as "state secrets." Russia's first printed newspaper for general distribution, *Vedomosti* [The News], was edited by Tsar Peter himself and

on scheduled days regardless of the quantities of mail which had been received by that time.[41]

During the mid-1600's A. L. Ordin-Nashchokin in particular was occupied with the further development of the Russian post. He was partly motivated by diplomatic objectives, for the Russo-Polish Treaty of Andrussovo (1667) specified that Russia would establish an efficient postal service to enable the two governments to communicate quickly and frequently on affairs of mutual interest. Ordin-Nashchokin also saw the postal needs of his increasingly commerce-oriented society, and often pointed out that a post "will be a great help for merchants in the speedy sending of their letters about trade." Ordin-Nashchokin disliked John of Sweden, however, and decided to pass the postal franchise to the Marselis family, which he favored. The reasons for his hostility to van Sweeden are not completely clear,[42] but in any event on May 25, 1668, he ordered that Johann van Sweeden's post be given to Leonhard Marselis, who would add to it new routes to Kurland and through Smolensk.[43]

For some reason John of Sweden continued to operate his post after the edict of May 1668; and when John died in that same year his widow, Maria, and his nephew, Hermann Löfken, actually concluded a new agreement with the *Prikaz Tainykh Del* for the supply of foreign newspapers and the maintenance of other postal services. Soon after this, however, Maria van Sweeden's post seems to have been discontinued, for on December 7, 1669, several foreign merchants petitioned the tsar for permission to use Maria's service, pointing out that a letter sent through her post cost six kopecks per *zolotnik,* whereas Marselis charged ten kopecks. But the request was refused, Leonhard's monopoly reaffirmed, and soon even the van Sweeden family was using his post.[44]

Leonhard Marselis moved quickly to organize his postal service. By September 17, 1668, the Moscow-Tver-Nov-

appeared for the first time on January 2, 1703. S. Marlinskii, "Pervaia dopetrovskaia rukopisnaia gazeta" [First pre-Petrine manuscript newspaper], *I. zh.,* No. 5 (1945), 74-75.

gorod-Riga line was already in operation, and on March 11, 1669, Marselis carried out his first run from Moscow to Vil'no. The post left the capital for Vil'no every Wednesday, for Novgorod every Thursday. From Moscow the cost to either city was two *altyn*, four *den'gi* (eight kopecks) per *zolotnik* (*one zolotnik* = exactly .15 ounce), from Novgorod to Riga or Vil'no, eight *den'gi* (four kopecks). Interestingly enough, letters from Pskov to Moscow or Novgorod were taken without the payment of a fee. A mailbag from Moscow would reach Novgorod in seven days; Vil'no to Moscow took eight days; Riga to Moscow required nine, ten, or eleven days. A letter from Moscow to Hamburg was delivered in twenty-one days at a cost of twenty-four kopecks per *zolotnik*. These rates were expensive for the time, but price reductions were made after 1668 for the post from Moscow to Novgorod, Pskov, and Riga, and in all probability to other cities as well.[45]

Although service between the major Russian cities was surprisingly efficient for a large, underdeveloped nation, it cannot be said that rationality always governed the development of the Russian post. This is illustrated by the way in which petty vindictiveness on the part of some government officials delayed the creation of an important new postal line. On June 5, 1669, Leonhard Marselis petitioned the *Posol'skii Prikaz* for permission to establish between May and September of each year a weekly postal route linking Moscow and Archangel via Iaroslavl' and Vologda. At the same time as Leonhard's petition (and as if to support it), five prominent foreign merchants asked the government to organize a Moscow-Archangel post, pointing out that while they were in Archangel for the annual fairs the mail they received in Moscow lay there, unread and unanswered. Also it was impossible to write from Archangel to Moscow concerning the arrival and departure of ships or the current state of the market at either city.[46]

Because Leonhard Marselis was in bad standing at the *Posol'skii Prikaz,* his project for an Archangel post was refused. Marselis' disfavor with the government (as explained in a *Prikaz* memorandum of October 30, 1669) was due to the fact that he had recently delivered newspapers to the *Prikaz* which were unsealed and the contents of which were already known in Moscow.[47] The translators of the *Posol'skii Prikaz* were highly indignant over this violation, and maintained that postmasters in foreign states would never unseal such newspapers, or if they did, they would be punished. Leonhard also offended the translators by noting those passages which should be translated; they hotly asserted that without Marselis' help they knew what to translate and what to ignore! [48] Piddling though this affair might appear, it delayed the establishment of a Moscow-Archangel post for some twenty-five years.[49]

Leonhard Marselis died suddenly and unexpectedly in 1670. The post remained in the Marselis family's hands until around April 1672, when it was taken from the elder Peter Marselis and given to Andrei Andrei'ch Vinius, son of Peter's former partner and rival, Andrei Vinius, and at that time a *d'iak* and translator in the *Posol'skii Prikaz*. Since A. A. Vinius went abroad on a government mission on October 22, 1672, the post was returned to the oldest of Marselis' sons, Petr Petrovich Marselis, head of his family after his father's death on July 10, 1672. Petr Petrovich himself died in August 1675, and by decree of December 4 of that year the Marselis post was returned once and for all to the young Andrei Vinius.[50]

The Marselis family may have found their post barely profitable, and for this reason may actually have wanted the government to take it from them. In any event, the Marselises did nothing to prevent the loss of their postal system and Vinius did not assume it as a private business venture. Rather, he converted the enterprise into a government institution and merely acted as its director, being the first Russian to hold the title of "postmaster" *(pochtmeister)*. This meant, of course, that the Russian post now joined the *iam* system as a government operation, although the *iam* couriers, overworked and underpaid as they were, continued to give tardy and indifferent service. Vinius failed to bring about significant reform of the *Iamskii Prikaz,* but he did succeed in stimulating some bridge construction and road improvements. His main efforts were directed toward extending the post into new areas and assuring its efficient and economical operation. In 1695 Andrei Vinius formally handed supervision of the Riga and Vil'no posts over to his son Matvei, but in effect the older man continued as the real director even of this line.[51]

Vinius paid foreigners in service of the Russian post in such cities as Vil'no, Warsaw, and Vienna,[52] while provincial masters were reimbursed with local postal fee collections, supplemented by payments from the *Posol'skii Prikaz* in case receipts of a particular station did not meet the salary specified by the state. Vinius himself received no salary as postmaster, but he was so well rewarded for the entirety of his efforts during this period[53] that he may be said to have profited—if indirectly—from his position as postmaster. And without a doubt Vinius did much for Russian postal development, for as a statesman (rather than a private operator) Vinius not only eliminated the earlier entrepreneurial conflicts which had characterized John of Sweden or the Marselises and the government, he also gained the support of such progressive colleagues as Matveev, Golitsyn, and Secretary of the Duma E. I. Ukraintsov.[54]

As postmaster Andrei Vinius proved to be the same kind of bold innovator as was his father in iron manufacturing. Before the younger Vinius the Russian post went only to the west; after his tenure in office postal service radiated from Moscow in all directions. Thus between 1677 and 1697 no fewer than five postal routes were established south of Moscow:
(1) Moscow-Kaluga-Sevsk-Kiev (which began to operate by 1680)
(2) Moscow-Kaluga-Sevsk-Akhturkha-Poltava-Zaporazh'e (late 1680's)
(3) Moscow-Tula-Mtsensk-Kursk-Belgorod (1689)
(4) Moscow-Tula-Novyi Oskol-Azov (1695–1697)
(5) Moscow-Kolomna-Tambov (1677 or 1678).
Two new lines were also organized to the west. In 1683 the collapse of the Vil'no route (which occurred as a result of

diplomatic developments) led the government to set up courier service from Moscow to Smolensk and Mignovich. The second post ran from Smolensk to Pskov and was established by royal decree of June 24, 1697. This postal service was quite efficient; with sixty-two carrier stations over a distance of 460 *versts,* it operated throughout the year.[55]

In 1693 a group of foreign merchants renewed efforts to gain an Archangel post. In a petition formally addressed to young Tsar Peter I, the merchants pointed out they paid thousands of rubles to the treasury in taxes each year, and that their economic activities enriched many Russians. They asserted that the healthy development of future trade depended upon communication between Moscow merchants and their agents in Archangel. For this reason the petitioners begged Peter to allow Andrei Vinius, an "experienced man," to open a Moscow-Archangel postal road. The tsar did this with a decree issued on June 8, 1693, and by the winter of that same year the Archangel-Moscow post was in operation. Here too we see rather effective organization and management, for although this route covered a distance of 1,046 *versts,* during the summer it was transversed in eight or nine days, in ten or eleven days in the spring and fall. The mail left Moscow once or twice each week.[56]

Andrei Vinius also helped establish a Siberian postal service, although most of the credit for this achievement must go to Prince V. V. Golitsyn, who hoped the post would aid in developing trade with China. The route stretched from Moscow to Kazan to Tobolsk, and by 1698 had been extended as far as Irkutsk and Nerchinsk. Postal stations were located every ten miles, peasants and even convicts being settled there with land grants under the condition that each house have three horses available for couriers, who were paid three *den'gi* for each ten *versts* traveled. Although service was relatively quick between Siberia and Russia (Patrick Gordon received a letter in Archangel from Tobolsk two months and twenty days after it was posted), there were only three postal runs per year, all in the summer.[57]

By the end of the seventeenth century the Russian post covered many parts of the empire and was functioning in a regular and competent manner. A letter usually reached Moscow from Azov in ten days; by express a courier traveled from Kiev to the capital in six or eight days, though regular service took two or three weeks. Of course there were mail losses, thefts, and inefficiencies, but on the whole much had been achieved toward linking the vast empire together through a system of postal communication. Patrick Gordon illustrates how important this service was to Russian men of affairs in this period, for on one day in 1666 he sent no fewer than seventeen letters (many of them abroad), and on another occasion in 1687 he posted twenty-five letters. Perhaps Kilburger best summarized the importance of this system when he remarked that "the post is an enterprise such that those engaged in trade are not able to dispense with it for the maintenance of continuous correspondence. . . ." Communications could be carried on with foreigners in Danzig (three weeks from Moscow), Hamburg (four weeks), or even England. Thus the Russian post of the seventeenth century not only brought Russians into closer contact with each other, it did something to bring Russia into the advanced capitalistic civilization of Western Europe.[58]

12

Status and Influence
of the Foreigner in Early Modern Russia

IT IS DIFFICULT TO estimate the number of foreigners who lived and worked in Russia in the sixteenth and seventeenth centuries. Olearius seems to tell us that at the time of his travels in the 1630's there were one thousand Protestant men, women, and children living in Moscow;[1] some fifty years later, in 1684, there were 690 individual house *(dvor)* owners in Moscow's foreign quarter *(nemetskaia sloboda)*. S. F. Platonov believed there were more than three hundred Dutch merchants residing in Russia throughout the entire seventeenth century, with perhaps a thousand of all nationalities.[2] As we saw in the preceding chapter, 2,422 European officers commanded some 55,000 Russian troops in 1665. On the basis of these facts and estimates, it seems reasonable to conclude that during the 1670's roughly the following numbers of foreign-born family heads lived in Russia: 2,700 officers, active and retired; 230 manufactory workers; 400 merchants — 100 Dutch,[3] 100 others of Western European origin, 200 Poles, Lithuanians, Greeks, and so forth; 130

218

Western artisans, engineers, watchsmiths, shipwrights, town-builders, and so forth; 150 translators and full-time government employees; about 30 manufacturers and entrepreneurs; and 12 doctors, apothecaries, astrologers, and men of university stature. If these figures are correct, then, about 3,650 foreigners were active at a single time in the 1670's—and this is a "conservative" rather than "generous" estimate.

Naturally a study of the activity and influence of these men must inquire into their overall level of competence, though the nature of the problem precludes a simple or unqualified conclusion. Foreign entrepreneurs such as Marselis, Akema, Vinius, and others seem to have obtained capable and experienced masters for their manufactories, and this was certainly the case with the "Venetian" masters active at Aleksei Mikhailovich's Izmailovo glass works. In fact, by the seventeenth century government authorities realized that just *any* specialist in a given area would not solve the needs of the economy, and for this reason people who wished to take service under the tsar had to present documents and letters concerning their knowledge and previous experience. Otherwise state officials might receive the hopeful worker in a manner such that he would regret coming to Russia to find employment. (Even some physicians who came to Russia without prior invitation were sent home.) But it would seem that true selectivity could not be maintained in the army, for many soldiers recruited at the time of the Thirty Years War were of poor character, and others from a later time proved lazy and incompetent. Patrick Gordon noted in his diary that a "significant part" of the foreign officers entering the Russian army in the early 1660's were "foul, low people. Many of them not serving [previously] as officers entered service in Russia at officers' ranks."[4] Another foreign observer at this time, Shleizing, was equally severe in his judgment of Western soldiers in the Russian army, saying:

> Some of them are called old, others new foreigners. The old foreigners were born in Russia [and] the foreign blood in them

has vanished; a great part of them have Russian manners, go about in Russian dress and are very poor in military affairs, [for they] remember little or even nothing about it. For the best officers these wretched birds who have landed here are simply splinters in the eye, they are so obnoxious. They have not returned to their homelands because their fathers and grand-fathers took eternal citizenship in the [Muscovite] state and many of them accepted the Russian faith. There are gallant people among the new foreigners, however, those who were sent for by the tsar from abroad and who earlier served the Swedish, Polish and other kings. . . .[5]

Only toward the end of the seventeenth century were the Russians able consistently to recruit talented officers of high character. In part this was due to the exodus from England after 1649 of such distinguished Scotch royalists as the Drummonds, Hamiltons, and Crawfords; in part because after 1685 French Huguenots were granted free entrance to all areas of the Russian state, with the right to establish their own settlements in Moscow or other cities.[6]

Apart from professional ability there is also the question of personal character. Here it would seem that a sober view of foreigners active in Russia at this time should give Western historians little cause for self-congratulation concerning the alleged superiority of foreigners over the Muscovites in matters of ethics and behavior. We have often quoted Heinrich von Staden, for example, who revealed himself as a murderer and thug at the time of Ivan the Terrible's *oprichnina*. In the midst of Shein's defeat in late 1632, foreign mercenaries in the tsar's service began going over to the Polish side; on December 2, Lesly accused a certain English Colonel Sanderson of treason and shot him on the spot. Such men as Peter Marselis or the soldier Arthur Aston were not above supplementing their primary activities with counterfeiting and theft. A report of Heinrich Butenant von Rosenbusch from 1678 indicates that his factory suffered constant damage from the drunkenness and fighting of his workers, and sometimes even killings occurred. Foreigners themselves noted the abundance of arguments, murders, and duels in the *Nemetskaia Sloboda,* and the Saxon government, considered the patron of foreigners in Moscow, informed its agents that even pastors in the Foreign Quarter were guided by bad motives and admitted that the number of cases constantly in the Moscow courts could well give the Russian government the most negative impression of the West.[7]

The factor most likely to attract a foreigner to service in Russia was the high level of wages offered both by the tsar and by foreign entrepreneurs. In addition to generous allowances of food and drink, European masters at Tula and elsewhere received 100 rubles or more per year.* Physicians were paid far more than that. Arthur Dee, for example, received an annual salary of 1,100 rubles plus drink, presents, an estate near Moscow, and a large house in the city which he sold for 1,600 rubles when he finally left Russia in 1634. When Olearius visited Russia in this same period he reported that Hartmann Gramann, the tsar's physician, was paid a yearly salary of 1,044 rubles "in addition to bread, grain, malt, honey, and other things for the household." Gramann also received fees of 50 rubles and cloth or furs when he administered bleedings or treatments, though boyars who received his services usually paid with "sables, bacon, vodka, or other provisions instead of money." Two foreign physicians working for the *Aptekarskii Prikaz* in 1645 received the sizeable sums of 288 rubles and 420 rubles per month — wnile pharmacists drew salaries of 80 and 100 rubles per month, an oculist 70 rubles, and a *lekar'* 20 rubles. Only high-ranking foreign officers received salaries comparable to these leading doctors. A colonel in the 1630's received 400 *efimki* per month, a company commander 150, a major 100, and others (many of whom were Russian rather than European) as follows:

*As we have seen, the payment of workers in other industries differed considerably. The highest-paid workers at Egidius Tabbert's cloth mill and the royal Vorontsovo leather manufactory received 45 rubles and 36 rubles, respectively, per year. Masters at the Pakhra river paper mill received from 110 to 60 rubles per year. The best wages were paid in the silk industry: masters received 130 or even 150 rubles annually, while the best Russian

quartermaster	60 *efimki* per month
lekar' (regimental)	60
lieutenant	45
ensign	35
priest	30
secretary	25
sergeant	14
executioner	8

Interpreters were also well paid in this period. *Perevodchiki* in the 1660's received 100, 80, 60, or 50 rubles per month (depending on the skill of the individual), *tolmachi* 40 to 15 rubles or less per month — and all were awarded daily rations of drink and food *(korm),* as well as estates and valuable gifts.[8]

In fact the tsar's "generosity" (i.e. gratuities for good service beyond regular salary) was an important element in the remuneration of many foreigners in state service. On one occasion Ivan IV rewarded the garrison of Wesenberg castle in Livonia for heroically resisting the enemy; among the men so favored was a German interpreter, Simon Kerklin, who was granted two fine imported horses, four hundred *chetverti* of land and the right to select for his own the finest house in Narva. When Heinrich von Staden entered Russian service as interpreter of German, Latin, and Latvian, he was immediately given an estate, some cloth, a silk caftan, some money, and a daily allowance of four and a half quarts of mead and four *den'gi* for food. Most important, perhaps, were the *pomestia* the tsar offered foreigners and their heirs for the duration of their service. Generals and staff officers usually received estates of eight hundred *sazhens,* senior officers holdings in the range of 450 *sazhens,* junior officers perhaps a third as much, and corporals, sergeants, even transport drivers, eighty *sazhens*. Sometimes foreigners experienced difficulties in receiving their pay. Promised salaries might be reduced for no apparent reason or paid tardily, in which case a bribe for the

---

apprentices were paid 20 rubles. In all cases masters and apprentices received, in addition to their wages, free housing and a daily sum for food and drink.

paymaster clerks often caused them to work more efficiently! In other instances the government might fall into an economizing mood, especially if the value or amount of work the foreigners performed declined noticeably. Thus at one point the salaries of inactive officers were cut, as were the pensions of widows and orphans "of [foreign] officers killed in battle or deceased in government service," and in 1682, 383 foreign soldiers received word that in the future their salaries would not be paid unless they were actually on duty. Those who did not wish to serve in this manner could either remain at their homes in Moscow or return to the West.[9]

Leaving Russia could be a problem, however, at least for those who worked in a satisfactory manner. In theory there should not have been difficulties, for a foreigner entering the tsar's service was usually assured that when he completed the agreed tenure of employment he could leave at any time. Certainly there are many instances of foreigners trusting to such agreements without later cause for regret. Under Boris Godunov the pharmacist Frengam left Russia and then returned after eight years with his entire family, while Polidanus, Arthur Dee, and other doctors also went and came at will. But some English physicians and apothecaries of the sixteenth and seventeenth centuries met such opposition in their desire to return home that others hesitated to take their place, although the tsars continually asked for them in their letters.[10] Von Staden's memoirs provide a dramatic illustration of the hazards a valued foreigner might face:

> It seldom happens that a foreigner manages to flee the country, since the road into the country is broad and clear, but the way out is extremely narrow, even if one has studied Muscovy [with care. But if a foreigner] is caught trying to flee the country, then only God can help him. His talents no longer count, and his money and property help him not at all.
>
> Doctor Eliseus Bomelius came to the Grand Prince from England during the great plague. He had acquired a lot of money and property, and had lined his pockets well. He requested a pass from the Grand Prince, saying that he wanted to send his servant to Riga to get some medicinal herbs which he

could not find in the Treasury. He took the pass himself and set out in the guise of his servant. He had changed all his money and property into gold and had it sewn into his clothes. When he arrived at the post station in Pskov, he wanted to buy some fish in the market. Although his beard was cut off, he was recognized by the way he spoke. The Russians found his money, and the good doctor was led back to Moscow in chains welded with lead.[11]

In other cases government opposition to departure would be expressed in more subtle ways: delays in hearing petitions for exit, silence, or threats of exile to Siberia. Soldiers most often were so treated—merchants and factory workers probably left with the greatest ease.[12] On the whole it seems that one's ability to return home quietly and in good order depended on such factors as the importance of the work performed, the availability of replacements, the temperament of the tsar or his officials, or the influence of the individual foreigner.[13]

At a time when the spirit of religious intolerance was burning brightly in Western Europe, it is not surprising to learn that Russians had strong feelings of superiority on account of their Eastern Orthodox faith, with corresponding elements of hostility and contempt for other creeds. The Muscovites were most opposed to Judaism and Catholicism, and this inevitably lessened the number of Catholics and Jews who might otherwise have been active in Russia during the sixteenth and seventeenth centuries. When the tsar sent Alexander Lesly to the West in 1631 "to hire military people good and faithful," he also admonished Lesly not to engage "the French and others of the Papal faith. . . . "[14] Lesly's orders were not mere rhetorical rumblings, for, as Olearius tells us at this very time,

> When the war at Smolensk [with Poland] was imminent, and there turned out to be some Catholics among the military commanders invited into the country, they were given some presents for having made the journey, and then were escorted across the border again by a good convoy. In the treaties the Russians concluded with us concerning the Persian trade, they

included a strict ban on persons of the Latin faith . . . among our company. Even the name [Catholic] is detested [among the Russians].[15]

Yet the tsar's government by no means systematically excluded Catholics or Jews from Russian service, the latter being accepted as physicians and residing in Moscow's foreign quarter by the 1680's. And if Lesly in 1631 was told to refuse Catholics employment in the army, two years later in 1633 the English merchant Glovert was told — if necessary — to go even to France to find makers of gold and silver thread. But "persons of the Latin faith" living in Russia did suffer certain disabilities. A Catholic church was not established in Moscow until 1696 despite continual complaints from Popes, Holy Roman Emperors, kings of Poland, and, on one occasion, Louis XIII. (The Roman church in Novgorod in the *Nemetskii Dvor* was only for Hanse merchants briefly in the city on business.) Catholic residents in Russia did well to receive their sacraments from Jesuit priests attached to Polish diplomatic embassies; in other cases Catholics were driven to seek the services of Protestant ministers.[16]

The Muscovites had no sympathy for Protestantism and were concerned to keep its influence from the native population. But the enmity that existed between the two Western branches of Christendom caused the Russians in principle to prefer the Reformed tradition to Rome, which had a well-established and ever-renewed record of conflict with Eastern Orthodoxy. The fortunes of Protestant churches in Russia, however, varied. As we have seen, the Danish government was concerned over the question of religious liberty for Protestants when the question of marriage between Waldemar and Irina arose in the 1640's, and negotiations finally collapsed over a mutual inability to solve religious differences. Danish doubts about Russian assurances of a liberal religious policy were justified, as was demonstrated by the destruction of a Lutheran and a Reformed church in Moscow in 1643 because of complaints from Orthodox clerics and attendant disorders among the population. But parishioners of the two churches (which were originally built at the time of Ivan the Terrible) quickly received permission to rebuild their churches in different areas, and apparently no further obstacles were raised to their operation.[17]

In fact, Protestants in Russia were not treated unreasonably, considering the religious climate in Europe as a whole during the sixteenth and seventeenth centuries. The Lutheran church organized with permission of Ivan the Terrible at Nizhnyi-Novgorod still existed when Olearius visited there, at which time the congregation numbered about one hundred, including Scots who were probably Calvinists. Kilburger tells us that in 1674 three Lutheran and one Reformed church were holding services in Moscow's Foreign Quarter, and their non-Russian adherents could worship there "as freely and unhindered as in any other place in the world." The Dutch also had a Reformed church in Archangel in 1674, and by this time Lutheran and Calvinist ministers had long pastored to the numerous foreign masters working for Marselis and Akema. According to von Staden, during the mid-sixteenth century "A foreigner [was] free to hold any faith he chooses, so long as he [did] not force his servants and maids to eat meat on the fast days, likewise on Wednesdays and Fridays." Olearius likewise bore witness to Muscovite toleration in dealing "with people of other nations and religions, such as Lutherans, Calvinists, Armenians, Tatars, Persians, and Turks."[18]

A foreigner in Russia always had the option of converting to the Russian Eastern Orthodox church and in this way becoming a subject of the tsar, a Russian "citizen." Depending on which clerics were consulted on this process, both Catholics and Protestants might do this even without undergoing rebaptism, and the material advantages of such a move were obvious. After conversion one could work in the tsar's bureaucracy, choose a residence outside of "foreign quarters," marry a Russian, and escape all the legal and economic disadvantages connected with being a "foreigner." Moreover, the very act of conversion could be profitable, for the tsar appointed a "godfather" *(krestnyi otets)* to aid and protect the convert, who could also expect to receive estates and sums of money. The tsar's own father-in-law, boyar I. D. Miloslavskii, acted as patron for Lesly and his wife when they accepted Orthodoxy, giving them valuable clothing, while the tsar himself made Lesly a present of three thousand rubles. Sometimes newly baptized foreigners would be as bold as Stepan Matveev, who openly petitioned Tsars Peter and Ivan in May 1687 for a present on the occasion of his conversion.[19]

Apparently such conversions began at the Time of Ivan the Terrible. A few English merchants connected with the Muscovy Company became Russian citizens, and Fletcher tells us that during the Livonian War:

> Of [Livonians] that are captiues [*sic*], there are many that take on them this second *Russe* baptisme to get more libertie, and somewhat besides towards their liuing, which the Emperor [Tsar Ivan IV] ordinarily useth to giue them.

In 1599 several long-time German "Moscow dwellers" converted and assumed the high merchant rank of *gostinym imenem*. Many foreigners underwent "this second *Russe* baptisme" under Michael and a still larger group under Aleksei Mikhailovich, especially soldiers, and even some Jewish and Polish doctors.[20]

As in the instance of Vinius' conversion,[21] this was an act which could also alienate the convert from his fellow foreigners in Russia,[22] for as Fletcher said disparagingly of one Englishman in his own time, this was an act which meant the apostate "forgot God, his faith, and countrie. . . ." At the very least such people would take new surnames (the Leslys became Avraam and Evdokiia), they would wear Russian clothing, speak Russian, and adopt many customs of their new homeland.[23] Colonel Augustus Elern endured much hostility from his erstwhile European friends in Russian service when he converted to Orthodoxy, as did Colonel Heinrich Egerat and General Bauman. Many other foreigners of more humble status became Russian at this time. In 1662 the foreign masters Andrei and Filipp Filippov accepted Orthodoxy, and in this period records of the Tula-Kashira iron factories show workers with forty, thirty, and twenty years of service, suggesting that several generations were born and reared there in this work. These men enjoyed immunity from receiving troops on billet and were granted privileges of duty-free trade.[24]

A foreigner who accepted Eastern Orthodoxy and Russian citizenship might visit the West with permission of the tsar, but he was expected not to revert to his former status. An unfortunate example of one who tried was the English Lady Anna Barnesly, a sister of Peter Marselis' wife Daria. She converted to Orthodoxy at the same time as her husband, the French Baron Pierre de Remon, but after his death Anna wished to return to Calvinism. For this she was sent to a monastery and endured great trials and privations, finally being released on the condition she would not reconvert to Calvinism.[25]

Some foreigners located in Moscow for years but never became Russian citizens, and finally returned home. The van Klenk family, for example, traded successfully in Russia and after several decades received titles of *gosti*. One of the family even arrived at the Kremlin in 1675 as the Dutch Ambassador, and was received quite favorably. But the van Klenks did not abandon Holland for Russia, and after a long while returned home. S. F. Platonov was harsh but just in saying, "For them, Moscow remained only a market to be utilized in the interests of Dutch trade and policy. And this the Klenks did with great skill."[26]

The most striking contrast to the problem of adaptation to life in Russia is presented by Peter Marselis and Andrei Vinius and their families. In many respects the two were alike. Of Dutch extraction, they both began their careers in Russia as international merchants, rose to success in that field, and then became pioneer iron manufacturers. Apparently it was the very similarity in the extent and nature of their ambitions that caused the dissolution of their partnership, and if each man experienced mixed fortunes in later years, both remained prominent in the economic life of later seventeenth-century Russia. But the two men were separated by a great difference in temperament and outlook: Andrei Vinius and his son became sterling examples of "Russified foreigners" who retained the best qualities of their Western European background, while the Marselis family — no less committed to Russia in terms of economic investments or time in residence — remained to the end spiritually alienated from the Russian environment.

The most striking external demonstration of this "spiritual isolation" was the care with which the Marselis family retained and cultivated its Calvinist faith. Certainly the Marselises were ambitious, greedy — even dishonest — and willing to make any number of concessions to the Russian situation to retain their interests there. But they never forgot or failed to cherish the role their ancestors played in the Reformation and the dedication to that cause sufficiently strong to force their forebears to flee from Holland to Hamburg during the stormy second half of the sixteenth century. Not that Peter Marselis was a missionary or religious fanatic! His basic thought seems to have been to tolerate in his Russian hosts those characteristics he hoped they would ignore in himself. If in time he came to be universally regarded as the leader of the entire Protestant cause in Russia, Marselis' sense of reality never slipped enough for him to try to spread his faith to the Russian population. He was careful merely to sustain both Lutheranism and Calvinism among his workers and combat discreetly tendencies toward conversion in the foreign community. This was a modest goal, but one which could be attempted with a minimum of risk. Even when he gambled, that was the kind of situation Peter Marselis liked best.

Marselis' political career also demonstrates the extent to which he retained the interests and mentality of a foreigner. To be sure, on any number of occasions Peter Marselis tried to serve the best interests of the Russian state, especially as a diplomat and personal envoy of the tsar; but these were situations and objectives which in no sense conflicted with his own economic and industrial interests. Not so the series of discussions preceding the issuing of the New Commercial Code (*Novotorgovyi Ustav*) of 1667, for in this instance the object of the Russian authorities was to erect a series of tariffs and trade duties to protect Russian merchants from the "unfair" competition of the wealthier and more highly organized merchant interests of the West. This conflicted with the advantages enjoyed and desired by Marselis and his foreigner friends, so Marselis' counter-proposal for new trade regulations opposed mercantilist acts which would have the effect of fettering international commerce, emphasizing, rather, the manner in which extensive foreign trade would bring precious metal to the state treasury.[27]

These ideas were so much at odds with the prevailing mood of Ordin-Nashchokin and other Russian statesmen at this time that Marselis' proposals had but little effect on the final Code of 1667. But two years later, in 1669, Marselis renewed his efforts to put aside the *Novotorgovyi Ustav* and institute *de facto* free trade in Russia. According to his new suggestions, foreign merchants should exchange *efimki* at the treasury for Russian coins which could then be used for trade in Russia without payment of customs. This would, he argued, encourage commercial activity from abroad and bring silver and gold into state coffers. After Marselis submitted his memorandum to the government, it was read at a meeting of Moscow merchants, which rejected the ideas of the "sly foreigner," saying he was "enticing the government with an abundant influx of efimki" to set aside government taxation and control of foreign trade and thereby "give foreigners domination over all Russian people." On this occasion leading Russian merchants vented real resentment and hostility toward the "foreigner" Marselis, saying,

> And he, Peter, proposed only a relatively small gain in efimki, while in return for that small gain he hoped to capture all the trade in Moscow and in other cities. In that memorandum he also asked that foreigners be allowed to bring to Moscow as well as to other cities gold coins and efimki, sell their wares to everyone, exchange their wares duty-free, and with that money purchase various goods in Moscow and in other cities. Through this idea he desires, together with other foreigners, to establish a monopoly over the trade of all the Russian people.[28]

Whether or not Marselis consciously intended to harm the

interests of Russian traders through a continuation of low tariffs and minimum government regulation of foreign commerce, the nature of his proposals and the reaction of Russian merchants to them provides one more example of Marselis' unwillingness to integrate himself fully into the Russian environment and accept its needs vis-a-vis the West.

Andrei Vinius took a completely different approach to the opportunities Russia presented an energetic entrepreneur. From the very beginning he had no sense of solidarity with his fellow foreigners, but certainly was anxious to ingratiate himself with the tsar. To gain a trade charter and the good will of the court, he broke the previously solid front of foreign merchants which dictated that no one would pay more than one ruble per *chetvert'* for grain from Michael's own private reserves. Vinius raised his price to one ruble, forty kopecks per *chetvert'* and for this sum was permitted to buy a quantity of grain so large as to earn the tsar profits of over 100,000 rubles and to require fifteen ships to send the purchase to Holland.[29] Vinius gained his objectives—a charter and the tsar's friendship—all of which compensated him amply for outraging his competitors, who feared Vinius' action would raise the entire price level of Russian grain in the future. As was later noted by a Swedish contemporary, even then Vinius was "more disposed towards Russians than foreigners," as he himself indicated in a letter to the tsar which began

> Majesty! In the year 1631, by your majesty's decree, we foreigners were permitted to buy . . . all sorts of bread from your majesty's bread supplies, and our brother foreigners traded your majesty's bread at a low price, but I, majesty, served your majesty faithfully and truly, and bought your majesty's bread supplies at a large straight-forward price without slyness and self-interest, and your state treasury gained much profit, and in the future you will be glad, your majesty, to be served by such a sincere soul.[30]

After Vinius brought the younger members of his family to Moscow, in 1646 he took the great step of converting to Orthodoxy. His action earned him the undying enmity of

Marselis and other Muscovite foreigners, but it pleased the tsar so much that Aleksei Mikhailovich made Vinius a nobleman with the title "commissioner of his royal majesty of the Russian state and Muscovite *gost'*, Andrei Denisov, son of Vinius." By this time Vinius was an important government figure who consistently defended Russian interests from abuse by foreigners. In 1646 he proposed a system of fortifications for Archangel which would not only keep out enemy vessels in wartime but prevent foreign merchant ships from navigating the Dvina secretly and without paying custom fees. At the same time Vinius was the driving force behind legislation that doubled trade duties on foreign commerce to gain the extra income needed to finance the reform and reorganization of the Russian army.* We can see why Vinius became the first foreigner to attain a high position in the political affairs of the Russian state,[31] and if his position in Russian affairs declined sharply in 1647–1648, by 1649 Vinius had gained new economic interests and from that time served the government continuously as a diplomat and statesman until he died.

Vinius' entire household was arranged along Russian lines. Women and men dined separately, and we have a revealing account of his wife on one occasion greeting her guests in the Russian manner by presenting them a cup of vodka and a kiss.[32]† Vinius had several daughters and a son, Andrei An-

---

*As a contrast to Vinius' defense of Russian economic interests, consider the following episode. In 1646 Peter Marselis and the foreigner Eremei Fentsel captured the foreign market in Russia which bought blubber oil *(vorvan')* for export. They cut their price to one-half, one-third, and even one-fourth of what was ordinarily offered for the product. Since the peasants of Kholmogory and Pomor'e had no alternative, they suffered impoverishment and misery by selling their oil to Marselis and Fentsel, who earned 400 per cent profits. A petition of Moscow merchants of 1646 complaining generally about the activities of foreigners in Russia singled out this case for extended discussion. Solov'ev, *Istoriia*, X, 476; Tsvetaev, *Protestanstvo*, p. 269; Kozlovskii, *Pervye pochey*, I, 82.

†In another instance, the Dutch diplomat Baltazar Koiet noted that in Vinius' household the women during meals sat in Russian fashion in a room separate from that of the men. *Posol'stvo Kundrata fan Klenda k tsariam Alekseiu* . . . [Embassy of Conrad van Klenk to Tsar Aleksei . . .] (St. Petersburg, 1900), pp. 435–436.

dreevich, who was born in 1641, raised in the "Orthodox spirit" and baptized at fourteen (in 1655) to be able to enter state service at that time. Andrei Andreevich Vinius was an educated and versatile man who was a merchant, a translator, and a nobleman, and involved at various times in Russian naval and postal affairs. He was especially successful as the director of the *Aptekarskii Prikaz* and was available for such special assignments as supervising "the affairs of the velvet master Zakharii Pavlov with his masters" from December 28, 1681, through 1684. Andrei Andreevich knew several languages, had a keen interest in geography and geology, and wrote a series of works on religious and ethical questions. By 1695 he was working for Peter on artillery affairs and later became an important state adviser and agent in the Russian iron industry. Correspondence between Andrei Andreevich and his son Matvei Vinius shows that the father had an ascetic view of life and insisted on the need for ambitious tasks and never-ending work. A. A. Vinius went through a period of disfavor with Peter the Great, left Russia for a time in 1706, but returned to Russia and died in state service in 1717.[33]

We must say something about influences of a noneconomic nature which may have derived from the presence and activity of foreigners in Russia during the sixteenth and seventeenth centuries. The most difficult (and interesting) aspect of this question, of course, is the cultural-spiritual impact of Westerners on the various classes of Russian society at the time. One would think, for example, that Russians coming into professional or commercial contact with "Muscovite foreigners" would acquire something from them in the realm of ideas, tastes, and feelings—and this should be all the more the case with those foreigners who lived in Russia for lengthy periods or even became Russian "citizens." For example, when Dutchmen, Germans, Englishmen, and other foreigners in Moscow were forced to move to the "new" Foreign Quarter in the mid-seventeenth century, the Poles and Lithuanians of the city were permitted to remain in their *Staropanskaia Sloboda* ("old Polish quarter") whence they assimilated into the Russian population.[34] Surely there was *some* "cultural" result of that social symbiosis and synthesis. But suppositions aside, can we prove that such influence actually occurred?

Clearly a number of important Russians in this period became "Westernized." Nikita Romanov, for example, the most wealthy person in Russia after the tsar, was a free-thinking patron of foreign music and dress, and was friendly with English merchants, one of whom gave the boyar's son, Fedor, Latin lessons. Artamon Matveev (1625–1682) was a cultivated boyar who married the Scottish Lady Hamilton after her family converted to Orthodoxy, and became one of the first Russians to arrange his life in the manner of a Western noble family. The Matveevs kept open house for their friends, at which time subjects of current interest were frankly discussed. Matveev knew Latin and Greek, and maintained a troop of actors who staged Biblical plays; because he became the tsar's leading minister after Ordin-Nashchokin's resignation in 1671, other Russian aristocrats began to dress in European fashion and to trim their hair and beards. A. S. Miloslavskii's home also presented a European air, with its illustrated ceilings and imported religious paintings. His wife appeared in men's company and their son received careful tutoring in the Western manner.

Other Russians in this period were touched by international influences. The statesman and iron manufacturer Boris Morozov adopted foreign clothing and often expressed regrets at not having received a good education when young. A. L. Ordin-Nashchokin and Prince V. V. Golitsyn were both learned men for their time. Ordin-Nashchokin once said, "there is no shame in borrowing what is good even from your enemies," and he had a good knowledge of Latin, Polish, German, and mathematics. Golitsyn appears to have been a truly cosmopolitan nobleman who conversed with foreigners in German, Latin, and Greek, who read widely in history, theology, and the classics, and was interested in legal, administrative, and military reform, the advancement of education, even the aboli-

tion of serfdom.[35] In fact, most of the tsars of seventeenth-century Russia had moved significantly beyond traditional medieval cultural horizons and mentalities. The story of
Peter the Great's childhood is too well known to need retelling
here,[36] but it is well to recall that his stepbrother and predecessor Fedor (1676–1682) knew some Latin and spoke Polish fluently, while Sof'ia (regent 1682–1689) was exposed to
Ukrainian learning from the monk Semen Polotsky and others.
Boris Godunov advocated setting aside old animosities with
Lithuania to secure good relations with the merchants of that
country, to whom he showed direct and personal kindness on
many occasions, even lending them money without interest.
Boris also aspired to marry his daughter to a foreigner and to
establish a university and other schools of Western type.[37]

But of all pre-Petrine tsars, Aleksei Mikhailovich was probably most deeply influenced by contact with foreigners in his
country. He often visited the *Nemetskaia Sloboda,* where he
saw a performance of *Orpheus* and was fired with the ambition
of establishing a theater of his own. With his support, by 1673
the German pastor Johann Gottfried Gregory was teaching
theater arts to twenty-six young Muscovites, and in the next
year the first ballet began in Russia, again thanks to the tsar's
patronage. For a time Aleksei Mikhailovich presented himself
as a candidate for the Polish throne, and in this period he began
to arrange his court life and ceremony on the Polish pattern,
hoping thus to demonstrate that in Russia, too, people were
civilized and knew how to live well. Not that Aleksei's interest
in Western civilization was feigned or insincere. He was
sufficiently fascinated with astronomy and astrology to have a
huge map depicting the location and courses of the stars placed
on the ceiling of the Kremlin dining halls, and the tsar's new
palace at Kolomenskoe and gardens at Izmailovo abounded
with such Western innovations as imported furniture, a large
fresco showing the universe as heliocentric, and windmills and
irrigation canals.[38]

In fact, the very presence of Western artifacts may have influenced the consciousness of some of the Russian ruling

class. Imported portraits, for example, perhaps enabled them to consider the human figure in a new way. In place of stereotyped and nonrealistic icons, Aleksei Mikhailovich at Kolomenskoe used pictures of Julius Caesar, Alexander the Great, and Darius, and on New Year's Day of 1667 the tsar received from his Dutch court painter a depiction of the fall of Jerusalem. In the same period a Dutchman painted the patriarch Nikon. Dmitrii Tsvetaev feels these developments were important culturally, for the import of mirrors around 1665, "together with the simultaneous introduction of realistic portraiture and naturalistic iconography, helped increase consciousness of the human body and its appearance."[39]

Western books also entered Russian life at this time in original copies and published or manuscript translations. Libraries were accumulated not only by such government institutions as the *Posol'skii Prikaz*[40] and *Aptekarskii Prikaz* (for medical instructors, pharmaceutical work, and the like), but also by private individuals interested in the West. On merely one occasion in 1669, Ordin-Nashchokin received eighty-two books in Moscow in Latin;[41] A. A. Vinius had a collection of 363 volumes in Dutch, German, Latin, French, Polish, and Estonian.[42] Golitsyn, Matveev, and Nikita Romanov also had libraries of foreign books, as did several educated prelates, though in these cases theological and religious subjects were dominant. During the period 1500-1699 at least 153 different titles were published in Russian translation.[43]

But there are some paradoxes in Russian Westernization during the sixteenth and seventeenth centuries which must be brought to light if we are to understand the development and its meaning. For example, there is a certain contradiction in the *intent* of the various parties in the process. As we have seen, the Russian government wanted Dutch and Swedish iron masters at Tula and elsewhere to "influence" Russian apprentices by teaching them the advanced skills of iron manufacturing. On the other hand, the state did not want those foreigners to infect Russians with ideas alien and uncongenial to the Russian tradition. Literally the Russian state hoped to use foreigners to bridge the technological gap between Russia and the West in order to consolidate and perpetuate — by maintaining military might and political independence — major elements of the cultural chasm existing between the two civilizations. But the foreigners involved in this process wished to minimize the technological knowledge they passed on to their Russian understudies, because the high wages and favored position of the European master were based on knowledge and skills he possessed which were unique and inimitable in the Russian environment. As for Protestantism, however, this was something a foreigner might have been quite willing to share with Russian colleagues[44]—except that this sort of influence would have been abhorred and combated by the tsar and his statesmen. We must not think, then, that the elements of Westernization as they operated in early modern Russia were equally satisfactory to all parties involved, or that each element shed its influence in a manner consistent with the wishes of all parties concerned.

Nor did Westernization in any one area of thought and learning occur at a steady and accumulative rate throughout this entire period. There were so many "backward steps" in the dissemination of scientific learning in Russia that the overall ascent from ignorance to learning forms a zigzag pattern rather than a gently ascending, unbroken line. Thus the Judaizer heretics of the late 1400's were aware of Euclid, but he was entirely forgotten in Russia throughout the sixteenth and seventeenth centuries, although Euclid was included in the curriculum of better Persian religious schools of the 1630's. Among other subjects, the Likhudy brothers taught physics at the Slavonic-Greek-Latin Academy after 1685, but when they were removed in 1694 instruction in physics did not reappear in Russia until after 1750. Likewise, the introduction of Copernican theories in published form in Russia in the 1710's did not exclude later expositions of "cosmological" problems without reference to Copernicus.[45] In fact, is it not amazing that Euclid and Copernicus represented "new" learning in a state as important as Russia as late as the *eighteenth century?*

Perhaps it is this realization that moved one Russian historian to remark that in an age of Bacon, Harvey, Leibnitz, and Descartes. Russians were only beginning "to chew medieval phantasmagorics with a scholastic sauce."[46]

There were, of course, powerful social forces in Russia which were unwilling to see Muscovite society approach the West to any degree. To be sure, there were such generalized obstacles as religious exclusiveness, national chauvinism, and provinciality—perhaps even jealousy springing from the fact that if foreigners were to come to Russia at all, as a matter of course they had to receive higher pay and enjoy more rights than Russians. But if we look at the interplay of classes and institutions in Russia in this period, we also detect a certain relationship between social alignment and attitudes toward the West. For example, the tsars were interested in using foreign officers to improve the fighting quality of the armies; but the *strel'tsy,* professional elements of the army who enjoyed good pay and extensive peacetime trade and artisan privileges, justifiably saw this "modernization" as a threat to their established position. So they emerged during the seventeenth century as a reactionary element opposed not only to army reform but to almost *any* form of Westernization, and their sentiments were sometimes expressed in armed clashes with foreign soldiers.[47] Russian nobles who witnessed an eclipse of their traditional pre-eminence also registered frequent objections to "unbaptized" commanders of Russian troops,[48] but the ordinary Russian soldier tended to admire his foreign officers, respecting them for their knowledge and experience.[49]

Although important boyar-merchants like the Stroganovs and Boris Morozov welcomed Western trade relations and industrial ideas, Russian tsars of the period had to contend with boyar and church opposition to close relations with the West. The mass of boyars opposed Ivan the Terrible's cultivation of the English, and Boris Godunov's plans to establish a university with scholars from the West were destroyed by a solid front of clergy and aristocracy. Orthodox opposition to

Western innovations was expressed in a variety of ways, ranging from destruction of Russia's first press in 1566, to labeling snuff and tobacco the work of satan, to a larger doubt that faith and a learning based on the ungodly arrogance of an inquisitive mind could really be reconciled or combined. At one point in the seventeenth century a Russian Orthodox bishop declared "abhorred of God is any who loves geometry; it is a spiritual sin," while the Patriarch Ioakim in 1690 refused the services of a foreign doctor sent him by the tsar. It is indicative of the age that imprisonment of the boyar Matveev was justified in part by his extensive use of Arabic (Moslem!) numerals in a handbook of medical advice. In fact, Russian prelates of this period had little use even for those Byzantine studies of society, nature, and man which did not fall within the rigid limits of official religious orthodoxy, and not until the Church lost its monopoly over the press under Peter the Great did secular books in Russia begin to appear freely and in large quantity.[50]

The tsars of sixteenth- and seventeenth-century Russia themselves opposed some forms of Western activity and influence, though often this seems to have represented capitulation to religious pressures. In 1628, for example, Michael succumbed to church demands that foreigners be forbidden to hire Orthodox for house service, "so that Christian souls would not be defiled and would not die without confession." This prohibition against keeping Orthodox servants was repeated in the law code *(Ulozhenie)* of 1649. Three years later, in 1652, a group of foreigners petitioned for the right to hire Russian domestics (promising that they themselves would keep fast days so as not to present an obstacle to their attendants), but this request was met with a categorical denial—and a suggestion that the petitioners themselves should adopt the Orthodox faith. Usually foreigners in this period were able only to engage Poles and Tatars for household work.[51]

Apart from commercial regulations and strictures, the most serious royal legislation against foreigners pertained to their places of residence in Moscow and elsewhere. By the 1630's Russian merchants were broadly distributed in those cities on the river trade routes from Archangel and Novgorod to Astrakhan and Kazan, including smaller towns such as Kholmogory, Vologda (where there were twenty Dutch merchants in 1675), Iaroslavl', Belozero, Rostov, and Kargopol. Foreign military instructors also lived and worked in such diverse places as Starorusskii *uezd,* Zaon'ezh, Tomsk, and Sevsk. From the beginning, it would appear, the practice had grown up of segregating foreigners in these and other areas into special "suburbs," *slobody,* where they would not come into contact with the Russian population. In part this custom developed in response to the Church's desire to keep European influence from the Russian people, in part from a natural desire of the foreigners themselves to escape the constant ridicule and abuse provoked by the very appearance of their clothing. (Foreign adoption of Russian dress had been prohibited by Michael upon insistence of the patriarch.[52])

There were, then, many "foreign quarters" in early modern Russia, notably at Novgorod and Pskov, in Vologda and Archangel (which dated from the 1550's), and also at Sevsk, Iaroslavl', Belgorod, Astrakhan, and Nizhegorodsk.[53] The most famous foreign quarter, however, was in Moscow. The first foreign colony there, founded by Ivan the Terrible, was scattered during the Time of Troubles and then repopulated after 1613 by merchants, artisans, and professional people. By that time foreigners were so numerous in Moscow that several suburbs of various nationalities existed, and some foreigners were forced to settle where they could — thus provoking hostile comments from conservative elements of the city.[54] In response to complaints, Michael and Aleksei Mikhailovich restrained foreigners from buying *dvory* in various parts of Moscow,[55] and finally in 1652 all Western Europeans were ordered to move to one large area just outside Moscow, northeast of the Kremlin, on the right bank of the Iauza river.[56] This settlement was formally called the New Foreign Quarter, or more popularly simply the Foreign Quarter.

By 1665 this area comprised one-fifth of the entire area of Moscow and represented a veritable microcosm of Western Europe, including a German school, four Protestant churches, European-type mansions with two and three stories and large windows, and broad straight streets.[57] In 1665 there were over two hundred household courts *(dvory)* in the Foreign Quarter;[58] by 1684 the number had risen to 690 *dvory,* some owned by Jewish families.

But what of our original inquiry? What was the cultural impact of foreign entrepreneurs—especially manufacturers—on Russian Westernization tendencies of the sixteenth and seventeenth centuries? Unfortunately, a definitive answer to this question does not appear possible. We know that Boris Morozov was a close friend of Andrei Vinius, that Peter Marselis was associated with I. D. Miloslavskii and Ordin-Nashchokin. But there is no way to assess the *specific influence* of those (or other) foreigners on *those* Russians. And even if N. A. Baklanova is correct in concluding that "foreign books entered into circulation in Russia through the foreigners who settled there and brought them for their personal use "[59] how are we to determine *precisely* the extent to which those particular books affected the thoughts or manners of the Russians who may have used them? This is the insoluble problem of cultural history. It is easy in the case of seventeenth-century Russia to detect Western influence in painting, architecture, and literature, and it is possible to talk about the "new" men of the period—but it is difficult or impossible to isolate any one change as the clear result of any one person, even though we may *feel* that Vinius, Marselis, and others must have had some influence outside the realm of pure economic activity.

Perhaps the best we can do is to say that an internal ferment in the consciousness of educated Russians appeared and developed in this period—especially after the 1630's—and that it was related *in a general way* to increasing diplomatic-commercial contact with the West, the presence and activity of foreigners in the Muscovite state, and a growing dominance of the state over the Church (which made possible the emergence of secular moods and viewpoints rationalized on the basis of "necessity of state"). If the economic dimensions of this Westernization process had cultural and intellectual ramifications — which our instincts tell us is likely — the nature of the problem apparently excludes definite or extended commentary.

13

Manufacturing in Early Modern Russia:
Some Generalizations and Conclusions

FIFTY-SEVEN MANUFACTORIES OF Western European type were built in Russia from the early 1500's to the mid-1690's. Although seven of these enterprises appeared during the sixteenth century and two between 1600 and the 1620's, the systematic and extensive development of Russian industry did not begin until the 1630's. The notable achievement of that period, of course, was the construction of the four Tula iron mills and the Coyet glass factory at Dukhanino. Nine more iron manufactories and three other enterprises were built during the next two decades, suggesting a steadily rising (if not dramatic) line of industrial growth. The 1660's saw the addition of only a small iron works, a glass and leather factory, and two paper mills, but from the 1670's to the mid-1690's Russian manufacturing was strengthened by thirteen new iron factories and twelve other enterprises. In summary, seven manufactories (12 per cent of the total) were built during the sixteenth century, two (4 per cent) between 1600 and the 1620's, twenty-two (39 per cent) from the 1630's to the 1660's, and twenty-six (45 per cent) during the last three decades of the seventeenth century.*

Foreigners organized the majority of these manufactories. In the iron industry before 1662 European merchants built ten iron factories, the state one, and Russian nobles three. From 1668 to the 1680's, however, the role of foreign capital fell slightly: in those years foreigners constructed seven new iron works, as compared with two by the state and two by Russian commoners. In the last decade of the century foreigners built one additional iron mill, Russian commoners two. Thus throughout this period foreign merchant-entrepreneurs organized eighteen iron factories (65 per cent), the state accounted for three (11 per cent), Russian nobles two (7 per cent), and Russian commoners five (17 per cent). In other manufactures, foreigners at this time dominated silk, cloth, leather, rope, and gunpowder, leaving Russians most important in sawmill activity and glass and paper production. The following figures clarify the interest of various sections of Russian society in establishing manufactories during the sixteenth and seventeenth centuries:

	Iron Manufactories	*Other Manufactories*	*All Manufactories*
Foreigners	18 (65%)	15 (52%)	33 (58%)
State	3 (11%)	9 (31%)	12 (21%)
Russian nobles	2 (7%)	1 (3%)	3 (5%)
Russian commoners	5 (17%)	3 (11%)	8 (14%)
Church	0	1 (3%)	1 (2%)
	28	29	57

Although the above data indicate that foreign entrepreneurs played a commanding role in the construction of Russian

*These figures exclude such enterprises as the state-owned glass manufactory which Iakov Romanov established on the Moskva river (because it never functioned); the Tsil'ma river copper works of the 1490's discussed on p. 39 (existence and nature uncertain); Aleksei Mikhailovich's large rope enterprise (possibly a large artisan shop); etc. Enterprises such as these were discussed to give a rounded picture of Russian industrial development, but I have no desire to use them to produce an inflated estimate of manufacturing in this period.

manufactories, the history of these enterprises shows that the actual influence of foreigners was greater still. The nobility, for example, was not an independent force in the overall course of Russian industrial development. The two aristocrats who built iron factories at this time (Miloslavskii and Morozov) were inspired to do so by direct contact with foreigners. To be sure, the Pavlovskii iron works remained in the hands of Morozov's family throughout twenty-five years of operation and three changes in title, but boyar Il'ia Miloslavskii soon tired of his Porotovskii manufactory and sold it to Akema and Marselis. The short-lived paper mill of the *pomeshchik* Savinov (dating from the 1560's) represented an interesting but fragmentary episode in the economic history of the period, and it failed to stimulate similar activity on the part of other Russian feudalists, though many of them were sufficiently wealthy to make the necessary investments. As for the Orthodox Church's paper mill of 1665, it was closed within two years and then reconstructed by John of Sweden. Russian commoners made a more serious effort than the church, state, and nobility to profit from the use of new technology. Nikita Demidov, the partners Aristov and Borin, Semen Kiprianov, and Vladimir Voronin established four large iron factories which operated for long and profitable periods. (The Stroganov works was probably a "small" enterprise.) Russian merchants also founded two sawmills (one of which was large) and a rather enigmatic paper mill. These seven manufactories added much to Russian industrial development, but they all appeared during the last thirteen years of the seventeenth century, when foreign capitalists had already built up a certain tradition of entrepreneurship and a reservoir of technological knowledge.

It is difficult to evaluate the role of the state in this process. The bare fact that the government built twelve manufactories (21 per cent of the modern enterprises) in this period may not be as impressive as it sounds. Some of the royal enterprises were opened with small expenditures of capital, others operated for only a short time. This does not damage the state's image as a successful entrepreneur, however (for private efforts, too, occasionally required little capital or were short-lived), as much as the fact that the tsar's agents did not usually operate such enterprises in a satisfactory manner. The Iauza Morocco tannery and Paulsen's silk shop functioned well, but their output was more costly than equivalent imported leathers and silks, and for this reason they were eventually closed. Only Aleksei Mikhailovich's Izmailovo and Chernogolovskii glass works were unqualifiedly successful, and they were built by workers commandeered from Coyet's manufactory and with supplies purchased from the ill-fated project of John of Sweden. Least satisfactory was the government's record in iron manufacturing. The Tula iron works experienced striking decline during their intervals of state ownership and control in 1647–1648 and 1663–1667, though their performances quickly returned to normal after being returned to Peter Marselis. *Prikaz* officials organized the Borodnikovskii and Obushkovskii iron works and launched them successfully, but these factories soon passed on to private ownership. As for the Iauza paper mill and the Onega-Olonets copper manufactory of the early 1670's, the results of their work were so insignificant that the enterprises were abandoned. In still other instances, industries were built and then closed because it was impossible to find the necessary workers to keep them going. This was true of the Iauza iron factory of 1649, the paper mill directed by Burtsev about 1641, and even the well-equipped glass works supervised by Iakov Romanov in 1691. Much of this construction indicates poor planning on the part of the government, even an *overenthusiasm* for industry which led to the building of some factories (evidently) without a careful consideration of whether the material and human resources would be forthcoming to make the original investment operative and profitable.

The state was most useful as an agent of industrial development when it backed private entrepreneurs with extensive charter rights, generous subsidies, and loans, and all but guaranteed markets and profits. As we have seen, foreign capitalists relied rather heavily on the tsar for financial assistance.

Vinius occasionally received three-thousand-ruble advances on factory deliveries, and after 1667 Marselis borrowed sums of five thousand, one thousand, and six hundred rubles to repair and expand his iron manufactories. When Filimon Akema obtained full ownership of the Ugodskii and Porotovskii iron factories in 1663, the state not only paid him five thousand rubles "compensation" for dividing the factories in a manner different from what the Dutch entrepreneur had requested and expected; the tsar helped Akema through a difficult period by paying his workers' wages for a length of time.

Whether the role of foreign entrepreneurs in early Russian manufacturing was a profitable one is another question entirely. At the time of their deaths John of Sweden, Filimon Akema, and Peter Marselis were indebted for the respective sums of 2,948, 11,000, and 20,000 rubles.[1] As for Egidius Tabbert's textile factory and the silk works of Arent Paulsen, their inabilities to sustain profitable operation are matters of clear record. Some of these difficulties may have stemmed from the fact that many manufactories required large investments of capital. The Marselis family claimed that Peter Marselis spent more than 60,000 rubles on his iron works.[2] Paulsen disbursed at least 5,650 rubles on his silk enterprise, and the Coyet family's Dukhanino glass mill was capitalized at 2,000 rubles.[3] Did these manufactories operate profitably? The desire of their owners to continue holding iron foundries and glass works at least suggests that the enterprises were advantageous—though it is possible, of course, that their masters looked upon the source of their indebtedness as the means of liquidating those debts and attaining profits in the future. Or perhaps Marselis and others suffered losses in entrepreneurial activities not related to their industrial interests, and used that situation to plead with the government for special favors and aid in manufacturing. The information on these deficits is indeed gathered from petitions begging the tsar to grant the petitioners certain considerations and requests—and some exaggeration was likely. But conjecture aside, the most we can say is that foreign capitalists of this period incurred considerable debts in organizing and managing their manufactories; they filled large orders while operating their enterprises; and they resisted the loss of their property—or struggled to regain and expand it—in every conceivable way. But it also seems that many manufacturers died with greater debts than their families were able immediately or conveniently to pay.

We have seen how the Russian state before Peter the Great tried to develop home manufactures because it wanted to have needed commodities of good quality, at a cheap price, and in good supply, so that in the future Russia could obtain a more "favorable balance of trade" by exporting manufactured items to the West. To what extent did Russian industrial development by the 1690's match these hopes and expectations?

First, Russia had only fair success in exporting the products of her manufactories. The English rope walks of the sixteenth century worked only for England's needs, and many Russian iron manufactories and sawmills counted on foreign markets to provide a large part of their profit margin. But all this did little to reverse the trade relationship between Russia and the West which dictated that Russia at this time needed military equipment and luxury goods on a scale such that continued import was a perpetual necessity. As for the desire of the government to use indigenous manufacturing to obtain a dependable supply of needed commodities, we must conclude that even where progress was most pronounced, imports remained at a significant level. Thus during the Russo-Polish war of 1654-1667 it was common for Russian agents in Holland and England to buy at a single time twenty thousand muskets and thirty thousand *puds* of gunpowder, or twenty thousand muskets and thirty thousand yards of fabric. And if the Russian army had the services of sixteen iron manufactories throughout the 1690's, in that same decade we see the following quantities of iron imported* from Sweden alone.[4]

---

*It is ironic, of course, that some Russian iron manufacturers, seeking the higher prices of foreign markets, exported their products at the very time the tsar's government was going to such pains to import as much iron as possible.

	Rod-iron	*Sheet-iron*
September 1692- August 1693	15,289 *puds*	2,423 *puds*
1693-1694	12,209	1,879
1694-1695	18,308	2,000
1695-1696	11,857	1,391
1696-1697	19,096	3,291
1697-1698	25,030	2,934
1698-1699	25,465	1,805

Likewise, the successes of glass manufacturing in Russia did not diminish the import of fine Western crystal and glass throughout the entire century.[5] And foreign paper remained much in demand in Russia at this time.[6]

Russian manufacturers were more successful in reducing state expenditures on military equipment. We have evidence of this as early as 1648, when Andrei Vinius, struggling to persuade the government to grant him sole ownership of the Tula iron works, boasted of the low prices the tsar paid for his commodities. Vinius pointed out that whereas imported cannon iron once cost one ruble, fifty kopecks (and Russian artisans demanded one ruble, thirty kopecks) the Tula factories delivered it for five *altyn* (fifteen kopecks); foreign cannon balls were twenty *altyn* (sixty kopecks) and more per *pud,* but from Vinius the price was twenty kopecks; the Tula equivalent of European angle-iron could be had at less than half the price of the imported product.[7]

The owners of the Tula works succeeded in raising their prices in following years, but on the whole it seems clear that the products of these enterprises generally enabled the government to save money by freeing itself from total dependence on foreign trade. This is illustrated by a letter of 1668 from Marselis to the tsar, in which he compares import prices of the 1630's with the current listings of his factories:

Considering this and other evidence, Kilburger seems quite mistaken in saying in 1674 that ". . . at the present time in Muscovy they are making so much iron that they are able to supply sufficiently the entire country" (Kurts, *Sochinenie Kil'burgera,* p. 120).

Items	Import prices of the 1630's	Tula-Kashirskie prices of 1668
rod-iron	75 kopecks per *pud*	50 kopecks
iron for doors and window-fittings	1 ruble 20 kopecks – 1 ruble 50 kopecks	90 kopecks
grenades	90 kopecks – 1 ruble or more	30 kopecks
cannon-balls	60 kopecks or more	50 kopecks
musket-barrels	75–80 kopecks or more	60 kopecks
swords	70–75 kopecks (each?)	60 kopecks
cavalry armor with spiked helmet	4–4½ rubles (per suit?)	2 rubles

In view of these price differentials, Marselis seemed quite justified in exclaiming: "And thanks to this [domestic iron manufacturing], mighty sovereign, much profit was made [by you], and in the future, thanks to this, there will be still more profits. . . ."[8]

But if the Russian iron products were inferior to those of Holland, Sweden, or Germany, their lower cost would necessarily appear in a different light. Blast furnaces and forges used in Western Europe during the seventeenth century were not able to produce what would be considered quality iron today; but in Russia the situation was even worse because of the nature of the country's ore deposits — which in the case of the Tula, Kashirskie, Zvenigorodskie, and Vepreiskii factories were in swamp beds and hence of poor quality. For this reason many of the cannon made in these iron works burst on the very first firing, although in some cases the barrels of faulty weapons were bound with iron hoops, which prolonged their lives considerably.

Nevertheless, evidence on the quality of Russian firearms in this period is confusing and contradictory. To take one example, we know that Vinius exported 960 light cannon to Holland in 1646–1647. Yet in 1674 the observant Kilburger criticized Russian cannon for being of inferior quality. S. G.

Strumilin refers to the export of Tula cannon to refute Kilburger's opinion, saying, ". . . It seems they [cannon made in Russian manufactories] could not have been so poor if they were purchased abroad both before and after Kilburger." Thus far one might be disposed to accept Strumilin's logic — but for the realization that Miloslavskii, the Russian Ambassador to the Dutch General States in the mid-1640's, alleged that the Tula capitalists delivered inferior cannon to the Russian government and reserved the best of their output for foreign export.[9] Yet the fact that the Russian government consistently accepted cannon and other goods from Russian iron manufactories during the seventeenth century suggests that these weapons, on the whole, must have been useful to the army. If a larger number were destroyed on first firing than might have been the case for products made in Western Europe, the Russians probably accepted it as one of their inevitable difficulties in army supply.[10] The frequent praise of knowledgeable foreigners also contributes to an optimistic picture of Russian artillery. Thus in March of 1674 a party of Swedish diplomats told their Russian guides that

> . . . they were unable to disdain [the Russian] infantry and cannon, all the more because a number of monarchs could not possess better infantry regiments. . . . And they went to the city to the Kremlin and looked at where cannon are made, and they, the diplomats, studiously looked at these cannon and, as a consequence, praised them.[11]

Although the place "where cannon are made" was undoubtedly a large state artisan works — (probably the *Pushechnyi dovr*), it seems likely that iron manufactories were forced to produce weapons of comparable value.

There is a final indication that some weapons reaching the army were of satisfactory quality, even if many others were wasted due to low quality. We know that cannon at Tula were tested and that the government had inspectors who could reject parts of a delivery they considered unfit. Ivan Pustynnikov and *d'iak* Ivan Lomakin, for example, refused a number of cannon around 1647 because their barrels were too thin. As a result, the discarded artillery just sat around the factory.[12]

In estimating the quality of Russian manufacturing we must also keep in mind that the output of all enterprises within a given industry was not necessarily the same. Although Morozov's enterprise and the Zvenigorodskie factories worked on low-quality swamp and bog iron, Akema's Ugodskii and Porotovskii iron works and Werner Muller's manufactory used iron ore that produced finished iron more costly than fine Swedish iron. The three large iron manufactories built in the 1690's by Evert Isbrants, Aristov-Borin, and Nikita Demidov also made iron products from superior ore.

A survey of the relationship between price and quality in Russian manufactures besides iron at this time produces a mixed picture. Available evidence would suggest that Russian glass, rope, gunpowder, and sawmill products were of high standard and reasonable cost—whereas leather, silk, and textiles were not competitive by international standards, not even on the Russian market.[13] The Russian effort to manufacture paper appears to have been a great and continual disappointment. Six paper mills were established between the 1560's and 1690's, but all of these enterprises were small and short-lived, and even the technology of the Iauza works was backward in comparison with recent developments in Holland and Germany. Savinov's factory of 1564 soon closed because of its inability to make satisfactory paper, and the paper of Nikon's mill of the 1660's was said to have been "black" and unsuitable for use as stationery. There is no information about the quality of the output of the state Pakhra river factory of 1673. We do know that the paper manufactured at the van Sweeden Iauza paper mill in the same period was of useful quality, but at a market price of one ruble per ream it did not compare favorably with imported paper priced from ninety kopecks to one ruble, sixty kopecks per ream.*

*One of the problems of paper manufacturing in Russia during the sixteenth and seventeenth centuries was the scarcity of thin rags, for at this time paper was made from rags and strengthened with glue made from sheep hooves. The rags were rotted in large piles, boiled, washed, and bleached with alum. This thin material was pulverized by water-driven millstones.

Why did capitalist manufacturing in Russia not make greater progress during the sixteenth and seventeenth centuries? Scholarly opinion on this question has been divided. Some historians have emphasized that the lack of raw materials, as well as Russia's primitive and inadequate communications system, presented an enormous barrier to rapid industrial modernization. As we have seen, poor or unaccessible raw materials did present a problem at this time,* and it is true that foreigners spoke with horror of the absence of orderly paths of communication in the Muscovite state. In spring and fall sudden floods produced the notorious Russian "roadlessness" (*rasputitsa*) for at least a month in each season, making travel almost impossible throughout the entire country. Although foreign engineers worked in seventeenth-century Russia, they evidently built no roads. For this reason in northern Russia it was still best to travel in winter, when sleds could draw a passenger as far as four hundred miles in three days.[14] Commercial travelers in the south relied most heavily upon the use of navigable rivers in late spring and summer, though rapids and cataracts would cause dangerous moments, while portages presented all the hardships of overland travel. One can appreciate, then, the difficulties which existed in Russia at this time in carrying raw materials and industrial commodities,[15] and the resulting obstacles to industrial growth.[16]

The thick mass which emerged from this process was then put through log rollers and, finally, made into paper (Novitskii, "K istorii," pp. 36–38). Concerning Russian paper manufacturing at this time see also Kurts, *Sochinenie Kil'burgera*, pp. 117, 143, 146, 148.

*Poor quality of Russian livestock and hemp does much to explain the failure of leather and textile manufacturing at this time. The virtual absence of known copper precluded a large or flourishing copper industry, and Russian bronze depended on copper imported from Sweden, Lublin, and Hamburg. As for the natural wealth of Siberia, it lay virtually untouched until the eighteenth century, and some large iron deposits in central Russia (even) could not be exploited by existing mining technology. Thus one cannot doubt the significance of the availability or nonavailability of raw materials as a factor in Russian industrial development, for when hemp, wood, brimstone, and saltpeter *were* at hand, outstanding rope factories, sawmills, and gunpowder works could be, and were, constructed. Likewise the fine birch and superior sand, fireclay, and galena of the Moscow area go far toward explaining the success of the glass manufactories at Dukhanino and Izmailovo.

Other historians have judged that the political situation in medieval Russia presented a major obstacle to industrial development. A. M. Pankratova, for example, stressed that the Mongol invasion of the 1240's adversely affected the national economy, while the two centuries of the Mongol "yoke" which followed delayed the building of an independent centralized state which could liquidate prevailing elements of feudal disunity, create a unified and stable internal market, and reach out for commercial relations abroad.[17] From this, other scholars have gone on to say that the state which did emerge after the fifteenth century was neither institutionally nor ideologically conducive to the emergence of capitalism. To quote Mikhail Pokrovsky:

> It is an absolutely mistaken opinion that political conditions forced the growth of Russian capitalism in the seventeenth and eighteenth centuries; but it is quite true that the political framework of *a state that was controlled by the nobles* prevented this capitalism from developing . . . [and created the] administrative havoc so well depicted by Mr. Milyukov in his book.[18]

Still other historians have emphasized limitations of a specifically economic nature, such as the absence of banking and credit facilities, a complex and inhibiting system of internal customs and road tolls, and even certain practices governing the role of the entrepreneur himself.[19] To this I would add that the Russian government did not always relate to promising entrepreneurs in a manner so as to develop their maximum potential. This was especially true of *Russian* entrepreneurs, who had little or no influence at court. The four Tumashev brothers, for example, built a significant artisan iron shop east of the Urals on their own resources and might have organized larger-scale iron production. But "the government did not support [Dmitrii Tumashev]; on the contrary, it constantly ordered him to search for precious stones and copper and silver ores." An episode concerning the artisan Grigorii Grigor'ev is equally indicative of the state's attitude toward Russian commoners who aspired to develop modern industry. In 1658 the *Prikaz Tainykh Del* sent Grigor'ev to Kodomenskii *uezd* to prospect for silver ore. He failed to locate silver but did discover iron deposits, and on his own initiative he began to smelt that metal. But since he had been sent for silver and not iron, neither the tsar nor the *Prikaz* supported Grigor'ev's activities. He did not receive a single kopeck; the iron work dragged on and gradually stopped. As a result, Grigor'ev had to return to Moscow, where he sat idle for a long while before obtaining work elsewhere. In Kuzin's opinion:

> . . . had Grigor'ev received the same help from the tsar as Marselis and Akema, he might have been able to organize an iron-working enterprise of no smaller dimensions. Without support his project declined and the ore found in Kodomskii *uezd* was either forgotten or utilized by local smiths and artisan-smelters.[20]

And Nikita Demidov, who began his career as a gunsmith and ended it as the greatest Russian industrialist of the eighteenth century, built his first factory entirely with his own resources. It appears, then, that before Peter the Great only foreigners could win the confidence of the Russian government and receive material assistance for the construction of new manufactories,[21] and this probably retarded the development of Russian industry.

But all these factors do not really explain why Russian manufacturing failed to make greater progress during the sixteenth and seventeenth centuries. To be sure, such things as lack of raw materials, problems of transport, belated political unification and centralization, collection of trade duties and road tolls—all have a retarding effect on the development of capitalistic industry, especially at the very beginning when perseverance in the face of such obstacles is likely to be especially difficult. But all countries which have experienced intensive capitalistic development faced similar problems and in some way overcame them. In a very real sense, recalling Russia's problems with geography and politics does not so much explain why her capitalistic development in this period was limited as it forces a rephrasing of the question to ask *why* those particular obstacles at that particular time had such a great effect. Posing the problem in this manner will account not only for the *geographical-political context* in which Russian capitalism appeared, but for the *substance* of its development.

Capitalism is above all a series of social relationships resting upon a certain technological foundation. Specifically, capitalism means that wage-workers sell their labor power to those who have invested capital in the technology required for the profitable and competitive production of commodities. Any analysis of capitalism's growth, whatever the stage, should focus upon those three factors: class relationships, the availability of capital, and the prevailing state of technology. Given the proper relationship among these three elements, the greatest natural barriers will be overcome; and if the social forces concerned with capitalistic activity are sufficiently powerful, the most confining political practices and institutions will be thrust aside.

Certainly Russia in the sixteenth and seventeenth centuries lacked neither capital nor access to the most modern industrial techniques of Western Europe. Foreigners such as Andrei Vinius, Peter Marselis, Heinrich Butenant von Rosenbusch, and Werner Müller gathered large fortunes from their commercial activities and were capable of minimizing the inevitable risks of investment in manufactories by obtaining large loans, advances, and gifts from the state. And there were Russian feudalists far wealthier than any foreigner in Russia at the time, among them Boris Godunov, Aleksei Mikhailovich (who had an annual income of 200,000 rubles), Nikita Romanov, Prince I. K. Cherkasskii, Morozov, Miloslavskii, Trubetskoi, Odoevskii, and, above all, the Stroganov family. As for technology, it scarcely presented an insuperable problem. It was possible for Marselis and other foreigners to bring Western European engineers and masters to Russia to build and operate manufactories. Most interesting, perhaps, is the fact that by the 1680's the Russians had taken great steps toward mastering for themselves many of the once esoteric secrets of Western engineering. Yet no more than forty-eight manufactories were built from the 1630's to the 1690's. Why were there not many more?

The answer to this question may lie in the "third factor" in a country's capitalist development, namely the state of class relationships in that society. Capitalism, as a mode of production, does not attain great strength until the disintegration of feudalism reaches an advanced stage. The essence of feudalism is the attachment of the great mass of the population to dispersed agrarian communities where "natural" relationships are dominant between men, and the rather small demand for commodities is satisfied by local markets and artisans. At the base of the entire movement *from* a feudal-agrarian *to* a bourgeois-industrial order is the separation of the agricultural worker — whether slave, serf, or yeoman peasant — from the land which is simultaneously the means of his livelihood and the source of his economic backwardness. Such dispossession of the peasants by their social betters usually follows in the wake of technological improvements in agriculture which make it possible to feed large groups of people no longer engaged in farming. In fact, such technological innovation actually creates a class of "unemployed" peasants no longer needed on the land, a class which is then forced to seek its living in a new way by selling labor power to entrepreneurs endowed with capital and ready to undertake commodity production in search of profits. A rising curve of inflation and the increasing dominance of cash relationships over earlier "natural" exchange are also likely features of this period, for it is the new importance of money that makes agricultural reform both necessary and possible — necessary because inflation generates pressures on the style of life to which the aristocrat is accustomed, possible because of the increased income available to landlords who place their produce on the open market. The dynamics of the consumer market — its tendency to provide increasing quantities of goods and to bring ever-fresh layers of the population into cash relationships — also make profits from industrial activity a reality for the early capitalist. A final element in this process is the development of a sharp polarization within the artisan community, as the more fortunate handicraftsman evolves into a nascent entrepreneur holding capital and exploiting labor-power, while his less successful fellows move toward the status of wage-laborers hired by those who are able to hold — and expand — the new instruments of production.

Based on this analysis, we conclude that *serfdom* was the main barrier to extensive capitalist development in Russia during this period. The manner in which serfdom bound the peasant to the land precluded the availability of large masses of wage workers, and in any case the natural economy and rapacious exploitation which were intensified by the serf order made such workers unnecessary. Few people had money to exchange for commodities — so their industrial demands remained minimal. Markets for cash goods were small and industrial possibilities limited. To be sure, we do find significant capitalist *tendencies* in Russia in this period, even apart from the construction of manufactories, notably the formation of an all-Russian market and the beginnings of international commerce, a certain emphasis on *obrok* (quit-rent) rather than *barshchina* (corvée) in feudal relationships between lord and serf, the use of wage-labor in such traditional activities as river shipping and in some handicrafts, and even polarization tendencies within the artisan community. But because agriculture remained the primary source of profit for the ruling order of tsar, church, and nobility, the condition of the agricultural worker changed not in the direction of greater freedom and social mobility but rather in the direction of greater entanglement in the economic cycle of the manorial system.

Thus Russian manufacturing lacked broad opportunities for growth. The needs of the state (especially for war) provided a certain market for native factories, as did the desire for luxury goods among some members of the ruling class. A few enterprises were designed solely for export activity. But if some manufacturers relied upon consumer demand for part of their profits, no more than a few were able to base themselves solely upon production for the open market.[22] The broad social changes had not yet occurred which might have created a situation in which the masses had sufficient purchasing power to justify foreign and native entrepreneurs undertaking intensive manufacturing activity. So industrialists in this period — for the most part — took advantage of opportunities to build their enterprises only when profitable operation seemed all but guaranteed. Foreigners no less than Russians accepted the feudal framework with its strange mixture of opportunities and limitations, and adapted themselves to the existing realities of economic life. Manufacturers relied upon royal patronage and privileges, and accepted ascribed serfs for unskilled labor. If the enterprises organized in this fashion strengthened the Russian economy and laid the foundation for further capitalistic advances in the next century, they had no discernable influence on the "feudal" economic patterns of the seventeenth century.

In fact, the most striking indication of the resiliency of feudal institutions vis-à-vis early capitalistic manufacturing is the further development of artisanry during and after the seventeenth century. Although the expansion of Russian handicrafts was not as great during the seventeenth century as it had been in the fifteenth and sixteenth centuries,[23] the number of artisans grew considerably during the Petrine period, reaching a high point "between 1750 and 1850, and particularly in the last twenty-five years of that period."[24] The state smiths at Tula, for example, grew from thirty masters in 1595 to seventy in 1635 and 1,161 in 1720. And the output of Russian iron artisans must have been fairly large: late in 1678 the tsar commanded the masters of Novgorod to make two thousand or three thousand rifle locks; Patriarch Makarii was told in Moscow in 1654 that the tsar's workmen in the Kremlin made seven thousand muskets each year, and that arms were also being prepared in "the majority of the other cities without limit."[25] As we have seen, iron artisans were able even to secure *de facto* monopolies on such commodities as nails, shoemakers' awls, "and other small tools" which Marselis, Akema, and other iron manufacturers did not care to produce.* The continued vigor of Russian artisanry is but one indication that the kinds of shifts within Russian society which would have laid the basis for a more rapid and extensive development of capitalist manufacturing were not taking place on a broad scale during the sixteenth and seventeenth centuries.

Yet the modern industrial enterprises of seventeenth-century Russia were extremely important for the more intensive development which was to come from the early 1700's to 1725. If nothing else, a number of workers acquired the experience which enabled them to act as cadres for the energetic industrial projects of Peter the Great. In the case of the glass industry, for example, this kind of influence of one century on the next was obvious and direct, for in 1724 a large mirror and crystal glass factory was built near Moscow by former masters of the state Izmailovo works. The new enterprise was also located in Chernogolovskaia *volost'*, took the Izmailovo manufactory as its model, and used raw materials which had been available to the tsar's glass mill. In another instance, Heinrich Münter, the former partner of Maria and Peter Coyet in their Dukhanino factory, assumed ownership in 1719 of a glass factory which had been built by P. Vestov, a Russian sugar manufacturer. The development of glass manufacturing in the Ukraine during the seventeenth century also was of special importance in preparing the way for an impressive growth of the industry in a later period.[26]

The impact of sixteenth- and seventeenth-century rope manufacturing upon Russian efforts in the following period is also apparent. A number of Russians learned rope-spinning at the English rope walks of Vologda and Kholmogory, and when these enterprises closed at the end of the sixteenth century Russians (and at least one foreigner) continued rope-making in the same area, although the scale of production was probably smaller than that of the English. By the 1690's Vologda and Nizhnyi-Novgorod were active centers of rope artisanry, and

---

*During the 1670's peasant forges were turning out steel, nails, shoemakers' awls (*kochediki* and *sapozhnye shili*), and "other small tools."

in 1697 and 1698 Peter I sent dozens of these masters to organize rope factories in Moscow and Voronezh, and, much later, in 1718, to St. Petersburg. The Russian paper industry before 1700, backward as it was, likewise laid the basis for striking improvements and expanded output during the eighteenth century.[27]

Even the rather dismal Russian efforts to create a seagoing fleet during the sixteenth and seventeenth centuries had a direct and seminal influence on the true founder of the Russian navy, Peter the Great. Queen Elizabeth of England, knowing Ivan the Terrible's interest in ships, sent him a sailboat as a token of her good will. The ship finally passed into the hands of Prince Nikita Romanov, and later it lay (in disrepair) in a shed at Izmailovo—until one day in 1687 young Tsar Peter discovered this "battered old English boat." With as much fancy as fact, perhaps, Peter was to maintain in later years that his passion for navigation dated from the time he discovered Elizabeth's gift. But it is also true that two years before the Izmailovo episode Peter had been fascinated with ship models which Kliuchevskii suggested were prepared for the building of the *Orel* in the 1660's. In any event, at this point the elements of the past came quickly into focus as factors working to shape the future. For

> Karsten Brandt, who had constructed that ship [the *Orël*], was engaged by Peter to repair the Elizabethan one, which, after sailing on the [Iauza] River at Moscow, was sent to Kronstadt by order of the Tsar, saluted by his ships of war, and returned eventually to Moscow, to be kept as a perpetual reminder of how, from so small a beginning, a fleet could arise.[28]

But the most significant aspect of earlier Russian industrial development for the later period was most certainly iron manufacturing. No fewer than nineteen iron factories continued to operate beyond the close of the seventeenth century, and they helped supply the army during the Great Northern War.* Equally important, perhaps, was the training of sev-

---

*At least fifteen of these enterprises, and perhaps two others, were producing iron goods even in the *mid*-eighteenth century, or *later*. In addition, two

enteenth-century iron masters which enabled them to build some of the most famous and important Petrine enterprises. The large Nev'ianskii and Kamenskii iron factories of the Urals, in particular, bore a direct genetic relationship to earlier enterprises and personalities. They were organized by the state early in the eighteenth century under the direction of A. A. Vinius and Semen Kiprianov, who had also organized the "new Zvenigorodskie" iron works in 1686 as the partner of the wealthy *gost'* Vladimir Voronin. The builders and first workers at these Urals works were actually from the Zvenigorodskie complex, and, despite the great distances involved, they brought with them equipment from the older factories. Without the manufactories and workers of the Moscow-Tula area, the Kamenskii and Nev'ianskii enterprises could never have been built so easily and quickly.[29]

The significance of Russian industrial development in the early modern period becomes even clearer through some brief comparisons with the iron industries of other countries. Leslie Aitchison has estimated the iron output of all European countries by the late 1400's at about sixty thousand tons per year.[30] Germany and France accounted for thirty thousand and ten thousand tons respectively of this figure, but presumably Russia did not even enter into Aitchison's calculations. By the first third of the seventeenth century Russian performance in this area was still modest. In the late 1630's Russia had only four iron manufactories at Tula, and they produced no more than 450 tons (25,000 *puds*) of pig iron each year. In 1625 Sweden alone obtained annually some 9,500 tons of pig and bar-iron from her iron factories.[31] So we see that Russia was still far behind the other major European powers.[32]

By the 1670's, however, Russian iron works were rolling about 2,700 tons (150,000 *puds*) of pig iron each year, and by the turn of the century output may have reached 4,500 tons (250,000 *puds*).[33] Therefore, if Swedish iron production increased fivefold between 1600 and 1720,[34] Russian produc-

glass works, a sawmill, and a gunpowder manufactory from this period were active during the early 1700's.

tion rose *ten times* from the 1630's to the late 1690's, and almost eight times *again* between 1700 and 1740. It is a strange and seldom appreciated fact that by 1725 Russia was the world's *leading producer of iron*. In 1740, having cast 31,975 metric tons* of pig iron, Russian manufactories far exceeded the achievement of the iron industries of France (25,979 metric tons), England (20,017 tons), and Germany (17,691 tons).[35] And Russia held its outstanding position in ferrous metallurgy until the beginning of the nineteenth century,[36] though it must be said that more than half of Russian iron production was exported, mainly to England. Soon after 1800, however, the Russian iron industry began to decline, and by 1860 Russia produced only 335,500 tons of pig iron, while England cast almost four million tons. Although we cannot analyze here the reasons for the relative rise and fall of Russian iron manufacturing during the eighteenth and nineteenth centuries, the importance of the seventeenth-century foundation for this entire course of development is clear.

Are we, then, justified in saying that Russia entered into a course of capitalistic development as early as the seventeenth century? If we take *capitalism* to be nothing more than the socio-economic system that was emerging in England or Holland at this time, we may be forced to conclude that Russia was *not* capitalistic. For Russian economic development in this period was different in many crucial respects: the sovereign was himself a vigorous entrepreneur who used his absolute political authority to advance private economic interests; even in the area of "private enterprise," property rights were uncertain and the state played a key supervisory role; the tsar ascribed Cossacks, *strel'tsy,* peasants, and others to foreign-built manufactories; and so on. Reflecting on these and other realities, such old-regime historians as Paul Miliukov and Michael Tugan-Baranovsky have concluded that "capitalistic" efforts in seventeenth-century Russia were vain and arbitrary attempts (largely on the part of the government) to

*One metric ton = 1.10231 short tons; one short ton = 2,000 lbs.

foster economic activities which differed qualitatively from the real thrust of the nation's economic institutions and practices.[37]

Nor has such skepticism concerning Russia's early capitalistic development been limited to earlier generations of economic historians. The distinguished Soviet scholar A. M. Pankratova denies that one may speak of capitalist relations in Russia, "*i.e.,* of class contradictions between a bourgeoisie and a proletariat," before the last two-thirds of the eighteenth century. An American student of Russian industrial development, William M. Blackwell, has maintained that

> Russia in the several decades prior to Peter the Great witnessed the building of its first factories, but these were little more than overgrown craftsmen's shops or loose agglomerations of individual workers in specific localities. There were no machines; Russian technology was primitive at best. Beyond some use of water power for mills, it was almost totally nonindustrial in its application, the work of occasional, dexterous hands in the employ of the church, the army, or the court. Science was nonexistent in a rigid, anti-rational religious environment obscurantist and hostile to any innovation that smacked of the West.

And Jesse D. Clarkson believes that during the sixteenth and seventeenth centuries, "In early Muscovy there is — apart from the Stroganovs and the monasteries — no indication of any capitalistic spirit, of rational calculation of economic activity for the sake of long time gain. . . ."[38]

My own research as presented in this book forces me to an opposite opinion. Clarkson's contention, in particular, is based upon a wholly inadequate understanding of the social and economic forces that were operating throughout this entire period. He is obviously unaware, for example, that Boris Morozov (to cite only one of many possible instances of "rational calculation" in a "capitalistic spirit" for the sake of entrepreneurial "gain") owned seventeen large potash factories whose output was esteemed even abroad, and which brought him an annual income of 24,000 rubles.[39] As for Blackwell's conclusion, I can only hope I have shown that

Russian opinion was far from hostile to foreign manufacturing activity,* and that the government constantly sought to encourage it in many ways. Nor is it correct to characterize Russian manufactories as "little more than overgrown craftsmen's shops" with "no machines." The Dutch Tula factories of the 1630's were technologically advanced by even the most stringent international standards, and Russian iron works built at the end of the century demonstrated striking advances in such areas as blast-furnace productivity and division of labor.[40] Finally, Pankratova may be correct in denying the existence of specific "class contradictions" between the proletariat *as a class* and manufactory owners *as a class* during the seventeenth century. But incontrovertible evidence urges us to think that, "contradictions" aside,[41] the two classes *did exist* and that the high wages of the former (which included free Russians) were exceeded only by the considerable profits of the latter, profits realized through exploitation of labor-power by such capitalists as Vinius, Marselis, Akema, and John of Sweden.

There is no reason to think of capitalism as an academic model whose features are to be derived from one particular country (England, for example), a model which the historian is then to apply in rigid fashion to other nations at other times to see if they, too, are to be called *capitalistic*. Most of the fifty-seven manufactories treated in this book were built by entrepreneurs who sought to realize profits from commodity production. We need not exaggerate either the number of these enterprises or the success of their activity to appreciate the nature and extent of the achievement and its significance for a later and more dynamic age. If the state and foreigners played a great role in this process — and if it occurred late in comparison with the West — Russia was not really so very different

---

*Peasant conflicts with the Marselises, Butenant von Rosenbusch, and other foreigners (pp. 123 ff., above) do not appear to have been caused by a principled hostility "to any innovation that smacked of the West," but rather by perfectly explicable conflicts of *class interest* which could have occurred — and did — as easily in Western Europe at this and in later times.

even in those respects from England, Sweden, or France. The first blast furnace in England was not set up until the 1490's, probably by a visiting Frenchman — a nationality which was important for a long time in English metallurgy, as were Germans, both as investors and skilled workers, throughout the entire sixteenth century. As for France, Colbert engaged numerous Swedish ironworkers to modernize French enterprises during the mid-seventeenth century. As in Russia at the same time, the foreigners were obliged to instruct native masters in their skills, but

> French workers complained that the Swedes, who were jealously guarding the Swedish secrets of production, would order them to leave every time a critical stage in the production process was reached. [A similar attitude was encountered by the English iron master Foley], who was anxious to learn the secrets of the Swedish rolling and slitting mills but saw no other way to do so than to disguise himself as a wandering minstrel in the hope of gaining admission to a Swedish ironmill.[42]

Even Sweden was not an isolated post of industrial enterprise. The first blast furnace did not enter the country before the mid-1400's, and Sweden attained a position of consequence only during the sixteenth century. Gustavus I (1523-1560) speeded the modernization of the country's iron industry by employing German masters who built both public and private works. French and English technology was also adapted to Sweden with splendid results, although Holland provided most of the entrepreneurs during the seventeenth century.[43] A Dutchman introduced modern copper-smelting into Sweden in the early 1600's, and the Swedish brass industry "was virtually controlled by immigrants" throughout the entire century.[44] The following words of Michael Roberts might well cause us to think of such Russian contemporaries as Ivan the Terrible or Aleksei Mikhailovich:

> All the early Vasa kings were keenly interested in developing the manufacture of arms and armour, in order that Sweden might ultimately become independent of foreign supplies; and most of them imported armourers and gunsmiths from aboard to supplement the skill of the local workmen. They had considerable success with this policy.[45]

Yet as late as 1600 Sweden had not a single paper mill, nor by 1611 a modern textile industry.[46]

As for England in this period, an anonymous writer of the mid-1500's estimated the home production of iron to be a mere half of what was needed for internal consumption and lamented the fact that this made England dependent upon supplementary imports from abroad, which not only depleted the nation's specie but imperiled its safety in time of war. The king, we are told, was compelled to rely on foreigners for "armour, all kinds of artillerie, anckers . . . , yron, steile, handgonnes, and manie other things" which had to be paid for "at the price the strainger will set."[47] For this reason English rulers of the sixteenth and early seventeenth centuries took active measures to develop home metallurgy,[48] in large part by inviting foreign masters to enter the country to build and operate iron and copper manufactories.

This was a time in which warfare between the great powers of Europe led most of them to borrow freely from others the technological wherewithal to sustain intense military and commercial competition. Russia began her "borrowing" later than the other powers, and she had not made as much progress as the others before the end of the seventeenth century. But, as we can see, the differences between Russia and the West in these respects were not differences of kind but rather of degree.

In 1965 the Soviet Union produced 62 million tons of pig iron and 91 million tons of steel, 190 million square meters of window glass, and almost 800 million square meters of silk. Four great Soviet iron enterprises in 1956 turned out more than 14 million tons of pig iron; in the same year the Balakhna paper mill alone accounted for nearly 200,000 tons of paper.[49] The difference between this period of the nation's industrial history and the epoch represented by the manufactories of Vinius, Marselis, Julius Coyet, and John of Sweden is all but phenomenal. After all, how is one to compare the fifty thousand *puds* of the Sorokinskii-Kaminskii iron works to the *four-thousand-fold* greater capacity of the Magnitogorsk, Kuznetsk, or Zaporozhal factories? Or the tremendous output of the Balakhna paper works to the seventy-five reams from Nikon's poor Iauza mill — "black" and suitable only for bookbinding? And if the Coyet family was proud to send eighty to ninety thousand bottles to the market in Moscow each year, could they have dreamed of an enterprise that would produce that many bottles in a matter of days?

Such comparisons and speculations are interesting, but there is no point in using them to belittle the work of earlier generations. For a man of insight knows that a tree grows by stages, a mountain is worn away through centuries, and each day has problems sufficient unto itself.

APPENDIX I

The Russian Ruble from the Sixteenth to the Eighteenth Century

Russian Currency of the Sixteenth and Seventeenth Centuries

1 ruble = 100 kopecks = 200 *den'gi*
1 *grivna* = 20 *den'gi*
1 *altyn* = 6 *den'gi*
1 *poltina* = 50 kopecks
1 *polupoltina* = 25 kopecks

Efimok (Joachimsthaler), see entry in Glossary.

The Changing Value of the Russian Ruble

One ruble of 1500 = at least 100 rubles of 1882
1501-1550 = 63-83
1551-1600 = 60-74

1601-1612 = 12
1613-1636 = 14
1651-1700 = 17

269

$$1701\text{-}1715 = 9$$
$$1730\text{-}1740 = 10$$
$$1741\text{-}1750 = 9$$

SOURCE: V. O. Kliuchevskii, "Russkii rubl' xvi-xvii vv. v ego otnoshenii k nyneshnemu" ("The Russian Ruble from the Sixteenth to Eighteenth Centuries in Its Relationship to the Ruble of Today"), in *Sochineniia (Works),* VII (Moscow, 1959), 236.

APPENDIX II

Some Russian Weights and Measures of the Sixteenth and Seventeenth Centuries

Linear Measures

Arshin = .71 meter, about 28 inches
Chetvert', chet' = .25 *arshin*
Sazhen = 2.13 meters, about 7 feet
Versta = 1.067 kilometers, about 0.6629 miles
          (about 3500 feet)
1 sazhen = 3 *arshiny* = 12 *chetverti*
1 versta = 500 *sazheny*

Weights and Volumes

Berkovets = 10 *puds,* 163.81 kilograms, 361 pounds
    avoirdupois
Chetvert', Chet' = 24 *puds;* 209 liters or about 8 bushels
    (volume)
Funt = about 408.24 grams, about 14.4 ounces avoirdupois;
    96 *zolotniki* = one *funt*
Grivna = about one *funt*

Pud =   16.381 kilograms, 36.113 pounds avoirdupois; 40
   funty = one *pud*
Shiffunt = 500 *funty*
Zolotnik = about 4.25 grams, exactly .15 ounce; see *funt*
1 pud = 40 funts = 3840 *zolotniki*

MAIN SOURCE: V. I. Dal', *Tolkovyi slovar' zhivogo velikorus-skogo iazyka (Explanatory Dictionary of the Living Great Russian Language)* (Moscow, reprinted 1955), in four volumes.

Russian Manufactories During the Sixteenth and Seventeenth Centuries

Unless otherwise specified, the dates below refer to the year in which the enterprise *began* operation, and the year it was closed. In case of doubt as to size, an enterprise has been classified "small" (S).

> L - Large enterprise (relative to that particular industry)
> S - Small enterprise
> * - Equipped with a blast furnace
> ** - May not have been a manufactory

Iron Manufactories

* (S)   1. Stroganov works, 1583- ?

Tula (Gorodishchenskie) iron manufactories:
  (S)   2. No. 1, 1637-before 1690
* (L)   3. No. 2, 1637-mid-18th century
  (S)   4. No. 3, 1637-before 1690

  (L)   5. No. 4, 1637-mid-18th century
* (S)   6. Vaga river, 1648 (soon closed)
* (S)   7. Iauza river, c. 1649 (soon closed)
* (L)   8. Pavlovskii, 1651-1686†

Kashirskie iron manufactories:

  (S)   9. Vedmenskii, built 1653-mid-18th century
  (S) 10. Salamykovskii, built 1653-mid-18th century
  (L) 11. Chentsovskii, built 1653-mid-18th century
  (L) 12. Elkinskii, built 1653-mid-18th century
* (S) 13. Porotovskii, mid-1650's-1673
* (L) 14. Ugodskii, built 1659-mid-18th century
* (L) 15. Vepreiskii (Aleksinskii), 1671-mid-18th century
  (S) 16. Borodnikovskii, 1669-1686†
  (S) 17. Obushkovskii, 1672-1686†

Olonets iron manufactories:

* (S) 18. Ust', early 1680's
  (S) 19. Spirovskii, early 1680's
  (S) 20. Lizhemskii, 1689
  (S) 21. Kedrozerskii, early 1690's

In reconstructed form, the Olonets factories continued to operate into the 19th century

  (L) 22. Istenskii, 1680-mid-18th century
  (L) 23. Sorokinskii, 1686-1705††
  (L) 24. Kezminskii, 1686-1705††
  (L) 25. Dugna river, built ca. 1690−mid-18th century
* (L) 26. Vora river, 1690's-18th century (?)
* (L) 27. Romanovskii, built 1693-1725 or later
* (L) 28. Demidov's Tula manufactory, 1687-1754

---

† These factories were collectively called the "Zvenigorodskie" enterprises.

†† Replaced the old "Zvenigorodskie" factories and were called the "new Zvenigorodskie" works.

Glass Manufactories

- (L) 1. Coyet's Dukhanino works, built 1634-1705 (?)
- (L) 2. Izmailovo, built 1669-after 1706
- (S) 3. Chernogolovskii, noted in documents of 1687

Paper Manufactories

- (S) 1. Utsa river, 1560's-before 1576
- (S) 2. Burtsev-Frum enterprise, 1630's-*ca.* 1641
- (S) 3. Burtsev-Shpil'kin Pakhra river, 1665-1667
- (S) 4. Pakhra river works above as reconstructed by John of Sweden, 1668-before 1685
- (S) 5. Iauza river, 1673-1682 †††
- (S) 6. Savka's mill near Moscow, noted in document of 1693

Gunpowder Works

- ** (L) 1. Moscow, of the French master Aleviz, destroyed 1531
- ** (S) 2. Iauza river, c. 1626
- (L?) 3. David Bacheracht's powder works near Moscow, built 1650
- (L) 4. Bacheracht's Iauza river works, *ca.* 1655-1673 and 1682-after 1693
- (S) 5. Izbrants' Vora river powder works, existed in 1698

Rope Walks

- (L) 1. Kholmogory, 1557-late 16th century (?)
- (L) 2. Vologda, *ca.* 1560-late 16th century (?)
- ** (S) 3. Karp Demulin's enterprise at Kholmogory, cited in documents of 1623

††† Paper manufactory No. 5 and gunpowder works No. 4 occupied the same buildings on the Iauza river.

Textile Mills

(S)   1. Flax-spinning works of English Muscovy Company at Kholmogory, late 16th century

(S)   2. Egidius Tabbert's Moscow mill, *ca.* 1684-*ca.* 1689

(L)   3. Franz Timmermann's sailcloth factory at Archangel, built 1693-*ca.* 1697

Sawmills

(S)   1. Butenant von Rosenbusch's sawmill near Archangel, operated in 1691

(S)   2. Grudtsyn's sawmill near Archangel, 1690's

(L)   3. Bazhenin brothers' sawmill near Archangel, 1690's-early 18th century

Copper Manufactories

(S)   1. Onega-Olonets area, early 1670's (soon abandoned)

(S)   2. Butenant's copper works in Foimogubskaia *volost'*, 1676-1680

Leather Tanneries

(S)   1. Enterprise located successively on the Iauza river, at Chasnikov, on Vorontsovo field, 1666-1676

Silk-Weaving Enterprises

(S)   1. Marco Chinopi's Kremlin shop, 1593/4-*ca.* 1597

(S)   2. *Barkhatnyi dvor* (velvet court) in Moscow, *ca.* 1632 - before 1650

(S)   3. Arent Paulsen's Moscow shop, 1682-1689

Notes

Introduction

1. See Meyer Reinhold, "Historian of the Ancient World: A Critique of Rostovtzeff," *Science and Society*, X (1946), 361–391. M. Rostovtzeff, *Social and Economic History of the Hellenistic World* (Oxford, 1959), I, 100–101; II, 1302–1307. M. Rostovtzeff, *Social and Economic History of the Roman Empire* (Oxford, 1926), pp. 142–179, 482–483. Henri Pirenne, *Histoire économique de l'Occident médiéval* (Bruges, 1951), pp. 15–50.

2. This feat is actually accomplished in William L. Langer, *et al.*, *Western Civilization; Paleolithic Man to the Emergence of Europen Powers* (New York, 1968), where the reader is at once assured that the economy of ancient Mesopotamia "became capitalistic" during the third millenium B.C., and that "[c]apitalism developed first in the most highly industrialized European areas of Flanders and Italy" at the end of the thirteenth century A.D. (pp. 37, 672). Both conclusions strike me as premature.

3. Marc Bloch, "The Advent and Triumph of the Water Wheel," in *Land and Work in Medieval Europe* (Berkeley and Los Angeles, 1967), p. 137. S. Lilley, *Men, Machines and History: The Story of Tools and Machines in Relation to Social Progress* (London, 1965), pp. 46, 78. Paul Mantoux, *The Industrial Revolution in the Eighteenth Century* (London, 1961), p. 25.

4. Maurice Dobb, *Studies in the Development of Capitalism* (New York, 1963), pp. 17–18.

278 *Notes*

5.　I. V. Stepanov, "Otkhod naseleniia na zarabotki v Povolzh'e v xvii v" [Movement of the population to wage labor in Povolzh'e during the seventeenth century], *Uchenye zapiski Leningradskogo gosudarstven-nogo universiteta* [Academic notes of Leningrad State University], XIV (1949), No. 112. N. V. Ustiutov, "Rabotnye liudi na Sukhono-Dvinskom vodnom puti v pervoi polovine xvii v." [Working people on the Suk-hono-Dvinsk water route during the first half of the seventeenth century], *I.z.,* VI (1940), 166–194. V. G. Geiman, "Solianoi promysel gostia I. D. Pankrat'eva v Iarenskom uezde v xvii veke" [Salt works of gost' I. D. Pankrat'ev in Iarenskii *uezd* during the seventeenth century], *Letopis' zaniatii arkheograficheskoi komissii* [Chronicle of the activities of the archeological commission], XXXV (1929). K. N. Serbina, *Ocherki iz sotsial'no-ekonomicheskoi istorii russkogo goroda: Tikhvinskii posad v xvi-xviii vv* [Studies in the social economic history of a Russian town: Tikhvinskii suburb during the sixteenth, seventeenth, and eighteenth centuries] (Moscow-Leningrad, 1951). V. I. Shunkov, "O feodal'nom stroe sibirskoi derevni" [Concerning the feudal structure of the Siberian countryside], *V.i.,* No. 6 (1952). *K. voprosu o pervonachal'nom nako-plenii v Rossii (xvii-xviii vv.): Sbornik statei* [On the question of primary accumulation in Russia (seventeenth and eighteenth centuries): A collection of articles], published in Moscow in 1958 by the Institute of History of the Academy of Sciences, contains valuable articles and bibliographical information on this subject.

6.　As the reader will see from the bibliography to this book, relevant articles by G. A. Novitskii, N. A. Baklanovna, I. V. Chekan, and others were published in the 1920's or 1930's. B. B. Kafengauz, S. G. Strumilin, A. M. Pankratova, E. I. Zaozerskaia, and P. G. Liubomirov have written monographs dealing with early Russian industry, but in all cases the pre-Petrine period is treated tangentially, usually in a few introductory pages or paragraphs, as it is in Roger Portal's fine study of the Urals iron industry during the eighteenth century. Short books by Baklanov-Mavrodin-Smirnov and N. N. Stoskova on the iron industry are valuable but do not fill the need for a broad study of manufacturing as a whole in Russia during the sixteenth and seventeenth centuries. Interesting pre-revolutionary studies of various early Russian industries were written by N. P. Likhachev, E. Lermontova, G. M. Belotserkovskii, Iosif Gamel', A. I. Zaozerskii, and others, but obviously these scholars could not benefit from later Soviet research and interpretation. Apart from a sketchy article by George Vernadsky and a splendid book by Erik Amburger, little has been contributed by historians of Russia living in the West to our understanding of Russian manufacturing during the early modern period.

1. The Town Life, Artisanry, and Commerce of Early Modern Russia

1.　M. N. Pokrovsky, *History of Russia from the Earliest Times to the Rise of Commercial Capitalism,* trans. and ed. J. D. Clarkson and M. R. M. Griffiths (Bloomington, Ind., 1966), p. 90.

2.　B. A. Rybakov, *Remeslo drevnei rusi* [Artisanry of ancient Russia] (Moscow, 1948), p. 522.

3. George Vernadsky, *The Mongols and Russia* (New Haven and London, 1953), p. 338.

4. Cited in Nicholas V. Riasanovsky, *A History of Russia* (New York, 1963), p. 79, with no indication of source.

5. *Ocherki istorii SSSR. Period feodalizma IX-XV vv. v dvukh chastiakh* [Studies in the history of the U.S.S.R.: Period of feudalism, ninth through fifteenth centuries, in two parts], part 2 (Moscow, 1953), 112. The chapters on economic history in this *Ocherki SSSR* series are based upon extensive archival work and contain useful information not easily available elsewhere.

6. Concerning the post-Mongol decline of Kievan enamel, filigree, niello technique, glazed polychrome ceramics, etc., see Vernadsky, *Mongols and Russia,* pp. 339–340.

7. Jerome Blum, *Lord and Peasant in Russia from the Ninth to the Nineteenth Century* (Princeton, N.J., 1961), p. 62.

8. S. M. Solov'ev, *Istoriia Rossii s drevneishikh vremen* [History of Russia from the most ancient times], IV (Moscow, 1960), 533, 543–547.

9. A. A. Zimin thinks *obrok* in kind, however, continued to be the basic form of peasant rent during the sixteenth century. See *Ocherki istorii SSSR: Period feodalizma, konets XV v.-nachalo XVII v.,* [Studies in the history of the U.S.S.R.: Period of feudalism, end of the fifteenth century to the beginning of the seventeenth century] (Moscow, 1955), pp. 50, 226.

10. *Ocherki istorii SSSR . . . konets XV v.-nachalo XVII v.,* pp. 261–262.

11. Lloyd E. Berry and Robert O. Crummey (eds.), *Rude and Barbarous Kingdom: Russia in the Accounts of Sixteenth-Century English Voyagers* (Madison, Milwaukee, and London, 1968), p. 67.

12. Baron Sigismund von Herberstein, *Notes upon Russia, Being a Translation of the Earliest Account of that Country Entitled Rerum Moscoviticarum Commentarii,* trans. and ed. R. H. Major (London, "Printed for the Hakluyt Society," 1852), II, 5. Berry, *Rude and Barbarous Kingdom,* p. 23. *Ocherki istorii SSSR . . . konets XV v.-nachalo XVII v.,* pp. 262–266.

13. S. V. Bakhrushin, *Nauchnye trudy* [Scholarly works] (Moscow, 1952), I, 29–35. For completeness Bakhrushin's survey supersedes N. D. Chechulin's roster of 210 urban trades, *Goroda Moskovskago gosudarstva v XVI veke* [Cities of the Muscovite state during the sixteenth century] (St. Petersburg, 1889), p. 339.

14. Peter I. Lyashchenko, *History of the National Economy of Russia to the 1917 Revolution,* trans. L. M. Herman (New York, 1949), p. 206.

15. *Ocherki istorii SSSR . . . konets XV v.-nachalo XVII v.,* pp. 246, 72–73.

16. Lyashchenko, *History of the National Economy of Russia,* p. 206. A. I.

Pashkov, *et. al., A History of Russian Economic Thought: Ninth Through Eighteenth Centuries,* ed. J. M. Letiche, trans. B. Dmytryshyn and R. A. Pierce (Berkeley and Los Angeles, 1964), p. 184; based upon archival information. Pavel Smirnov, *Moskovskie tkachi XVII v. i ikh privilegii* [Muscovite weavers of the seventeenth century and their privileges] (Tashkent, 1928), p. 3.

17. Giles Fletcher noted that during 1588–1589 the Volga, Dvina, and Kola rivers and the Pereiaslavl' area were important for various kinds of fish. He adds: "Their chief towns for fish are Iaroslavl', Beloozero, Novgorod, Astrakhan', and Kazan', which all yield a large custom to the emperor every year for their trades of fishing which they practice in summer, but send it frozen in the wintertime into all parts of the realm." From Fletcher's *Of the Russe Commonwealth* as reprinted in Berry, *Rude and Barbarous Kingdom,* pp. 122–123.

18. *Ocherki istorii SSSR ... konets XV v.-nachalo XVII v.,* pp. 35, 78, 66–68.

19. *Ibid.,* pp. 68–69. Berry, *Rude and Barbarous Kingdom,* p. 121. Lyashchenko, *History of the National Economy of Russia,* pp. 160, 162.

20. *Ocherki istorii SSSR ... konets XV v.-nachalo XVII v.,* pp. 57, 257.

21. George Vernadsky, *Kievan Russia* (New Haven and London, 1948), p. 111.

22. George Vernadsky, "Iron Mining and Iron Industries in Medieval Russia," *Etudés dédiées à la mémoire d'Andreé Andréadès* (Athens, Greece, 1939), p. 363.

23. B. A. Kolchin, *Tekhnika obrabotki metalla v drevnei Rusi* [Technique of metal-working in ancient Russia] (Moscow, 1953), pp. 22–39. A. M. Pankratova, *Formirovanie proletariata v Rossii (xvii-xviii vv.)* [Formation of the proletariat in Russia (seventeenth and eighteenth centuries)] (Moscow, 1963), p. 36. N. N. Stoskova, *Pervye metallurgicheskie zavody Rossii* [First metallurgical factories of Russia] (Moscow, 1962), p. 14.

24. Kolchin, *Tekhnika,* p. 23. Pankratova, *Formirovanie,* p. 37.

25. Pokrovsky, *History of Russia,* p. 95. Thomas Esper, "Military Self-Sufficiency and Weapons Technology in Muscovite Russia," *Slavic Review,* hereafter cited as *S.R.,* XXVIII (June 1969), 187–191, 197. P. P. Zabarinskii, "550 letie russkoi artilleri" [550 years of Russian artillery], *Sbornik issledovanii i materialov artilleriiskogo istoricheskogo muzeia krasnoi armii* [Collection of studies and materials of the Historical Artillery Museum of the Red Army], I (1940), 54–55. Rybakov, *Remeslo,* pp. 602–605. Arthur Voyce, *Moscow and the Roots of Russian Culture* (Norman, Okla., 1964), pp. 55–56.

26. Von Herberstein, *Notes upon Russia,* I, 98. *Ocherki istorii SSSR . . . konets XV v.-nachalo XVII v.,* pp. 55, 240, 336.

27. *Ocherki istorii SSSR . . . konets XV v.-nachalo XVII v.,* p. 54. S. G. Strumilin, *Istoriia chernoi metallurgii v SSSR* [History of ferrous metallurgy in the U.S.S.R.] (Moscow, 1954), I, 16–32. Bakhrushin, *Nauchnye*

trudy, I, 56-72. Pankratova, *Formirovanie,* pp. 129-130, 42.

28. Serbina, *Ocherki . . . Tikhvinskii posad, pp. 82-84, 92-94.*

29. *Ibid.,* pp. 112-119, 121-130.

30. *Ocherki istorii SSSR . . . konets XV v.-nachalo XVII v.,* p. 250.

31. *Ibid.,* pp. 254, 75. Heinrich von Staden, *The Land and Government of Muscovy: A Sixteenth-Century Account,* ed. and trans. Thomas Esper (Stanford, 1967), p. 81.

32. M. G. Rabinovich writing in *Ocherki istorii SSSR . . . konets XV v.-nachalo XVII v.,* pp. 262-266. Bakhrushin, *Nauchnye trudy,* 1, 39.

33. Berry, *Rude and Barbarous Kingdom,* pp. 31-32.

34. Von Herberstein, *Notes upon Russia,* I, 113.

35. A. A. Zimin accepts Jerome Horsey's contention that by the mid-1500's the Church owned one-third of Russia's arable land. See *Ocherki istorii SSSR . . . konets XV v.-nachalo XVII v.,* p. 223.

36. Von Staden, *Land and Government of Muscovy,* p. 80.

37. Raymond H. Fisher, *The Russian Fur Trade, 1550-1700* (Berkeley and Los Angeles, 1943), pp. 20-21, 36, 48-67, 192, 207-209.

    In 1595, when the Russian government sent an embassy to Holy Roman Emperor Rudolf II, Russian furs arrived in the West in the most dramatic way. To advance their diplomatic objectives Russian statesmen made Rudolf a present of 1,003 timbers (a timber being forty skins tied between two boards) of sable, 519 timbers of marten, 120 black fox skins, 337,000 ordinary fox pelts, 3,000 beaver skins, 1,000 wolf skins, and 74 elk skins. Quite overcome, Rudolf employed many large rooms of his palace to display his great and curious treasure. In Russia these furs had been valued at 44,645 rubles; but a group of Prague merchants set a Western value on these furs of 400,000 rubles—a figure which did not include the black fox skins, which the appraisers declared quite simply to be priceless! Adam Olearius, *The Travels of Olearius in Seventeenth-Century Russia,* ed. and trans. Samuel H. Baron (Stanford, 1967), p. 179. Fisher, *Russian Fur Trade,* pp. 110, 138. Cf. Walther Kirchner's unconvincing contention that Russian fur exports declined in value after (and because of) the Reformation and Counter-Reformation (*Commercial Relations Between Russia and Europe, 1400 to 1800: Collected Essays* [Bloomington, Ind., 1966], p. 13).

38. Fisher, *Russian Fur Trade,* pp. 231-232. Pokrovsky, *History of Russia,* p. 258. Berry, *Rude and Barbarous Kingdom,* p. 119.

39. *Ibid.,* pp. 118, 120. C. Bickford O'Brien, *Russia Under Two Tsars, 1682-1689, the Regency of Sophia Alekseevna* (Berkeley and Los Angeles, 1952), p. 69.

40. Pokrovsky, *History of Russia,* p. 265. *Ocherki istorii SSSR . . . konets XV v.-nachalo XVII v.,* pp. 118-121.

41. *Ibid.,* p. 120. Pokrovsky, *History of Russia,* p. 265.

42. Von Staden, *Land and Government of Muscovy*, p. 37. Olearius, *Travels.* pp. 6–11. Pokrovsky, *History of Russia*, pp. 267–269.

43. See George Vernadsky, *The Tsardom of Moscow, 1547–1682* (New Haven and London, 1969), pp. 659–661. George V. Lantzeff, *Siberia in the Seventeenth Century: A Study of the Colonial Administration* (Berkeley and Los Angeles, 1943), p. 147. Fisher, *Russian Fur Trade*, pp. 220–226.

44. *Ibid.*, pp. 217–218.

45. *Ibid.*, pp. 214–217. Vernadsky, *Tsardom ·of Moscow*, pp. 653–659.

2. First Steps Toward Industrial Modernization

1. Karl Marx, *Secret Diplomatic History of the Eighteenth Century* and *The Story of the Life of Lord Palmerston*, ed. Lester Hutchinson (London, 1969), p. 114.

2. Vernadsky, *Mongols and Russia*, pp. 170–172, 197, 204–205. Pokrovsky, *History of Russia*, p. 95.

3. Dmitrii Tsvetaev, *Protestanstvo i protestanty v Rossii do epokhi preobrazovanii* [Protestantism and protestants in Russia before the (Petrine) reform period] (Moscow, 1890), p. 17. George Vernadsky, *Russia at the Dawn of the Modern Age* (New Haven and London, 1959), pp. 18–19. James H. Billington, *The Icon and the Axe: An Interpretative History of Russian Culture* (New York, 1966), pp. 84–85. M. Tikhomirov, *Srednevekovaia Moskva v xiv-xv vekakh* [Medieval Moscow during the fourteenth and fifteenth centuries (Moscow, 1957), pp. 125–131, 147–153.

4. J. L. I. Fennell, *Ivan the Great of Moscow* (London, 1961), p. 319. For a different view of Sof'ia's marriage, see Manfred Hellmann, "Moskau und Byzanz: 1. Die Heirat Ivans III. mit der Byzantinerin Zoë-Sofija," *J.G.O.*, XVII (1969), 322–338.

5. Voyce, *Moscow*, p. 18.

6. I. I. Smirnov, *et al., A Short History of the U.S.S.R.* (Moscow, 1965), p. 88. A. A. Kuzin, *Istoriia otkrytii rudnykh mestorozhdenii v Rossii do serediny xix v.* [History of the opening of ore deposits in Russia until the mid-nineteenth century] (Moscow, 1961), pp. 52–53. L. Maleev, "Altaiskii gornyi okrug" [The Altaisk mining area], *R.S.*, CXXXIX (1909), 301.

7. Iurii Tolstoi, *Pervyia sorok let snoshenii mezhdu Rossieiu i Anglieie, 1553–1593* [First forty years of relations between Russia and England, 1553–1593] (St. Petersburg, 1875), p. v. Inna Lubimenko, "Trud inozemtsev v Moskovskom gosudarstve" [Labor of foreigners in the Muscovite state], *Arkhiv istorii truda v Rossii* [Archive of the history of labor in Russia] (Petrograd [sic], 1923), p. 56. Pashkov, *History*, p. 101. Thomas Esper, "Russia and the Baltic, 1494–1558," *S.R.*, XXV (1966), 466–467.

8. S. F. Platonov, *Moskva i zapad v xvi-xvii vekakh* [Moscow and the West during the sixteenth and seventeenth centuries] (Leningrad, 1925), pp. 9–10.

9. *Ibid.*, p. 10. Tsvetaev, *Protestanstvo*, pp. 30–31.

10. Platonov, *Moskva i zapad*, pp. 10–11. Tsvetaev, *Protestanstvo*, p. 31.

11. Walther Kirchner, *Rise of the Baltic Question* (Newark, Del., 1954), p. 95.

12. Tolstoi, *Pervyia sorok let*, p. iii. Platonov, *Moskva i zapad*, p. 12.

13. T. S. Willan, *Early History of the Russia Company, 1553–1603* (Manchester, 1956), p. 63. Tolstoi, *Pervyia sorok let*, p. iv.

14. *Ibid.*, p. ii. N. I. Kostomarov, *Sobranie sochineniia* [Collected works], book viii, XX (St. Petersburg, 1905), 89.

15. There is a good summary of the provisions of this charter in Solov'ev, *Istoriia*, VI, 521ʹ–522. The original document is not extant, but an early copy prepared by the company is reprinted in *The Principal Navigations, Voyages, Traffiques and Discoveries of the English Nation . . . by Richard Hakluyt* (London and New York, 1907; 1929 ed.), I, 313–318.

16. Inna Lubimenko, "Moskovskii rynok kak arena bor'by Gollandii s Angliei" [Muscovite market as an arena of struggle of Holland with England], *Russkoe proshloe* [Russian past], No. 5 (1923), 3. Pashkov, *History*, pp. 166–167.

17. E. Zviagintsev, "Angliiskii dvor v Moskve" [English settlement in Moscow.] *I.zh.*, No. 10–11 (1941), 143. Willan, *Early History*, pp. 63–65.

18. Tolstoi, *Pervyia sorok let*, pp. 30–31 (emphasis added, spelling modernized).

19. *Ibid.*, p. 39. Willan, *Early History*, p. 65.
    Conflicting opinions about whether there were military goods in English-Russian trade may be found in Willan, *Early History*, p. 66; Anthony Jenkinson, *Early Voyages and Travels to Russia and Persia* (New York, n.d.), I, lix–lx, Walther Kirchner, "Entrepreneurial Activity in Russian-Western Trade Relations During the Sixteenth Century," *Explorations in Entrepreneurial History*, VIII (1955–1956), 250–251. Especially good is Thomas Esper's "A Sixteenth-Century anti-Russian Arms Embargo," *J.G.O.*, XV (1967), 180–196.

20. Inna Lubimenko, "The Struggle of the Dutch with the English for the Russian Market in the Seventeenth Century," *Transactions of the Royal Historical Society*, fourth series, VII (1924), 27–33. Lubimenko, "Moskovskii rynok," pp. 4–5. Alexandra Kalmykow, "A Sixteenth-Century Russian Envoy to France," *S.R.*, XXIII (1964), 701.

21. A. S. Muliukin, *Priezd inostrantsev v moskovskoe gosudarstvo* [Arrival of foreigners to the Muscovite state] (St. Petersburg, 1909), pp. 63–71, 124–126, 167–168, 173. Kirchner, *Rise of Baltic Question*, p. 251. Lubimenko, "Trud inozemtsev," p. 54. Kuzin, *Istoriia otkrytii*, p. 53.

Tolstoi, *Pervyia sorok let,* p. 37. Mildred Wretts-Smith, "The English in Russia during the Second Half of the Sixteenth Century," *Transactions of the Royal Historical Society,* fourth series, III (1920), 99.

22. Zviagintsev, "Angliiskii dvor," p. 143. *Istoriko-statisticheskii obzor promyshlennosti Rossii* [Historical-statistical survey of the industry of Russia], (St. Petersburg, 1886), II, 3, 39, 64. Wretts-Smith, "English in Russia," p. 101. Lubimenko, "Moskovskii rynok," p. 3. Jenkinson, *Early Voyages,* II, 208.

Much information on the English rope industry in the Russian northeast during the sixteenth century may be found in Willan, *Early History,* pp. 40, 55–56, 271, 280–281. Inna Lubimenko asserts that as late as 1638 the English still had rope walks at Kholmogory and Archangel, but this opinion does not seem to be shared by other scholars and my own research was unable to confirm it. Cf. Inna Lubimenko, "Letters Illustrating the Relations of England and Russia in the Seventeenth Century," *E.H.R.,* XXXII (1917), 95–96, and P. G. Liubomirov, *Ocherki po istorii russkoi promyshlennosti xvii, xviii i nachalo xix veka* [Studies in the history of Russian industry of the seventeenth, eighteenth, and early nineteenth centuries] (Moscow, 1947), p. 512.

23. Lubimenko, "Trud inozemtsev," p. 72.

24. Wretts-Smith, "English in Russia," p. 100.

25. Jenkinson, *Early Voyages,* I, lxx-lxxi. Tsvetaev, *Protestanstvo,* pp. 721-722.

26. Lubimenko, "Trud inozemtsev," p. 70. Rafael Barberini, *Puteshestvie v Moskoviiu* [Journey to Muscovy], *Syn otechestva* [Son of the fatherland], No. 7 (1842), 23. N. P. Likhachev, *Bumaga i drevneishiia bumazhnyia mel'nitsy v moskovskom gosudarstve* [Paper and the earliest paper mills in the Muscovite state] (St. Petersburg, 1891), p. 86. G. Novitskii, "K istorii promyshlennosti i truda vo vtoroi polovine 17 veka. Bumazhnaia mel'nitsa na reke Iauza" [Toward the history of industry and labor during the second half of the seventeenth century. The paper mill on the river Iauza], *Arkhiv istorii truda v Rossii* [Archive of the history of labor in Russia] (Petrograd, 1924), p. 28.

27. K. A. Pazhitnov, *Ocherki istorii tekstil'noi promyshlennosti dorevoliutsionnoi Rossii: khlopchatobumazhnaia, l'nopen'kovaia i shelkovaia promyshlennost'* [Studies in the history of the textile industry of pre-revolutionary Russia: cotton, flax-hemp, and silk industry] (Moscow, 1958), pp. 162, 303. K. A. Pazhitnov, *Ocherki istorii tekstil'noi promyshlennosti dorevoliutsionnoi Rossii: sherstnaia promyshlennost'* [Studies in the history of the textile industry of pre-revolutionary Russia: woolen industry] (Moscow, 1955), pp. 8, 187. Bakhrushin, *Nauchnye trudy,* I, 165–166. Kostomarov, *Sobranie sochinenii,* XX, 413.

28. Jenkinson, *Early Voyages,* II, 211, 270 (original emphasis, spelling modernized).

29. Kuzin, *Istoriia otkrytii,* pp. 14–15. V. N. Kashin, "Tul'skaia oruzheinaia

sloboda v xvii yeke" [Tula armaments settlement in the seventeenth century], *Problemy dokapitalisticheskogo obshchestva* [Problems of pre-capitalist society], Nos. 1-2 (1935), 132-137.

The crucial feature of manufacturing technology, of course, was harnessing waterpower for the operation of industrial machinery. A. A. Kuzin and V. V. Danilevskii believe that even before the sixteenth century Russian peasants and artisans built and used waterwheels. Even if this is true, A. A. Vvedenskii's book on the Stroganov family (see footnote 30 below) makes one doubt that Russian manufactured goods of the sixteenth century were actually the product of an indigenous development of waterpower in the service of industry. We do not know who built the Utsa paper mill of the 1560's, but there is no reason to think that the technicians were Russians operating without knowledge of Western technology. See V. V. Danilevskii, *Russkaia tekhnika* [Russian technology] (2nd ed.; Leningrad, 1948), pp. 273-277.

30.   A. A. Vvedenskii, *Dom Stroganovykh v xvi-xvii vekakh* [Stroganov house during the sixteenth and seventeenth centuries] (Moscow, 1962), pp. 24-27, 45, 177-178.

31.   Erik Amburger, *Die Familie Marselis, Studien zur russischen Wirtschaftsgeschichte* (Giessen, 1957), pp. 92, 97. Vvedenskii, *Dom Stroganovykh*, p. 179.

3. Andrei Vinius and the Beginnings of Iron Manufacturing

1.   George Vernadsky, *Political and Diplomatic History of Russia* (Boston, 1936), pp. 191-192. *Tri veka* [Three centuries] (Moscow, 1912), I, 77-78.

2.   J. L. H. Keep, "The Regime of Filaret, 1619-1633," *S.E.E.R.*, XXXVIII (1959-1960), 357.

3.   Voyce, *Moscow*, pp. 162-163. Liubomirov, *Ocherki*, p. 511. Pankratova, *Formirovanie*, p. 217. Amburger, *Die Familie Marselis*, pp. 94-95. B. B. Kafengauz, *Istoriia khoziaistva Demidovykh v xviii-xix vv* [History of the Demidovs' economic holdings in the eighteenth and nineteenth centuries] (Moscow-Leningrad, 1949), p. 28. Kuzin, *Istoriia otkrytii,* p. 16. Tsvetaev, *Protestanstvo,* pp. 50-53.

4.   The following numbers of iron artisans were registered in these Russian towns during the 1620's: Kholmogory (63), Nizhnyi-Novgorod (49), Pavlovo-Nizhegorodskoe (11), Solikamsk (16), Tula (38), Velikii Ustiug (47), Kaluga (44), Vologda (49), Sol'-Galitskaia (20), Tot'ma (10). See S. G. Strumilin, *Istoriia chernoi metallurgii v SSSR* (Moscow, 1954), I, 31. N. I. Pavlenko, *Razvitie metallurgicheskoi promyshlennosti Rossii v pervoi polovine xviii veka: promyshlennaia politika i upravlenie* [Development of the metallurgical industry of Russia during the first half of the eighteenth century: industrial policy and administration] (Moscow, 1953), pp. 29-30. R. S. Livshits, *Razmeshchenie promyshlennosti v dorevoliutsionnoi Rossii* [Distribution of industry in pre-revolutionary Russia] (Moscow, 1955), pp. 24-25.

5.   Kuzin, *Istoriia otkrytii,* p. 17.

6.   Iosif Gamel', *Opisanie tul'skago oruzheinago zavoda v istoricheskom i tekhnicheskom otnoshenii* [Description of the Tula armaments factory in its historical and technical aspects] (Moscow, 1826), p. 10 (documents). Stoskova, *Pervye metallurgicheskie*, pp. 37–38. E. I. Zaozerskaia, *Razvitie legkoi promyshlennosti v Moskve v pervoi chetverti xviii v.* [Development of light industry in Moscow during the first quarter of the eighteenth century] (Moscow, 1953), p. 30.

7.   Kuzin, *Istoriia otkrytii*, p. 17. Pankratova, *Formirovanie*, pp. 128–129. Zaozerskaia, *Razvitie*, pp. 26–30.

8.   Pankratova, *Formirovanie*, p. 217.

9.   See Ioann Kobentsel', "Pis'mo o Rossii v xvi v." [Letter about Russia during the sixteenth century], *Zh.m.n.p.*, XXXV (1842), 150. Concerning Barberini, see *Syn otechestva*, No. 7 (1842), 23. Concerning the "anonymous Englishman," Voyce, *Moscow*, pp. 44–46. Lloyd E. Berry (ed.), *The English Works of Giles Fletcher the Elder* (Madison, Wisc., 1964), p. 241.

10.   Von Herberstein, *Notes upon Russia*, I, 98; II, 63.

11.   S. Konovalov, "Anglo-Russian Relations, 1620–4," *O.S.P.*, IV (1953), 97, and "Anglo-Russian Relations, 1617–1618," *O.S.P.*, I (1950), 92, 94.

12.   *Ibid.*, p. 64.

13.   Konovalov, "Anglo-Russian Relations, 1620–4," pp. 65, 77–83.

14.   Platonov, *Moskva i zapad*, pp. 64–65, 83.

15.   Tolstoi, *Pervyia sorok let*, p. xx. Konovalov, "Anglo-Russian Relations, 1620–4," pp. 68, 71, 85. Ruth Schoener, "Zur Frage eines englisch-russischen Bundnisses in Jahre 1623," *J.G.O.*, 182–195.

16.   During the first half of the seventeenth century tiny Holland accounted for no less than two-thirds of the world's shipping. At the same time powerful Dutch banks lent money to Dutch merchants at $3\frac{1}{2}$ to 4 per cent annual interest. S. A. Pokrovskii, *Vneshniaia torgovlia i vneshniaia torgovaia politika Rossii* [External trade and the external trade policy of Russia] (Moscow, 1947), p. 55.

17.   As early as 1624 the Dutch had invested about two million florins (400,000 rubles) in Russian trade, compared to the mere £ 80,000 (130,000 rubles) invested by the English at the height of their activity, in 1583. See Lubimenko, "Struggle of the Dutch," pp. 32, 39–40, 50. Lubimenko, "Moskovskii rynok," p. 8. I. M. Kulisher, *Ocherk istorii russkoi torgovli* [Study of the history of Russian trade] (Petrograd, 1923), pp. 129–131.

18.   Lubimenko, "Moskovskii rynok," p. 9. A. Lappo-Danilevskii, "Inozemtsy v Rossii v tsarstvovanie Mikhaila Fedorovicha" [Foreigners in Russia during the reign of Mikhail Fedorovich], *Zh.m.n.p.*, CCXLI (October 1885), 66.

19.   Platonov, *Moskva i zapad*, p. 14. Pankratova, *Formirovanie*, p. 133.

20. The tsar's officials had instructed Lesly to travel abroad and hire two or three colonels and the necessary number of captains to command 4,000 "good" rank-and-file mercenaries. We know Lesly recruited at least 2,200 men in northern Germany, and other large numbers of mercenaries were raised for the tsar at this time in the West. Significantly Lesly had difficulty in obtaining permission in Holland to purchase military equipment, but de Willem and van Lier Abmachungen finally were able to sell him 5,000 muskets, 750 pairs of pistols, 500 carbines, 2,000 swords and scabbards, 2,000 suits of armor, 100,000 pounds of gunpowder, and 200 halberds. *S.G.G.i D.,* III, 316–322. Tsvetaev, *Protestanstvo,* p. 374. Amburger, *Die Familie Marselis,* pp. 74–75, 79, 96.

21. Violet Barbour, *Capitalism in Amsterdam in the Seventeenth Century* (Ann Arbor, Mich., 1963), p. 39. Amburger, *Die Familie Marselis,* pp. 95–96. *S.G.G. i D.,* III, 335–336.

22. Duke Frederick of Schleswig-Holstein sent an embassy to Moscow in the summer of 1632 to establish friendly trade relations between the two states. To show their sovereign's good will, Frederick's ambassadors presented the tsar with a gift of eleven cannon, fully equipped, and expressed readiness to assist the Russians in recruiting and transporting masters and soldiers for service in Moscow. The Swedes, hoping to purchase Russian grain, also sent a present on 19 November 1634: ten bronze cannon, fully equipped, plus 2,000 muskets. Actually, Russians had been making extensive purchases in Sweden by this time. In 1631 two tsarist agents were sent there to buy 10,000 muskets with ammunition and 5,000 bayonets, and in the next few years (notably in 1632, 1640, and 1641) Russia obtained other quantities of Swedish muskets, swords, saltpetre, copper, and iron.

See Tsvetaev, *Protestanstvo,* pp.171–176, on Schleswig-Holstein. On Sweden, Solov'ev, *Istoriia,* IX, 161–162, and especially *Russko-shvedskie ekonomicheskie otnosheniia v xvii veke. Sbornik dokimentov* [Russian-Swedish economic relations during the seventeenth century. A collection of documents] (Moscow-Leningrad, 1960), pp. 85–87, 95–97, 104, 107–110, 114, 117–118, 182, etc.

23. On 29 November 1630, Tsar Michael wrote Charles I concerning the commission of John Cartwright, an Englishman in Muscovite service, to buy 2,000 good muskets and ammunition. On 20 May 1631 the English king informed Filaret that English merchants would supply the Russian requests with no charge for transportation. In January 1632, Cartwright returned to England to purchase for Russia "... five thousand good swords, in sheaths and with belts...." Charles seems to have cooperated with the Russians because they had restored certain "ancient privileges" to English merchants and because the English were hoping (in vain) to buy large amounts of Russian grain. See S. Konovalov, "Twenty Russian Royal Letters (1626–34)," *O.S.P.,* VII (1958), 120, 123, 136, 148–149. Inna Lubimenko, "Letters Illustrating the Relations of England and Russia in the Seventeenth Century," *E.H.R.,* XXXII (1917), 100–102.

24. Platonov, *Moskva i zapad,* pp. 62–63. M. S. Anderson, "English Views

of Russia in the 17th Century," *S.E.E.R.*, XXXIII (1954–55), 141. Lubimenko, "Moskovskii rynok," pp. 4, 19. Kostomarov, *Sobranie sochinenii*, XX, 251–253. S. Konovalov, "Patrick Gordon's Dispatches from Russia, 1667," *O.S.P.*, XI (1964), 14. Aleksei Mikhailovich's expulsion edict (dated 1 June 1649) is reprinted in *S.G.G.i D.*, III, 455–456.

25. The contemporary English resident of Russia, Dr. Samuel Collins, explained Holland's ascendancy over England: "The Dutch fell upon Moscow like locusts and took away bread from the English. They were much more numerous and wealthier than the English, spared nothing for the attainment of their goals, and scattered things in all directions where something advantageous might be obtained. They were received in Russia more favorably than the English because they presented the boyars with gifts and in this way gained their patronage. They also endeavored to denigrate and ridicule the English: they drew caricatures and spread slander and thus gave the Russians a negative picture of us. They depicted us in the image of a tail-less lion with three toppled crowns, and as a great pack of large dogs with clipped ears and tails. . . . And these depictions made a great impression on the Russians." Cited in Russian translation in Kulisher, *Ocherk*, pp. 124–125

26. Amburger, *Die Familie Marselis*, pp. 97, 210. Stoskova, *Pervye metallurgicheskie*, p. 5.

27. L. V. Cherepnin, "Russian 17th-Century Baltic Trade in Soviet Historiography," *S.E.E.R.*, XLIII (1964–65), 21. Pokrovskii, *Vneshniaia torgovlia*, p. 53. Barbour, *Capitalism*, p. 128. K. V. Bazilevich, "Elementy merkantilizma v ekonomicheskoi politike pravitel'stva Alekseia Mikhailovicha" [Elements of mercantilism in the economic policy of the government ot Aleksei Mikhailovich], *Uchenye zapiski Moskovskogo . . . universiteta* [Scholarly notes of Moscow . . . University], XII (1940), 5. *Russko-shvedskie*, p. 561; also pp. 75–77. V. A. Kordt, *Otchet Al'berta Burkha i Iogana fan Feltdrilia . . .* [Report of Albert Burkh and Iogan fan Feltdril' . . .] (St. Petersburg, 1902), pp. cccxlvi, ccclix, 64–65, 159. Gamel', *Opisanie*, p. 7 (documents).

28. Kordt, *Otchet*, pp. cccxliv–cccxlv, cclvii. Tsvetaev, *Protestanstvo*, p. 395.

29. Gamel', *Opisanie*, pp. 1–4 (documents). *R.S.*, XL (1909), 430ff.

30. A. S. Muliukin, *Ocherki po istorii iuridicheskago polozheniia inostrannykh kuptsov v Moskovskom gosudarstve* [Studies in the history of the judicial position of foreign merchants in the Muscovite state] (Odessa, 1912), p. 216. Gamel', *Opisanie*, pp. 3–4 (documents).

31. Amburger, *Die Familie Marselis*, pp. 98, 100. Gamel', *Opisanie*, p. 12. Stoskova, *Pervye metallurgicheskie*, pp. 21–22.

32. Amburger, *Die Familie Marselis*, pp. 21, 26–29. Olga Crisp, review of Amburger's *Die Familie Marselis* in *S.E.E.R.*, XXXVII (1958–59), 276. Kurts, *Sochinenie Kil'burgera*, p. 453. *S.G.G. i D.*, III, 109, 371.

33. Gavrilo's son Leonhard established himself in the commercial life of

Hamburg; the other three sons were more adventurous and sought their opportunities in the backward but developing north and northeastern areas of Europe. Gabriel the Younger and Selio were active in Norway and Denmark, respectively, while Pieter (Peter) turned to Russia. In each case a similar pattern developed:

> All were under the particular protection of the King of Denmark, who bestowed upon them titles of nobility, while in return the Marselis business was an important factor in the Danish state economy. The sphere of interest of the Marselises' was the same in all the countries concerned: armaments, mining, postal services, all based financially on successful commercial transactions. [Crisp, review of Amburger, *Die Familie Marselis*, p. 276.]

Equally interesting is the fact that in each case the Marselis brothers became important to their individual governments of Norway, Denmark, and Russia. This is an indication of their daring and adaptability, as is the fact that the Marselises even appeared as prospective colonizers of Africa. Consult Amburger, *Die Familie Marselis,* pp. 27, 29–67 and Walther Kirchner, review of *Die Familie Marselis* in the *American Slavic and East European Review,* XVII (1958), 547.

34. Olearius, *Travels,* pp. 122–123. Kurts, *Sochinenie Kil'burgera,* pp. 432, 453. Tsvetaev, *Protestanstvo,* p. 718. Amburger, *Die Familie Marselis,* pp. 81–91. Reviews of Amburger's *Die Familie Marselis* by Kirchner (p. 547) and Crisp (p. 276), already cited.

35. Akema's son, Thielman, died around the same time as his father, *ca.* 1676. A daughter, Anna, became the second wife of Peter Marselis in 1655, and then, in 1676, four years after his death, married Thomas Kellermann, a Dutch merchant in Moscow who was also involved in manufacturing. Akema's brother, Gillis (Russian equivalent Elisei) was also active in Russia as a merchant; Filimon Akema brought a sister (whose name is now unknown) to Moscow in the 1630's. She married Thomas Andrews, a partner in the iron works. and they had two sons: Richard (who became a partner of his uncle) and Boldwin (d. 1705), also an iron manufacturer in Russia. (See Amburger, *Die Familie Marselis,* pp. 127, 180, 211.)

These details are interesting for the picture they provide of the personal, marital lives of Dutch merchants who permanently relocated in Russia, and suggest that these foreigners did not actually "mix" much with the Russian population. Moreover, these facts urge us to think that iron manufacturing in seventeenth-century Russia was a well-developed, self-contained process which perpetuated to an amazing extent an inter-relationship in the lives of those originally involved in its organization.

36. Amburger, *Die Familie Marselis,* pp. 101, 211. Gamel', *Opisanie,* pp. 12–13.

37. G. D. Bakulev, *Tul'skaia promyshlennost', istoriko-ekonomicheskii och-*

erk [Tula industry, a historical-economic study] (Tula, 1952), p. 18. G. M. Belotserkovskii, *Tula i tul'skii uezd v xvi i xvii vekakh* [Tula and the Tula region during the sixteenth and seventeenth centuries] (Kiev, 1914), pp. 9, 11. Stoskova, *Pervye metallurgicheskie*, p. 20.

38. The Swedish traveler Kilburger noted that the Tula dams were provided with strong foundations by stone obtained 90 *versts* from the factory site. Kurts, *Sochinenie Kil'burgera*, p. 167.

39. Gamel', *Opisanie*, pp. 8–13. Stoskova, *Pervye metallurgicheskie*, pp. 20–21, for an enlightening discussion of the advantages of the final location over the initially-conceived site.

40. Gamel', *Opisanie*, pp. 10–11. Stoskova, *Pervye metallurgicheskie*, pp. 80, 88–89. Baklanov, *Tul'skie*, p. 83.

41. Strumilin, *Istoriia*, i, 108. Amburger, *Die Familie Marselis*, p. 103. I. P. Kozlovskii, *Pervye pochty i pervye pochtmeistery v moskovskom gosudarstve* [First posts and first postmasters in the Muscovite state] (Warsaw, 1913), I, 173. Gamel', *Opisanie*, pp. 16-18 (documents).

42. Vinius delivered 100 *puds* of rod iron and 43½ *puds* of sheet iron and was paid according to the prearranged price. Gamel', *Opisanie*, p. 15.

43. As we shall see later, this argument broke out in November 1647 over whether or not the entrepreneurs' ten-year monopoly had expired. In saying that their blast furnace did not function until 1640, Marselis and Akema were insisting they had the right to work the manufactories for three more years, until 1650; by contending that the furnace's activity began in 1637, the state was asserting that the capitalists had received their due and that confiscation did not violate the original charter of 1632. (See pp. 87–88.)

44. *Krepostnaia manufaktura v Rossii* [Peasant manufacturing in Russia], hereafter cited as *K.m.*, I (Leningrad, 1930), 248; also 78–80.

45. Leslie Aitchison, *A History of Metals* (New York, 1960), II, 342. H. R. Schubert, *History of the British Iron and Steel Industry from c. 450 B.C. to A.D. 1775* (London, 1957), p. 157. Stoskova, *Pervye metallurgicheskie*, pp. 75–76.

46. An observer of this process in the early 1650's described it as follows:

> They have marvellous furnaces in which they smelt ore in order to separate it from the soil. . . . Ore is melted in the furnaces, made like water and poured from the aperture into troughs dug into the ground with moulds for cannons, cannon balls, and other objects; in each trough there are 40, 50 holes with moulds on all sides. When they are full, they pull out the objects from the moulds, not even using a hammer, without effort or difficulty. In this way they make thousands of objects every day. [*Puteshestvie Antiokhiiskago Patriarkha Makariia v Rossii v polovine xvii veka* (Journey of Makarii, Patriarch of Antioch,

to Russia in the mid-seventeenth century), (Moscow, 1896), 11, 197.]

47. Stoskova, *Pervye metallurgicheskie,* pp. 82–83, 85.

48. This would probably be for sale on the open market to peasant artisans, or perhaps for delivery to the state, in which case the bars and rods might be delivered to royal artisans and transformed at their forges into some sort of commodity or used for construction. *Sviaznoe zhelezo* (joint- or angle-iron) was used to strengthen corner structures of stone buildings, to affix ledges and cabinets to walls, etc.

49. Stoskova, *Pervye metallurgicheskie,* pp. 85–86. Kafengauz, *Istoriia,* p. 26.

50. *K.m.,* I, 24.

51. The hydrologic nature of factory power during the seventeenth century limited the actual length of the "work year" at Tula. Winter freezing, spring floods, and summer low waters led to periods of inevitable inactivity. Moreover, there was no work on Sundays and some holidays (save for the necessary continual stoking and care of the blast furnace). Considering these and other factors, Strumilin concluded that in a calendar year the Tula factories operated for no more than 250 days—and often only 200 days (*Istoriia,* I, 130). Factory documents dating from 1662 indicate that a work year at the Tula iron manufactories was officially considered to be 300 days, but for some reason this excluded only Sundays and holidays (*K.m.,* I, 26). This suggests that work of some sort continued at the manufactory even when an absence of water brought the blasting works, boring shops, etc., to a temporary halt. In England at this time similar circumstances limited the smelting period to thirty or thirty-five weeks per year, mostly during the autumn and winter months (Aitchison, *History of Metals,* II, 398).

52. Stoskova, *Pervye metallurgicheskie,* p. 74. Strumilin, *Istoriia,* I, 98–99, 104–105. Victor S. Clark, *History of Manufactures in the United States* (New York, 1949), I, 170.

53. Although it dates from a slightly later period, the technology of this factory differed little, if at all, from the Tula enterprises. See pp. 95–96.

54. *K.m.,* I, 24–26, 33, 37. Strumilin, *Istoriia,* I, 122. For general information on these questions consult Schubert, *History,* p. 161.

55. From factory inventories of 1647, 1662–1664, and 1690 we have a list of some of the foreign workers (70 masters and 38 submasters) engaged at Tula. Twenty-two masters and 20 submasters were employed in the hammering shops. Eight masters and 7 submasters were occupied at the blast furnace as smelters *(plavil'shchiki)* or cannon-casters *(pushechniki),* the two tasks being similar. Twelve masters and 4 submasters were called *sovmestitely,* literally "pluralists," i.e., men employed in two or more specialties. The remaining foreigners were smiths *(kuznetsy)* of various types: iron-sheet makers *(doshchatniki),* barrel-borers *(stvol'nye zavarshchiki),* cuirassiers *(latniki),* nail-makers, lock-makers, sword-makers, cannon muzzle polishers *(vertel'shchiki),* and polishers *(tochil'-*

shchiki). See *K.m.,* I, 8–21 and *passim.* Also N. B. Baklanov, V. V. Mavrodin, and I. I. Smırnov, *Tul'skie i kashirskie zavody v xvii v.* [Tula and Kashirskie factories in the seventeenth century] (Moscow-Leningrad, 1934), pp. 67–68.

56. For example, the team of a master and two assistants described above, which could produce two cannon in 24 hours, would also clean three or four cannon and bore the detonators in that same period. Here we observe not only high productivity but also looseness in the "division of labor" sufficient to permit the same men to be occupied at such radically different tasks. *K.m.,* I, 24–25.

57. Muliukin, *Ocherki,* p. 92. *Russko-shvedskie,* pp. 115, 118–119. Amburger, *Die Familie Marselis,* p. 104.

58. Pankratova, *Formirovanie,* pp. 219, 223. Amburger, *Die Familie Marselis,* p. 104.

59. Pankratova, *Formirovanie,* pp. 227–228. Gamel', *Opisanie,* pp. 1–4 (documents). Baklanov, *Tul'skie,* p. 71. *K.m.,* I, xxvii.

60. Speaking of iron factories in the Urals during the following century, one historian noted that ". . . the usual work day for those employed full time ran for eleven hours in winter and thirteen hours in summer. Night work was exceptional, except in the smelters, where two shifts were used to keep the furnaces in continuous operation . . . ." (Blum, *Lord and Peasant in Russia,* p. 311). In view of the rather static technology of this period, it seems likely that this statement also applies to Russian iron manufactories of the seventeenth century. I have discovered no evidence that women or young boys were used in any aspect of the factory activity at Tula or in any other Russian iron manufactory during the seventeenth century.

61. Pankratova, *Formirovanie,* p. 228.

62. Strumilin, *Istoriia,* I, 113–114. I. V. Chekan, "Tul'skie i kashirskie zheleznye zavody xvii veka" [Tula and Kashirskie iron factories of the seventeenth century], *Ocherki po istorii torgovli i promyshlennosti v Rossii v 17 i v nachale 18 stoletiia* [Studies in the history of trade and industry in Russia during the 17th and beginning of the 18th centuries] (Moscow, 1928), p. 158.

63. There are actually some cases of Solomenskaia peasants working as assistants, or even submasters, within the factories, in the production process. This work was more highly paid and not so onerous or burdensome. *K.m.,* I, 31, 37, 122.

64. Strumilin, *Istoriia,* I, 115, 113. *K.m.,* I, 1–8.

65. *Ibid.,* 190, 193–194, 198, 206–207, 265, 325. Kuzin, *Istoriia otkrytii,* p. 20. Stoskova, *Pervye metallurgicheskie,* p. 63. Lilley, *Men, Machines, and History,* pp. 72–77.

66. Kafengauz, *Istoriia,* p. 30. *K.m.,* I, 206–207, 29–30, 198, 194. Kuzin, *Istoriia otkrytii,* pp. 20–22.

67. Kafengauz, *Istoriia*, pp. 30–31. Strumilin, *Istoriia*, i, p. 108. *K.m.*, I, 11–13. Gamel', *Opisanie*, p. 10.

68. Kurts, *Sochinenie Kil'burgera*, pp. 168–169.

69. Baklanov, *Tul'skie*, p. 68. *K.m.*, I, 13.

70. *K.m.*, I, 14. Gamel', *Opisanie*, p. 14 (documents). Stoskova, *Pervye metallurgicheskie*, p. 76. Strumilin, *Istoriia*, I, 105.

71. Evgenii Vil'chinskii, "Andrei Denis'evich Vinius," *R.S.*, CXL (1909), 438. Strumilin, *Istoriia*, I, 105.

72. *Ibid.*, 109.

4. The Downfall of Andrei Vinius

1. Gamel', *Opisanie*, p. 13. Tsvetaev, *Protestanstvo*, p. 397. *K.m.*, I, 260.

2. *Ibid.*, 260, 262. This charter is also available in *S.G.G. i D.*, III, 408–410.

3. Kozlovskii, *Pervye Pochty*, I, 77–78.

4. Tsvetaev, *Protestanstvo*, p. 397.

5. Amburger, *Die Familie Marselis*, p. 105. Chistyi had gone abroad under Tsar Michael on an unsuccessful mission to buy silk. (N. A. Baklanova, "Privoznye tovary v moskovskom gosudarstve vo vtoroi polovine xvii veke" [Imported goods in the Muscovite state during the second half of the seventeenth century], *Ocherki po istorii torgovli i promyshlennosti v Rossii v 17 i v nachale 18 stoletiia* [Studies in the history of trade and industry in Russia during the seventeenth and early eighteenth centuries], IV (1928), 21. Solov'ev provides interesting information on Chistyi (vols. IX and X, *passim*) and Olearius describes his tragic death during the Moscow uprising of 1648 (Olearius, *Travels*, pp. 206, 208–209).

6. Amburger, *Die Familie Marselis*, pp. 105–106.

7. Tsvetaev, *Protestanstvo*, p. 397. Readers interested in this type of proceeding should consult H. W. Dewey, "Old Muscovite Concepts of Injured Honor *(Beschestie)*," *S. R.*, XXVII (1968), 594–603.

8. Tsvetaev, *Protestanstvo*, pp. 396–398. Proceedings cited in Solov'ev, *Istoriia*, X, 616–617.

9. Amburger, *Die Familie Marselis*, p. 106. Tsvetaev, *Protestanstvo*, pp. 398–400.

10. *K,m.*, I, 15–16. Tsvetaev, *Protestanstvo*, pp. 400–401. Solov'ev, *Istoriia*, X, 617. Amburger, *Die Familie Marselis*, p. 106.

11. *Ibid.*, pp. 106–107. Gamel', *Opisanie*, p. 14. Solov'ev, *Istoriia*, X, 615–616. Muliukin, *Ocherki*, p. 213.

12. Solov'ev, *Istoriia*, X, 616. Muliukin, *Ocherki*, p. 226.

13. Amburger, *Die Familie Marselis*, p. 104. Concerning Vinius' management of the factories, see Vil'chinskii, "Andrei Denis'evich Vinius," pp.

434–439 and *K.m.,* I, 14.

14. The date of the government's seizure assumes that factory activity began at Tula in 1637. At this time Marselis and Akema asserted that the iron manufactories did not function until 1640, but this was probably a distortion calculated to postpone the expiration of their privileges for another three years, until 1650. It should be noted, incidently, that Morozov quietly withdrew from partnership in the Tula enterprises just before the confiscations of 1647 (Amburger, *Die Familie Marselis,* pp. 106–107). I am unable to explain why Morozov was unable (or unwilling) to prevent this catastrophe from befalling his friend Andrei Vinius.

15. Telepnev had prospected for copper on behalf of the state in the Perm area in 1645 and 1646. One of his first actions at Tula was to compile an extensive description and inventory of the manufactories, 44 extremely valuable pages of which have survived until the present time. See *K.m.,* I, 8–21.

16. The Vaga enterprise was located in Volodskaia *gubernaia,* well over 600 kilometers northeast of Moscow. As early as 1644 Vinius had been urging his partners to speed their plans to establish a blasting factory at this location, and by the end of that year a court *(dvor)* for the iron works had been established on the Shelash'e river in Vazhskii *uezd.* Now construction of the factory proceeded as quickly as possible, and it began operation on 6 October 1648. Actually the partners received some government cooperation in their Vaga river project. They obtained, for example, two fuel masters from the Pyskorskii copper enterprise in Perm *gubernaia;* the smelting master in the Vaga factory was evidently a Russian, Kiril Savel'ev, who had been trained at Tula by Christian Wilde. Only cannon balls were smelted at this new manufactory.

17. Despite his opposition to foreigners' converting to Eastern Orthodoxy, Marselis remained close to some key government figures, in part because of his generous gifts and bribes. Kozlovskii, *Pervye pochty,* I, 89–90.

18. Amburger, *Die Familie Marselis,* pp. 107–108.

19. *Ibid.,* p. 108. Gamel', *Opisanie,* p. 16. Muliukin, *Ocherki,* p. 227.

20. Amburger, *Die Familie Marselis,* pp. 108–109.

21. Gamel', *Opisanie,* pp. 5–9 (documents).

22. *Ibid.,* pp. 16–17 (documents). Stoskova, *Pervye metallurgicheskie,* p. 26. Amburger, *Die Familie Marselis,* p. 109.

23. Gamel', *Opisanie,* pp. 17 (documents), 19. Strumilin, *Istoriia,* I, 112. Amburger, *Die Familie Marselis,* p. 109.

24. In 1634, for example, at a time when he was deeply involved in the organization of his iron factories, Vinius received the right to establish a new commercial warehouse in Pskov. Kozlovskii, *Pervye pochty,* I, 172. Muliukin, *Ocherki,* p. 289.

25. *D.k A.I.,* III (1848), 199. Muliukin, *Ocherki,* pp. 64, 65–66. Stoskova,

Pervye metallurgicheskie, p. 26. *K.m.*, I, 209–210.

26. Consult Index for information on these departments: *Iamskii prikaz*, *Pushkarskii p.*, *Aptekarskii p.*, *Sibirskii p.*, *Posol'skii p.*

27. *Russko-shvedskie*, p. 183. Amburger, *Die Familie Marselis*, pp. 117, 210. Tsvetaev, *Protestanstvo*, p. 403.

5. Surging Ahead

1. *K.m.*, I, 14, 16. Kurts, *Sochinenie Kil'burgera*, p. 455.

2. Tsvetaev, *Protestanstvo*, p. 402. Lubimenko, "Trud inozemtsev," p. 68. Chekan, "Tul'skie," p. 146. Amburger, *Die Familie Marselis*, pp. 109–110.

3. Kurts, *Sochinenie Kil'burgera*, p. 455. Strumilin, *Istoriia*, I, 118.

4. Stoskova says the Vaga works were closed by Peter in 1693–1694 *(Pervye metallurgicheskie*, pp. 42–43), but provides no references to support this contention. Documents I have examined do not mention this factory after 1649, nor was it involved in the ownership controversies and exchanges of 1662, 1663, and 1667.

5. There may have been other foreign masters at this factory, since Amburger reports that a "millmaster" ("Muhlenmeister") here had worked for Vinius in 1640 *(Die Familie Marselis*, p. 110).

6. Gamel', *Opisanie*, pp. 32–35 (documents). Tsvetaev, *Protestanstvo*, p. 713.

7. Gamel', *Opisanie*, p. 35 (documents). Amburger, *Die Familie Marselis*, p. 110:

8. See the long citation from one of his letters, dated 17 April 1651, in Ivan Zabelin, "Bol'shoi boiarin v svoem votchinnom khoziaistve xvii veka" [A great boyar and his *votchina* economy of the seventeenth century], *Vestnik Evropy* [Messenger of Europe], February 1871, pp. 486–487.

9. N. A. Baklanova, "Zvenigorodskie zheleznye zavody v xvii v." [Zvenigorodskie iron factories in the seventeenth century], *Moskovskii krai v ego proshlom* [Moscow *krai* during its past], part 2 (Moscow, 1930), 91.

10. Zabelin, "Bol'shoi boiarin," pp. 487–488.

11. See pp. 189–192 for a discussion of the relationship between government *prikazy* and Russian iron manufactories of the seventeenth century.

12. Baklanova, "Zvenigorodskie," p. 91. Kurts, *Sochinenie Kil'burgera*, p. 90.

13. *K.m.*, I, 31–32. Gamel', *Opisanie*, p. 20.

14. *K.m.*, I, 35–36, 39.

15. Baklanov, *Tul'skie*, p. 31. Stoskova, *Pervye metallurgicheskie*, p. 89. *K.m.*, I, 31, 33, 37, 38. Gamel', *Opisanie*, p. 20.

16. *K.m.*, I, 95, 213, 215–217, 277–278. Baklanov, *Tul'skie*, pp. 15–16.

17. Gamel', *Opisanie*, pp. 21–22. Kafengauz, *Istoriia*, p. 25.

18. *Ibid.* Gamel', *Opisanie*, p. 22.

6. Crisis in the Affairs of Peter Marselis

1. Strumilin, *Istoriia*, I, 61. Amburger, *Die Familie Marselis*, pp. 124–125.

2. All specialists in Russian history are indebted to Professor Amburger's extensive work in Western archives for clarifying the reasons for Marselis' downfall. Heretofore it had not been properly understood or analyzed. The closest that material published in the first volume of *Krepostnaia manufaktura* comes to an explanation of the affair is a document saying Marselis' calamity befell him "for his guilt" *(za viny*, p. 246); another document mentions his "thievery" *(vorovstvo*, p. 213). Gamel' spoke vaguely of "some sort of political reason" for the confiscation *(Opisanie*, p. 23), while the generally valuable *Tul'skie i kashirskie zavody* of Baklanov, *et al.* (p. 16) explains Marselis' disgrace as the result of failures in diplomatic assignments, although the references of the footnote given as the source of this statement do not support it in any way. Mavrodin, the historian responsible for the above error, even speculates over some sort of denunciation of Marselis by his partner Akema (!), " . . . which is not at all unlikely if we consider the presence of such events earlier in their partnership and the further conduct of Marselis . . . ." Stoskova follows in this confused and unhappy tradition by attributing Marselis' disaster to "political considerations," without explaining what she means by "politicheskie soobrazheniia" *(Pervye metallurgicheskie*, p. 26). See Amburger, *Die Familie Marselis*, p. 125.

3. *Ibid.*, p. 126.

4. *K.m.*, I, 210–211.

5. Fonvizin's report on the Tula-Kashirskie factories (dated 1 September 1663) is contained in *ibid.*, pp. 40–92; his description of the Porotovskii and Ugodskii factories (dated 8 December 1663) is reprinted in the same volume, pp. 92–186.

6. *Ibid.*, pp. 25–26, 211. Stoskova, *Pervye metallurgicheskie*, p. 27. Gamel', *Opisanie*, p. 11. Amburger, *Die Familie Marselis*, pp. 126–127.

7. *Ibid.*, pp. 211, 103. *D.k A.I.*, V, 57–59.

8. Amburger, *Die Familie Marselis*, pp. 124–125, 135.

9. *Ibid.*, pp. 136–139. Solov'ev, *Istoriia*, XI, 530–531. Bazilevich, "Elementy merkantilizma," p. 30.

10. Amburger, *Die Familie Marselis*, pp. 144–145, 146–147, 150. *K.m.*, I, 219–220, 251–252.

11. E. S. Iarantseva writing in Pashkov, *History*, p. 226.
    From 26 May 1661 the Tula-Kashirskie iron factories were under the

jurisdiction of the *Oruzheinaia palata;* in February 1667 they were assigned to the *Pushkarskii Prikaz* (cannon department). After the division of the iron works between Akema and the state in December 1663, the Tula-Kashirskie enterprises were directed (in succession) by *stol'nik* Afanasii Fonvizin, *striapchii* Nikita Vodov, Ivan Pomaskov, Ivan Pafomov, and Timofei Mitkov. Gamel', *Opisanie,* p. 23. *D.k A.I.,* V, 392.

12. *K.m.,* I, 220, 257, 397, 399, 401.

13. *Ibid.,* pp. 228–235, 257, 239, 242–243.

14. *Ibid.,* pp. 229, 257–258, 371–372.

15. *Ibid.,* pp. 228–229, 397, 399, 401.

16. *Ibid.,* pp. 258, 290–292.

17. *Ibid.,* pp. 238–240. Amburger, *Die Familie Marselis,* p. 151.

18. *K.m.,* I, 219–222, 391–392. Pashkov, *History,* pp. 226–227.

19. *K.m.,* I, 219–222, 373–377, 382.

20. *Ibid.,* p. 370.

21. Prices for the following commodities were agreed upon in advance, though quantities were to be specified upon the actual placing of orders:

halberds of standard design	5 *altyn* apiece
cavalry armor and spiked helmets	2 rubles per suit
musket barrels	20 *altyn* apiece
swords	20 *altyn* apiece
iron-tipped lances	4 *den'gi* apiece
axes of halberds	5 *altyn* apiece
thin roofing plates	1 ruble 16 *altyn* 4 *den'gi* per *pud*
plow with plowshare blades	6 *altyn* 4 *den'gi* per plow
plowshare blades	3 *altyn* 2 *den'gi* per blade
shovels and spades	6 *altyn* apiece
iron for nails, chains, wagon parts,	23 *altyn* 2 *den'gi* per *pud*

and other small items

D.k A.I., IX, 4, 49. *K.m.,* I, 224, 253–254, 269–270.

22. *Ibid.,* p. 276.

23. *Ibid.,* pp. 446–447, 254–255, 363–366, 266, 283. *D.k A.I.,* V, 389–393. Consult *D.k A.I.,* V, 389–401, for documents showing the prices of goods from the Tula-Kashira factories during the period 1668–1671.

24. *Puteshestvie . . . Makariia,* II, 197.

25. *K.m.,* I, 391–393, 406.

26. In 1668, following a great fire in Archangel, Marselis served as architect and delivered for reconstruction of the city 8,728 *puds* of bar-, angle-, and latticed iron, plus 793 *puds* of sheet-iron for doors and window-fittings. (*K.m.,* I, 220; also pp. 403, 405).

27. Many state orders for construction materials at this time were earmarked for the building of stone churches. For example, the *Posol'skii*

Prikaz ordered from Marselis 300 sheets of iron for the doors and windows of a stone church being erected at Kolomen'skoe (*K.m.*, I, 397–398), and such requests were by no means rare (*ibid.*, pp. 402–403, 406, 420–421, 423, 428, 433–438). In 1671 Marselis even made a new clapper for one of the bells in the *Uspenskii sobor* (*ibid.*, p. 412).

28. *Ibid.*, pp. 430, 432.

29. Kilburger's book (already cited as *Sochinenie Kil'burgera*) was translated into Russian with extensive notes and commentaries by Professor B. G. Kurts. The original German title was *Kurzer Unterricht von dem Russischen Handel wie selbiger mit aus-und eingehenden Waaren 1674 durch ganz Russland getreiben worden.*

30. Peter Marselis' death in Moscow on July 10, 1672, is discussed in this volume on p. 119. Petr Petrovich Marselis·died in Moscow on August 7, 1675, at which point his son, Christian, received title to the iron factories until his own death in 1690. Peter Marselis had two children from his second marriage: a daughter whose name is now unknown and a son, called by his contemporaries "Peter the Younger," who was apparently a merchant and not at all involved with his family's industrial undertakings. Peter the Younger was married in Moscow in 1691 and died there on December 22, 1696 (Amburger, *Die Familie Marselis*, pp. 20, 208).

31. Kurts, *Sochinenie Kil'burgera*, p. 166.

32. *Ibid.*, p. 166.

33. *Ibid.*, pp. 168, 463.

34. In 1654 Paul of Aleppo saw the following: "As it was necessary sometimes to wipe dry the stone floor of the patriarchal cathedral, the tsar asked of Tula, and lo! they made large four-cornered [iron] slabs which were superb and brilliant like silver. And they paved the entire floor of the cathedral   and altar with them, even down to the doors and threshold. . . ." (*Puteshestvie . . . Makariia*, II, 196–197).

35. Kilburger mentions the sale of "Gegossene Stücke" in Moscow (p. 116); if they were from Tula, this would indicate that by 1674 cannon were being cast from forged iron. For the situation in 1668, see *K.m.*, I, 370.

36. Kurts, *Sochinenie Kil'burgera*, p. 166.

37. *Ibid.*, pp. 166–167.

In 1674 the Marselis brothers were making a pair of large cannon costing 150 rubles for their friend, the King of Denmark. Factory documents from the following year mention three such cannon for Christian V (*K.m.*, I, 271, 285, 300). The Marselis factory also used sheet iron to make armor and *spalten* (the word is Kilburger's and its meaning was unclear to both B. G. Kurts and me; Kurts says [*Sochinenie Kil'burgera*, p. 239], "Spalten" may mean spade, shovel, hatchet, ovendoor, or even pots and pans of crude type). Kilburger also observed large salt-pans at the Tula factory, but they sold poorly and were in storage. The Marselises made saber blades, but Kilburger said of them, ". . . not many are produced, and they are completely bad" *(ibid.,* p. 167).

38. From the rupture of his partnership with Peter Marselis in 1661 until his death in 1675, Filimon Akema ceased to play a pioneering or expansive role in Russian iron manufacturing—a fact which suggests that in his earlier association with Marselis, Akema moved in the shadow of his aggressive partner. After receiving full ownership of the Ugodskii-Porotovskii iron works in 1663, Akema was apparently satisfied to supervise their operations, obtain large profits, and develop the quality of his metallurgical art to a level high enough to win the approval even of a critical foreign observer like Kilburger.

39. Kurts, *Sochinenie Kil'burgera,* p. 168.

40. *Ibid.,* p. 116.

41. His charter covering the Ugodskii-Porotovskii factories after 1663 specified that Akema would deliver annually to the state 11,250 *puds* of rod iron and 3,750 *puds* of angle-iron, the former at 16 *altyn* 4 *den'gi* per *pud* unless the market price was less, in which case ". . . upon examination angle- and rod iron . . . will be accepted from Filimon and his relatives at market price, with a discount" *(D.k A.l.,* V, 56, 58). Iron from the factories in excess of state orders could be sold "on the side" at home or abroad, with permission of the tsar *(K.m.,* I, 262). In fact, by 1674 Akema was working almost exclusively for the Russian open market (Baklanov, *Tul'skie,* pp. 133–134).

42. Kurts, *Sochinenie Kil'burgera,* pp. 168, 169.

43. O'Brien, *Russia Under Two Tsars,* p. 53; see also p. 76. *K.m.,* I, xxvi.

44. Some of these expeditions involved skilled technicians from Western Europe. Consult Kuzin, *Istoriia otkrytii,* pp. 27–28. Kurts, *Sochinenie Kil'burgera,* pp. 458–460.

45. *K.m.,* I, 283, 286. Stoskova, *Pervye metallurgicheskie,* pp. 28, 48, 89. Amburger, *Die Familie Marselis,* pp. 163–164.

46. *R.I.B.,* XXIII, 1144–1145, 1151–1152, 207–208.

47. *Ibid.,* XXI, 199, 259; XXIII, 87, 97. Kurts, *Sochinenie Kil'burgera,* p. 168.

48. Baklanova, "Zvenigorodskie," p. 99. *R.I.B.,* XXI, 256–258; XXIII, 85, 103.

7. Iron Manufacturing in the Far Northwest

1. *D.k A.l.,* V, 73–74. Amburger, *Die Familie Marselis,* p. 176. *Krepostnaia manufaktura,* Vol. II, *Olonetskie mednye i zheleznye zavody* [Peasant manufacturing, Olonets copper and iron factories], hereafter cited as *K.m.,* II (Leningrad, 1931), 90–99, 141.

2. *Ibid.,* xiv, 141. *D.k A.l.,* V, 74.

3. Kurts, *Sochinenie Kil'burgera,* pp. 165, 168. Amburger, *Die Familie Marselis,* p. 177.

4. *Ibid.*, p. 175.

5. *D.k A.I.*, ix, 46. *K.m.*, II, xv; I, 461–463.

   Despite his legal rights to do so, Marselis did not establish copper or iron factories in the Tsyl'ma area, nor did any other seventeenth-century entrepreneur. Contemporary sources, however, indicate that two large copper mines existed in this part of Archangel *krai.* The first was 228 miles north of where the Mezen river flows into the White Sea, on the Pendora river, and was described to Kilburger as containing " . . . good copper ore with large black veins." The second mine was eighteen miles away, on a small river joining the Mezen from the south; this copper ore was imbedded in rocks and sulphuric stone (Kurts, *Sochinenie Kil'burgera,* p. 165). I have been unable to learn how or where this copper ore was used.

6. Amburger, *Die Familie Marselis,* pp. 163–164, 177, 208.

7. *K.m.*, I, 250–251.

8. This document vaguely indicates that some arrangement for sharing the factory benefits had been worked out between Anna (Akema) Marselis, Peter Marselis' widow and second wife, and her husband's three surviving sons. In 1674 Petr Petrovich Marselis also moved to consolidate his family's industrial interests by paying Thomas Kellermann, his father's partner in the Vepreiskii factory, 20,000 rubles for Kellermann's 75 per cent share in that enterprise (Kurts, *Sochinenie Kil'burgera,* pp. 165–166). Two years later, in 1676, Anna Marselis married Thomas Kellermann (Amburger, *Die Familie Marselis,* p. 211).

9. *K.m.*, II, 264–265; I, 297–299.

10. Two days before his death Petr Petrovich and his partner Harmen van der Gaten received a charter summarizing their right to exploit the mines in Olonetskii *uezd* " . . . which *gost'* Semen Gavrilov was in charge of . . ." as well as ore-bearing areas on the Tsyl'ma and Pizhma rivers in Pustozerskii *uezd.* As we shall see, this document was superseded by the charter given Christian Marselis in 1678 (see footnote 13 of this chapter). Aleksei Mikhailovich specified that Petr Petrovich Marselis was to use his own money and hire people at his own expense; we know that even in 1674 Petr Petrovich was already trying (evidently with difficulty) to hire coppersmiths through his family's old friend, the king of Denmark *(K.m.,* II, xv, 130, 133–134, 126–128. Kurts, *Sochinenie Kil'burgera,* p. 165. *D.k. A.I.*, VI, 399–401).

11. *K.m.*, I, 299–300. Amburger, *Die Familie Marselis,* pp. 177–178.

12. After 1676 sources no longer mention van der Gaten in connection with any of Christian's economic interests.

13. According to this charter (dated 10 February 1678), the partners were free of *obrok* and taxes on these factories for seven years, after which 10 per cent of factory output would be delivered to the state without charge. The remaining factory produce could either be sold in Russia or exported, although in the latter instance foreign *efimki* had to be ex-

changed for rubles at the rate of 50 kopecks per *efimok*. The tsar prom- ised Christian Marselis and von Rosenbusch a monopoly on metallurgy in this area and even provided that, if they discovered new ores on royal land or the land of monasteries, *votchiniki* or *pomeshchiki,* they could utilize those areas, build factories on them, and ". . . hire at a free price those people living on those lands." If the entrepreneurs discovered gold, silver, precious stones, or mica, one-eighth of these materials would be delivered to the state without charge. See *K.m.,* II, 130–134, 141–142.

14. *Ibid.,* xvi, 132. Amburger, *Die Familie Marselis,* p. 178.

15. *K.m.,* II, xxi, 131, 146, 137–138. Kafengauz, *Istoriia,* p. 22. Kuzin, *Istoriia otkrytii,* p. 25.

16. *K.m.,* II, 147–148.

17. *Ibid.,* pp. 146–147.

18. Evidence indicates, however, that as time went by and Butenant ex- panded the scale of his iron manufacturing the number of foreigners increased, and after 1699 the factory even had the services of a Protes- tant minister, Pastor Johann Pestel. Perhaps the Russian and Karelian iron artisans were employed provisionally until foreign replacements could be obtained. Interestingly enough Dr. Andersen and Joris contin- ued to work in this area under Butenant, only now the "experiments" of Dr. Andersen involved iron rather than copper! *K.m.,* II, xxiii. Gamel', *Opisanie,* pp. xix, 113–114.

19. *K.m.,* II, 139–140, 151, 156. Kuzin, *Istoriia otkrytii,* p. 25.

20. *K.m.,* II, xxii–xxiii, 1–3, 54. Kuzin, *Istoriia otkrytii,* p. 25.

21. *K.m.,* II, xxii–xxiii, 54–55, and p. 41 of the subject index.

22. *Ibid.,* pp. 157–159.

23. *Ibid.,* pp. 153–156.

24. *Ibid.,* pp. xviii, 170, 159–160. Concerning Prince Golitsyn's interest in the Butenant iron manufactories, see *ibid.,* pp. 133, 137, 138, 152, 153, 155, 162.

25. *Ibid.,* pp. 162–164.

26. *Ibid.,* pp. 165–169, 172–174.

27. *Ibid.,* pp. 177–181, 181–182, 184, 185–186.

28. *Ibid.,* pp. 189–197.

29. The last Marselis to have full title to all the family's iron factories was Petr Petrovich, who died in August 1675. On 18 February 1676, his widow (and Christian Marselis' mother), Margarethe Böcker von Del- den, married Paul Menesius, a foreigner and a general in the tsar's army. According to the agreement between the Marselis and Butenant families, the Olonets iron works were to be jointly managed by Menesius and Andrei Butenant von Rosenbusch, son of Heinrich. With the death of Paul Menesius on 9 November 1694, the Olonets enterprises became the full property of Andrei Butenant von Rosenbusch. His father, Heinrich,

incidentally, is mentioned in government documents as late as 10 August 1696 *(D.k A.I.,* XII, 387–389), but it appears that Andrei carried on the actual operation of his family's enterprises from the early 1690's *(K.m.,* II, 144, 148, xxi. Amburger, *Die Familie Marselis,* pp. 181–182, 208).

30. *K.m.,* II, 144. Amburger, *Die Familie Marselis,* pp. 191–192.

31. *K.m.,* II, 149–150.

32. *Ibid.,* pp. xviii–xix, xxi–xxii, 144, 150.

33. Strumilin, *Istoriia,* I, 119. Stoskova, *Pervye metallurgicheskie,* p. 49. *K.m.,* II, 144, xxi–xxii.

8. Expansion and Russification

1. Amburger, *Die Familie Marselis,* p. 128. Gamel', *Opisanie,* pp. 23–24.

2. The Russians called Werner Müller Vakhramei Petrovich Miller. Before 1678, one of Miller's most noted activities was the export of Russian ship-building wood to Holland, for which he held a ten-year *privilegium* from the tsar.

3. *K.m.,* I, 303–305. Amburger, *Die Familie Marselis,* p. 128.

4. This charter, with information on the state of affairs at the factory given in this paragraph, is reprinted in *K.m.,* I, 303–310.

5. Baklanov, *Tul'skie,* p. 21. Stoskova, *Pervye metallurgicheskie,* p. 46. Amburger, *Die Familie Marselis,* p. 130.

6. This enterprise does not figure in our estimate of the achievements of iron manufacturing in Russia during the seventeenth century. It is mentioned here only to provide a rounded picture of earlier discussion. See Gamel', *Opisanie,* p. 24.

7. Lyashchenko, *History of National Economy,* p. 225. Baklanova, "Zvenigorodskie," pp. 99–100.

8. Kafengauz, *Istoriia,* p. 26. Baklanova, "Zvenigorodskie," p. 101. Amburger, *Die Familie Marselis,* pp. 180, 211. Strumilin, *Istoriia,* I, 119. Stoskova, *Pervye metallurgicheskie,* pp. 56–57.

9. *K.m.,* I, 145. Stoskova, *Pervye metallurgicheskie,* p. 48. Kafengauz, *Istoriia,* p. 23.

10. Gamel' *Opisanie,* p. 26. *Pod'iachii* Sergei Severgin's report (dated 30 March 1690) is reprinted in *K.m.,* I, 108–186.

11. Specifically, only the second and fourth enterprises at Tula were really functioning, and even at the second works both the main blast furnace and its spare were idle. The seven functioning iron manufactories included the following equipment: two blast furnaces, eight hammer shops (with nine hammers in use and as many in reserve), fourteen hearths, and thirty waterwheels to operate the bellows, hammers, and hearths. These blast furnaces had an annual combined output of 50,000 *puds* (about 900 tons) of pig iron, from which the masters could derive 33,000 *puds* of quality

iron. In 1690 ore was still obtained from Dedilov. *K.m.*, II, 111–138. Strumilin, *Istoriia*, I, 126. Kafengauz, *Istoriia*, pp. 25, 31. Chekan, "Tul'skie," p. 154. Baklanov, *Tul'skie*, p. 102.

12. Some of Naryshkin's iron factories were situated on the land of local *pomeshchiki* and monasteries, and he, as their new owner, assumed the annual payments in money and kind which previous entrepreneurs had rendered for use of this land. The Bolotov family, for example, received for the Elkinskii manufactory " .'. . thirty rubles and iron and all sorts of iron products at 15 *puds* per year." The Vepreiskii works was on the property of the Cheliusktins, who received compensation of " . . . 22 rubles in money, and 15 *puds* of salt, and 6 plows *(soshniki)* with blades, and 6 axes per year" (Chekan, "Tul'skie," pp. 149–150. Stoskova, *Pervye metallurgicheskie,* map between pp. 20–21).

13. *D.k A.I.,* XII, 20–21. Stoskova, *Pervye ·metallurgicheskie,* pp. 29–31.

14. Kafengauz, *Istoriia*, p. 23. Concerning Evert Isbrants, also consult Amburger, *Die Familie Marselis*, pp. 186, 189, 201, 203.

15. Liubomirov, *Ocherki*, p. 517. Stoskova, *Pervye metallurgicheskie,* pp. 57–58. Strumilin, *Istoriia*, I, 119.

16. Professor Jerome Blum draws the following picture of Demidov: "He was a skillful manager, a shrewd and ruthless businessman, and the employer of thousands. He was fully aware of his own great power and was knowledgeable in the ways of holding his sovereign's favor. Yet Nikita lived near his forges in a small wooden house (a stone house was a sign of affluence in Russia), never learned to read or write, never drank – in this he was spectacularly unlike the usual peasant – and refused to take the honors and decorations offered him by the tsar until five years before his death, when he finally accepted a patent of nobility" (*Lord and Peasant,* p. 300).

17. Concerning Nikita Demidov's early life, consult Kafengauz's definitive study, *Istoriia*, pp. 82–98. Concerning his Tula factory, see *ibid.,* pp. 87–90; also Stoskova, *Pervye metallurgicheskie,* p. 48.

18. Pavlenko, *Razvitie*, p. 48.

19. Amburger, *Die Familie Marselis*, p. 174. Lubimenko, "Trud inozemtsev," p. 66.

20. Maleev, "Altaiskii gornyi okrug," pp. 302–305. Kuzin, *Istoriia otkrytii,* pp. 34–35, 39–51. *Sibir' xvii-xviii vv.* [The Siberia of the seventeenth and eighteenth centuries] (Novosibirsk, 1962), pp. 97–108.

21. Danilevskii, *Russkaia tekhnika*, p. 28.

22. Amburger, *Die Familie Marselis*, p. 93. Roger Portal, *L'Oural au xviiie siècle, étude d'histoire économique et sociale* (Paris, 1950), pp. 16–17. Kafengauz, *Istoriia*, p. 50. Stoskova, *Pervye metallurgicheskie,* p. 15. Strumilin, *Istoriia*, I, 57–58. Nikolai Abramov, "O zheleznykh i oruzheinykh zavodakh v Sibiri v xvii i pervoi polovine xviii stoletii" [Con-

cerning iron and weapons factories in Siberia during the seventeenth and first half of the eighteenth centuries], *Vestnik imperatorskago russkago geograficheskago obshchestva* [Messenger of the Imperial Russian Geographical Society], part xiii (1860), 183–194.

23. Amburger, *Die Familie Marselis*, pp. 174–175. Liubomirov, *Ocherki*, p. 517. Kafengauz, *Istoriia*, pp. 24, 50. V. V. Danilevskii gives a strange account of the Pyskorskii copper works. First, he states (incorrectly) that the enterprise was water-powered. Second, Danilevskii believes that the only contribution made to the project by the Saxon "Arist Pettsol'd" was ". . . some very unfortunate advice concerning the selection of a new place for this factory" (*Russkaia tekhnika*, p. 28). Danilevskii names eleven of the Russian masters associated with the Pyskorskii and asserts that Russians were exclusively responsible for running the factory (*ibid.*, pp. 28, 478)— which does not really appear to be true.

24. *D.k A.I.*, V, 61–67.

25. A. A. Preobrazhenskii, "Predprinimateli Tumashevy v xvii v." [Tumashev entrepreneurs during the seventeenth century], *Russkoe gosudarstvo v xvii veke* [Russian state during the seventeenth century] (Moscow, 1961), pp. 113–123. Kuzin, *Istoriia otkrytii*, pp. 37–39, 122, 123.

26. *D.k A.I.*, V, 61–67.

27. Kuzin, *Istoriia otkrytii*, p. 39. Also see pp. 254–255, above.

28. Kafengauz, *Istoriia*, p. 50.

29. Strumilin, *Istoriia*, I, 61. Kafengauz, *Istoriia*, pp. 24, 50.

30. Kuzin, *Istoriia otkrytii*, p. 35.

31. Information about this activity for the years 1683–1698 is to be found in *D.k A.I.*, X, 322–341.

9. Other Russian Manufactures of the Seventeenth Century

1. A. A. Zimin, *Reformy Ivan Groznogo* [Reforms of Ivan the Terrible] (Moscow, 1960), p. 145. Baklanova, "Privozne tovary," pp. 24, 45, 51–59, 63, 102–103. I. M. Kulisher, *Ocherk istorii russkoi promyshlennosti* [Study of the history of Russian industry] (Petrograd, 1922). Lappo-Danilevskii, "Inozemtsy," p. 67.

2. Baklanova, "Privoznye tovary," p. 24.

3. The Russians exported furs, leather goods, hemp, cereals, wood, honey, wax, potash, tar, resin, lard, fish glue (up to 300 *puds* per year), salmon (about 25,000 *puds* per year), caviar (as much as 20,000 *puds* annually), seal blubber, mica, rhubarb, hog bristles, corned beef, and such primitive "finished" products as rope and *vatman* cloth, carded flax, and scutched hemp. Actually the government was aware of the disadvantage—and even the losses, when the market was bad—connected with conducting

foreign trade on the basis of raw materials. Losses sustained in 1668 by the sale of Izmailovo flax in Riga led to the idea of marketing *poloten* cloth, which came from artisan production. The exact outcome of this experiment is unknown, but for our purposes it is interesting to note it involved two foreign masters in the tsar's service, Andrew Hoffman and "Ivan Rykhtar." O'Brien, *Russia Under Two Tsars,* p. 77. Kostomarov, *Sobranie Sochinenii,* XX, 14, 29, 371. Kurts, *Sochinenie Kil'burgera,* pp. 100–101. The Riga episode and its aftermath are discussed in A. I. Zaozerskii, *Tsar' Aleksei Mikhailovich v svoem khoziastve* [Tsar Aleksei Mikhailovich and his economy] (Petrograd, 1917), pp. 248–249.

4. Kurts, *Sochinenie Kil'burgera,* pp. 104, 284–285. Kostomarov, *Sobranie Sochinenii,* XX, 361. *Puteshestvie . . . Makariia,* IV, 4. N. A. Baklanova, "Stekliannye zavody v moskovskom gosudarstve xvii veka" [Glass factories in the Muscovite state of the seventeenth century], *Ocherki po istorii torgovli i promyshlennosti v Rossii v 17 i v nachale 18 stoletiia* [Studies in the history of Russian trade and industry during the seventeenth and early eighteenth centuries], IV (1928), 120. Berry, *English Works of Giles Fletcher,* p. 183.

5. M. A. Tseitlin, *Ocherki po istorii razvitiia stekol'noi promyshlennosti v Rossii* [Studies in the history of the development of the glass industry in Russia] (Moscow-Leningrad, 1939), p. 18. Baklanova, "Stekliannye zavody," p. 120. Baklanova, "Privoznye tovary," pp. 44-45.

6. Baklanova, "Stekliannye zavody," pp. 121, 123. Amburger, *Die Familie Marselis,* pp. 94–95, 200.

7. Baklanova, "Stekliannye zavody," p. 122. *S.G.G.i D.,* III, 351–352.

8. Baklanova, "Stekliannye zavody," pp. 122–123. Amburger, *Die Familie Marselis,* p. 200.

9. *R.I.B.,* VIII, 295–297. Baklanova, "Stekliannye zavody," pp. 123–125. Kurts, *Sochinenie Kil'burgera,* pp. 323–324.

10. Amburger, *Die Familie Marselis,* p. 201. Baklanova, "Stekliannye zavody," pp. 125–127.

11. *Ibid.,* pp. 133, 138. Zaozerskii, *Tsar' Aleksei Mikhailovich,* p. 148. *R.I.B.,* XXI, 1444–1445.

12. Zaozerskii, *Tsar' Aleksei Mikhailovich,* pp. 148–149. *R.I.B.,* XXI, 1450; XXIII, 1160. Baklanova, "Stekliannye zavody," pp. 132, 134–136. Kurts, *Sochinenie Kil'burgera,* p. 325. Zaozerskii, *Tsar' Aleksei Mikhailovich,* pp. 150–152. Ivan Zabelin, *Sochinenie* [Works], I: *Domashnii byt Russkikh tsarei v xvi xvii st.* [Home life of the Russian tsars during the sixteenth and seventeenth centuries] (Moscow, 3rd ed., 1895), 518–519, 547–548.

13. *Ibid.,* 518–519, 527, 534, 547–549. Lubimenko, "Trud inozemtsev," p. 71. Baklanova, "Stekliannye zavody," pp. 129–130, 137. Kurts, *Sochinenie Kil'burgera,* pp. 119, 324–325.

14. *Ibid.,* p. 119. Liubomirov, *Ocherki,* p. 191. Baklanova, "Stekliannye zavody," p. 137.

15. Kurts, *Sochinenie Kil'burgera*, p. 325. Baklanova, "Stekliannye zavody," p. 138.

16. For further details, consult Baklanova, "Stekliannye zavody," pp. 139–140. Concerning glass manufacturing during the eighteenth century, see Liubomirov, *Ocherki*, pp. 191–200.

17. We might add that there was a certain amount of glass-making on the left bank of the Ukraine during the second half of the seventeenth century. We know that Iuska Gutnik and Colonel Perekrest owned glass factories in Lebedinskii *uezd*, and other small manufactories operated in the same period. The Ukrainian product was finer than Russian glass and was shipped to Moscow and sold all year long at the *gostinyi dvor* (Liubomirov, *Ocherki*, pp. 519, 191–192. Kurts, *Sochinenie Kil'burgera*, p. 119).

18. Solov'ev, *Istoriia*, IX, 94. Liubomirov, *Ocherki*, pp. 160–162, 517–518. Pokrovsky, *History of Russia*, p. 283.

19. Kurts. *Sochinenie Kil'burgera*, p. 100. *R.I.B.*, VIII, 160–161.
    Inna Lubimenko asserts that the English still had rope works at Kholmogory and Archangel as late as 1638 ("Letters," pp. 95–96), but my own research has been unable to confirm this, nor does Lubimenko's opinion seem to be shared in other secondary works (cf. Liubomirov, *Ocherki*, p. 512).

20. Tolstoi, *Pervyia sorok let*, pp. 299, 309. Zaozerskii, *Tsar' Aleksei Mikhailovich*, pp. 142–145. Muliukin, *Ocherki*, pp. 204–205. Amburger, *Die Familie Marselis*, pp. 202–203.

21. *Ibid.*, p. 203. Liubomirov, *Ocherki*, p. 513.

22. Kurts, *Sochinenie Kil'burgera*, pp. 112, 116.

23. *Istoriko-statisticheskii obzor*, Vol. II, part 3, section nine, p. 2. Likhachev, *Bumaga*, pp. 3, 29–30, 33–34, 51–56. Tsvetaev, *Protestanstvo*, p. 716.

24. Shpil'kin was by trade a cloth merchant of the *sukonnaia sotnia* and a *tseloval'nik*, i.e., literally, one who "kissed the cross" upon entering state service. These were merchants compelled to perform duties on behalf of the tsar, usually of an economic nature. In Shpil'kin's case this service (apparently) involved the management of a royal manufactory.

25. Novitskii, "K istorii," pp. 28–29. Likhachev, *Bumaga*, pp. 83–84.

26. Amburger, *Die Familie Marselis*, pp. 118, 155–157. *D.k A.I.*, XI, 111–112. Excerpts from John's petition are reprinted in Baklanova, "Stekliannye zavody," p. 131.

27. *D.k A.I.*, XI, 111.

28. *Ibid.*, p. 111. Novitskii, "K istorii," pp. 30, 39. Amburger, *Die Familie Marselis*, p. 204.

29. Amburger, *loc. cit.* Baklanova, "Stekliannye zavody," p. 131–132.

30. Surviving documents do not explain why the tsar refused the loans needed to complete the van Sweeden glass manufactory. The fact that

John had already received state loans totaling 2,948 rubles (still unpaid, as of 1668) might have discouraged the authorities from increasing investment in still-uncompleted industrial undertakings — especially as they pertained to "light," nonmilitary manufacturing. *D.k A.I.*, XI, 111, 112).

Another possible explanation makes for fascinating speculation. As we have seen, Aleksei Mikhailovich took measures after 1656 to establish his own glass works. This enterprise, the Izmailovo factory, was finally completed between the autumn of 1668 and February 1669 — just after (please note) the death of John of Sweden. Is it possible that the tsar, already facing competition from the Coyet family's Dukhanino factory, did not wish to broaden that competition by assisting — or even permitting — the completion of yet another privately-owned glass manufactory? Certainly we know that Aleksei Mikhailovich was high-handed enough to take (by royal fiat) no fewer than eight skilled glass masters from the rival Dukhanino enterprise, where he also purchased glassmaking equipment at bargain prices. An Italian known to the Russians as M. Vatolinyi and working for the *Tainyi Prikaz* (the government office responsible for the tsar's glass factory) also bought "...from the foreign woman Ivanova, wife of John of Sweden, from the widow Ovdot'ia... pots and copper frying pans and all sorts of various copper and iron equipment and ashes..." for the sum of 138 rubles 20 *altyn*. *R.I.B.*, XXIII, 1337.

31. *D.k A.I.*, XI, 111, 112.

32. I have been unable to establish the reasons for this change in ownership, but probably Maria van Sweeden died in 1676 and Herman Löfken (known to the Russians as Eremei Levkin), a nephew of John of Sweden, was her heir. John's family continued to live in Russia. The name "vanSweden" often appears in the postal books of 1698–1701, and on 23 January 1695 Patrick Gordon's journal takes note of a wedding of the son of the foreign merchant Adolf Goutman and a daughter [granddaughter?] of John of Sweden (Kozlovskii, *Pervye pochty*, I, 70).

33. *R.I.B.*, XXIII, 1337, 1342. *D.k A.I.*, XI, 112. Kurts, *Sochinenie Kil'burgera*, p. 318. Amburger, *Die Familie Marselis*, p. 204. Baklanova, "Stekliannye zavody," p. 132.

34. Zaozerskaia, *Razvitie*, p. 56. Novitskii, "K istorii," pp. 32, 34. Kurts, *Sochinenie Kil'burgera*, p. 117.

35. We hope that this will clarify any gaps of information on p. 151, above. After 1665 David Bacheracht operated the gunpowder works which he organized on the Iauza river quite near Moscow's *Pushkarskii Prikaz* and the "new" foreign quarter *(Nemetskaia Sloboda)*. The tsar took the factory in 1671, when Bacheracht died, and had the enterprise converted to paper manufacturing in 1673 in the manner just described. In 1676 the state passed the enterprise on to Herman Löfken, etc.

36. *D.k A.I.*, VII, 312. Amburger, *Die Familie Marselis*, p. 204.
Professor Amburger is not quite correct, however, in concluding from

this that paper-making disappeared in Russia until foreigners established the first Petrine paper factory in 1705. The receipt book of the Voskresenskii Novoierusalimskii monastery near Moscow for 1963 speaks of receiving four rubles *obrok* from "Savka," who had built a paper mill on the monastery's land. No other details concerning this factory are available today (Liubomirov, *Ocherki*, p. 519), but apparently Savka's enterprise was separate from any of the earlier efforts described in these pages.

37. Kostomarov, *Sobranie Sochinenii*, XX, 413.

38. *D.k A.I.*, V, 211.

39. G. A. Novitskii, "Iz istorii nasazhdeniia sukonnykh fabrik v 17 veke" [From the history of the establishment of cloth factories during the seventeenth century], *Trud v Rossii* [Labor in Russia], No. 2 (1924), 20–21. *D.k A.I.*, V, 211; XI, 111–112. Kurts, *Sochinenie Kil'burgera*, p. 171.

40. Professor Novitskii believes that Russian statesmen in this period were sufficiently far-sighted to refuse new entrepreneurs long-term monopolies, thus keeping open the possibility of competition from other foreign capitalists ("K istorii," p. 27). While this may be largely true, the policy was not applied consistently.

41. *D.k A.I.*, XI, 109–111. Novitskii, "K istorii," pp. 22, 25–27.

42. *Ibid.*, pp. 29–30. Pazhitnov, *Ocherki . . . sherstnaia*, p. 9. *D.k A.I.*, X, 312–313, 413–414.

43. Novitskii concluded that Tarbet's enterprise failed because of the state of the national economy at that time, namely " . . . the dominating position of artisan industries and the capture of the market by merchant capital, [as well as] the fall in demand for cloth which was noted by Kilburger in 1674." Zaozerskaia agrees " . . . the entire enterprise was estranged from Russian conditions, and probably for this reason decayed after five years." See "Iz istorii," p. 31, and *Razvitie*, p. 49, respectively.

44. Zaozerskaia, *Razvitie*, p. 46. Amburger, *Die Familie Marselis*, p. 214. Novitskii, "K istorii," p. 31. O'Brien, *Russia Under Two Tsars*, pp. 76–77.

45. *D.k A.I.*, XII, 23–28. Zaozerskaia, *Razvitie*, pp. 49–50. Amburger, *Die Familie Marselis*, p. 199. A. L. Iakobson, *Tkatskie slobody i sela v xvii veke (Kadashevo, Khamovniki, Breitovo i Cherkasovo)* [Weaving suburbs and towns during the seventeenth century (Kadashevo, etc.)] (Moscow-Leningrad, 1934), p. 37.

46. According to Pokrovsky, the above-mentioned 225,000 pairs of yufts annually exported during the 1650's was valued at 335,000 rubles. Fletcher reported that Russians once exported 100,000 cattle hides each year, though at the time of his visit in 1588–1589 the quantity was down to about 30,000. Fletcher found Russian cowhide was "of small sise" but called their elk "very faire and large." Pokrovsky, *History of Russia*, pp. 257–258. Berry, *English Works of Giles Fletcher*, pp. 179–180.

47. *Istoriko-statisticheskii obzor,* Vol. II, part 3, section seven, pp. 1–3. Bakhrushin, *Nauchnye trudy,* I, 77–82. Kurts, *Sochinenie Kil'burgera,* pp. 100, 104, 269.

48. Liubomirov, *Ocherki,* p. 518. *S.G.G.i D.,* III, 350–351. Zaozerskaia, *Razvitie,* p. 53.

49. G. A. Novitskii, "Pervye moskovskie manufaktury xvii veka po obrabotke kozhi" [First Muscovite manufactories of the seventeenth century for leather-making], in S. ·V. Bakhrushin (ed.), *Moskovskii krai v ego proshlom* [Moscow *krai* in its past] (Moscow, 1928), p. 48. The Iauza factory is described in detail by Novitskii in *ibid.,* pp. 48–50, 52. See also *R.I.B.,* XI, 1356; XXIII, 1601, 1640–1641. Zaozerskaia, *Razvitie,* p. 52. Zaozerskii, *Tsar' Aleksei Mikhailovich,* pp. 152–154.

50. Zaozerskii, *Tsar' Aleksei Mikhailovich,* p. 153. Novitskii, "Pervye," pp. 51, 53–56.

51. *Ibid.,* p. 56. Zaozerskaia, *Razvitie,* p. 52. Liubomirov, *Ocherki,* p. 170.

52. Novitskii, "Pervye," p. 53. Zaozerskii, *Tsar' Aleksei Mikhailovich,* p. 156. Zaozerskaia, *Razvitie,* p. 52.

53. Evidence indicates that Aleksei Mikhailovich had another leather works organized in the Moscow area during the 1670's, but surviving documents do not disclose the nature or·duration of its activity. Another state tannery was built in this period on the Kliaz'ma river, near Timonin, but again, we have not sufficient information to describe or analyze the enterprise. There is no reason to think that either shop employed foreigners or was anything but an artisan works (Novitskii, "Pervye," pp. 58–59).

54. *Istoriko-statisticheskii obzor,* II, 185–186. Pazhitnov, *Ocherki . . . khlopchatobumazhnaia,* p. 303. Kurts, *Sochinenie Kil'burgera,* pp. 150–151. Baklanova, "Privoznye tovary," p. 31. Kostomarov, *Sobranie Sochinenii,* XX, 418–422. Pashkov, *History,* pp. 206, 221–222. *P.S.Z.R.I.,* I, 665–670.

55. Muliukin, *Ocherki,* p. 98. See also Amburger, *Die Familie Marselis,* pp. 71, 198, and Zaozerskaia, *Razvitie,* p. 41.

56. E. Lermontova, *Shelkovaia fabrika v pravlenie tsarevny Sofii Alekseevnyy* [The silk factory in the reign of Tsarevna Sof'ia Alekseevna] (Petrograd, 1915), p. 43. Zaozerskaia, *Razvitie,* p. 43. In general, see *D.k A.I.,* XI, 110, 113.

57. *R.I.B.,* XXI, 1121.

58. Zaozerskii, *Tsar' Aleksei Mikhailovich,* pp. 134–135.

59. *Ibid.,* pp. 135, 137. Zaozerskaia, *Razvitie,* pp. 41–42. *R.I.B.,* XXI, 1177, 1341; XXIII, 1237, 1289, 1488. *D.k A.I.,* XI, 112–113; X, 175–177.

60. *Ibid.,* X, 174; XI, 173. Zaozerskaia, *Razvitie,* pp. 44–45. Lermontova, "Shelkovaia fabrika," pp. 46–48.

61. *Ibid.,* pp. 48–49. *D.k A.I.,* X, 173, 174, 182, 183. Zaozerskaia, *Razvitie,* p. 45.

62. *D.k A.I.,* X, 180–182, 184–185, 186–187.

63. Although it was clearly understood from the beginning of his entrepreneurship that the silk factory would be financed entirely by Paulsen and that he would not plead economic hardship to avoid any of the obligations set forth in his charter, Paulsen had often requested and received various forms of state aid. For example, on 11 November 1682, the government granted Paulsen 100,000 bricks and 300 barrels of lime to construct a new silk factory. On 12 December 1681, Paulsen had gone so far as to request outright relief from his 2,000 rubles' debt to the state. At that time half the debt was cancelled, and later, on 28 February 1684, it was decided that half of the remaining obligation could be settled with cloth from the silk enterprise (*D.k A.I.,* X, 174–176, 179–180, 183–184).

64. Zaozerskaia, *Razvitie,* p. 46. Lermontova, "Shelkovaia fabrika," pp. 53–55. Kulisher, *Ocherk,* p. 88. *D.k A.I.,* X, 190–191.

65. Paulsen's raw silk was obtained by the *Posol'skii Prikaz* from Armenian merchants. Factory records reveal the following quantities as received (from Lermontova, "Shelkovaia fabrika," p. 57):
    1685   2½ *puds*
    1686   3 *puds* 16 *funts* + 30 *funts* of velvet
    1687   3 *puds* 30 funts
    1688   4 *puds* 7 *funts*
    1689   2 *puds* 16 *funts*

66. *D.k A.I.,* X, 182, 187–188, 192–198.

67. Lermontova, "Shelkovaia fabrika," pp. 60–69. Kulisher, *Ocherk,* p. 88.

68. Liubomirov, *Ocherki,* p. 104. Zaozerskaia, *Razvitie,* p. 48. Lermontova, "Shelkovaia fabrika," pp. 69–70. Concerning the silk industry during the eighteenth century, see Liubomirov, *Ocherki,* pp. 105–128.

69. Lubimenko, "Trud inozemtsev," p. 72. Pokrovsky, *History of Russia,* p. 260. Gamel', *Opisanie,* p. 23. Kostomarov, *Sobranie Sochinenii,* XX, 377. Lubimenko, "Struggle of the Dutch," pp. 42, 43.

70. This line of entrepreneurship demonstrates the great technological disparity between Russia and the West in this period. Although the sawmill was well established in Europe by the sixteenth century, Russians a full century later did not even have use of the *hand-saw,* which had been known to the ancient Egyptians! Actually a massive demand for lumber did not exist in Russia at this time, and even the largest manufactories of the seventeenth century relied on individual Russian and foreign carpenters for their construction. Lest one lose perspective, however, one should remember that it was the Dutch who introduced the sawmill into England and England's American colonies, and that this, too, occurred in the seventeenth century. A Dutchman built the first sawmill in England near London in 1663. It had to be removed because of the pressure of workers who feared it would deprive sawyers of their trade, and " . . .

apprehensions of the same sort prevented a renewed attempt when proposed in 1700; and the populace actually destroyed one as late as 1767." J. Leander Bishop, *A History of American Manufactures from 1608 to 1860* (Philadelphia and London, 1868), I, 93. Also Liubomirov, *Ocherki,* pp. 237, 683–684, 686–693. Barbour, *Capitalism,* pp. 19–20, 69.

71. Kordt, *Otchet,* p. ccciv.

72. Liubomirov, *Ocherki,* p. 693.

73. *Ibid.,* p. 694. *P.S.Z.R.I.,* III, 112. Liubomirov, *Ocherki,* pp. 518, 694–695.

74. *Ibid.,* pp. 696–698.

10. The Russian State's Industrial Policy

1. During the 1630's an average of 450,000 rubles was collected annually at Moscow alone in the "fifth" tax (20 per cent *ad valorem*), most of it on domestic commerce. By contrast we know that during the first half of the century from 26,000 to 40,000 rubles were collected each year at Archangel, and an average of 12,000 rubles at Astrakhan during the 1640's. It is clear, then, that foreign trade provided relatively significant revenues to the tsar's government. M. N. Pokrovsky, *Ocherk istorii russkoi kul'tury* [Study of the history of Russian culture], I (Moscow, 1915), 102. Lappo-Danilevskii, "Inozemtsy," p. 98.

2. Kirchner, *Commercial Relations,* p. 8.

3. C. Bickford O'Brien, *Muscovy and the Ukraine, from the Pereiaslavl Agreement to the Truce of Andrussovo* (Berkeley and Los Angeles, 1963), pp. 35–36.

4. Bazilevich, "Elementy merkantilizma," p. 33.

5. Report dated 8 February 1684, and reprinted in *D.k A.I.,* X, 178–179, 184.

6. Concerning the advantages anticipated from Efim Fimbrant's chamois factory, see his charter of 31 March 1634, reprinted in *S.G.G.iD.,* III, 350–351.

7. Report dated 9 April 1684, and reprinted in *D.k A.I.,* XI, 110.

8. The clerk *(d'iak)* who actually wrote out this statement was Harmen van der Gaten, but he may have used earlier reports written by Peter Marselis (see *D.k A.I.,* IX, 46–48).

   It is interesting to compare the ideas in this memorandum to those set forth in a petition from Peter Marselis to Aleksei Mikhailovich in the late 1660's. After enumerating his deliveries to the state during 1668, Marselis remarks: "And before the establishment of a Russian iron industry those military supplies were ordered from above . . . at a high price." Marselis then gives an extended comparison of the costs of iron goods from his factories and from Western Europe, and concludes:

   > And thanks to this, mighty sovereign, much profit
   > was made, and in the future thanks to this, there will

be still more profits. And that money which was once
sent abroad for military supplies now remains in the
Muscovite state and goes for peace. And many people
are sustained by this and many Russian people learn
this handicraft, [all this] to the glory of your Russian
kingdom [*K.m.*, I, 220–221].

9.   Keep, "Regime of Filaret," p. 349.

10.   *R.I.B.*, VIII, 295–300.

11.   *K.m.*, I, 301–303.

12.   See, for example, the complaint launched by Andrei Vinius and Peter
Marselis in July 1641, published in *Russko-shvedskie*, pp. 118–119.

13.   *D.k A.I.*, V, 410–411, etc.

14.   Muliukin, *Ocherki*, pp. 220–224.

15.   *S.G.G.i D.*, III, 352.

16.   *D.k A.I.*, V, 60.

17.   Kafengauz, *Istoriia*, p. 21.

18.   *D.k A.I.*, X, 184.

19.   This charter was granted to Iakov Galaktinovich and A. A. Vinius, son of
Andrei Vinius, the Tula iron manufacturer (Kuzin, *Istoriia otkrytii*, p.
30). Although this document indicates an interest on the part of A. A.
Vinius in the entrepreneurial activities for which his father was famous, it
appears this factory was never built. I have been unable to discover other
manufacturing projects contemplated or launched by A. A. Vinius.

20.   Again we observe discrimination against "light" industry as compared to
government treatment of iron manufacturing. Julius Coyet was granted
an *obrok*-free period of 15 years, but he could import materials needed by
the factory on a customs-free basis for only 5 years; the Hamburg silk
master Arent Paulsen was permitted to bring materials from Western
Europe without payment of duty only during the actual organization of
his silk enterprise; duty-free import of raw silk, etc., thereafter was
possible only through Armenian and Indian merchants.

21.   Kafengauz, *Istoriia*, p. 21. *K.m.*, II, 146.

22.   Muliukin, *Ocherki*, p. 216. *K.m.*, I, 272–273; II, 135.

23.   Shipment of 23 January 1670. See *K.m.*, I, 393, 397.

24.   *Ibid.*, pp. 366, 373–375, 381–382.

25.   Baklanov, *Tul'skie*, pp. 131–132.

26.   *K.m.*, I, 301. *Puteshestvie . . . Makariia*, II, 197.

27.   Muliukin, *Ocherki*, p. 96.

28.   *K.m.*, I, 289; II, 147.

29.   In other cases the tsar provided construction materials while a factory

was being built. During the 1630's Andrei Vinius got hammers for his Tula works from the *Posol'skii Prikaz (K.m.,* I, 10) and when Arent Paulsen reconstructed his silk-weaving enterprise in 1682, government officials granted him 100,000 bricks and 300 barrels of lime from the tsar's own brickyards and lime-pits.

30. *K.m.,* II, 127–130.

31. It is true that *pomestia* (estates) with serfs owing feudal services and dues to the *pomeshchik* were granted to foreigners and their heirs, but this was only for the duration of satisfactory service rendered to the tsar. Olearius tells us that a scandal involving the Lesly family's alleged contempt for Eastern Orthodoxy caused the Patriarch to pressure the tsar to revoke the use of such estates by non-baptized foreigners. A royal decree to this effect was finally issued (reprinted in *P.S.Z.R.I.,* I, No. 103), but since the state lacked the means to pay so many officers cash salaries, this legislation was seldom enforced. But Lesly and some 50 other foreigners were sufficiently shaken by the episode to convert to Orthodoxy! As the century drew to a close, the feeling grew among conservative Russians that it was not good to give Russian peasants in this manner even to those foreigners who *had* converted to Orthodoxy. But the practice continued (Olearius, *Travels,* p. 245. Muliukin, *Ocherki,* pp. 190–194. Platonov, *Moskva i zapad,* p. 129).

32. Muliukin, *Ocherki,* pp. 127–145, 225–228.

33. Kuzin, *Istoriia otkrytii,* pp. 31, 26. *K.m.,* I, 441–442.

34. The English preferred to use Russian workers at their sixteenth-century rope walks at Vologda and Kholmogory because the Russians were satisfied with lower wages. In the case of state-owned iron enterprises, foreign masters met their pedagogical obligations with regard to Russian apprentices. Under Tsar Mikhail, for example, foreigners at the Neg-linnaia artisan works cast a large number of cannon and bells, and ". . . here Russians also learned foundry work fairly well" (V. O. Kliuchevskii, *Kurs Russkoi istorii* [The course of Russian history] in *Sochineniia* [Works] (Moscow, 1957), III, 266).

35. *K.m.,* II, xix–xxi, 157–158, 176, 185, 190. *D.k A.I.,* XII, 322–325.

36. *K.m.,* II, 165–166.

37. *Ibid.,* I, 328–345, 196.

38. Baklanov, *Tul'skie,* p. 21.

39. See Kozlovskii, *Pervye pochty,* I, 90, for discussion of this figure.

40. *K.m.,* I, 313–315. S. G. Strumilin, *Ocherki ekonomicheskoi istorii Rossii* [Studies in the economic history of Russia] (Moscow, 1960), pp. 65–69.

41. *K.m.,* I, xxviii.

42. The example given here is from the Vinius-Galkin charter of 1676, discussed by Kuzin, *Istoriia otkrytii,* p. 130.

43. This was the provision of the charters given to the Marselis brothers in

314 *Notes*

1674, Butenant in 1696, etc. (consult Kafengauz, *Istoriia,* pp. 21–22). Peter Marselis' charter of 12 March 1638 specified that he and his workers had the right to be judged at the *Posol'skii Prikaz* in civil suits, and that Peter—by kissing the cross—would have his word accepted by those present (*S.G.G.i D.,* III, 370–373). Evidently the latter privilege did not apply in disputes with the government.

44. *K.m.,* I, 205, 196–197, 200–204, 204–206.

45. *Ibid.,* 243–246; II, 130–131, 135–139.

46. Kuzin, *Istoriia otkrytii,* pp. 27–28. Danilevskii, *Russkaia tekhnika,* p. 32.

47. *K.m.,* II, 126–128.

48. *Ibid.,* p. 147.

49. *K.m.,* I, 307–309.

50. Zaozerskii, *Tsar' Aleksei Mikhailovich,* pp. 5–6. Pankratova, *Formirovanie,* p. 177. On the *Tainyi Prikaz's* economic responsibilities in general, see Zaozerskii's book, pp. 17–21, 39–47.

51. *R.I.B.,* XXI, 74–75, 1747.

52. The term I am translating as "heavy plow" is *kosulia,* which is a " . . . northeastern *sokha* (light northern plow); a heavy *sokha* or light *plug* (heavy southern plow) with a plowshare with cutter and mold-board" (Dal', *Tolkovyi slovar',* II, 174).

53. Zaozerskii, *Tsar' Aleksei Mikhailovich,* pp. 16–17; but compare p. 113.

54. *R.I.B.,* XXI, 1624–1625, 1623, 1608–1609, 1721, 1609–1610, 1695. Baklanov, "Zvenigorodskie," p. 98.

55. Pavlenko, *Razvitie,* p. 91.

56. Chekan, "Tul'skie," p. 147, *R.I.B.,* XXI, 157, 159, 179, 680. *D.k A.I.,* V, 391–392, 401; IX, No. 16.
    Frequent changes of jurisdiction are also found in the histories of state-owned manufactories. The *Prikaz Tainykh Del* organized the Iauza river tannery in 1666. When the enterprise was relocated in 1669–1670 it was placed under the *Prikaz Vladimirskoi chetverti (prikaz* for Vladimir affairs), and then handed in rapid succession to such unlikely institutions as the *prikaz* for Ukrainian affairs *(Malorossiiskii Prikaz), prikaz* for Galician affairs *(Prikaz Galitskoi chetverti),* and finally the "new" pharmaceutical *prikaz (Prikaz Novoi Apteki),* which indirectly brought the leather factory back to the *Prikaz Tainykh Del,* since this government office supervised the new pharmaceutical *prikaz.* These changes were purely administrative and had no effect upon the actual operation of the tannery *(R.I.B.,* XI, 1356; XXIII, 1640–1641. Novitskii, "Pervye," p. 52. Zaozerskaia, *Razvitie,* p. 52. Zaozerskii, *Tsar' Aleksei Mikhailovich,* pp. 152–154).

57. *D.k A.I.,* V, 273–274. *K.m.,* I, 360–361; 322–323, 347–348, 354–355, 360–361, 376; 187–195, 321–323; 385–389.

11. Activities of the Foreigner in
Early Modern Russia

1. V. O. Kliuchevskii, *Skazaniia inostrantsev o moskovskom gosudarstve*
    [Account of foreigners concerning the Muscovite state] (Petrograd,
    1918), p. 93. Berry, *English Works of Giles Fletcher*, pp. 235–236.
    Alexander Vucinich, *Science in Russian Culture: A History to 1860*
    (Stanford, 1963), p. 16. Pokrovsky, *Brief History*, p. 85. (On the use of
    German mercenaries in the 1648 Moscow uprising, see Olearius, *Trav-
    els*, pp. 209–210). Ustrialov, *Istoriia*, I, 171–180. Stanislas Zolkiewski,
    Expedition to Moscow, a Memoir (London, 1959), pp. 55, 58, 61, 78–
    80, 102–103.

2. Tsvetaev, *Protestanstvo*, p. 1. Lesly's instructions are reprinted in
    S.G.G.i D., III, 316–322. Concerning his mission, see Tsvetaev, *Protes-
    tanstvo*, p. 374, and Amburger, *Die Familie Marselis*, pp. 74–75, 79, 96.
    Concerning van Dama, see Kliuchevskii, *Kurs*, III, 264. See *S.G.G.i D.*,
    III, 322–330, 338–339, for valuable documentary material on other
    mercenary projects of this time.

3. Lappo-Danilevskii, "Inozemtsy," p. 104. Tsvetaev, *Protestanstvo*, pp.
    279, 706. Olearius, *Travels*, p. 51. Ustrialov, *Istoriia*, I, 104, 180–181.
    Solov'ev, *Istoriia*, IX, 161. O. L. Vaynshtein, *Rossiia i 30-letnaia voina
    1618–1648 gg.* [Russia and the Thirty Years' War of 1618–1648] (Mos-
    cow, 1947), pp. 92–102. Platonov, *Moskva i zapad*, p. 128. *Tri Veka*,
    III, 3–4. *R.I.B.*, VIII, 122, 130, 138, 141.

4. Platonov, *Moskva i zapad*, p. 128. Ustrialov, *Istoriia*, I, 181–182. Bill-
    ington, *Icon and the Axe*, p. 112. P. Miliukov, *Gosudarstvennoe khoziai-
    stvo Rossii v pervoi chetverti xviii stoletiia i reforma Petra Velikago*
    [State economy of Russia during the first quarter of the eighteenth centu-
    ry and the reform of Peter the Great] (St. Petersburg, 2d ed., 1905), pp.
    52–53.

5. Kliuchevskii, *Skazaniia*, p. 108. Tsvetaev, *Protestanstvo*, p. 710. Smir-
    nov, *Short History of the U.S.S.R.*, p. 136.

6. But foreigners should not receive all the credit for Russian stone fortifica-
    tions of this period. For example, the Russian master Fedor Kon' built
    two walls which George Vernadsky termed: "masterpieces in the art of
    fortification": the white stone wall *(belyi kamennyi gorod)* around Mos-
    cow's *bolshoi posad* in 1586–1591, and a stone wall surrounding
    Smolensk in 1597–1600 *(Tsardom of Moscow*, p. 216).

7. Zaozerskii, *Tsar' Aleksei Mikhailovich*, pp. 161–162, 279–280. Lubi-
    menko, "Trud inozemtsev," p. 62. *S.G.G.i D.*, III, 330. Ustrialov,
    Istoriia, p. 104. *D.k A.I.*, III, 61–65. Billington, *Icon and the Axe*, p. 113.
    On the technology of architecture, defense walls, etc., in Muscovite
    Russia, see Danilevskii, *Russkaia tekhnika*, pp. 130–133.

8. Baklanova, "Privoznye tovary," pp. 7–8. Von Staden, *Land and Gov-
    ernment of Muscovy*, p. 43. Solov'ev, *Istoriia*, IX, 306. Lubimenko,
    "Trud inozemtsev," p. 62.

9. Iu. Got'e and S. Bakhrushin, "Kul'turnye i politicheskie sviazi Rossii i

316   *Notes*

Anglii v xvi-xvii vekakh" [Cultural and political connections of Russia and England during the sixteenth and seventeenth centuries], *I. zh.*, No. 12 (1941), 66. Pashkov, *History*, p. 189.

10. Kolchin, *Tekhnika*, p. 12. M. V. Dovnar-Zapol'skii, *Torgovlia i promyshlennost' Moskvy xvi-xvii vv.* [Trade and industry of Moscow during the sixteenth and seventeenth centuries] (Moscow, 1910), pp. 5–6. Kurts, *Sochinenie Kil'burgera*, pp. 149, 93, 122, 428–430. Tsvetaev, *Protestanstvo*, p. 722. See Walther Kirchner, *Commercial Relations*, especially pp. 26–34, 124–125.

11. *S.G.G.i D.*, IV, 179.

12. Tsvetaev, *Protestanstvo*, pp. 722–724. Kurts, *Sochinenie Kil'burgera*, p. 428. Pashkov, *History*, p. 207.

13. *D.k A.I.*, XII, 22; V, 211. Konovalov, "Patrick Gordon's Dispatches," p. 9. Tsvetaev, *Protestanstvo*, pp. 723–724, 725. Pashkov, *History*, p. 227.

14. *D.k A.I.*, V, No. 80.

15. *Ibid.*, XII, 22–23; V, 230–234. Solov'ev, *Istoriia*, XI, 567, 569.

16. *D.k A.I.*, V, 229, 236, 240, 244, 245, 270–271, 272.

17. The *voevoda* of Astrakhan, Prince Prozorovskii, defended the city against Stenka Razin, whose forces included, we should note, a flotilla of 200 small boats. Prozorovskii was assisted by naval captain David Buthler and the English colonel Thomas Bailey, commander of a detachment of Muscovite troops. Prozorovskii and Bailey fell during the capture of Astrakhan; Buthler, Struys, Boyle, and other foreigners in the tsar's service there were sufficiently fortunate to escape with their lives (Vernadsky, *Tsardom of Moscow*, pp. 621–622).

18. *D.k A.I.*, XII, 22–23. Tsvetaev, *Protestanstvo*, pp. 724–725. Ustrialov, *Istoriia*, I, 106.

19. For example, in February 1674 ship-builders in Muromsk *uezd* were ordered to make 200 ships, and 3,150 *puds* of construction iron were requested for this purpose from the Marselis iron factories. Petr Petrovich Marselis delivered over 3,185 rubles' worth of rod iron and sheet-iron to Muromsk. *K.m.*, I, 421–423.

20. Lubimenko, "Trud inozemtsev," p. 58. Wretts-Smith, "English in Russia," p. 98. Article "Di, Artemii" in *E.S.*, X (St. Petersburg, 1896), 568. The English meaning of the Latin title of Dee's treatise might be rendered: "A fascicle introducing and advancing secret hermetic knowledge with explanation." For information about foreign physicians and apothecaries in Russia during the sixteenth and seventeenth centuries, see Erik Amburger, *Beiträge zur Geschichte der deutschrussischen kulturellen Beziehungen* (Giessen, 1961), pp. 25–30.

21. A notable exception to the tsar's monopoly was the typically enterprising Stroganov family, which had *lekari*, doctors' assistants *(fel'dshery)*. and pharmacists from Holland and elsewhere in several of their enter-

prises during the 1580's and later. Tsvetaev. *Protestanstvo,* p. 727.

22. The *Aptekarskii Prikaz* (pharmaceutical chancellery) was organized in 1620 at the Kremlin and had such tasks as recruiting foreign physicians and pharmacists, preparing medicines, procuring quality vodka, honey, and candies for the royal table (and for sale). Before 1672 the *Prikaz* served members outside the tsar's family only with the sovereign's special permission, but in March of that year Aleksei Mikhailovich organized a "new pharmacy" (called the *Novaia Apteka*) "...for the sale [of medicine] to all ranks of people," the original organization (now called *Staraia Apteka,* or "old pharmacy") continuing to serve only the tsar. The *Novaia Apteka* soon developed into a sizeable enterprise employing (by January 1677) three doctors, two pharmacists with four apprentices, an alchemist, four *lekari,* an interpreter, four important bureaucrats, and four watchmen. The two pharmacies were so large and well equipped that they earned lavish praise from such foreign visitors as Olearius and Shleizing. A. A. Vinius was a particularly successful director of these pharmacies, and several distinguished foreigners served in the same capacity. Kurts, *Sochinenie Kil'burgera,* pp. 181, 538–544. Platonov, *Moskva i zapad,* pp. 131–132. Lubimenko, "Trud inozemtsev," p. 59.

23. Platonov, *Moskva i zapad,* p. 132. Lubimenko, "Trud inozemtsev," p. 59. V. Liubavskii, "Biblioteka aptekarskogo prikaza" [Library of the pharmaceutical prikaz], *Bibliotekar'* [The librarian], No. 1 (January 1950), 30–31. A. Lebedianskaia, "Pervaia voenno-meditsinskaia shkola na Rusi; seredina xvii v." [First military-medical school in Russia; mid-seventeenth century], *Voenno-istoricheskii zhurnal* [Military-historical journal], No. 3 (March 1941), 97–100.

24. See the article by N. V. Khaliaev on "Postnikov, Petr Vasil'evich" in *E.S.,* XI, 710. Platonov, *Moskva i zapad,* pp. 132–133. Vucinich, *Science in Russian Culture,* p. 28. Lubimenko, "Trud inozemtsev," pp. 59–60. Extensive primary material on the arrival of doctors and pharmacists between 1600 and 1640 may be found in *R.I.B.,* VIII, 83–327. On the history of medicine in Russia see Tsvetaev, *Protestanstvo,* pp. 727–730. Muliukin, *Priezd inostrantsev,* pp. 78–91. Authoritative works are available by Wilhelm Michael von Richter, *Geschichte der Medicin in Russland* (Moscow, 1815) in two volumes, and M. Lakhtin, *Meditsina i vrachi v Moskovskom gosudarstve* [Medicine and doctors in the Muscovite state] (Moscow, 1906).

25. Lubimenko, "Trud inozemtsev," p. 58.

26. For example, Olearius, born Adam Oelschläger (1603–1671), took his Master of Philosophy at the University of Leipzig in 1627 in philosophy, literature, mathematics, astronomy, and geography, and published physical-astronomical treatises. He joined Leipzig's faculty and was invited to take service under Tsar Michael in 1639 (see *S.G.G.i D.,* III, 373) and again in 1643 – declining both offers after due reflection. He visited

Russia during the 1630's and 1640's. See Olearius, *Travels*, pp. 1-13.

27. Billington, *Icon and the Axe*, pp. 123, 677. Danilevskii, *Russkaia tekh-nika*, pp. 128-130. Lubimenko, "Trud inozemtsev," pp. 56, 63-64.

28. *Ibid.*, p. 72. Muliukin, *Ocherki*, pp. 94, 205-206, 210. Liubomirov, *Ocherki*, pp. 519-520. Tsvetaev, *Protestanstvo*, p. 715.

29. Lubimenko, "Trud inozemtsev," p. 72.

30. *Ibid.*, pp. 72-73. Muliukin, *Ocherki*, p. 206. Tsvetaev, *Protestanstvo*, pp. 717-718. Billington, *Icon and the Axe*, p. 149. Olearius, *Travels*, pp. 326-327.

31. Fimbrant was granted a charter four years later, in 1634, to make elk leather *(losinye kozhi)*, but I have discovered no evidence that he actually built such an enterprise (Solov'ev, *Istoriia*, IX, 306. See also p. 174 of this study).

32. Kirchner, "Entrepreneurial Activity," p. 246. Lubimenko, "Trud in-ozemtsev," p. 56. Tsvetaev, *Protestanstvo*, pp. 370-379. *S.G.G. i D.*, III, No. 93.

33. See pp. 58-59, above.

34. Baklanova, "Privoznye tovary," pp. 21, 23-24. Gamel', *Opisanie*, pp. 24-25. Ustrialov, *Istoriia*, I, 105.

35. Lappo-Danilevskii, "Inozemtsy," p. 104. Solov'ev, *Istoriia*, IX, 166, 281. Ustrialov, *Istoriia*, I, 106.

36. Kotoshikhin tells us there were 50 *perevodchiki* (who provided written translations) and 70 *tolmachi* (oral interpreters) in the employ of the *Prikaz*—presumably at a single time (Kotoshikhin, *O Rossii*, p. 97). The *tolmach'* was of lower professional standing and received a much smaller salary than the *perevodchik*. On the subject of foreign interpreters in Russia, see Lubimenko, "Trud inozemtsev," p. 61, and Muliukin, *Priezd inostrantsev*, pp. 76-78.

37. Kozlovskii, *Pervye pochty*, I, 18-32. The *iam* system is discussed by Gustave Alef, "The Origin and Early Development of the Muscovite Postal Service," *J.G.O.*, XV (1967), 1-15.

38. Von Staden, *Land and Government*, pp. 38, 39, 43. Berry, *Rude and Barbarous Kingdom*, p. 53. Olearius, *Travels*, pp. 180-181.
     Von Herberstein's information on the *iam* system is all the more interesting because of its early date, being based upon the Austrian ambassador's visit of 1517: "The ruler has postal routes to all parts of the dominion, with an adequate number of horses, in different places, thus when a courier is sent anywhere, he gets a horse on demand without delay [and] is free to choose any horse he might wish. When I travelled quickly from Novgorod the Great to Muscovy, the master of the post, who is called in their language *iamshchik*, took care to have led to me sometimes thirty, at other times forty or fifty, horses at sunrise, but I did not need more than twelve. Each one of our men, therefore, took a horse

which looked suitable to him. Then whenever the horses were tired we arrived at another post which they called *iama,* we immediately changed horses and kept the saddle, bridle, and bit. Anyone was permitted to ride horses at top speed and if any horses by chance fell, or could not last, it was permissible to seize another from any nearby house, or from anyone whom one by chance met on the way, excepting only the courier of the ruler, and to take the horse with impunity. The *iamshchik* is accustomed to look for horses exhausted and left en route, to restore another to him from whom it was taken, and to pay the price according to the length of the trip. Ordinarily from ten to twenty versts cost six *dengi.* In that way my servant travelled by post horses from Novgorod to Moscow, a distance of six hundred versts, that is one hundred and twenty German miles, in seventy-two hours. That is something all the more to be marvelled at since the horses are little and are cared for more negligently than by us, and yet perform such labors" *(Notes upon Russia,* I, 108–109).

39. Even during the 1630's–1640's, however, some *iam* lines must have been served efficiently, for according to Olearius at that time it was "... easily possible by means of the *iam* to cover the distance from Novgorod to Moscow, which is reckoned 120 leagues, in six or seven days, and in winter, by sleigh, faster yet." This schedule essentially agrees with von Staden's information of the mid-sixteenth century, quoted directly above. In fact Olearius had a high opinion of the *iam,* which he called "a good system" *(Travels,* pp. 181, 180). Gustave Alef also speaks highly of the *iamskaia gon'ba,* believing it provided much quicker service than was available in Western Europe during the fifteenth and sixteenth centuries. Alef provides detailed and informative comparisons between the Russian *iam* and Western posts of the period ("Origin and Early Development of the Muscovite Postal Service," pp. 1–4).

40. Kozlovskii, *Pervye pochty,* I, 33–37, 50–54, 145. Kurts, *Sochinenie Kil'burgera,* pp. 406–407, 410. Rozhkov, *Russkaia istoriia,* V, 27.

41. *R.I.B.,* XXI, 1065. *S.G.G.i D.,* IV, 628. Kozlovskii, *Pervye pochty,* I, 58, 61–63. Kurts, *Sochinenie Kil'burgera,* p. 408.

42. Ordin-Nashchokin might have wanted simply to make the post more satisfactory to its customers, for although van Sweeden's service was open to all merchants and public officials, the former continued to ship letters and packages abroad through private couriers, and a Hamburg company, referring to John's extremely high rates, asked permission of the tsar to conduct its own communications. On the other hand, we know that Ordin-Nashchokin expressed to the tsar the necessity of guarding " ... against the foreign merchants secretly hiring and sending someone with letters, as in former years, and thus depriving your treasury of taxes, by sending precious things, stones and pearls and gold in bags and in bundles ... via the mails." Cited in Pashkov, *History,* p. 227.

43. Kozlovskii, *Pervye pochty,* I, 63–68, 100. Zaozerskaia, *Razvitie,* p. 34.

44. Kozlovskii, *Pervye pochty,* I, 69–70, 135. Solov'ev, *Istoriia,* XI, 399, 401.

45. Kozlovskii, *Pervye pochty,* I, 108–111, 113–120, 163. Kurts, *Sochinenie Kil'burgera,* p. 160. *S.G.G.i D.,* IV, 223–224.

46. Kozlovskii, *Pervye pochty,* I, 137–138.

47. As we have seen, news from the foreign press was considered a secret of state at the time. Kilburger also sheds light on the government attitude toward this question in 1674: "As soon as the post arrives in Moscow, the packages must be brought sealed to the 'Posol'skii prikaz' . . . and opened there, so that private persons will not know earlier than the court what is happening within and without the country, but even more, so that everyone will realize that he might incur suspicion through correspondence which is improper, and, for the state, harmful, keeping in mind that all letters fall into the hands of the chief chancellor. As is the case here in Sweden, through the post they receive weekly all Dutch, Hamburg, and Königsberg news, both published and written. This must always be translated into the Russian language and read by the tsar" (Kurts, *Sochinenie Kil'burgera,* pp. 160–161).

    One must not think, of course, that the Russian government was unique in its desire to follow private correspondence which touched upon the interests of the state. When Louis XI (1461–1483) established a *poste royale* he permitted his nobles to utilize the service, but insisted that their letters be examined before dispatch to prevent politically dangerous communications from reaching their addressees (Alef, "Origin and Early Development of the Muscovite Postal Service," p. 4). But it seems that the rejection of Leonhard Marselis' proposed Archangel post was part of a personal vendetta which transcended his "mere" violation of state security.

48. Kozlovskii, *Pervye pochty,* I, 138.

49. Leonhard Marselis and his father did not reply to these complaints until April of the following year. To dramatize their position, Peter Marselis entered the *Posol'skii Prikaz* on 30 April 1670 with unopened mailbags which had just arrived from Vil'no. Peter said he had been ordered to do this, and was complying. But he repeated his earlier request to be permitted to deliver the bags unsealed, lest he be disgraced by everyone's thinking the tsar did not trust him. From Kilburger's evidence four years later, however, it would appear the Marselises were not allowed to open the mailbags (Kurts, *Sochinenie Kil'burgera,* pp. 138–139).

50. Kozlovskii, *Pervye pochty,* I, 91, 158, 164. Amburger, *Die Familie Marselis,* pp. 154–160.

51. Kozlovskii, *Pervye pochty,* I, 145–154, 164, 192, 394–399. Tsvetaev, *Protestanstvo,* p. 727. Kotoshikhin, *O Rossii,* p. 124.

52. *S.G.G.i D.,* III, 493–495.

53. For example, during the 1680's Vinius received an estate of 1,000 *cheti* and drew a yearly salary of 120 rubles.

54. Kozlovskii, *Pervye pochty,* I, 343–344, 303, 191–192, 302.

55. *Ibid.,* pp. 508–517.

56. *Ibid.*, pp. 419, 421-432, 438-441, 458-459. *S.G.G.i D.*, III, 639-640.

57. Kozlovskii, *Pervye pochty*, I, 504-507. Kurts, *Sochinenie Kil'burgera*, p. 409. *Akty Istoricheskie* [Historical acts]. V, Nos. 294, 295.

58. Kurts, *Sochinenie Kil'burgera*, pp. 160, 408-411. Kozlovskii, *Pervye pochty*, I, 520, 522.

12. Status and Influence of the Foreigner

1. Some historians have interpreted Olearius to say there were 1,000 Protestant family *heads* in Russia at this time. For example, S. F. Platonov does in *Lektsii po russkoi istorii* [Lectures on Russian history] (St. Petersburg, 1907), p. 315. I personally do not find that his words indicate this (see *Travels*, p. 278), and if they did I would regard the estimate as excessive. Tsvetaev, *Protestanstvo*, p. 250, discusses conflicting interpretations of Olearius' statement.

2. Platonov, *Lektsii*, p. 315.

3. In 1675 twenty Dutch merchants lived in Vologda alone. See p. 240 of this chapter.

4. Muliukin, *Priezd inostrantsev*, pp. 118-121. Lubimenko, "Trud inozemtsev," p. 56. Tsvetaev, *Protestanstvo*, pp. 279-281. *Istoriia Moskvy* [History of Moscow], I (Moscow, 1952), 490.

5. Cited in Platonov, *Moskva i zapad*, pp. 128-129.

6. A royal *ukaz* of 21 January 1689 also promised the Huguenots honor and high rank for good service, and the right to leave Russia at any time. *P.S.Z.R.I.*, III, No. 1331.

7. Tsvetaev, *Protestanstvo*, pp. 279-280, *D.k A.I.*, IX, 90. *Istoriia Moskvy*, I, 490. Vernadsky, *Tsardom of Moscow*, p. 351.

8. Tsvetaev, *Protestanstvo*, p. 273. Olearius, *Travels*, p. 201; on Dr. Hartmann Gramann see also in Olearius pp. xii, 86, 150. 256. *D.k A.I.*, III, 1-2. Lappo-Danilevskii, "Inozemtsy," pp. 93-94. Kotoshikhin, *O. Rossii*, p. 97. Lubimenko, "Trud inozemtsev," p. 61.

9. Von Staden, *Land and Government*, pp. 63, 14. *D.k A.I.*, XII, 29-30. *P.S.Z.R.I.*, I, No. 85. Anderson, "English Views," pp. 150-151. Kliuchevskii, *Skazaniia*, p. 112. Platonov, *Moskva i zapad*, p. 129.

10. Lubimenko, "Trud inozemtsev," p. 60. Ustrialov, *Istoriia*, I, 104-105. Anderson, "English Views," pp. 151-152. Wretts-Smith, "English in Russia," p. 99.

11. Von Staden, *Land and Government*, pp. 69-70.

12. One instance when seven Swedish masters left the Tula iron factories could serve even now as a standard of efficiency for modern bureaucratic states. Since the men had completed the agreed duration of their stay, they requested permission to return home without "hinderance" or "delay." The petition was submitted on 9 February 1645 and answered on 16 February, and by 20 February the workers and their families were

on their way back to Sweden, *K.m.,* I, 311-312. Kuzin, *Istoriia otkrytii,* p. 25.

13. One could also leave easily if his presence became an annoyance to the authorities. Von Herberstein tells us that Vasilli III praised the German artillerists "Nicholas" and Johann Jordan for the skill they displayed in defending Moscow and Riazan (respectively) against the Mongols in 1521, and promised to reward the two men. "Each of them therefore confidently hoped that they should receive liberal rewards from the prince; but nothing was given them, although they often wearied the prince on the subject, and reminded him of his promises. Disgusted at length with the prince's ingratitude, they begged their discharge, that they might visit their country and kinsfolk, from whom they had been long absent; which was allowed them, with a grant from the prince of ten florins to each, in addition to their former stipend" *(Notes upon Russia,* II, 62, 64, 66).

14. *S.G.G.i D.,* III, 311.

15. Olearius, *Travels,* p. 283.

16. Lappo-Danilevskii, "Inozemtsy," p. 74. Olearius, *Travels,* p. 282. Tsvetaev, *Protestanstvo,* p. 131. Ustrialov, *Istoriia,* I, 106-108.

17. Tsvetaev, *Protestanstvo,* pp. 2-9. Muliukin, *Priezd inostrantsev,* pp. 139-143. Platonov, *Moskva i zapad,* p. 65. *S.G.G.i D.,* III, 404. *Istoricheskie akty,* III, 114-115, 385. Ustrialov, *Istoriia,* I, 106-107.

18. Tsvetaev, *Protestanstvo,* p. 122. Kurts, *Sochinenie Kil'burgera,* pp. 163, 182. Amburger, *Die Familie Marselis,* 130, 193-198. Von Staden, *Land and Government,* p. 69. Olearius, *Travels,* pp. 277, 248, 281-282, 293.

19. Tsvetaev, *Protestanstvo,* pp. 11, 342, 344-348, 378-379. *D.k A.I.,* XII, 319-320. Lappo-Danilevskii, "Inozemtsy," 94-97. *Istoriia Moskvy,* I, 491. Olearius, *Travels,* p. 246. *R.I.B.,* VIII, 205-233, 266, 278-284, 294-295.

20. Wretts-Smith, "English in Russia," pp. 91-92: Berry, *English Works of Giles Fletcher,* p. 280. Lubimenko, "Trud inozemtsev," p. 59. Bakhrushin, *Nauchnye trudy,* I, 180.

21. See pp. 80, 84, above.

22. Olearius says, "The foreign apostates in Moscow are especially malicious to their former coreligionists, who suffer more from them than from the Russians" *(Travels,* pp. 248-249). Andrei Vinius is a good illustration of the truth of this statement, as we shall soon see in this chapter. Olearius, incidentally, gives interesting information on the actual process of abjuration and conversion *(ibid.,* pp. 233n, 242-249). He had a low opinion of such action, which he termed "apostasy," claiming it was done merely for material considerations. Tsvetaev thought there was usually conviction behind adoption of Orthodoxy *(Protestanstvo,* pp. 343-344). I suspect most converts were indifferent to specific questions of religious principle, and I would call their actions opportunistic but not quite hypocritical.

23. The process of Russification might go farther than dress and manners, for as Platonov points out, ". . . many foreigners who had been 'of yore' in Muscovite service . . . took on, together with Orthodoxy, an indigenous mental outlook" (*Moskva i zapad*, p. 128).

24. Berry, *English Works of Giles Fletcher*, pp. 280–281. Tsvetaev, *Protestanstvo*, p. 378. *Istoriia Moskvy*, I, 490. Kuzin, *Istoriia otkrytii*, pp. 25–26. *K.m.*, I, xxvii, 28, 124.

25. A good discussion of this case will be found in Olearius' writings (*Travels*, pp. 246–248).

26. Platonov, *Moskva i zapad*, pp. 125–126.

27. Bazilevich, "Elementy merkantilizma," pp. 30–32.

28. Solov'ev, *Istoriia*, XIII, 103. Bazilevich, "Elementy merkantilizma," p. 32. Pashkov, *History*, pp. 207–208.

29. Other details on Vinius' grain purchase may be found on pp. 59–61, above.

30. Cited in Kordt, *Otchet*, p. cccxliii.

31. Amburger, *Die Familie Marselis*, pp. 103, 210. Platonov, *Moskva i zapad*, p. 126. Lubimenko, "Trud inozemtsev," p. 68. Gamel', *Opisanie*, p. 9 (documents). *D.k A.I.*, III, No. 13. Kozlovskii, *Pervye pochty*, I, 173. Tsvetaev, *Protestanstvo*, p. 396. Solov'ev, *Istoriia*, X, 478, 615; concerning Vinius' role in the Russian government, see *ibid.*, p. 460.

32. *Istoriia Moskvy*, I, 490. For a discussion of this Russian custom and its significance, see Olearius, *Travels* pp. 42, 158-159.

33. Platonov, *Moskva i zapad*, p. 127. Kozlovskii, *Pervye pochty*, I, 192–193, 196–224, 246–269, 214–216, 222, 224, 270–278; see pp. 176–182 for a survey of bibliographical information about the young Andrei Vinius.

34. E. Zviagintsev, "Slobody inostrantsev v Moskve xvii veka" [Settlements of foreigners in Moscow during the seventeenth century], *I.zh.*, Nos. 2–3 (1944), 85.

35. Kliuchevskii, *Kurs*, III, 274. Wretts-Smith, "English in Russia," pp. 95–96. Zviagintsev, "Angliiskii dvor," p. 143. Olearius, *Travels*, pp. 130, 138, 214. L. R. Lewitter, "Poland, the Ukraine and Russia in the 17th Century," *S.E.E.R.*, XXVII (1948-1949), 421. Bernard Pares, *A History of Russia* (New York, 1956), p. 186. Voyce, *Moscow*, p. 37. O'Brien, *Russia Under Two Tsars*, pp. 50–52. Vucinich, *Science in Russian Culture*, p. 26. Pashkov, *History*, p. 210. *E.S.*, XXXVI, 779.

36. See two articles in *J.G.O.*: Erich Franz Sommer, "Der junge Zar Peter in der Moskauer Deutschen Sloboda," V (1957), 67–105; Reinhard Wittram, "Peter des Grossen erste Reise in dem Westen," III (1955), 373–403.

37. Vernadsky, *Political and Diplomatic History*, p. 218. Pares, *History*, p. 186. Isaak Massa, *Kratkoe izvestie o moskovii v nachale xvii v.* [Brief account of Muscovy at the beginning of the seventeenth century] (Moscow, 1937), pp. 52–55, 187–188.

38. Voyce, *Moscow,* pp. 36–37. Kliuchevskii, *Kurs,* III, 272–273, 270. Billington, *Icon and the Axe,* p. 149. On Aleksei Mikhailovich's personality and attitudes, see Platonov, *Lektsii,* pp. 363–376, and S. F. Platonov, "Tsar' Aleksei Mikhailovich, opyt' kharakteristikii" [Tsar Aleksei Mikhailovich, a view of his character], in *Tri veka* [Three centuries], I (Moscow, 1912), 85–114.

39. Billington, *Icon and the Axe,* pp. 136, 149, 150, 686. Tsvetaev, *Protestanstvo,* p. 737.

40. In 1653 princes Repnin and Obolenskii purchased in Lublin and L'vov for the *Posol'skii Prikaz* a Slavonic-Russian lexicon, Piasetskii's Chronicle, a dictionary in German-Latin-Polish, a book on Russia by Guagnini, a Bible in Polish, an anthology of Polish writings, and a copy of the Polish constitution (Baklanova, "Privoznye tovary," p. 113). This list gives us an idea of the sort of foreign materials contained in the *Posol'skii Prikaz's* library.

41. Baklanova, "Privoznye tovary," p. 113.

42. The contents of this library are described in Kozlovskii, *Pervye pochty,* I, 245.

43. Most of these books were translated during the last 50 years of this 200-year period:

    1500–1550   7 titles translated and published
    1500–1600   19 titles
    1600–1650   13 titles
    1650–1700   114 titles

    These 153 books may be broken down into the following categories:

    37 religious subjects
    18 historical
    15 literary
    15 cosmography and geography
    12 encyclopedias, dictionaries, and reference books
     9 astronomy
     8 medicine
     6 jurisprudence and politics
     5 military
     4 natural sciences
    20 miscellaneous

    Consult *Moskva v ee proshlom i nastoiashchem* [Moscow in its past and present], VI (Moscow, n.d.), 88.

44. James H. Billington remarks on Swedish efforts to spread Lutheranism in Russia, and he believes the Reformed Church carried on some missionary work, too. It is possible that Protestantism had some effect on the Old Believer schism of the seventeenth century (*Icon and the Axe,* pp. 152–153). We know that John of Sweden made at least one convert at this time—a Tatar servant woman who was baptized in the Dutch Reformed Church and who then married a foreign officer in Russian state service (Kozlovskii, *Pervye pochty,* I, 68–69).

45. Vucinich, *Science in Russian Culture,* pp. 34, 21, 23, 19.

46. *Moskva v ee proshlom*, VI, 89.

47. Voyce, *Moscow*, p. 50. *Istoriia moskvy*, I, 490. John Keep shows that by the 1670's (if not before) the *strel'tsy* had acquired a sense of corporate identity. Their attitudes are discussed in "The Muscovite Elite and the Approach to Pluralism," *S.E.E.R.*, XLVIII (April 1970), 119–123.

48. Anderson, "English Views," p. 151. Tsvetaev, *Protestanstvo*, pp. 707–708.

49. Olearius says the following of the Moscow uprising of 1648: "When the Germans had gathered a considerable mercenary force . . . , they were surprised that the rioters very readily made way for them and even addressed them cordially: 'You are honest Germans, who do us no harm. We are your friends and have no intention ever to do you any harm.' " Olearius then notes that "Previously, they very often quarreled with the Germans and were hostile" *(Travels*, pp. 209–210).

50. Lubimenko, "Trud inozemtsev," p. 53. Lewitter, "Poland," pp. 159–160, 161. Got'e and Bakhrushin, "Kul'turnye i politicheskie sviazi," pp. 66, 68. Voyce, *Moscow*, p. 37. Pares, *History*, p. 188. Zviagintsev, "Angliiskii dvor," p. 141. Vucinich, *Science in Russian Culture*, pp. 3, 29, 34.

51. Tsvetaev, *Protestanstvo*, p. 334. *Istoriia Moskvy*, I, 486–487. See in general on this subject Muliukin, *Ocherki*, pp. 112–126, and Olearius, *Travels*, pp. 254–255n.

52. *A.I.*, III, 312, 335, 397. *R.I.B.*, II, 615. Lappo-Danilevskii, "Inozemtsy," pp. 79–80. Tsvetaev, *Protestanstvo*, pp. 264, 265–266, 708. Zviagintsev, "Slobody inostrantsev," pp. 84–85. Vucinich, *Science in Russian Culture*, p. 16. Kliuchevskii, *Skazaniia*, pp. 209–210. Olearius, *Travels*, pp. 129–130.

53. Tsvetaev, *Protestanstvo*, pp. 21, 258–259, 264–266.

54. In 1643 Marselis admitted to the Danish government that the Moscow clergy had recently complained over the presence of foreigners in *poganyi prud*, an area of Moscow where Marselis himself lived, and that merchants of the city in 1638 had lodged a specific protest over Marselis' occupancy of his house! (Tsvetaev, *Protestanstvo*, p. 75.) Marselis may have relocated in the Foreign Quarter after 1652. At that time he and Filimon Akema also had homes in Vologda, probably for the times they were in the city on business trips. Akema's main house was at his Salamykova factory in 1662; at the end of the century Christian Marselis and his family lived near the fourth Tula iron works. *(Ibid.*, p. 264. *K.m.*, I, 33. Stoskova. *Pervye metallurgicheskie*, p. 29.)

55. *Istoriia Moskvy*, I, 487–488. Ustrialov, *Istoriia*, I, 107–108. Voyce, *Moscow*, pp. 36, 52–53, 82.

56. For Aleksei Mikhailovich's decree, see *P.S.Z.R.I.*, I, No. 85. At least twenty influential foreign doctors and merchants (e.g., *gosti* Klenk and Fogler) who were not converts to Orthodoxy obtained dispensations from this order *(Istoriia Moskvy*, I, 489. Ustrialov, *Istoriia*, I, 107–108).

57. *Novoinozemskaia Sloboda*, or, more commonly, *Nemetskaia Sloboda*.

See Olearius on the formation of the "Foreign Quarter" *(Travels,* pp. 279–281). Also Tsvetaev, *Protestanstvo,* especially Chapter IV, and V. V. Nechaev, "Inozemskiia slobody v Moskve v xvi i xvii vv." [Foreign quarters in Moscow during the sixteenth and seventeenth centuries], *Moskva v ee proshlom,* IV, 18–43. Voyce, *Moscow,* pp. 36, 52–53.

58. Of these *dvory,* 142 belonged to officers (including 16 widows), while merchants had 23, artisans 24, pastors and translators 3 each, *lekari* and pharmacists 2 each, etc. Most of these families were Lutheran (they had three churches), others were Reformed (one church), while the French and Italian families and a few others were Catholic (Tsvetaev, *Protestanstvo,* pp. 256–257. Zviagintsev, "Slobody inostrantsev," pp. 83, 85).

59. Baklanova, "Privoznye tovary," p. 113.

13. Manufacturing in Early Modern Russia

1. Concerning Marselis, see the petition from his family published in *K.m.,* I, 252.

2. Some 15,000 rubles of this amount came from Peter Marselis' brother in Amsterdam, Gabriel *(K.m.,* I, 252. Chekan, "Tul'skie," p. 146. Amburger, *Die Familie Marselis,* p. 112). Later documents of the mid-1690's claim the Marselises spent at least an additional 23,000 rubles prospecting for copper in the far north and bringing copper masters to Russia, who were finally sent home "...with many labors and great losses..." *(K.m.,* II, 144; cf. pp. 130–131, 154). That these figures are not exaggerations is suggested by the fact that just before 1675 Marselis' son Petr Petrovich paid his father's partner, Thomas Kellermann, 20,000 rubles for Kellermann's share in the Vepreiskii works.

3. I arrived at Paulsen's figure on the basis of his initial loan of 2,000 rubles (300 of which were spent on supplies in Hamburg), 3,000 rubles expended in bringing masters to Russia, plus another 650 rubles spent relocating the enterprise from the old "velvet court" to the Foreign Quarter in Moscow in early 1683. It is most likely, however, that Paulsen spent more than 5,650 rubles on his factory. Other enterprises were not so costly. Vasilii Burtsev spent 400 rubles on the Church's paper mill on the Iauza during the 1660's, while it cost John of Sweden 290 rubles to reestablish his paper factory on the same location. Two relocations of the state Morocco tannery of the mid-1660's cost 158 and 250 rubles.

4. *Russko-shvedskie,* p. 554. See also Solov'ev, *Istoriia,* X, 617. Amburger, *Die Familie Marselis,* p. 118. Kafengauz, *Istoriia,* pp. 34–44. For information about Russian purchases in the Netherlands in 1690, see *D.k A.I.,* XII, 361.

5. For example, in 1671 64 dozen phials and 170 bottles were imported into Archangel; in 1672 six tons of miscellaneous glass work, two boxes of crystal dishes, four large and several small baskets of "Helbrunskii" wine glasses and thin mugs; in 1673 nine tons of glass work, one box of phials and large wine glasses; etc. European mirrors were so fashionable in this

period that every Russian gentleman considered it a duty to give his lady a small mirror. (Kurts, *Sochinenie Kil'burgera*, pp. 119, 128, 139. Kostomarov, *Sobranie Sochinenii*, XX, 376. Baklanova, "Privoznye tovary," pp. 84–85.)

6. In 1651 royal agents were ordered to buy "... not less than 300 reams [of paper] per year" in Archangel, and this supplied only a few of the smaller *prikazy*. In 1671 a total of 28,479 reams of paper were brought through Archangel, and in 1673 the figure was 8,033 reams plus "two bales" of paper. Collins accounted (in part) for these large amounts by noting that the government clerks " . . . leave large spaces between the lines of letters, and in this way they use up [such] an improbable quantity of paper" (!) (Kurts, *Sochinenie Kil'burgera*, pp. 117, 143, 146, 148, 318–319).

7. Bakulev, *Tul'skaia promyshlennost'*, p. 14. Chekan, "Tul'skie," p. 161. Gamel', *Opisanie*, pp. 8–9 (documents).

8. *K.m.*, I, 220–221.

9. Gamel', *Opisanie*, p. 14 (documents). Strumilin, *Istoriia*, I, 105. Solov'ev, *Istoriia*, X, 615–616.

10. In 1649 it was revealed that no fewer than 72 of the 104 cannon made by Julius Coyet (evidently in an artisan workshop) perished in this way. But the authorities must have been satisfied with his work, for Coyet's original wages of 25 rubles per month were doubled and then soon doubled again (Kurts, *Sochinenie Kil'burgera*, p. 467).

11. Kurts, *Sochinenie Kil'burgera*, pp. 466–467.

12. Amburger, *Die Familie Marselis*, p. 101. *K.m.*, I, 12.

13. The poorest imported Persian yuft of leather sold for six to seven *altyn* in Russia, and compared favorably with a yuft of Moscow leather which cost 20 *altyn* to produce. For that price one could buy the finest Persian leather, something far superior to the best Russian efforts of that time (Novitskii, "Pervye," p. 56). As for silk, the following figures compare the cost of production at the state-owned Moscow silk works after 1684 with the cost of equivalent eastern imports at Astrakhan:

Type of silk	*Moscow production cost*	*Equivalent import price at Astrakhan*
smooth velvet	4 rubles 9 *altyn* 5 *den'gi*	1 ruble 26 *altyn* 4 *den'gi*
shaggy velvet	4 rubles 16 *altyn* 2½ *den'gi* "	"
Kamka	3 rubles 2 *altyn* 2½ *den'gi*	17 *altyn* 2 *den'gi*
brocades	from 2 rubles 30 *altyn* 1 *den'ga* to 2 rubles 18 *altyn* 1½ *den'gi*	1½ ruble

(Pavlenko, *Razvitie*, p. 48)

14. Anthony Jenkinson writing in Berry, *Rude and Barbarous Kingdom*, pp.

57–58.

15. On one occasion Vinius informed Moscow officials that they had not been receiving cannon balls and other equipment from Tula " . . . because the ground has been frozen with snow since fall." Vinius went on to say that these goods ". . . have been placed in storage until spring" (*K.m.*, I, 12).

16. Vernadsky, *Kievan Russia,* p. 194. Lubimenko, "Trud inozemtsev," p. 62.

17. Pankratova, *Formirovanie,* p. 33.

18. Pokrovsky, *History of Russia,* p. 283 (emphasis added, J.T.F.). Pokrovsky is referring to Miliukov's study cited here as *Gosudarstvennoe khoziaistvo.*

19. V. N. Kashin goes quite far in developing the latter point: "Before he put the first large iron-working 'mill factory' in Russia into operation in 1639, Vinius endeavored to stifle the possibility of widespread utilization of this new technology by anyone but himself. This has been ignored in Russian literature on the history of industry, and Vinius has been depicted solely as an enterprising innovator to whom the Russian iron industry is indebted for the application of waterpower and of highly-developed technology in general. At the base of this silence rests the traditional conception of the creative role of representatives of the ruling classes as the only possible source of the development of Russian industry" ("Tul'skaia oruzheinaia sloboda," p. 132).

20. Kuzin, *Istoriia otkrytii,* pp. 39, 27.

21. Even foreigners were not always supported in their ambitions. Olearius tells us that the state would not assume the expenses of gold prospecting, even if initial finds suggested a project would be quite rewarding. Entrepreneurs were forced to finance their own surveys. The tsar would lend money for this if security were posted, but in the event of failure, losses were borne entirely by the prospector. Olearius describes a once-wealthy English merchant who sought gold on these terms and ended in debtors' prison for his pains. Surely this lack of "generosity" in state policy hindered maximum industrial development in Russia during the sixteenth and seventeenth centuries (*Travels,* p. 125).

22. I have been able to confirm that six manufactories worked for private commercial outlets: the Stroganov iron works of the 1580's; Akema's Ugodskii and Porotovskii iron factories (after 1663); the two large "new Zvenigorodskii" iron enterprises of Voronin and Kiprianov; and the Coyet family's Dukhanino glass mill. At least two sixteenth-century rope walks seem to have exported their products. Most of the other Russian manufactories of this period probably found the state to be their largest (or sole) customer.

23. Pankratova, *Formirovanie,* p. 139.

24. Blum, *Lord and Peasant,* p. 302.

25. Bakulev, *Tul'skaia promyshlennost',* p. 16. *D.k A.I.,* IX, 122–123; XII,

17. *Puteshestvie . . . Makariia*, IV, 45.

26. Zaozerskaia, *Razvitie*, p. 55. Liubomirov, *Ocherki*, pp. 192–193.

27. Liubomirov, *Ocherki*, pp. 518, 146; on paper manufacturing during the eighteenth century, see pp. 146–160.

28. Mairin Mitchell, *The Maritime History of Russia, 848–1948* (London, 1949), pp. 311, 315. See also Vasili Klyuchevsky, *Peter the Great* (New York, 1961), pp. 13–15.

29. Kafengauz, *Istoriia*, pp. 20, 26, 51–55. N. I. Pavlenko, *Istoriia metallurgii v Rossii xviii veka* [History of metallurgy in Russia of the eighteenth century] (Moscow, 1962), pp. 71ff., discusses the influence of the Tula manufactories on Russian metallurgy of the eighteenth century. Portal (*L'Oural*, pp. 28–51), presents a splendid account of the first iron factories in the Urals.

We should also note that the charter provisions for iron entrepreneurs during the seventeenth century were taken as the basis for agreements between the state and prospective industrialists during the eighteenth century. Thus there is also a certain continuity in mercantilist policy between the two centuries (Kafengauz, *Istoriia*, pp. 22–23).

30. Aitchison, *History of Metals*, II, 346.

31. Michael Roberts, *Gustavus Adolphus, a History of Sweden, 1611–1632*, I (London, 1953), 105.

32. In 1642 England and Sweden had a combined iron output of 75 to 80 thousand tons per year, which was nearly as much as the rest of Europe combined. Apparently except for those two countries (and Russia), there was but little increase in European output from the 1530's until the late 1600's (John U. Nef, *Western Civilization since the Renaissance: Peace, War, Industry and the Arts* [New York, 1963], pp. 80–81).

33. Kafengauz, *Istoriia*, p. 33.

34. Eli F. Heckscher, *An Economic History of Sweden* (Cambridge, Mass., 1954), p. 93.

35. Alexander Baykov, "The Economic Development of Russia," *Economic History Review*, second series, VII (1954), 139.

36. In 1800 Russia produced 162,427 short tons of pig iron; England, 156,000 tons (Blum, *Lord and Peasant*, pp. 294–295).

37. Paul Milioukov, *et al.*, *Histoire de Russie*, I (Paris, 1932), 370–373. M. Tugan-Baranovskii, *Russkaia fabrika v proshlom i nastoiashchem* [The Russian factory in the past and present] (St. Petersburg, 1898), pp. 4–7.

38. Pankratova, *Formirovanie*, pp. 9–10, 32. William L. Blackwell, *The Beginnings of Russian Industrialization, 1800–1860* (Princeton, 1968), p. 15. Clarkson, *History*, p. 100.

39. Morozov also had leather and large-scale linen works, distilleries, brickyards, flour mills, fisheries, stores, and numerous other enterprises. His 300 serf villages contained tens of thousands of peasants whose output

permitted Morozov to gather large profits from the domestic and foreign grain trade. From his colossal fortune (through "rational calculations" in a "capitalistic spirit") he loaned the state no less than 80,000 rubles at a high rate of interest. This brought him considerable "gain"! (Lyashchenko, *History,* pp. 212, 214. Pashkov, *History,* pp. 204–205. Pankratova, *Formirovanie,* pp. 188–197.)

For information concerning numerous other Russian "millionaires" during and after the 1630's, see Pokrovskii, *Ocherk,* I, 100; Liubomirov, *Ocherki,* pp. 513–516; Lyashchenko, *History,* pp. 211–213, 224–225.

40. As we have seen, the blast furnace of the Tula factories of the 1630's produced 100 to 120 *puds* of pig iron each 24 hours (see pp. 70–71, above). One furnace at Demidov's first factory (also at Tula) sixty years later turned out 150 to 170 *puds* of pig iron daily, and in other Demidov works of the early eighteenth century the best furnace smelted 270 to 330 *puds* (approximately 5 to 6 tons) daily (Stoskova, *Pervye metallurgicheskie,* p. 75). Isbrants and Aristov-Borin also built two large iron manufactories during the 1690's.

41. In fact there *were* sharp class struggles in and around several manufactories at this time—some quite protracted. Other such episodes may have occurred without being recorded in extant primary material.

42. Aitchison, *History of Metals,* II, 400, 401–402, Henry Hamilton, *The English Brass and Copper Industries to 1800* (New York, 1926), pp. 76–78, 82, 88, 97–98. Heckscher, *Economic History of Sweden,* p. 95.

43. Heckscher, *Economic History of Sweden,* pp. 43–44, 70–72, 97, 101–109. Roberts, *Gustavus Adolphus,* II, 37; also pp. 30, 89 concerning the role of Germans in Swedish industry of the sixteenth century.

44. Roberts, *Gustavus Adolphus,* pp. 91, 117–118.

45. *Ibid.,* 31. On the military and industrial reforms of Gustavus II Adolphus (1611–1632), see *ibid.,* pp. 225, 235–236, 238–271.

46. Roberts, *Gustavus Adolphus,* I, 498; II, 116.

47. E. Lamond (ed.), *A Discourse on the Common Weal of this Realm of England* (London, 1929), pp. 34, 42, 63, as cited in Schubert, *History,* p. 174.

48. Aitchison, *History of Metals,* II, 392–395.

49. *Ezhegodnik Bol'shoi Sovetskoi Entsiklopedii, 1966* [Annual supplement of the comprehensive Soviet encyclopedia, 1966] (Moscow, 1966), p. 82. *Forty Years of Soviet Power in Facts and Figures* (Moscow, 1958), pp. 89, 98.

Glossary

Terms are in the singular form, often followed by the plural form in parentheses.

Ambar (ambary). A building of considerable size; a barn.

Angle-iron. Synonymous with "joint-iron." See *sviaznoe zhelezo.*

Aptekarskii prikaz. Pharmaceutical *prikaz,* 1594–1714. Government chancellery for supervision of pharmacies, recruitment of medical specialists, organization of medical schools and libraries, etc. Moscow's first pharmacy existed primarily to serve the royal family, and when a "new pharmacy" *(novaia apteka)* was organized in 1672 to attend freely other members of the ruling elite, the original institution continued its traditional function under the name *staraia apteka,* "old pharmacy."

Arshin. See Appendix II.

Atlas. A smooth and glossy type of silk cloth.

Baiberek. Brocade: silk cloth with gold and silver designs woven into the fabric.

Bar-iron. See *Prutovoe zhelezo.*

Barshchina. Feudal services rendered by a peasant to his lord in labor; similar to the Western term *corvée. CF. obrok.*

Beloe zhelezo. Literally, "white iron." Unlike *seroe zhelezo* (grey iron), white iron was fragile and brittle in metalworking and hence subjected to a second stage of iron smelting (see *krichnyi peredel, syrodutnyi protsess*). Because it shrank little in size, grey iron went directly into casting and may be understood as basically the equivalent of cast iron or pig iron (see *chugun*).

Berdysh. Halberd, a weapon consisting of an axe blade with an elongated pikehead at the end of a staff usually about five or six feet in length. The *partizan* is a similar weapon, except the pike is more important; in the halberd, the axe is predominant.

Berkovets. See Appendix II.

Bloom. See *kritsa, krichnoe zhelezo*.

Boiarskaia duma. An advisory council to the Russian sovereign consisting of important boyars.

Boyar. A high member of the old Russian aristocracy, as distinguished from the newer service-noble *(pomeshchik)*. Boyars received titles from the tsars, headed *prikazy* and held other important offices, and sometimes participated in the deliberations of the *boiarskaia duma*.

Brocade. See *baiberek*.

Bunt. Rebellion, uprising.

Cast iron. See *chugun*.

Chernye krestian'e. "Black" peasants, i.e., peasants who were free by virtue of living on "black land" *(chernaia zemlia)*, which simply meant areas where serfdom had not yet been introduced. The black peasants owed taxes and service only to the tsar, and were, in effect, state peasants.

Chet (Cheti). In all cases the same as *chetvert'*.

Chetvert' (Chetverti). Length and measure: see Appendix II. Also a central office in Moscow for the administration of certain provincial areas. Seems to have been the equivalent of a *prikaz*. Also a geographical area, equivalent of an *oblast'* or *okrug*, e.g., *Novgorodskaia chetvert', Ustiuzhskaia chetvert'*.

Chugun. Cast iron (pig iron). Lower-quality iron cast immediately from a smelting furnace without forging or futher refinement. Cf. *krichnoe zhelezo, krichnyi peredel, uklad, kovanoe zhelezo*.

Cuirass. See *latnik*.

Datochnye liudi. Peasants who discharged the obligation of their estates (both *pomestia* and *votchiny*) to provide a proportionate number of recruits for the army.

Den'ga. A "Moscow penny." See Appendix I.

D'iachek. A junior *d'iak*, clerk.

D'iak. A secretary, clerk, or administrative assistant of considerable standing. *D'iaki* (pl.) worked in the *prikazy* or other government offices in Moscow and in the provinces. Cf. *pod'iachii*.

Dogovornyi zapis. "Agreement document," a contract between a capitalist and his employees stating wages, terms of work, etc.

Domennyi zavod. Rendered in this study as "blasting factory," "cast-iron factory," "smelting works." The primary stage of iron manufacturing occurred in *domennye zavody* (pl.); *chugun* (cast iron, pig iron) was smelted from iron ore in blasting furnaces *(domnitsy).* If a higher-quality iron *(uklad, kovanoe zhelezo)* was desired, a second stage of iron manufacturing occurred in an "iron working factory" *(zhelezodelatel'nyi zavod, zhelezoobrabaty-vaiushchyi zavod).* "Iron factory" in the generic term embraced both types of iron enterprises.

Domnitsa. "Blasting furnace" which produced cast (pig) iron *(chugun)* at a blasting factory *(domennyi zavod).*

Doshchatnik. One who made iron sheets, *doski.*

Doshchatoe zhelezo. Sheet iron, used for roofing, town gates, gates of large houses, etc. Red-hot iron sheets were "rolled up" at a hearth, under blows of a hand hammer, into musket barrels.

Doska (Doski). Iron cast in the form of boards, planks, or sheets. Cf. *doshchatoe zhelezo.*

Dragun (Draguny). Dragoon. Soldier armed with a carbine and capable of fighting on horseback or on foot.

Dumnyi d'iak. A high secretary (clerk) who attended meetings of the *boyarskaia duma* in an administrative capacity. This rank was immediately below that of *okolnichii* and was the highest form of *d'iak.*

Dvor. As used during the seventeenth century, a word of several meanings: (1) court, square, yard, in the sense of the open area within an interconnected series of buildings; by extension, the entire complex of such buildings; (2) house *(dom; izba);* (3) a state building, e.g., *monetnyi dvor* (mint), *pechatnyi dvor* (publishing house); (4) a trading area, e.g., *gostinyi dvor;* rows of shops and stores; (5) palace, mansion. Cf. German *Hof,* French *Cour.*

Efimok (efimki). Russian term for the German silver thaler *(Joachimsthaler),* which had originated in Bohemia in the sixteenth century and was the most common larger coin in seventeenth-century Russia. Under Aleksei Mikhailovich, Joachimsthalers were often counterstamped with Russian symbols and then circulated as Russian coin.

Fining. See *krichnyi peredel.*

Forge. See *gorn.*

Funt. See Appendix II.

Furma. See *Tuyère.*

Golova. Literally "head." As military officers, *golovy* (pl.) were commanders of *strel'tsy* regiments or raised units of provincial service gentry for service under regimental *voevody* in a particular campaign. *Golovy* were also heads of separate departments of the customs and financial administration.

Gorn. Forge, hearth.

Gost' (Gosti). Literally "guests," *gosti* comprised a small group of the highest-ranking Russian and foreign merchants. Attainment to this select group came only through appointment by the tsar. *Gosti* enjoyed such privileges as the right to trade abroad, to buy a *votchina,* exemption from certain taxes and fees, etc. The *gostinaia sotnia* was a larger, self-elected group of wealthy merchants varying in number from 100 to 350 individuals who did not enjoy the same rights, privileges, and social prestige as the *gosti.* The *sukonnaia sotnia* was a rank below the *gostinaia sotnia;* its members were involved in the textile trade. Members of all three groups were obligated to service in the state financial institutions and performed various important functions in the tsar's system of domestic and foreign trade.

Gostinnyi dvor. A marketplace in Moscow where foreign merchants could display and wholesale their goods.

Gramota. In seventeenth-century Russia, a written document.

Grivna (grivny). Monetary: see Appendix I. Measure: see Appendix II.

Halberd. See *berdysh.*

Hearth. See *gorn.*

Iam (Iamskaia gon'ba). The earliest regular system of post and transportation in Russia, it consisted of a series of stations usually manned by volunteers and supported by a tax on the local population. Each station provided horses or wagons for *iam* couriers or approved travelers passing on to the next station on the line on government business.

Izba. Usually a smaller building, as indicated by such English words as "hut" or "cottage."

Joachimsthaler. See *efimok.*

Joint-iron. See *sviaznoe zhelezo.*

Kadashevets. A cloth artisan who inhabited a special suburb in Moscow for masters of that trade *(kadashevyi dvor).* Sometimes used by the tsar as messengers, agents, factors, etc.

Kamka. A type of Chinese silk cloth with large free patterns.

Kazennyi dvor (Kazennyi prikaz). Literally "the Treasury court," 1512—1700. The tsar's own treasury. Provided the royal family's wardrobe, personal articles, and utensils, and managed the sovereign's textile enterprises (satins, velvets, taffetas, silks, etc.). Also supervised the state fur trade monopoly.

Kholodnolomkoe zhelezo. Cold-short iron. Cf. *krasnolomkoe zhelezo.*

Kochedyki. Awls for bast shoes.

Kopeck. See Appendix I.

Korm. Literally, "fodder," "forage," "food." In Russian industry it signified a periodical cash allowance (usually daily) for food; probably accompanied by a ration of drink.

Kosulia. See *sokha*.

Kovanoe zhelezo. Forged iron of a higher quality than *chugun* (cast iron, pig iron).

Krai. A small area of land, an administrative area.

Krasnolomkoe zhelezo. Red-short iron. CF. *kholodnolomkoe zhelezo*.

Krichnoe zhelezo. Bloomery iron. Iron in its primary stage, still containing a high percentage of impurities and demanding further working to obtain a higher-quality metal.

Krichnyi peredel. Process of reducing the amount of carbon and other impurities in pig iron to obtain a higher-quality, more malleable type of iron. This forging ("fining") occurred in hammering shops (*molotovye; molotovye zavody, ambary*) equipped with anvils and water-driven hammers and bellows. See *syrodutnyi protsess*.

Kritsa (Kritsy). "Bloom." A hot, malleable mass of wrought iron ready for further working.

Kustar'. Artisan, handicraftsman.

Kuznets. Artisan blacksmith. *Kuznitsa*, forge shops (smithy forge) having hearths but usually no water-driven hammers.

Latnik. *Cuirass*-maker, a *cuirass* being a piece of close-fitting armor for protecting the chest and back.

Lemeshnoe zhelezo. Strip-iron.

Masterskaia palata. One of several sections of the *Oruzheinaia palata*. One *masterskaia palata* specialized in making clothing and personal effects for the tsar, another for the tsaritsa.

Moiré. Cloth bearing a watered or wavy pattern pressed by engraved rollers.

Molotovyi master. A worker who operated a hammer at a forge.

Muchnaia mel'nitsa. Grain mill, driven either by hand or by such "natural forces" as wind or water.

Nemetskaia sloboda. Sometimes translated the German Quarter, i.e., the Foreign Quarter. A suburb on the Iauza river on the outskirts of Moscow where foreigners in Russian service and residence were concentrated after 1652. There were other smaller *nemetskie slobody* in Russia outside Moscow.

Novotorgovyi ustav. "New trade code" issued on May 7, 1667. Much of its content dealt with the trade activity of foreigners in Russia, the object of the document being to increase state revenues through new and higher trade duties and to protect native capital from being disadvantaged by wealthier, more highly organized foreign merchant interests. Thus foreigners could not trade among themselves, were prohibited from retail trade in Russia, were restricted in places and times of their activity, etc. Superseded by the *Tamoz-*

hennyi ustav (customs statutes) of 1755.

Oblast'. An old Russian word referring to "land," "area," "territory." Under the Petrine territorial reforms early in the eighteenth century, *okrugy* formed *oblasti* (pl.), which in turn comprised *gubernii*.

Obogashchenie. Separation of iron ore from stones and debris by washing or sifting.

Obrezi. Iron plowblades.

Obrok. A cash payment. When it involved payment from a subject to the tsar, *obrok* might be understood as "tax"; from a peasant to his lord, "quit rent" (cf. *barshchina*); from a factory owner to a landlord for use of land, "rent."

Okhochie liudi. Literally "willing people," "volunteers." Peasants offering to work at a factory, sometimes for lower wages than those already being paid for a particular type of work. In another sense, peasant army volunteers who often comprised combat regiments. Cf. *datochnye liudi*.

Okolnichii (Okolnichie). An office second only to that of boyar. An *okolnichii* might head a *prikaz,* and would hope to be elevated to the rank of *boyar* before retirement.

Okrug. A given area of land under a single *nachal'nik* (head, chief).

Oruzheinaia palata. The "armaments palace," an armory established early in the sixteenth century in Moscow to produce sidearms and hand firearms. Closed in the 1720's.

Otbelka. The blanching, polishing, and finishing of cannon with grindstones and other devices.

Partizan. See *berdysh*.

Pekhota. The infantry. *Pekhotinets (pekhotintsy),* infantryman (infantrymen).

Perevodchik. A translator whose work was done in writing. Cf. *tolmach'.*

Physicians. In theory, in seventeenth-century Russia (as elsewhere in Europe) physicians were sharply divided into professional categories, beginning with the *doktor* (doctor) who gave counsel and commanded but did not personally administer treatments or medicines, this being the task of the *lekar'* (pl. *lekari*), "subdoctors." The pharmacist *(aptekar)* assisted both; below him were surgeons *(khirurg;* pl. *khirurgi)* and bone specialists *(kostopravye-khrurgi).* The *fel'dsher* was a physician's assistant, or male nurse. A *zeleinik* was a folk-remedier who worked with herbs, grasses, soils, etc., *zelënyi* being the Russian adjective "green."

Pig iron. See *chugun*.

Pishchal' (Pischali). (H) arquebus.

Pis'mennyi otpusk. Literally "written leave." A document from an employer stating that the worker holding the *otpusk* left the factory in good standing and could be hired elsewhere.

Plank iron. See *doska, doshchatnoe zhelezo.*

Plavil'shchik. A smelting master working at a blast furnace.

Plug. See *sokha.*

Poddatnye liudi. Workers provided by the tsar for unskilled work at a factory, etc.

Pod'iachii (Pod'iachie). Clerks, secretaries, scribes, who worked in *prikazy* and in other government institutions. They assisted *d'iaki* and may be understood as "undersecretaries," "sub-*d'iaki.*"

Pod-master. Literally "submaster." A skilled worker who had not yet attained the full status of master.

Podriadchik. A contractor; commercial agent of the tsar's government.

Pogost. A term similar to *volost';* comprised of several hamlets *(derevni)* under common government administration and tax collection. Also a church area containing a church, the house of the priest, cemetery, etc. Modern meaning: cemetery.

Poltina. See Appendix I.

Polupoltina. Literally, "one half a poltina." See Appendix I.

Pomeshchik (Pomeschiki). The holder of a *pomest'e (pomestia),* which were small landed estates given as fiefs to lesser noblemen and retained by them through continuous military service to the tsar. Already a widely developed form of land tenure by the sixteenth century; by the mid-seventeenth century these holdings had, in effect, become patrimonial. Cf. *votchinnik.*

Poruchik. Army lieutenant.

Posad. Suburb, settlement. A particular area or part of a city containing individuals (e.g., artisans) who were free, tax-paying subjects of the tsar. Cf. *kadashevets.*

Poshlina. Trade duty.

Posol'skii prikaz. Foreign office, 1549–1720. Chancellery which conducted diplomatic relations with foreign governments.

Praporshchik. Army ensign.

Prikaz. Chancellery, office, department, ministry. *Prikazy* were central government bodies which (1) handled various affairs of state (e.g., the *posol'skii prikaz,* the foreign office, conducted diplomatic relations with foreign states); (2) managed the affairs of a given part of the country (e.g., *sikirskii prikaz,* the Siberian chancellery); (3) attended to personal affairs of the tsar or directed his economic interests (e.g., *prikaz tainykh del, kazennyi prikaz*). Normally headed by a boyar and staffed by *d'iaki* and *pod'iachie.* The *prikaz* system crystallized by the mid-sixteenth century; despite consolidations and reforms (especially in 1680), the *prikazy* were not really planned or coordinated and were often characterized by overlapping function and authority. There were forty-two prikazy by mid-seventeenth century. Replaced by the college system of Peter I early in the eighteenth century.

Prikaz bol'shogo dvortsa. Prikaz of the Grand Palace, 1621–1718. Managed many of the tsar's economic enterprises and activities, estates and villages, etc.

Prikaz bol'shoi kazni. Grand Exchequer, 1621–1718. Supervised collection of direct taxes from the urban merchant-artisan population, directed money affairs and certain royal industrial enterprises and activities; after 1680 collected bar taxes and trade duty.

Prikaz tainykh del. Privy chancellery, 1654–1676. Managed some of the tsar's personal affairs, had extraordinary power to oversee and improve the operation of all other government bureaus and offices, handled political crimes and investigations. Increasingly took on economic directorships and responsibilities.

Prikhodnaia-raskhodnaia kniga. Receipt and expenditure book of a factory, government institution, etc.

Prutovoe zhelezo. Rod-iron. Sometimes used as construction material in stone houses, around windows, for example.

Pud ((Pudy). See Appendix II.

Pushechnik. A cannon caster.

Pushechnyi dvor. "The cannon yard," an armaments enterprise established in Moscow in 1479 by Aristotle Fioraventi. State-owned, based upon pre-manufacturing technology. Also called *pushechnaia izba* (the cannon house).

Pushkar. Gunner; cannon-smith (less common).

Pushkarskii prikaz. Cannon *prikaz,* 1577–1700. Office which directed affairs pertaining to the import and maintenance of cannon, construction of forts, engineering projects, etc. The *pushkarskii prikaz* normally organized and managed artisan works on the model of the *pushechnyi dvor,* and was sometimes involved in the operation of iron manufactories.

Pustosh'. The modern meaning is "wasteland." In sixteenth-seventeenth century Russia, however, a *pustosh'* was simply an unused "field" or plot of land, swamp, forest, etc., and might be economically useful.

Razriad. Office of Military Affairs, an administrative department in Moscow. *Razriady* (pl.), in a completely different sense, were administrative territorial units in seventeenth-century Siberia and elsewhere. *Razriad* also designated cadastres of provincial nobility.

Reitar (Reitary). Cavalryman (cavalrymen).

Rod-iron. See *prutovoe zhelezo.*

Rozsyl'shik. Ore prospector.

Ruble. See Appendix I.

Rudokop. Miner.

Sapozhnye shili. Shoe awls.

Sazhen (Sazheny). See Appendix II.

Sheet iron. See *doshchatnoe zhelezo.*

Shiffunt. See Appendix II.

Skupshchik. "Middleman," a merchant who obtained artisan goods in quantity and carried them to more distant and profitable markets.

Smola. The word seldom appears with a precise, self-explanatory meaning in old Russian documents. In general, it indicates "resin," a common juice derived from coniferous trees, thick and not soluble in water. In a more liquid form *smola* indicates "pitch" or "tar," useful in waterproofing ships, etc. *Smola* in hard form should be understood as "rosin," the substance derived by distilling oil of turpentine from crude turpentine.

Smuta (Smutnoe vremia). A series of economic crises, class struggles, dynastic conflicts, and foreign wars lasting in Russia from 1601 until 1612. Usually translated "Time of Troubles."

Sokha. A word of diverse meaning. Concerning the post it designated an area of one hundred houses which paid a tax to maintain the *iam* service's local station. The *sokha* plow was a light instrument in use in the northeast; cf. *kosulia,* which was a heavy *sokha* or a light *plug* (a heavy southern plow) equipped with a plowshare with cutter and mould-board.

Sovmestitel'. Literally a "pluralist." A master employed in two or more specialties.

Starosta. "Elder." The elected head of a village, *volost',* town, or suburb.

Stol'nik. Literally "courtier of the table." Administrative officials of middle rank, *stol'niki* (pl.) might assist a boyar in directing a *prikaz,* attend the tsar during receptions of foreign dignitaries, etc.

Strelets (Strel'tsy). From the Russian verb "streliat'," to shoot. The *strel'tsy* were professional soldiers, "musketeers," also armed with swords, pikes, and battleaxes. Some were mounted but most were infantrymen. From the time of their introduction by Ivan IV, they enjoyed special commercial rights and received homes, plots of land, and salaries in money and grain. A *strelets* regiment was commanded by a *golova.* Sometimes they might be assigned by the state to entrepreneurs for fairly menial industrial services.

Striapchii (Striapchie). Royal courtiers attending to food, clothing, and other household matters of the tsar. Comparable to *stol'niki* in importance of office.

Strip-iron. See *lemeshnoe zhelezo.*

Stvol'nyi prikaz. Gun-barrel *prikaz,* 1647–1666. Administered the production of barrels for hand firearms; was subordinated to the *Oruzheinaia palata.* (The Russian word *stvol* means "gun barrel.")

Stvol'nyi zavarshchiko. A barrel borer.

Submaster. See *pod-master.*

Sukonnaia sotnia. See *gost'.*

Sviaznoe zhelezo. Angle-iron, joint-iron, iron strips used in construction to brace and stabilize various parts of a building. *Sviaznoe zhelezo s obukhami* was bent joint-iron bolted into the corners of brick buildings (corner-iron); *sviaznoe zhelezo s obukhami i s zasovami'* referred to joint-iron with "catches" (bolts) on each end which would fit into the bricks forming the corner of a house. Joint-iron gave structural support to the walls.

Syrodutnyi protsess. The "two-stage" process in iron manufacturing whereby cast iron is obtained from iron ore during the first stage and higher-quality iron forged from the cast iron during the second stage. See *krichnyi peredel.*

Tamozhnaia. A building in which trade duties were collected.

Tochil'shchik. A polisher of weapons.

Tolmach'. An interpreter; one who translates oral conversation. Of lower professional status than *perevodchik.*

Tseloval'nik. From the Russian verb "tselovat'," to kiss. Literally, "one who has kissed the cross," i.e., taken an oath. *Tseloval'niki* were elected or appointed merchants who worked in the cities and provinces at collecting taxes and customs duties, or in the state monopolies for the sale of wine, salt, etc. They drew no salaries and were prohibited from trading during their tenure in office.

Tuyère. The pipe or nozzle through which air is forced into a blast furnace, forge, etc. Russian *furma,* pl. *furmy.*

Uezd. Administrative unit of local government; cf. *volost'.*

Ugol'nyi master. "Fuel master," a specialist in the selection and conversion of firewood into charcoal fuel for blast furnaces, etc. This burning took place in special pits dug in the ground.

Ukaz. English *ukase.* A royal edict having the force of law.

Uklad. Iron of unusually high quality, being the product of extensive refining and standing midway between iron (see *zhelezo)* and steel *(stal').* Usually obtained from artisan furnaces.

Ulozhenie. The new law code issued in 1649. It provided the first systematization of Muscovite laws since 1550 and was not superseded until 1835.

Versta (Versty). See Appendix II.

Vertelnaia. A boring shop for cannon.

Vertel'shchik. A polisher of cannon muzzles.

Voevoda (Voevody). An important military as well as administrative official in medieval Russia, usually a high-born member of the aristocracy. A *voevoda* governed a *uezd* from the principal town of that *uezd;* in the event of a mobilization, *voevody* led regiments of provincial services gentry and their peasant soldiers during the campaign. See *golova, volost'.*

Volost'. An administrative unit in Russia comprising several villages. Several *volosti* (pl.) formed an *uezd*. Each *uezd* had a town as its center and was governed from there by a *voevoda*. Tsar Mikhail inaugurated a move toward administrative centralization by consolidating *uezdy* (pl.) into larger territorial units, *razriady*. This policy aimed at a better organization of national defense, and was continued by Aleksei Mikhailovich.

Votchinnik (Votchinniki). The holder of a *votchina (votchiny)*, which from early times were large patrimonial estates held without service obligation to the sovereign. (Cf. alodial land tenureships of medieval Western Europe.) By the sixteenth century, however, the services of *votchinniki* to the state were scarcely fewer or less burdensome than those obtained from *pomeshchiki*.

Yuft. Skin of a grown bull or cow processed by Russian fashion into leather; in practice, used in Russia to refer to imported leather as well.

Zheleznyi riad. Literally the "iron row." A row of shops in Moscow where iron goods, tools, and weapons could be purchased.

Zhelezo. Iron.

Zhelezodelatel'nyi (or Zhelezoobrabatyvaiushchyi) zavod. An enterprise which produced higher-quality iron from the cast (pig) iron *(chugun)* produced at a blasting factory *(domennyi zavod)*. Might be understood as "forging factory."

Zolotnik. See Appendix II.

A Note on Sources

1. Published State Documents, Decrees, and Correspondence

This was the single most important type of material used in the preparation of this study. The first two volumes of *Krepostnaia manufaktura v Rossii* [Peasant manufacturing in Russia] (55–56)* were especially valuable, for they contain extensive descriptions of the iron factories of the Tula-Kashira area compiled by government inspectors between 1647 and 1690, documents concerning the entrepreneurs, their privileges and relations to the government, and information relative to the output of the iron enterprises, its marketing and prices, and data on the workers and peasants of the manufactories. *Dopolnenie k Aktam Istoricheskim* [Supplement to historical acts] (21) and *Sobranie gosudarstvennykh gramot . . .* [Collection of state documents . . .] (115) also contain a wealth of petitions, government decrees, factory reports, and the like. Volumes XXI and XXIII of *Russkaia Istoricheskaia Biblioteka* [Russian historical library] (110) draw heavily on records of the *tainyi prikaz* (privy chancellery) from the 1660's to 1676, which makes them indispensable for a study of the Zvenigorodskie iron works while they were under government own-

---

* Numbers following the bibliographical citations in this essay refer to the bibliography which follows.

343

ership, as well as for information on state involvement with the silk, glass, and leather industries. *Polnoe Sobranie Zakonov Rossiiskoi Imperii* [complete collection of the laws of the Russian empire] and *Russko-shvedskie ekonomicheskie otnosheniia* . . . [Russian-Swedish economic relations . . .] (111), while not as important as the above works, are still worthy of note.

Several publications deal with English-Russian diplomatic, commercial, and industrial relationships from the 1550's to the mid-seventeenth century. The most interesting of these for my purposes was published by Iurii Tolstoi in St. Petersburg in 1875 (120). The documents in this volume are given in both Russian and English (or Latin, where necessary) and are prefaced by a valuable – if quaint – fifty-two-page historical introduction by the editor-translator. S. Konovalov assembled a large quantity of similar material in six issues of the *Oxford Slavonic Papers* between 1950 and 1964 (45–49). And one must not overlook Inna Lubimenko, "Letters Illustrating the Relations of England and Russia in the Seventeenth Century," printed in England in 1917 (69).

II. Writings of Travelers and Contemporaries

V. O. Kliuchevskii's *Skazaniia inostrantsev o moskovskom gosudarstve* [Accounts of foreigners concerning the Muscovite state] (42) is still the definitive survey and analysis of this subject. The most notable single work of this type of literature for the economic historian is Johann Philipp Kilburger's account of Russian industry and trade in the year 1674 (59). This Swedish merchant's keen eye and high sense of accuracy allowed him to provide unique and valuable information on Russian manufactories, commodities, and price levels of the period. Of no less value is Professor B. G. Kurts's extensive "Explanation and Additions" (pp. 243–589) to Kilburger's essay, based on the reports of other foreigners, published documents and archival material, and monographs. Anthony Jenkinson's *Early Voyages and Travels to Russia and Persia,* in two volumes (34), is useful for English industrial projects and activities during the last half of the sixteenth century, as is Hakluyt's *Principal Navigations . . . of the English Nation* (29). Students of Russian-Western relations – both economic and cultural – during the sixteenth century should also consult the works of Rafael Barberini (9), Giles Fletcher (13), and Heinrich von Staden (128).

For the seventeenth century Grigorii Kotoshikin's classic description of Russia at the time of Aleksei Mikhailovich (52) contains background information of a political and social nature which is relevant to economic developments of the time, while Samuel H.

Baron's fine new translation of Olearius' writings (10) is invaluable for this and a slightly earlier period. The arch-deacon Paul of Aleppo accompanied his father, Makarius, the Patriarch of Antioch, on a visit to Russia in 1653–1654. Paul's account of this trip, translated from the Arabic by G. Murkos and published in Moscow in five volumes from 1896 to 1900 (107), contains colorful and extraordinary data on Russian iron factories and ordnance, and should not be ignored by the student of almost any aspect of Russian life during the mid-seventeenth century. The Polish soldier Stanislas Zolkiewski's *Expedition to Moscow: A Memoir* (139) provides material concerning Russian military problems during the Time of Troubles. Writings of the Dutch diplomats Isaak Massa (80) and Albert Burkh (50) touch on the economic activities of their countrymen in Russia during the first third of the seventeenth century.

III. General Histories of Russia

S. M. Solov'ev's encyclopedic *History of Russia from the Earliest Times* (116) provides a considerable amount of factual information concerning early Russian economic development. The third volume of Kliuchevskii's masterful *Kurs russkoi istorii* [The course of Russian history] (41) contains arresting interpretations and insights, as well as some historical material which one might not find elsewhere.* This is also true (if to a lesser degree) of the Bolshevik historian M. N. Pokrovskii (100 – 102). My own research has led me to respect N. A. Rozhkov's stimulating and provocative *Russkaia istoriia v sravnitel'no-istoricheskom osvenshchenii* [Russian history in comparative-historical presentation] (109) and to regret that it is not more appreciated by contemporary specialists in Russian history. George Vernadsky's *Russia at the Dawn of the Modern Age* (125) is useful for Russian commercial and industrial activity during the fifteenth and sixteenth centuries. Pushkarev's *Obzor russkoi istorii* [Survey of Russian history] (106) should be consulted for a good overall discussion of the Russian army, its difficulties and reforms during the late medieval period, questions of state administration and finance, and so forth.

IV. General Economic Histories of Russia

A. I. Zaozerskii's book on Tsar Aleksei Mikhailovich and his vast economic empire (137) is a classic of pre-revolutionary economic

---

*The third volume of Kliuchevskii's *Kurs* has been recently translated by Natalie Duddington under the title, *A Course in Russian History: The Seventeenth Century* (Chicago, Quadrangle Books, 1968).

historiography. Some unreliable features in the discussion of the state glass industry are more than offset by the author's striking picture of Alexis as entrepreneur, and most of the information on the tsar's economic activities is still accurate and useful. P. G. Liubomorov's *Ocherki* [Essays] on the history of Russian industry from the seventeenth to the early nineteenth century (67) are based on careful scholarship and probably comprise the best single book with which to begin a study of this subject. A leading general survey of Russian economic history in English is Peter Lyashchenko's *History of the National Economy of Russia* (74); Lyashchenko provides the kind of material which helps place the early history of Russian manufacturing in a broader context. Although Jerome Blum's *Lord and Peasant in Russia* (15) does not often utilize recent Soviet archival work on Russian agricultural history, his discussion and analyses are generally reliable and valuable in establishing, again, the historical context of the unfolding of industrial developments. Blum also devotes a few pages to Russian handicrafts and manufactures.

A. M. Pankratova's *Formirovanie proletariata v Rossii* [Formation of the proletariat in Russia] (92) is a solid and monumental study containing much data on the interrelated development of artisanry and factory labor along with useful sidelights on some of the Russian factories of the seventeenth century. Published posthumously in 1963, it shows the author to have been, at her best, a scholarly, nondogmatic Marxist historian, and makes one regret that she did not devote more energy to serious work of this sort.

Erik Amburger's *Die Familie Marselis* (2) is clearly one of the best major studies of Russian economic history in the pre-Petrine period to have appeared in the West. Amburger utilized broad archival material in Holland, Germany, and Denmark. His book is not only indispensable for a knowledge of the Marselises and their iron manufacturing interests in the late Muscovite period; it is also rich with general information on foreign commercial and entrepreneurial activities in Russia during the seventeenth century. The author does not engage, however, in much interpretation or analysis of his material. Reviews of *Die Familie Marselis* by Olga Crisp (18) and Walther Kirchner (39) are of supplementary value.

V. Histories of the Iron Industry and Other Forms of Manufacturing

B. A. Kolchin, *Tekhnika obrabotki metalla v drevnei Rusi* [Technology of metalworking in ancient Russia] (44) is largely based on archaeological work and deals mainly with the Kievan period. It is useful for its observations on the technical aspects of iron artisanry and for the insights which this gives into early factory iron production.

To a lesser extent this may also be said of Vernadsky's brief article "Iron Mining and Iron Industries in Medieval Russia" (126). G. B. Belotserkovskii's book on the town of Tula during the sixteenth and seventeenth centuries (12) provides valuable data on the iron artisans whose activity in the area served as a background to the first Russian efforts at iron manufacturing.

Iosif Gamel's account of the Tula iron manufactories (25) was the first effort at a serious study of the subject. Published in 1826, the book contains descriptions and interpretations which are on the whole still reliable, along with a large number of important documents in the appendix. The collective work of Baklanov, Mavrodin, and Smirnov (5) is of importance for detailed explanations of the technology and organization of the Tula, Kashirskie, Porotovskii, and Ugodskii iron factories. The authors also raise interesting theoretical questions about the nature of Russian industry in this period, as does A. A. Kuzin in his pioneering study *Istoriia otkrytii rudnykh mestorozhdenii v Rossii* [History of the opening of ore deposits in Russia] (60). V. N. Kashin's scholarly article on the Tula armaments settlement in the seventeenth century (36) deals at length with the factories of the area. Kashin presents an interesting case for regarding Russian manufacturing at this time as an indigenous product of the Russian genius and environment, but is so chauvinistic and unwilling to admit Russian indebtedness to foreign capitalists and technicians that the reader must struggle on the basis of his own resources for a more balanced, historical view. The same mixture of praise and criticism must be accorded V. A. Danilevskii's erudite history of *Russkaia tekhnika* [Russian technology] (19), which devotes considerable attention to iron manufacturing.

The two most outstanding monographs on the Russian iron industry are by S. G. Strumilin (118) and B. B. Kafengauz (35). Strumilin, in particular, is interested in the seventeenth century and in Russian iron artisanry. N. N. Stoskova's recent book on the first Russian iron manufactories (117) is a short work designed for students and the general reader, but it is written with accuracy and care, and clarifies several questions of factory dates and technology. Two splendid books by N. I. Pavlenko (95) and Roger Portal (104) deal with Russian iron manufacturing in the eighteenth century and are helpful in evaluating the significance of Russian metallurgy in the seventeenth century for the subsequent development which came under Peter the Great and his successors. Vvedenskii's study of the Stroganov family (131) is the most important source of information on the first Russian iron manufactory, built in Siberia during the late 1570's and early 1580's.

For the artisan background of the nonferrous manufactures of seventeenth-century Russia, the reader should consult one of the true masterpieces of Soviet historiography: *Remeslo drevnei rusi* [Artisanry of ancient Russia], published by B. A. Rybakov in 1948. Rybakov treats his subject only through the fifteenth century, which means that he does not even touch on manufacturing. But the book is useful for understanding the artisan background of manufactures such as glass, leather, and textiles. The best general treatment of factory activity of this sort is E. I. Zaozerskaia's *Razvitie legkoi promyshlennosti v Moskve v pervoi chetverti xviii v.* [Development of light industry in Moscow during the first quarter of the eighteenth century] (136). Despite the suggestion of her title, Madame Zaozerskaia provides a wealth of information on the seventeenth century.

During the 1920's Professor G. A. Novitskii produced three interesting articles on seventeenth-century efforts at the manufacture of cloth, paper, and leather (86–88). In the last article the author also discusses the mercantilist policy of the Russian state and its efforts to stimulate industrial development through favors and concessions to foreigners. Unfortunately, other historians have not added much to Novitskii's research in these areas, though two earlier studies present some information which Novitskii did not include in his essays. These are N. P. Likhachev's splendid book on the beginnings of paper manufacturing in Russia (65) and Volume II of the *Istoriko-statisticheskii obzor promyshlennosti Rossii* [Historical-statistical survey of the industry of Russia (33), which devotes considerable attention to textile manufacturing in the seventeenth century. Pazhitnov's books on the Russian woolen, cotton, and silk industries (96–97) are superficial in their treatment of the seventeenth century, but E. Lermontova's pre-revolutionary study of the silk "factory" built under Sof'ia Alekseevna is a scholarly work of great value for that particular industry (63).

A. I. Zaozerskii's book on the economic activities of Aleksei Mikhailovich (137) contains a great amount of information on the "light" industry of the seventeenth century, but his discussion of glass manufacturing has been completely superceded by N. A. Baklanova's lengthy article on the first glass manufactories built in the Muscovite state (7). *Russkaia Istoricheskaia Biblioteka* (110), *Dopolnenie k Aktam Istoricheskim* (21), *Sobranie gosudarstvennykh gramot i dogovorov* (115), and the writings of Kilburger (59) are indispensable sources for the study of nonmetallurgical industries in this period.

VI. Commercial Studies

In various ways commercial activity prepared the way for the origin and development of manufacturing in Russia during the sixteenth and seventeenth centuries. S. V. Bakhrushin's investigations of trade activity in this period (4) are particularly valuable for an understanding of the growth of an all-Russian market, the territorial division of labor, and the revival of cities and towns. With regard to foreign commerce, N. A. Baklanova's article on imported goods in the Muscovite state during the second half of the seventeenth century (6) is worthy of careful attention, as are older studies by Kostomarov (51) and Dovnar-Zapol'skii (22). Walter Kirchner's "Entrepreneurial Activity in Russian-Western Trade Relations During the Sixteenth Century" (38) contains interesting information on Italian economic influences in this early period.* T. S. Willan's *The Early History of the Russia Company, 1553–1603* (132) is an adequate study of English activity, but the author makes no use of Russian sources or secondary works. Two articles of Inna Lubimenko (70, 72) and Violet Barbour's *Capitalism in Amsterdam in the Seventeenth Century* (Ann Arbor, Mich., 1963) provide useful data on the ever-expanding Dutch involvement with Russian commerce in the late medieval period. An article published by Professor L. V. Cherepnin in English in the *Slavonic and East European Review* ("Russian 17th-Century Baltic Trade in Soviet Historiography" [17]) gives historical information on this subject as well as important bibliographical references.

VII. Cultural Relations with the West

The cultural influence of Western Europe on Russia in the pre-Petrine period is a complex subject of enormous interest which has not yet been subjected to thorough and systematic investigation by students of Russian history. The available literature is, however, useful in various ways. First, it clarifies the context in which foreign activity of a specifically entrepreneurial type emerged and developed; second, it provides a considerable amount of information on the individual capitalists both as manufacturers and as people. The writings of I. P. Kozlovskii (54) and Dmitrii Tsvetaev (123) are of greatest value for these purposes. The former historian published a two-volume study of the Russian post, the first volume being a monograph and the second a collection of relevant documents. Tsvetaev's book treats Protestantism and Protestants in Russia before Peter the Great. Both are solid, erudite essays which far transcend the deceptively narrow limits of their subjects. Unfortunately, these works are bibliographical rarities and seldom used by contemporary historians.

A. S. Muliukin is the author of two splendid books dealing with the legal-juridical aspects of foreign activities in late medieval Russia

---

*An anthology of Kirchner's writings was published in 1966 as *Commercial Relations Between Russia and Europe, 1400 to 1800: Collected Essays.*

(84, 85). These monographs are especially useful for their information on the mercantilist policy of the Russian state, and also contain some unique data on the capitalists themselves. S. F. Platonov's *Moskva i zapad v xvi-xvii vekakh* [Muscovy and the West during the sixteenth and seventeenth centuries] (99) gives a splendid account of Hans Schlitte's mission to the West in search of skilled workers for Tsar Ivan the Terrible, as well as Polish efforts to block such forms of Russian "modernization." Inna Lubimenko (73) and Lappo-Danilevskii (61) each have to their credit excellent articles on foreign soldiers, scholars, merchants, and manufacturers in Russia during the sixteenth and seventeenth centuries. Volume VIII of *Russkaia Istoricheskaia Biblioteka* (110) contains 245 pages of documents concerning foreigners in the Muscovite state between 1600 and 1640. Von Staden (128), Fletcher (13), Olearius (10), and Kilburger (59) were contemporary travelers who provided invaluable information on Russian life for the contemporary historian.

The English seem to have been the most thoroughly studied nationality with regard to cultural and commercial impact on Russia in the pre-Petrine era. Besides literature cited in other places in this essay, valuable books and articles have been published by Iosif Gamel' (26), Mildred Wretts-Smith (133), and E. Zviagintsev (140, 141).

James H. Billington's *The Icon and the Axe: An Interpretative History of Russian Culture* (14) is a pretentious and sometimes inaccurate book, but it does contain useful information concerning Western influence on the Russian Army and ordnance during the seventeenth century. Arthur Voyce's more modest and reliable *Moscow and the Roots of Russian Culture* (129) discusses the activities of foreigners in Russia during the sixteenth century.

VIII. Mercantilism

The greatest amount of material used to prepare this chapter came from the same sources, articles, and monographs which served as a foundation for the discussion of Russian industrial development. There are a few references, however, which deal specifically with this subject. For my purposes the most useful of these were two books on the legal position of foreigners in sixteenth- and seventeenth-century Muscovy by A. S. Muliukin (84, 85), and two studies from the Soviet period. The first of these articles is by K. V. Bazilevich, "Elementy merkantilisma v ekonomicheskoi politike pravitel'stva Aleksei Mikhailovicha" ["Elements of mercantilism in the economic policy of the government of Aleksei Mikhailovich"] (11). Of even greater value was a collective work edited by A. I. Pashkov, trans-

lated (not always accurately) and published in English under the title
*A History of Russian Economic Thought: Ninth Through Eighteenth
Centuries* (94). Despite heavyhanded Stalinist interpretations of
some historical problems, Pashkov's book is useful in tracing the
growth of the Muscovite state, the political and economic problems
facing the government at various times, and the overall evolution of
commercial and industrial policy. Discussions of Boris Morozov and
A. L. Ordin-Nashchokin are particularly informative.

IX. Technology, Western Economic History

I used a considerable amount of literature on the economic and
technological history of Western Europe, and a number of the most
relevant titles have been cited in footnotes in the text. H. R. Schubert's *History of the British Iron and Steel Industry from c. 450 B.C.
to A.D. 1775* (113) and the second volume of Leslie Aitchison's
A History of Metals (1) were especially useful in attaining some
understanding of the technical aspects of iron manufacturing in
Europe from the fifteenth to the seventeenth centuries. For purposes
of comparative development, I sometimes contrasted and compared
Sweden and Russia. Two works were extremely useful here: Eli
Heckscher, *An Economic History of Sweden* (30) and Michael Roberts, *Gustavus Adolphus, A History of Sweden, 1611–1632* (108),
in two volumes.

A final word concerning methodology and interpretation. In the
process of researching this topic and bringing my notes and thoughts
into order and coherence, I came to respect Karl Marx for his keen
understanding of the vast and complex historical phenomenon which
historians refer to as the "transaction from feudalism to capitalism."
The first and third volumes of *Das Kapital* (77, 78) are particularly
useful in the study of this problem, as is Marx's manuscript recently
published in English under the title *Pre-Capitalist Economic Formations* (79). I also learned much from the splendid work of two
British Marxist historians, Maurice Dobb (20) and Eric J. Hobsbawm
(31, 32). The economic development of Western Europe and of
Russia has been sufficiently different, however, for the specialist in
Russian history to be compelled to approach his subject with a minimum of the kinds of preconceived notions which one so early gains
from a study of England, France, and other Western countries. And
if Russian economic history is viewed in this way, the student may
even emerge with a somewhat different set of generalizations and
conclusions than would be the case if the object of his attentions
were the enclosure movement in England, mercantilism in early mod-

ern France, or the revival of trade in Genoa and Pisa during the eleventh century. *Honi soit qui mal y pense!*

Selected Bibliography

Following is a list of the most important books and articles cited in the text. An asterisk (*) indicates that the bibliographical item is discussed in the Note on Sources, which directly precedes this bibliography.

*1. Aitchison, Leslie. *A History of Metals.* Vol. II. New York, 1960.

*2. Amburger, Erik. *Die Familie Marselis, Studien zur russischen Wirtschaftsgeschichte.* Giessen, 1957.

3. Anderson, M. S. "English Views of Russia in the 17th Century," *S.E.E.R.,* XXXIII (1954–1955), 140–160.

*4. Bakhrushin, S. V. *Nauchnye trudy* [Scholarly Works]. Vol. I: *Ocherki po istorii remesla, torgovli i gorodov russkogo tsentralizovannogo gosudarstva xvi–nachaia xvii v.* [Studies in the history of artisanry, trade, and cities of the Russian centralized state during the sixteenth and early seventeenth centuries]. Moscow, 1952.

*5. Baklanov, N. B., V. V. Mavrodin, I. I. Smirnov. *Tul'skie i kashirskie zavody v xvii v.* [The Tula and Kashirskie factories in the seventeenth century]. Moscow-Leningrad, 1934.

*6. Baklanova, N. A. "Privoznye tovary v moskovskom gosudar-stve vo vtoroi polovine xvii veke" [Imported goods in the Muscovite state during the second half of the seventeenth

353

century], in *Ocherki po istorii torgovli i promyshlennosti v Rossii v 17 i v nachale 18 stoletiia* [Studies in the history of trade and industry in Russia during the seventeenth and early eighteenth centuries], IV (1928), 5–118. ·

*7. _____. "Stekliannye zavody v moskovskom gosudarstve xvii veka" [Glass factories in the Muscovite state of the seventeenth century], in *Ocherki po istorii torgovli i promyshlennosti v Rossii v 17 i v nachale 18 stoletiia* [Studies in the history of trade and industry in Russia during the seventeenth and early eighteenth centuries]. IV (1928), 119–141.

*8. _____. "Zvenigorodskie zheleznye zavody v xvii v" [The Zvenigorodskie iron factories in the seventeenth century], in *Moskovskii krai v ego proshlom* [Moscow *krai* during its past], Part 2 (1930), pp. 91–101.

*9. Barberini, Rafael, *Puteshestvie v Moskoviiu* [Journey to Muscovy], in *Syn otechestva* [Son of the fatherland], No. 7, 1842.

*10. Baron, Samuel H., trans. and ed. *The Travels of Olearius in Seventeenth-Century Russia.* Stanford, Calif., 1967.

*11. Bazilevich, K. V. "Elementy merkantilizma v ekonomicheskoi politike pravitel'stva Alekseia Mikhailovicha" [Elements of mercantilism in the economic policy of the Government of Aleksei Mikhailovich]. *Uchenye zapiski Moskovskogo... universiteta... istoriia* [Scholarly notes of Moscow... University... history], XII (1940), 3–34.

*12. Belotserkovskii, G. M. *Tula i tul'skii uezd v xvi i xvii vekakh* [Tula and Tula *uezd* during the sixteenth and seventeenth centuries]. Kiev, 1914.

*13. Berry, Lloyd E. *The English Works of Giles Fletcher the Elder.* Madison, Wisc., 1964.

*14. Billington, James H. *The Icon and the Axe: An Interpretative History of Russian Culture.* New York, 1966.

*15. Blum, Jerome. *Lord and Peasant in Russia, from the Ninth to the Nineteenth Century* Princeton, 1961.

Burkh, Albert. See Kordt, V. A.

Chamberlayne, Thomas. See Konovalov, S.

16. Chekan, I. V. "Tul'skie i kashirskie zheleznye zavody xvii veka" [The Tula and Kashirskie iron factories of the seventeenth century], in *Ocherki po istorii torgovli i promyshlennosti v Rossii v 17 i v nachale 18 stoletiia* [Studies in the history of trade and industry in Russia during the seventeenth and early eighteenth centuries], IV (1928), 143–161.

*17. Cherepnin, L. V. "Russian 17th-Century Baltic Trade in Soviet Historiography," *S.E.E.R.*, XLIII (1964–1965), 1–22.

*18. Crisp, Olga. Review of Erik Amburger, *Die Familie Marselis*, in *S.E.E.R.*, XXXVII (1958–1959), 275–278.

*19. Danilevskii, V. A. *Russkaia tekhnika* [Russian technology]. 2nd ed., Leningrad, 1948.

*20. Dobb, Maurice. *Studies in the Development of Capitalism*. New York, 1963.

*21. *Dopolnenie k Aktam Istoricheskim* [Supplement to historical acts]. Vols. III, V, IX–XII. St. Petersburg, 1848–1872.

*22. Dovnar-Zapol'skii, M. V. *Torgovlia i promyshlennost' Moskvy xvi-xvii vv* [Trade and industry of Moscow during the sixteenth and seventeenth centuries]. Moscow, 1910.

23. Esper, Thomas. "Russia and the Baltic, 1494–1558," *Slavic Review*, XXV (1966), 458–474.

fan Feltdril', Iogan. See Kordt, V. A.

24. Fennell, J. L. I. *Ivan the Great of Moscow*. London, 1961.

Fletcher, Giles. See Berry, Lloyd E.

*25. Gamel', Iosif. *Opisanie tul'skago oruzheinago zavoda v istoricheskom i tekhnicheskom otnoshenii* [Description of the Tula armaments factory in its historical and technical aspects]. Moscow, 1826.

*26. Gamel', I. *Anglichane v Rossii v xvi i xvii stoletiiakh* [The English in Russia during the sixteenth and seventeenth centuries]. 2 vols. St. Petersburg, 1865 and 1869.

Gordon, Patrick. See Konovalov, S.

27. Got'e, Iu. and S. Bakhrushin, "Kul'turnye i politicheskie sviazi Rossii i Anglii v xvi–xvii vekakh" [Cultural and political connections of Russia and England during the sixteenth and seventeenth centuries], *I.zh.*, No. 12 (1941), 64–70.

28. Grey, Ian. *Ivan III and the Unification of Russia*. London, 1964.

*29. Hakluyt, Richard. *The Principal Navigations, Voyages, Traffiques, and Discoveries of the English Nation*. Vol. I. London and New York. 1929.

*30. Heckscher, Eli F. *An Economic History of Sweden*. Trans. Goran Ohlin. Cambridge, Mass., 1954.

*31. Hobsbawm, E. J. "The General Crisis of the European Economy in the 17th Century," *Past & Present*, No. 5 (May 1954), 44–65.

*32. _____. "The Seventeenth Century in the Development of

Capitalism," *Science & Society*, XXIV (1960), 97–112.

*33. *Istoriko-statisticheskii obzor promyshlennosti Rossii* [An historical-statistical survey of the industry of Russia]. Vol. II. St. Petersburg, 1886.

*34. Jenkinson, Anthony. *Early Voyages and Travels to Russia and Persia.* Ed. by E. Delmar Morgan and C. H. Coote. 2 vols. Originally published by Hakluyt Society, republished by Burt Franklin, New York, n.d.

*35. Kafengauz, B. B. *Istoriia khoziaistva Demidovykh v xviii–xix vv* [History of the Demidov economic holdings in the eighteenth and nineteenth centuries]. Moscow-Leningrad, 1949.

*36. Kashin, V. N. "Tul'skaia oruzheinaia sloboda v xvii veke" [Tula armaments settlement in the seventeenth century], *Problemy dokapitalisticheskogo obshchestva* [Problems of pre-capitalist society], No. 1–2 (1935), 111–141; No. 5–6 (1935), 76–99.

37. Keep, J. L. H. "The Regime of Filaret, 1619–1633," *S.E.E.R.*, XXXVIII (1959–1960), 334–360.

Kilburger, Iogann Filipp. See Kurts, B. G.

*38. Kirchner, Walther. "Entrepreneurial Activity in Russian-Western Trade Relations During the Sixteenth Century," *Explorations in Entrepreneurial History*, VIII (1955–1956), 245–251.

*39. _____. Review of Erik Amburger, *Die Familie Marselis,* in *American Slavic and East European Review*, XVII (1958), 547–548.

40. _____. *Rise of the Baltic Question.* Newark, Del., 1954.

*41. Kliuchevskii, V. O. *Kurs russkoi istorii* [The course of Russian history], in *Sochineniia* [Works]. Moscow, 1956–1958.

*42. _____. *Skazaniia inostrantsev o moskovskom gosudarstve* [Account of foreigners concerning the Muscovite state]. Petrograd, 1918.

43. Kolchin, B. A. *Chernaia metallurgiia i metalloobrabotka v drevnei Rusi (domongol'skii period)* [Ferrous metallurgy and metalworking in ancient Russia (pre-Mongol period)]. *Materialy i issledovaniia po arkheologii SSSR* [Materials and studies on the archaeology of the USSR], No. 32 (1953).

*44. _____. *Tekhnika obrabotki metalla v drevnei Rusi* [Technology of metalworking in ancient Russia]. Moscow, 1953.

*45. Konovalov, S. "Anglo-Russian Relations, 1617–18," *O.S.P.*, I (1950), 64–103.

*46. _____. "Anglo-Russian Relations, 1620–4," *O.S.P.*, IV

(1953), 71–131.
*47. ———. "Patrick Gordon's Dispatches from Russia, 1667," *O.S.P.*, XI (1964), 8–16.
*47a. ———. "Thomas Chamberlayne's Description of Russia, 1631," *O.S.P.*, V (1954), 107–111.
*48. ———. "Twenty Russian Royal Letters (1626–1634)," *O.S.P.*, VII (1958), 117–156.
*49. ———. "Two Documents Concerning Anglo-Russian Relations in the Early Seventeenth Century," *O.S.P.*, II (1951), 128–144.

*50. Kordt, V. A., ed. *Otchet Al'berta Burkha i Iogana fan Feltdrilia o posol'stve ikh v Rossiiu v 1630 i 1631 gg. s predlozh eniem ocherka snoshenii Moskovskago Gosudarstva s respublikoiu Soedinennykh Niderlandov do 1631 g* [Report of Albert Burkh and Iogan fan Feltdril' concerning their embassy to Russia in 1630 and 1631, with an introductory study of the relations of the Muscovite state with the Republic of the United Netherlands until 1631]. St. Petersburg, 1902.

*51. Kostomarov, N. I. *Sobranie sochinenii* [Collected Works]. Book VIII, Vol. XX: *Ocherk torgovli moskovskago gosudarstva v xvi i xvii stoletiiakh* [A study of the trade of the Muscovite state during the sixteenth and seventeenth centuries]. St. Petersburg, 1905.

*52. Kotoshikhin, Grigorii. *O Rossii v tsarstvovanie Aleksiia Mikhailovicha* [Concerning Russia during the reign of Aleksei Mikhailovich]. 3rd ed., St. Petersburg, 1884.

53. Kozlovskii, I. P. "Andrei Dennis'evich Vinius," *R.S.*, CXL (1909), 444–447.

*54. ———. *Pervye pochty i pervye pochtmeistery v moskovskom gosudarstve, opyt izsledovaniia nekotorykh voprosov iz istorii russkoi kul'tury vo 2-i polovine xvii veka* [The first posts and first postmasters in the Muscovite state, an attempt at an investigation of several questions from the history of Russian culture in the second half of the seventeenth century]. 2 vols. Warsaw, 1913.

*55. *Krepostnaia manufaktura v Rossii* [Peasant manufacturing in Russia]. Vol. I: *Tul'skie i kashirskie zheleznye zavody* [Tula and Kashirskie iron factories]. Leningrad, 1930.

*56. *Krepostnaia manufaktura v Rossii* [Peasant manufacturing in Russia]. Vol. II: *Olonetskie mednye i zheleznye zavody* [Olonets copper and iron factories]. Leningrad, 1931.

57. Kulisher, I. M. *Ocherk istorii russkoi promyshlennosti* [Study

of the history of Russian industry]. Petrograd, 1922.

58. ———. *Ocherk istorii russkoi torgovli* [Study of the history of Russian trade]. Petrograd, 1923.

*59. Kurts, B. G. *Sochinenie Kil'burgera o russkoi torgovle v tsarstvovanie Alekseia Mikhailovicha* [Report of Kilburger on Russian trade in the reign of Aleksei Mikhailovich]. Kiev, 1915.

*60. Kuzin, A. A. *Istoriia otkrytii rudnykh mestorozhdenii v Rossii do serediny xix v* [History of the opening of ore deposits in Russia until the middle of the nineteenth century]. Moscow, 1961.

*61. Lappo-Danilevskii, A. "Inozemtsy v Rossii v tsarstvovanie Mikhaila Fedorovicha" [Foreigners in Russia during the reign of Mikhail Fedorovich], *Zh.m.n.p.*, CCXLI (October 1885), 66–106.

62. Lebedianskaia, A. P. "Ocherki iz istorii pushechnogo proizvodstva v Moskovskoi Rusi" [Studies from the history of cannon production in Muscovite Russia], in *Artilleriiskii istoricheskii muzei krasnoi armii. Sbornik issledovanii i materialov* [Historical Artillery Museum of the Red Army. Collection of studies and materials], I (1941), 57–84.

*63. Lermontova, E. "Shelkovaia fabrika v pravlenie tsarevny Sof'ii Alekseevny" [A silk factory during the reign of tsarevna Sof'ia Alekseevna], *Zapiski otdeleniia russkoi i slavianskoi arkheologii imperatorskago russkago arkheologicheskago obshchestva* [Notes of the Department of Russian and Slavic Archaeology of the Imperial Russian Archaeological Society], XI (1915), 43–74.

64. Lewitter, L. R. "Poland, the Ukraine and Russia in the 17th Century," *S.E.E.R.*, XXVII (1948–1949), 157–171, 414–429.

*65. Likhachev, N. P. *Bumaga i drevneishiia bumazhnyia mel'nitsy v moskovskom gosudarstve* [Paper and the earliest paper mills in the Muscovite State]. St. Petersburg, 1891.

66. Lilley, S. *Men, Machines and History: The Study of Tools and Machines in Relation to Social Progress.* London, 1965.

*67. Liubomirov, P. G. *Ocherki po istorii russkoi promyshlennosti xvii, xviii i nachalo xix veka* [Studies in the history of Russian industry of the seventeenth, eighteenth, and early nineteenth centuries]. Moscow, 1947.

68. Livshits, R. S. *Razmeshchenie promyshlennosti v dorevoliutsionnoi Rossii* [Distribution of industry in pre-revolutionary Russia]. Moscow, 1955.

*69. Lubimenko, Inna. "Letters Illustrating the Relations of England and Russia in the Seventeenth Century," *E.H.R.*, XXXII (1917), 92–103.

*70. _____. "Moskovskii rynok kak arena bor'by Gollandii s Angliei" [Muscovite market as an arena of struggle of Holland with England], *Russkoe proshloe* [Russian past], No. 5 (1923), 3–23.

71. _____. "A Project for the Acquisition of Russia by James I," *E.H.R.*, XXIX (1914), 246–256.

*72. _____. "The Struggle of the Dutch with the English for the Russian Market in the Seventeenth Century," *Transactions of the Royal Historical Society*, 4th series, VII (1924), 27–51.

*73. _____. "Trud inozemtsev v Moskovskom gosudarstve" [Labor of foreigners in the Muscovite state], in *Arkhiv istorii truda v Rossii* [Archive of the history of labor in Russia]. Petrograd, 1923, pp. 52–74.

*74. Lyashchenko, Peter I. *History of the National Economy of Russia.* Trans. L. M. Herman. New York, 1949.

Makarii (Patriarch). See *Puteshestvie . . .*

75. Maleev, L. "Altaiskii gornyi okrug" [Altaisk mining area], *R.S.*, CXXXIX'(1909), 301–326.

76. Mantoux, Paul. *The Industrial Revolution in the Eighteenth Century. An Outline of the Beginnings of the Modern Factory System in England.* London, 1961.

*77. Marx, Karl. Capital. Vol. I: *A critical Analysis of Capitalist Production.* Moscow, 1961.

*78. _____. *Capital.* Vol. III: *The Process of Capitalist Production as a Whole.* Chicago, 1909.

*79. _____. *Pre-Capitalistic Economic Formations.* Trans. Jack Cohen. Ed. and with an Introduction by E. J. Hobsbawm. New York, 1964.

*80. Massa, Isaak. *Kratkoe izvestie o moskovii v nachale xvii v* [Brief account of Muscovy at the beginning of the seventeenth century]. Trans. Aleksandr Morozov. Moscow, 1937.

81. Meyendorff, A. F. "Anglo-Russian Trade in the 16th Century," *S.E.E.R.*, XXV (1946–47), 109–121.

82. Miliukov, P. *Gosudarstvennoe khoziaistvo Rossii v pervoi chetverti xviii stoletiia i reforma Petra Velikago* [State economy of Russia in the first quarter of the eighteenth century and the reform of Peter the Great]. 2nd ed., St. Petersburg, 1905.

83. *Moskva v ee proshlom i nastoiashchem* [Moscow in its past

and present]. Vol. VI. Moscow, n.d.

*84. Muliukin, A. S. *Ocherki po istorii iuridicheskago polozheniia inostrannykh kuptsov v Moskovskom gosudarstve* [Studies in the history of the judicial position of foreign merchants in the Muscovite state]. Odessa, 1912.

*85. _____. *Priezd inostrantsev v moskovskoe gosudarstvo, iz istorii russkago prava xvi i xvii vekov* [Arrival of foreigners to the Muscovite state, from the history of Russian law of the sixteenth and seventeenth centuries]. St. Petersburg, 1909.

*86. Novitskii, G. A. "Iz istorii nasazhdeniia sukonnykh fabrik v 17 veke" [From the history of the establishment of cloth factories during the seventeenth century], *Trud v Rossii* [Labor in Russia], No. 2 (1924), 19–31.

*87. _____. "K istorii promyshlennosti i truda vo vtoroi polovine 17 veka. Bumazhnaia mel'nitsa na reke Iauza" [Toward the history of industry and labor during the second half of the seventeenth century. Paper mill on the river Iauza]. *Arkhiv istorii truda v Rossii* [Archive of the history of labor in Russia]. Petrograd, 1924, pp. 28–42.

*88. _____. "Pervye Moskovskie manufaktury xvii veka po obrabotke kozhi" [First Muscovite manufactories of the seventeenth century for the working of leather], in S.V. Bakhrushin, ed., *Moskovskii krai v ego proshlom* [Moscow krai in its past]. Moscow, 1928, pp. 47–60.

89. O'Brien, Carl B. "Agriculture in Russian War Economy in the Later Seventeenth Century," *American Slavic and East European Review,* VII (1949), 167–174.

90. _____. *Muscovy and the Ukraine, from the Pereiaslavl Agreement to the Truce of Andrussovo.* Berkeley, Calif., 1963.

91. _____. *Russia Under Two Tsars, 1682–1689; The Regency of Sophia Alekseevna.* Berkeley, Calif., 1952.

Olearius, Adam. See Baron, Samuel H.

*92. Pankratova, A. M. *Formirovanie proletariata v Rossii (xvii–xviii v.v.)* [Formation of the proletariat in Russia (seventeenth and eighteenth centuries)]. Moscow, 1963.

93. Pares, Bernard. *A History of Russia.* New York, 1956.

*94. Pashkov, A. I. (ed. Soviet edition). John M. Letiche (ed. English trans.). *A History of Russian Economic Thought: Ninth Through Eighteenth Centuries.* Trans. with collaboration of Basil Dmytryshyn and Richard A. Pierce. Berkeley, Calif., 1964.

Pavel Aleppskii. See *Puteshestvie . . .*

*95. Pavlenko, N. I. *Razvitie metallurgicheskoi promyshlennosti Rossii v pervoi polovine xviii veka; promyshlennaia politika i upravlenie* [Development of the metallurgical industry of Russia during the first half of the eighteenth century; industrial policy and administration]. Moscow, 1953.

*96. Pazhitnov, K. A. *Ocherki istorii tekstil'noi promyshlennosti dorevoliutsionnoi Rossii: khlopchatobumazhnaia, l'nopen'- kovaia i shelkovaia promyshlennost'* [Studies of the history of the textile industry of pre-revolutionary Russia: cotton, flax-hemp and silk industry]. Moscow, 1958.

*97. _____. *Ocherki istorii tekstil'noi promyshlennosti dorevoliutsionnoi Rossii: sherstnaia promyshlennost'* [Studies of the history of the textile industry of pre-revolutionary Russia: the woolen industry]. Moscow, 1955.

98. Platonov, S. F. *Lektsii po russkoi istorii* [Lectures on Russian history]. 5th ed., St. Petersburg, 1907.

*99. _____. *Moskva i zapad v xvi-xvii vekakh* [Muscovy and the West during the sixteenth and seventeenth centuries]. Leningrad, 1925.

*100. Pokrovsky, M. N. *Brief History of Russia*. Trans. by D. S. Mirsky. 2 vols. New York, 1933.

*101. _____. *History of Russia from the Earliest Times to the Rise of Commercial Capitalism*. Trans. and ed. by J. D. Clarkson and M. R. M. Griffiths. Bloomington, Ind., 1966.

*102. _____. *Ocherk istorii russkoi kul'tury* [Study of the history of Russian culture]. Vol. I. Moscow, 1915.

103. Pokrovskii, S. A. *Vneshniaia torgovlia i vneshniaia torgovaia politika Rossii* [External trade and the external trade policy of Russia]. Moscow, 1947.

*104. Portal, Roger. *L'Oural au xviiie siècle, étude d'histoire économique et sociale*. Paris, 1950.

105. Preobrazhenskii, A. A. "Predprinimateli Tumashevy v xvii v." [The Tumashev entrepreneurs during the seventeenth century], in *Russkoe gosudarstvo v xvii veke* [The Russian state during the seventeenth century]. Moscow, 1961.

*106. Pushkarev, S. G. *Obzor russkoi istorii* [A survey of Russian history]. New York, 1953.

*107. *Puteshestvie Antiokhiiskago Patriarkha Makariia v Rossii v polovine xvii veka, opisannoe ego synom, arkhidiakonom pavlom Aleppskim* [Journey of Makarii, Patriarch of Antioch, to Russia in the mid-seventeenth century, written by his son, the Arch-Deacon Pavel of Aleppo]. Trans. from the Arabic by G. Murkos. 5 vols. Moscow, 1896–1900.

*108. Roberts, Michael. *Gustavus Adolphus, A History of Sweden, 1611–1632.* 2 vols. London, 1953–1958.

*109. Rozhkov, N. A. *Russkaia istoriia v sravnitel'no-istoricheskom osveshchenii (osnovy sotsial'noi dinamiki)* [Russian history in comparative-historical presentation (The foundations of social dynamics)]. Vols. IV and V. Moscow-Leningrad, 1928.

*110. *Russkaia. Istoricheskaia Biblioteka* [Russian historical library]. Vols. VIII, XXI, XXIII. St. Petersburg, 1884-1907.

*111. *Russko-shvedskie ekonomicheskie otnosheniia v xvii veke. Sbornik dokumentov* [Russian-Swedish economic relations during the seventeenth century. A collection of documents). Moscow-Leningrad, 1960.

*112. Rybakov, B. A. *Remeslo drevnei rusi* [Artisanry of ancient Russia]. Moscow, 1948.

*113. Schubert, H. R. *History of the British Iron and Steel Industry from c. 450 B.C. to A.D. 1775.* London, 1957.

 114. Serbina, K. N. *Ocherki iz sotsial'no-ekonomicheskoi istorii Russkogo goroda, Tikhvinskii posad v xvi–xviii vv.* [Studies in the social-economic history of a Russian town, the Tikhvinskii settlement during the sixteenth, seventeenth, and eighteenth centuries]. Moscow-Leningrad, 1951.

*115. *Sobranie gosudarstvennykh gramot i dogovorov khraniashchikhsia v gosuaarstvennoi kolegii inostrannykh del* [Collection of state documents and agreements kept in the State College of foreign affairs]. Vols. III and IV. Moscow, 1822, 1828.

*116. Solov'ev, S. M. *Istoriia Rossii s drevneishikh vremen* [History of Russia from the most ancient times]. Vols. VI, IX, X, XI, XIII. Moscow, reprinted 1960–1962.

*117. Stoskova, N. N. *Pervye metallurgicheskie zavody Rossii* [The first metallurgical factories of Russia]. Moscow, 1962.

*118. Strumilin, S. G. *Istoriia chernoi metallurgii v SSSR* [History of ferrous metallurgy in the USSR]. Vol. I. Moscow, 1954.

 119. _____. *Ocherki ekonomicheskoi istorii Rossii* [Studies in the economic history of Russia]. Moscow, 1960.

*120. Tolstoi, Iurii. *Pervyia sorok let snoshenii mezhdu Rossieiu i Anglieie, 1553–1593* [First forty years of relations between Russia and England, 1553–1593]. St. Petersburg, 1875.

 121. *Tri veka* [Three centuries]. Vols. I and III. Moscow, 1912.

 122. Tseitlin, M. A. *Ocherki po istorii razvitiia stekol'noi promyshlennosti v Rossii* [Studies in the history of the development of the glass industry in Russia]. Moscow-Leningrad, 1939.

*123. Tsvetaev, Dmitrii. *Protestanstvo i protestanty v Rossii do epokhi preobrazovanii* [Protestantism and Protestants in Russia before the reform period]. Moscow, 1890.

124. Ustrialov, N. *Istoriia tsarstvovaniia Petra Velikago* [History of the reign of Peter the Great). Vols. I and II. St. Petersburg, 1863.

*125. Vernadsky, George. *A History of Russia*. Vol. IV: *Russia at the Dawn of the Modern Age*. New Haven, 1959.

*126. _____: "Iron Mining and Iron Industries in Medieval Russia," in *Études dédiées à la mémoire d'André Andréadès*. Athens, 1939, pp. 361–366.

127. Vil'chinskii, Evgenii. "Andrei Denis'evich Vinius," *R.S.*, CXL (1909), 428–439; CXLIII (1910), 433–440.

*128. Von Staden, Heinrich. *The Land and Government of Muscov. A Sixteenth Century Account*. Trans. and ed. by Thomas Esper. Stanford, Calif., 1967.

*129. Voyce, Arthur. *Moscow and the Roots of Russian Culture*. Norman, Okla., 1964.

130. Vucinich. Alexander. *Science in Russian Culture: A History to 1860*. Stanford, Calif., 1963.

*131. Vvedenskii, A. A. *Dom Stroganovykh v xvi–xvii vekakh* [House of the Stroganovs during the sixteenth and seventeenth centuries]. Moscow, 1962.

*132. Willan, T. S. *The Early History of the Russia Company, 1553–1603*. Manchester, 1956.

*133. Wretts-Smith, Mildred. "The English in Russia During the Second Half of the Sixteenth Century," *Transactions of the Royal Historical Society*, 4th series, III (1920), 72–102.

134. Zabarinskii, P. P. "550 letei russkoi artillerii" [550 years of Russian artillery], *Sbornik issledovanii i materialov artilleriiskogo istoricheskogo muzeia krasnoi armii* [Collection of studies and materials of the Historical Artillery Museum of the Red Army], I (1940), 54–57.

135. Zabelin, Ivan. *Sochinenie (Works)*. Vol. I: *Domashnii byt Russkikh tsarei v xvi i xvii st.* [Home life of the Russian tsars during the sixteenth and seventeenth centuries]. 3rd ed., Moscow, 1895.

*136. Zaozerskaia, E. I. *Razvitie legkoi promyshlennosti v Moskve v pervoi chetverti xviii v.* [Development of light industry in Moscow during the first quarter of the eighteenth century]. Moscow, 1953.

*137. Zaozerskii, A. I. *Tsar' Aleksei Mikhailovich v svoem khoziastve* [Tsar Aleksei Mikhailovich and his economy]. Petrograd, 1917.

138. Zimin, A. A. *Reformy Ivan Groznogo* [Reforms of Ivan the Terrible]. Moscow, 1960.

*139. Zolkiewski, Stanislas. *Expedition to Moscow: A Memoir.* Trans. from the Polish by Jedrzej Giertych. London, 1959.

*140. Zviagintsev, E. "Angliiskii dvor v Moskve" [English settlement in Moscow], *I.zh.*, No. 10–11 (1941), 141–144.

*141. _____. "Slobody inostrantsev v Moskve xvii veka" [Settlements of foreigners in Moscow during the seventeenth century], *I.zh.*, No. 2–3 (1944), 81–86.

Index

365

A Note on the Author

JOSEPH T. FUHRMANN is Associate Professor of History at Tusculum College in Greeneville, Tennessee. Born in Gadsden, Alabama, he studied at Emory University and Indiana University, where he received a Ph.D. after work in the Russian and East European Institute. He has also written on Grigorii Skovoroda, the first Russian philosopher, and is at work on a large study of the origins of Christianity in Russia.